THE BOOK PEOPLE ARE TALKING ABOUT!

"It's a brand-new genre in nonfiction writing. A combination of brilliant, scientific thinking that reads like poetry and teaches like a state-of-the-art guide to better talking."

DALE LARSON, PH.D.
Associate Professor of Psychology
Santa Clara University

"Jerry Goodman has distilled a valuable aid to intimate communication—which all of us are starved for. It is good psychology and a fine gift to humanity. Very readable, too!"

M. BREWSTER SMITH, PH.D
Past President of the
American Psychological Association

"Goodman and Esterly's book offers excellent help. Don't be a victim or perpetrator of 'loaded questions,' 'crowding,' or 'quick-cure advising.' This book is the cure for foot-in-mouth disease."

TOM GREENING, EDITOR
Journal of Humanistic Psychology

CONTENTS

Dedicated to my 13-year-old son, Sasha Goodman—with regrets that this book stole some of our talk time.

ACKNOWLEDGMENTS

I AM unable to disclose my gratitude to every person who donated a taped conversation to this book; some preferred anonymity. All of them know that this book couldn't have been done without their willingness, because I told them so. I talked with them. I hope their generosity will end up helping others talk better. I also regret not including the names of more than 200 men, women and children who anonymously participated in research on the SASHAtape programs containing many of the elements shaping this book.

Glenn Esterly, my gifted collaborator, suffered through the task of bringing simple clarity to academic thinking without damaging the "psychology." He was remarkably unselfish all the way, insisting that the writing carry my voice. His writing mastery and light touch with the ideas eventually transformed my ability to say it more simply. Glenn taught me to tame some powerful scholarly urges and respect the reader's needs. It wasn't easy. The ordering of ideas, the distribution of talk samples and the analyses were moved like chess pieces through his judgment. When a well-published creative writer patiently puts aside his high-powered, rapid process to worry through some sixth draft of a subtle psychology idea, it demonstrates a serious belief in the work. As needed, he took on the role of writer, editor, tutor and ordinary reader. He never forgot the reader.

Special thanks is due Wayne Satz for instigating the collaboration.

I've also chosen to give personal thanks to all the other people who criticized, edited, and typed the drafts, tested the impact of chapters on friends and relatives, argued with my hypotheses, and supported me with many conversations about this book. They are listed alphabetically without detail, along with others who wished to be named but not generally identified as contributors of conversations: Bob Wilson Bates, Dr. Debra Borys, Philippa Brophy, Dr. Bonnie Burstein, Jack Chambers, Dr. Cynthia Cohen, Dr. James W. Davis, Sherry Dunay-Hilber, Jeri Engle, John Feltman, William Gottlieb, Dr. Marion Jacobs, Dr. Dale Larson, Nerissa Leonardo, Dr. Chalsa Loo, Dr. Lou Medvene, Joanne Miller, Mary Miller, Gordon Molsen, Harold Moses, Roberta Mulliner, Beverly O'Neil, Chuck Roppel, Lon Schultz, Mei-Ling Shapiro, Jane Sherman, Dr. John Shlien, Cindy Spring and Carla Wanetick. And thanks to certain gambling buddies whose anonymity was essential.

INTRODUCTION

CHANGING TALK A LITTLE CHANGES LIVES
A LOT

HERE'S MY position: Improve one way of communicating and watch all of your relationships improve.

That notion is now becoming a conventional academic fact. The recent *Handbook of Communication Science* repeatedly drives home the point that changing any of our talk habits for asking questions, getting heard, giving advice, showing emotions, taking talk-turns, explaining thoughts and making others feel understood will change the quality of our interpersonal relations. It starts by fixing little skills.

This book was written to improve its readers' skills in making talk better for themselves—and for those close to them. It's organized around my method for simplifying the working parts of face-to-face communication. My framework breaks down the complexities of talk into six easily recognizable elements. Those six elements have been researched by colleagues and former students at various universities for more than a decade now and are documented as real verbal "tools." The talk skills that derive from using those tools well have been used by thousands of people—parents, couples, counselors, physicians, journalists, athletes, and by last count, even a couple of TV talk show hosts and a hermit.

Gaining knowledge of how these six tools work, singly and together, allows us to harness a wide spectrum of elusive communication phenomena. They can be used like a scorecard for understanding the fast action of conversation.

THE SIX COMMUNICATION TOOLS
THAT SHAPE THIS BOOK

I think of the talk tools at this point as members of a colorful family with basic characteristics that can be summarized (and oversimplified, here) along these lines:

- *Disclosures.* They're the dramatists of conversation. The same thing that happens in good drama—cycles of tension moved by characters' concealment or disclosure—goes on constantly when people talk. In the drama of human relationships, disclosures routinely take part that bring people closer together . . . or drive them farther apart.
- *Reflections.* These carry a precious communication commodity—empathic understanding—by feeding back the essence of important feelings and thoughts. Like mild-mannered Clark Kents, reflections go unappreciated until you get a behind-the-scenes look at their super potency in establishing and maintaining intimacy.
- *Interpretations.* Personified, these are kind of like doctors, lawyers or news analysts—they try to deliver diagnoses or link cause-and-effect or classify. At best, they bring meaning to confusion; at worst, they hopelessly botch up relationships.
- *Advisements.* By turns, these are like parents, teachers or military officers. Their major mission is to guide—from tiny suggestions to outright commands. Covering the general area of "advice," these things have a credibility problem from years of being overused and thrown around insincerely.
- *Questions.* These are meant to gather information, on the surface. But they often arrive in disguise—frequently, their main purpose is to convey advice, interpretations or self-disclosures.
- *Silences.* The pauses in our talk and between talking turns are pretty much taken for granted, but they're really the power brokers of communication—they manage a major item known as "attention."

In themselves, these talk tools aren't "good" or "bad." But taken as a complete set, they perform most of the psychological give-and-take and carry most of the meaning that bounces back and forth every minute in communication. Understood well, they can be used to cut through the confusing ups and downs of intimacy.

It's difficult for a cautious academic like me to write such stuff, but I don't feel reckless about the possibilities. I'm not promising rapid, profound understanding of the ways people connect and disconnect; I do insist that a good grasp of these talk tools makes interpersonal communication easier to understand—and easier to improve.

HOW TO USE THIS BOOK

THE SIX chapters of Part 1—"The Intimate Science: Explained"—explore the inner workings of person-to-person talk. They use a variety of natural conversations to illustrate events, habits, and hidden rules that go unnoticed in the flow of conversation. Obviously, reading such stuff could enlarge your capacity for understanding talk, and perhaps increase your communication skills—but the intention is to create vivid portraits of the six talk elements without many "how-to" distractions. Each element has a chapter of its own where it is displayed as a *tool* for talking—a talk tool.

These six chapters can be read purely as entertainment. It's not necessary to read them in order, but I believe traveling through the sequence from one to six would be the most satisfying approach. If you decide to read chapters randomly in Part 1, you may need to stop once or twice and refer to an earlier chapter for clarification before going on.

The six chapters of Part 2—"The Intimate Science: Mastered"—are about initiating self-change and assisting self-improvement; in short, Part 2 is a self-help guide. It's about learning skills, diagnosing bad habits, and applying this book to real-life situations. Once again the chapters are dominated by conversation examples, but now they're used as instructional aids that guide the reader to try something new. All of the chapters in Part 2 end with a "Practicing" section containing several tested methods for improving mastery over a single talk tool and making sense of another person's talk. There are exercises, games, routines, gimmicks, even systems that can be used by an individual (or a couple or a small group; but more about that in a moment).

A crucial point: Getting the most out of each chapter in Part 2 requires a *prior* reading of its corresponding chapter in Part 1. For example: If you want to develop greater skill or better habits in managing the interruptions, conversational crowding, awkward silences, and talk clutter that go along with imbalances in giving and getting attention, you should read chapter 6 ("Silences") *before* reading chapter 12 ("Mastering Silences"). Of course, some readers may wish to solve a minor problem with a specific talk tool, and go directly to a chapter in Part 2. That might work, because each "Mastering" chapter contains an analyzed conversation or two that can serve as a minimal preparation for the proper use of that chapter's self-improvement techniques. But the best bet for mastering the intimate science is to have it explained first—in other words, to read all of Part 1 before exploring any of Part 2.

Helping someone else pay attention to a troublesome talk habit or enhance their communication is tricky business and needs to be approached with deliberate care—but Part 2 offers several suggestions and some successful examples of how to initiate change in someone close. Even recommending pertinent sections or chapters for others to read can produce some impressive results. Many sections on annoying habits won't insult the recipient of a friendly "talk lesson."

Couples who want to improve or repair their communication will find a wealth of information and direction. Dozens of illustrations that untangle the hidden dynamics of common communication breakdowns appear in Part 1. And Part 2 is filled with a variety of step-by-step procedures (and games) designed specifically for the special ways that couples talk. Take five minutes to glance through the "Purpose" statements in the "Practicing" sections for a picture of the possibilities for couples. These exercises are effective not only for intimate or romantic couples but also for people who work together, parent/child pairs, and students wanting to learn about person-to-person talk.

Any small group needing to improve their interaction—families, self-help groups, classrooms, work teams—will find an exercise, experiment, or game for every talk tool. There are even a few games that can be played at adult parties, and a couple that can be played by groups of kids.

How have *I* used this book? Writing it has been an escape from my tight little academic tower. The wonderful struggle to make talk plain provided more than the fun of discovery—it brought the joy of seeing all this work on communication and intimacy collected in one place to be read by thousands. More than that, paying such close attention to talk over all these years has changed my own talking style, giving me more freedom to communicate. I hope it does something like that for you.

PART I

THE INTIMATE SCIENCE: EXPLAINED

CHAPTER 1

DISCLOSURES

"NO DISCLOSURES, NO INTIMACY."

IT'S BEEN more than ten years since I sold my race car, but I still miss it a lot. Sometimes the longing to be on the track fills my mind with vivid memories. I can almost reexperience those eerie, still moments in my car on the starting line as we all silently waited to fire our engines. Moments to wonder what a grown man was doing in such a childishly risky event. I felt both serious and silly at once. And when we took off, the still-ness turned to loud, violent speed and gave the illusion of a race course shrinking with each lap. The few seconds that it took to maneuver through each corner involved so many decisions that it created a sense of slow motion.

I loved that experience of space-shrinking and time-stretching. It's hard to put behind me. Over the years, I've rekindled those wonderful memories of my little open-wheeled formula car by relating racing stories to friends. But after a while, it became evident that some of my long-winded tales were boring. So now I keep those memories to myself. It makes me a little sad.

That was a self-disclosure.

No big confession. No real risk. Nothing of special interest, except to me and my friends. But if I made the same disclosure during a conversation, it would make me a little more transparent, a bit more knowable to my listener. Such simple revelations of personal history are requirements for initiating friendships. Without a good supply of them, people remain only acquaintances.

3

RISKY DISCLOSURES

A series of simple low-risk self-disclosures may initiate friendship, but deepening friendship demands more vulnerability. Getting close means taking risks, showing more than usual. It means risking some damage to pride by disclosing an unvarnished truth, a private thought, an embarrassing impulse, a romantic feeling, an undignified desire, the first rush of love, or any confession of classified information that might make someone think less of us or put us in emotional jeopardy. These riskier revelations that give away power and leave us vulnerable can paradoxically bring us the strength and protection of intimacy. They are special confessions that connect hearts; not necessarily confessions of cardinal sin but more the unveiling of a person's inner life—warts and all.

To distinguish them from less dangerous, more mundane acts of openness, I've labeled them *risky disclosures*. They put the discloser at psychological risk. That emotional risk-taking is a key ingredient for creating interpersonal trust, which is a key ingredient for friendship and love. (The function of self-disclosing for maintaining close relationships, reducing stress, initiating personal change, and enhancing job satisfaction has generated a whopping number of scientific articles in the last 25 years. My sorely missed friend, the late Sidney Jourard, started it all with his ideas linking self-disclosure to healthy personality. His popular book, *The Transparent Self*, set the standard for exploring the mysteries of how and why people open up to each other.)

Many mental health problems have their roots in the inability, unwillingness, or fearful refusal of people to disclose painfully private facts to friends or family. Emotional isolation produces sickness—we need to disclose to stay sane. At the same time, confessing imperfections, unbecoming thoughts, shameful urges, or any of those disappointing dimensions of our lives makes us vulnerable to the judgments of our listeners—vulnerable to being viewed as less of a person. So we typically seek out the right time, place, and person before the necessary confessing of a risky disclosure: privacy, a nonjudgmental ear, empathic understanding, and a common bond all reduce the danger. It usually comes down to the degree of psychological safety.

For some, the safety never arrives—and neither does intimacy, friends, or lovers. No disclosures, no intimacy. Close relationships build over time as disclosures are put on the table, like pieces of a jigsaw puzzle. We use them more frequently at three special times in the course of a relationship: at the beginning, during conflict, and during growth spurts in intimacy. Eventually, they fit together and form much more complete pictures of people. Almost every dramatic turning point in real-life (and fictionalized) human relations pivots on the act of self-disclosure. I've seen high-risk disclosures turn doubt into trust, hope into despair, neutrality into respect, boredom into lust (and vice versa).

The power of disclosure to change relationships is illuminated by a film example from the Steve Martin/Lily Tomlin movie *All of Me*, in which a woman's very *existence* pivots on an act of disclosure. (Unfortunately, the psychologically safe situation that allows her disclosure occurs after she becomes a ghost.) This dialogue example might seem unusual at first, coming as it does from a film comedy, but it has a fundamental truth that applies to the way people really live. The example illustrates how risky disclosures become essential acts that dramatically change real relationships. (It also shows how fiction writers routinely depend on such disclosures for story twists.)

In the film, a sickly heiress named Edwina (Tomlin) uses her wealth and a magic trick to buy the body of a beautiful young woman to inhabit, but by accident she ends up sharing half of Roger's (Martin's) body. Edwina, of course, completely messes up Roger's life (including his sex life when she ruins his lovemaking by making him think about dead kittens). He grouses, but she claims she'll find a way to leave his body and get into the younger woman's, as intended.

EDWINA: Oh, stop being such a martyr. As soon as I'm not dead anymore, I'll pay you for your troubles.

ROGER: Pay me? Oh, Jesus, I just realized why no one showed up at your memorial service. You forgot to hire mourners.

EDWINA: You are an insensitive horse's ass, do you know that?

ROGER: Oh, drop dead.

[Edwina's wounded by Roger's cutting insight about her memorial service. She's too hurt to continue fighting and will try getting compassion by disclosing an embarrassing truth.]

EDWINA: For your information, there is a perfectly good reason nobody showed up at my memorial service.

ROGER: Yeah, what?

EDWINA: I don't have any friends.

[Her risky negative self-disclosure leaves the glib Roger speechless. The relationship is about to be rearranged. His silent attention is the stuff real life is made of when someone opens up with a whopper. The constant bickering and crowding stops. He compassionately makes room for her to continue as his anger melts and the dialogue turns tender.]

EDWINA: *(Continuing after a long pause)* I'm looking back at an entire lifetime and I don't have one friend. I never had . . . *(Starting to sob)* any friends. I've had only nannies and tutors and servants and nurses.

[She cries harder after expanding on her humiliating position, and Roger shows regret for having been so rough on her. Her confession is one of the most difficult to express, a very risky disclosure. Most experienced therapists, I'd bet, would agree that it's easier to admit having been dishonorable, greedy, cowardly, or even cruel than to disclose a serious disconnection from all other humans—being friendless, lonely, unworthy of a close companion. The film's writer, Phil Alden Robinson, either made a fine intuitive stroke or used some basic wisdom to pivot his plot on such a compelling disclosure.]

EDWINA: *(Continuing)* Once my parents hired a clown to entertain me. But he didn't like me. And when my parents weren't in the room, he'd just sit there. He didn't lift a *finger* to amuse me!

ROGER: That's a *terrible* clown.

Edwina took another risk to illustrate she was not only friendless but unliked. Touched by her vulnerability, Roger begins to feel close and wants to help. He even tries to cancel the validity of her blunt honesty by blaming the clown. Just like in real life (and just as scientific research has found), Edwina's unflattering self-disclosures bring kindness and depth to the couple's screen relationship. The dialogue from then on is flavored with sincere disclosures from *both* characters. The film demonstrates a psychological dynamic of what actually happens in conversations: Disclosures beget disclosures.

Edwina's awful confessions might have come out of desperation, a sense of nothing more to lose. At any rate, they shocked Roger into a caring silence and then turned his biting ridicule into compassion. Their relationship turned upside-down (or right-side-up) after just a couple of extremely risky disclosures.

The Reveal/Conceal Ordeal in Romance

Sometimes a single risky disclosure triggers the first blush of romance, but more often it takes dozens of much less humiliating disclosures to create intimacy. And before that, during early courting, the costly habit for most couples is: When in doubt, don't tell. It's a rule that protects us from embarrassment. When that happens, pride is saved but the potential for closeness is lost.

A peculiar thing about saving pride by putting up a front is that the mask is often transparent. Face-saving in human relations usually suffers a blown cover. It's a weak sham. But it's all we've got to keep from showing what we are inside. The drama of this classical ordeal was illuminated by Woody Allen (as Alvy) and Diane Keaton (as Annie) in *Annie Hall*. They did a convincing job of demonstrating the way potential lovers cautiously try to size up each other and move closer without letting something embarrassing slip out that might look unattractive. Risky disclosures usually come gradually, after a sequence of milder ones.

The interplay between concealment and disclosure creates most of the ordeal of new romance. In this scene, Annie has driven Alvy uptown as far as her apartment. After she parks, he starts to leave.

ANNIE: Hey, well, listen . . . hey, you wanna come upstairs and uh . . . and have a glass of wine and something? Aw, no, I mean . . . I mean, you don't have to, you're probably late and everything else.

ALVY: No, no, that'll be fine. I don't mind. Sure.

ANNIE: You sure?

ALVY: No, I got time.

ANNIE: Okay.

ALVY: Sure, I got . . . I got nothing, uh, nothing till my analyst's appointment.

[Alvy's revelation of being a therapy patient lays bare a variety of private facts. The risky disclosure usually tells more than can be absorbed immediately, but the possibilities frequently unfold in minutes. Now Annie can know that he has felt dissatisfied with his life and helpless to the point of becoming a patient; he's paying someone to listen to him; he can afford all those expensive conversations; he's chosen a therapy that's fallen into some disrepute as old-fashioned; he's probably eager to get her acceptance of his status as a patient; and he's inviting her closer scrutiny by divulging a fact practically guaranteed to draw further questions.]

ANNIE: Oh, you see an analyst?

ALVY: Y-y-yeah, just for 15 years.

[A funny line for a serious confession. "Just for 15 years" reveals a king-sized commitment of time and money. Almost everyone who's submitted to long-term analysis has bumped into some ridicule of their enterprise. No doubt, Alvy has purposely displayed a bit of wordplay here to beat his potential accuser to the punch. He's wanting to be vulnerable—to reveal the magnitude of his dependency on analysis—but also wanting to cushion any ridicule by ridiculing himself. Making fun of himself is also a disclaimer of any naivete about the absurd aspects of his situation. His style of disclosing opens the door for greater intimacy while defusing some of the risk.]

Once they're in her apartment, the conversation is colored by small talk without significant disclosure. The dialogue shows them taking a breather by avoiding focus on their immediate impulses or anxieties—pretty realistic writing. Annie has just finished a nervously told, over-detailed, bizarre story about the death of a relative, almost as if she wants to match his risky disclosures, but can't, so she discloses about someone else. It happens all the time. Maybe the secret to Allen's comedy is its authenticity. Maybe his dialogue is drawn from vivid recall (or real tape recordings) and made even more realistic by partial ad-libbing during filming. I doubt that the writing springs forth from isolated imagining. In any case, Alvy isn't amused by Annie's death story.

ALVY: Yeah, it's a great story. . . . It really made my day. Hey, I think I should get outta here, you know, cause I think I'm imposing, you know . . .

[A mock disclosure, a manipulation that pretends to worry about imposing. The meaning of his talk is: "Could I get a further expression of interest on your part?"]

ANNIE: Oh really? Oh, well . . . uh, uh, maybe, uh, maybe, we uh—

ALVY: *(Interrupting)* And . . . uh, yeah, uh . . . uh, you know, I . . . I . . . I . . .

[They're both nervous and indecisive, but they wind up wandering out to the terrace, drinking wine.]

ANNIE: Well, I mean, you don't have to go you know.

[There's the expression of interest he stimulated with mock worry about imposing.]

ALVY: No, I know, but . . . but, you know, I'm all perspired and everything.

ANNIE: Well, didn't you take, uh . . . uh, a shower at the club?

ALVY: Me? No, no, no, 'cause I nev—I never shower in a public place.

ANNIE: Why not?

ALVY: 'Cause I don't like to get naked in front of another man, you know—it's, uh . . .

ANNIE: *(Laughing)* Oh, I see, I see.

ALVY: You know, I don't like to show my body to a man of my gender.

[Again, a risky disclosure that could expose him to ridicule is tempered by making fun of his own phobia. But even *with* the humor in the line, there's the chance that she could assess him as less attractive, less desirable, even weird. Most guys who've been in analysis for 15 years and can't use public showers wouldn't bring that stuff up during the first encounter with a new woman. A real-life Alvy, making such rapid-fire, compulsive disclosures to a sheer stranger, could be seen as just plain weird, aside from any wit.]

Quick confessions, however, do show up in early courtship. They can show up inappropriately early when the eagerness to connect overrules our reserve. Research reported in the *Handbook of Interpersonal Communication* shows these unexpected, out-of-sequence disclosures tend to make their owners appear troubled, deviant, even disliked.[1] These *premature disclosures* come unexpectedly, before the gradual escalation of vulnerability in a relationship. Allen's instincts and skills have Alvy's premature disclosures coming so rapidly, so comically that he disarms Annie—and the audience. Alvy's mating display is so unusually succumbing (for a man) that it colors the courtship with a special tenderness. The character becomes romantic instead of ridiculous. When premature disclosure becomes a regular fixture in anyone's acquaintanceship repertoire, though, I term it *promiscuous disclosure*, a repeated revealing of vulnerabilities to new acquaintances without discrimination. It's a sad habit that pretends at intimacy or feigns familiarity. Promiscuous disclosures used romantically carry some of the same disadvantages of sexual promiscuity, sabotaging chances for durable intimacy and increasing the risk of chronic emotional numbness. Alvy walks the tightrope here.

ANNIE: Yeah. Oh, yeah. Yeah, I see. I guess—

ALVY: —'cause, uh, you never know what's gonna happen.

ANNIE: *(Sipping her wine)* Fifteen years, huh?

[She hasn't forgotten the psychoanalysis. Disclosures are the main attraction for a newly met romantic couple. A bit later, Alvy points at some framed photographs and asks if they're hers.]

ANNIE: Yeah, yeah, I sorta dabble around, you know. *(As she talks, Annie's unexpressed feeling, her self-talk, pops on the screen: "I dabble? Listen to me—what a jerk.")*

[Annie's private put-down of herself illustrates the typical split between what we feel and say with new acquaintances. The secret self-ridicule of her talking style shows a common experience that sets up the reveal/conceal ordeal. It's a simple, profound theme: We want to get closer to others, but we're afraid we might look like jerks doing it. None of us is as tough or invulnerable as we often pretend, especially those supercool macho men and defiantly aloof women who are probably the biggest sissies about telling tender truths that lurk just below the surface of conversation. Of course, insecurity about opening up too soon is often a practical emotion. But the price of concealing in close relations is ultimately more costly and painful than showing something shameful.]

ALVY: They're . . . they're . . . they're wonderful, you know. They have . . . they have, uh . . . a . . . quality. *(Alvy's hidden thought on screen: "You are a great-looking girl.")*

[He says her photographs look wonderful, but it's *her* he's looking at. Expressing admiration to a stranger can be experienced as a loss of interpersonal power, or immature or insincere. So there's good reason for concealing serious romantic attraction early in relationships.]

ANNIE: Well, I . . . I . . . I . . . would like to take a serious photography course soon. *("He probably thinks I'm a yo-yo.")*

ALVY: Photography's interesting, 'cause you know, it's—it's a new art form, and a, uh, a set of aesthetic criteria have not emerged yet. *("I wonder what she looks like naked.")*

[The fun in these subtitles is a vivid reminder of the absurdly funny juxtapositions between our talk and the flow of hidden thoughts that parade through our minds during conversations. On those rare occasions when we make known the here-and-now flow of behind-the-scenes thought, the result is guaranteed to stimulate conversation. Very risky— and often rewarding—fun.]

ANNIE: Aesthetic criteria? You mean, whether it's, uh, a good photo or not. *("I'm not smart enough for him. Hang in there.")*

ALVY: The—the medium enters in as a condition of the art form itself. That's—*("I don't know what I'm saying—she senses I'm shallow.")*

ANNIE: Well, well, I . . . to me . . . I . . . I mean, it's . . . it's . . . it's all instinctive, you know . . . I mean, I just try to uh, feel it, you know? I try to get a sense of it and not think about it so much. *("God, I hope he doesn't turn out to be a shmuck like the others.")*

ALVY: Still, still we—you need a set of aesthetic guidelines to put it in social perspective, I think. *("Christ, I sound like FM radio. Relax.")*

Self-doubt, sexual impulses, suspicions about another's personality are common experiences for new couples. And neither Alvy nor Annie would be shocked to realize the other has such experiences. So the reason they hide—and people in new relationships typically hide—isn't so much to protect each other from some awful, unimaginable feelings that can be guessed anyway; the hiding is to protect themselves and the budding relationship from being overwhelmed with the intense reality of their needs and fears. Mutual attraction drives them to sincerely disclose, but their fears make them ring false.

Allen has typically played guys who are indecisive, worried, needy, and vulnerable—and reveal all that with risky disclosures. Lo and behold, women tend to love them for it.

Private Use of Public Confession

Like it or not, the most listened to and repeated poetry in the world is currently found in popular songs. It's usually bad poetry, but that doesn't stop us from occasionally using a line because the scenes touch our daydreams, memories, and everyday private feelings. Public songs evoke private emotions. The lyrics are usually about the coming and going of love. And the songs frequently take the form of someone confessing, complaining, exulting, spilling the beans, or sharing a heart-to-heart message. In other words, love songs are often nothing more than dressed-up risky disclosures.

In 1943, Harold Arlen wrote a classic, "One for My Baby (And One More for the Road)," in which a depressed guy, broken-hearted, tells his bartender:

> *". . . I'm gloomy*
> *You simply gotta listen to me*
> *Until it's talked away."*

His self-disclosure is about the end of a love affair. The bartender (whose occupational hazard is having to hear many sad self-disclosures) pours the drink and listens to the lament:

> *"I'm feeling so bad*
> *This torch I've found, must be drowned*
> *Or it soon might explode."*

A classic song about the classical event of drowning sorrow with drink and disclosure.

Twenty years and thousands of broken-heart songs later, John

Lennon and Paul McCartney wrote another classic combining self-deprecation, depression, and disclosure:

> *I'm not half the man I used to be*
> *There's a shadow hanging over me . . .*
> *Why she had to go, I don't know*
> *She wouldn't say*
> *I said something wrong*
> *Now I long for Yesterday.*

Other songs reveal the unfolding of a plot to recapture a heart, exposing daydreams, despair, the memory of ecstasy, simmering urges to be wild and fancy-free, bitterness and those old favorites—jealousy, resentment, and revenge. But the all-time, world-champion disclosure across all songs, countries, and generations is that excruciatingly painful confession of true love:

> *I love you*
> *There's nothing to hide*
> *It's better than burning inside*
> *I love you*
> *No use to pretend*
> *There, I've said it again.*

> *You made me love you*
> *I didn't wanna do it*
> *I didn't wanna do it.*

> *I can't help it if I'm still in love with you.*

> *I love you*
> *I honestly love you.*

Lyricists understand there's no end to our interest in variations on such themes. They're the stuff our real and fantasy disclosures are made of. They're about things we frequently feel and seldom risk saying. Sometimes lyrics make public certain feelings, thoughts, or events that people experience and *never* tell. They are made for our empathy. We can use them to massage our private aches. Songwriters can get away with thinly camouflaging blatantly sexual images because the blunt disclosures are just beneath the metaphors. Sometimes the stories feed our secret fantasies. Cole Porter had the heroine of one song divulge casual willingness to sexually succumb to a brand new acquaintance because her true love left and she needs distraction:

> *You can't know how happy I am that we met*
> *I'm strangely attracted to you*
> *There's someone I'm trying so hard to forget*
> *Don't you want to forget someone, too?*
> *It's the wrong time, and the wrong place*
> *Tho' your face is charming, it's the wrong face*
> *It's not his face, but such a charming face . . .*
> *That if some night you're free . . .*
> *It's alright with me.*

Revealing such needs out loud to a strange man (especially in the mid-1950's when the song made the "Your Hit Parade") would seem unusually bold, especially said candidly, in everyday, awkward language. The present-tense disclosure unashamedly says she's willing to get physical, even though there's no love. Her invitation to a stranger to substitute for her first choice was heard in homes all over 1953 America—including many where quick sex without love was considered repugnant.

The display of private emotions amid lyrical phrases allows a certain brief elegance that isn't there in actual conversations.

Those dreamy rhymed messages or snappy, smart declarations carried by a tune and metered out by a rhythm section can sound awkward in the real world. Listening to difficult disclosures packaged in poetry that easily rolls off talented voices allows us to absorb some of the joy or sorrow of an imaginary confessor. If the song strikes at the right time, it might help us rework an unresolved feeling or remind us of something in our personal history, or cause us to empathize with the hero or heroine. That's one reason music evokes our secret selves.

Nowadays, we blab more easily about our sex lives. There's less scandal in being "strangely attracted" to a new, charming face. So, to make songs spicy, modern lyrics disguise deeper, darker impulses that would shock if said plain and live. An internationally popular song by the Swedish ABBA ("Summer Night City") describes a restless urge for going to the city to find some recreational sex in the park. This risky disclosure is sung in lovely, plaintive tones by two wholesome-looking women in the group:

> In the sunlight, feel like sleeping,
> I can't take it for too long,
> My impatience slowly creeping
> Up my spine and growing strong
> (chorus)
> Summer Night City. Summer Night City.
> Walking in the moonlight
> Lovemaking in the park
> Waiting for the sunrise
> Dancing in the dark.
>
> I know what's waiting there for me
> Tonight I'm loose and fancy free
> When the night comes with the action
> I just know it's time to go
> Can't resist the strange attraction
> From that giant dynamo
> Lots to take and lots to give
> Time to dream and time to live . . .
> It's elusive all this glitter . . .
> And tomorrow
> When it's dawning
> And the first birds start to sing

> *In the pale light*
> *Of the morning*
> *Nothing's worth remembering*
> *It's a dream*
> *It's out of reach*
> *Scattered driftwood on the beach.*

The dutiful recantation, the confession of an emotional hangover at the end, show us that the song's discloser is sorry. And the repentance has allowed us to hear about that shameless, lustful impatience running loose in the city on a summer night. For some, such a desire is unthinkable; for others, it's thinkable but unmentionable. But most of us have revealed unmentionable things when our basic need to be known (for better or worse) overpowers shame. It's that essential act of speaking the unspeakable that can be seen frequently in pop lyrics. That act occurs rarely in real life. Maybe our fascination with risky disclosures in song lyrics, movies, and novels has to do with how frightening they are—and how *necessary* they are for moving even closer to special people in our lives, for tightening our personal connections.

Tightening connections, or at least maintaining them, is the customary motive for our use of greeting cards. Traditionally, their printed messages disclose sentiment that says, "I'm thinking of you," "Sorry you're sick," "Congratulations," or "Sorry your loved one died." They can be efficient implements for expressing complex emotions or touchy topics. Cards that acknowledge bereavement may be the most popular because they show concern without intrusion and replace the hard-to-handle, painfully awkward, direct disclosure to someone's grief. In recent years, manufacturers have produced new products that disclose emotions previously reserved for conversation. There are greeting cards that confess regret about nasty things said in argument or tell of remembering lost love after a separation or express the wish to right a variety of wrongs. Some even do our dirty work in telling people how we dislike something they've done (put-down cards).

Sending manufactured messages comes from the old American custom of showing care with handmade folk-art cards containing proverbs. Now we select messages made by others because we're too busy or unable to use our own words or unwilling to mess around with direct talk. I think we overdo the greeting card habit at the expense of more personal self-expression. A survey sponsored by the Greeting Card Association found the average person sends 25 cards a year, excluding Christmas. Almost one-third of the survey respondents said they were moved to tears by a card received during the past year. That finding reminded me of a TV commercial depicting a young woman handing her father a greeting card. His eyes moisten as she says something like, "I've been wanting to say that for a long time." The printed card conveyed a moment of affection, an important emotion that has remained unexpressed over their years together. Something unspeakable. A disclosure of gratitude, admiration, or love too risky for talk. Picking cards off a rack to fulfill personal communication needs is better than zero communication, but that practice may be the symptom of a problem: too little risky disclosing in close relationships.

The confessions of song lyrics and greeting cards are only part of the story. Unveiled secrets serve as the substance of autobiographies, the hook of soap operas, the scandal of politics, the spice of news, and the turning point of novels. Maybe that's because they are the terror of our intimacy. The incessant printing, filming, and singing of deliciously private, tender, sordid, noble, risky disclosures for public use shows not only our fascination but also a national struggle to manage this form of communication in our personal lives.

FLOODED DISCLOSURE: EXCEEDINGLY PRIVATE PREOCCUPIED TALK

The exceedingly private act of succumbing to reverie, of slipping into a daydream, can take us to the center of ourselves—a risky place. Getting lost in thought, whether it's wandering through a lovely memory, following the trail of some sour resentment, or reliving an old argument, usually puts us in potentially vulnerable territory. The vulnerability is created by the need to reveal our inner talk. Self-disclosures expose private musings from a safe, silent world to the scrutiny, judgment, and memory of another soul. The psychologically risky act of bringing a memory to light, sharing a daydream, confessing a personal preoccupation, is an overworked attention-grabbing device in drama—and pure fascination in real life.

As a culture, we're fascinated by the spontaneous revelation of reveries: "A penny for your thoughts." That offer might be accepted when made by an intimate friend or a mate at a safe moment, but many ruminations couldn't be purchased for a thousand dollars. (On the other hand, some people pay therapists thousands of dollars to hear the ongoing flow of their private preoccupations.) As a society, we're fascinated by those special situations in which someone lost in thought is able to talk about their interior journey. It's like listening to an explorer report from an intriguing location.

There are times, though—many times—when the discloser becomes so preoccupied with an unresolved problem or a compelling memory that it floods out all other topics. *Flooded disclosure* occurs when the "need to talk about it" dominates the conversation. It's the flip side of bottling up risky disclosures. As the discloser becomes preoccupied with reliving, problem solving, complaining, or justifying (or just plain being excited), the flooding pushes everything else to the background—including the listener.

Flooded *listeners* are usually less than fascinated by disclosure overload. They may seek relief by somehow diverting their attention: changing topics, complaining, or even leaving the conversation. So the intriguing experience of hearing a reverie revealed becomes a burdensome experience when overdone. Then, "A penny for your thoughts" becomes "Could I give you a few bucks to keep quiet?" The overload might come as Grandpa's fond remembrances activate another old "war story"; the thrilled high-schooler blathers on forever in quasi-ecstasy about the neat guy who smiled twice at her in art class; and the husband home from work falls deeply into an automatic hour-long reiteration about the problem in the office that just won't go away.

When our thoughts flood our talk in an effort to master some compelling emotion, the best of us are capable of disregarding the listener. Doing a flooded disclosure episode is akin to being swept away by our inner life. Relieving ourselves by flooding once in a while is a necessity for mental health. Flooded disclosure episodes aren't merely mistakes made in an overly talkative mood but a working component in the natural therapeutics of normal conversation.

Still, there are people who tend to produce flooded disclosures daily—not just at times of distress, excitement, or loneliness but whenever an unsuspecting listener leaves the door ajar. Sometimes even a suspecting listener gets flooded. It's hard to escape. Habitual flooders inspire anger. Their overwhelmed victims feel crowded out, bored, or insulted by the self-absorbed, repetitious, obsessive talk marathons.

Show me a heavy-duty flooder and I'll show you a lonely person. Flooders are both funny and poignant. Funny because sometimes they're so wrapped up in the message that they appear to be talking to themselves, mowing down listeners with their preoccupation. Poignant because the impetus to flood could be caused by a major unresolved problem or sheer loneliness or nostalgia for long-past experiences—some emotion that's too intense, aching, or worrisome to keep concealed.

Whatever the cause, self-absorbed unilateral flooding has been an interpersonal irritant over the centuries. An aphorism from the fourth century B.C. by Democritus of Abdera: "To do all the talking and not be willing to listen is a form of greed." In 1738, Voltaire added to the name-calling: "The secret of being a bore is to tell everything." Jonathan Swift (1667–1745), in his "Hints Toward an Essay on Conversation," complained about peers prone to flooded disclosing who "without any ceremony will run over the history of their lives; will relate the annals of their diseases, with the several symptoms and circumstances of them; will enumerate the hardships and injustice they have suffered in court . . . in love, or in law."

The following dialogue (captured in an answering machine tape) stars a modern flooder who has been "in a damn emotional crisis for five rotten months, just because I'm a single woman." Jessie is facing the prospect of losing her dream of "having a baby with the right man."

At 34, she's tasting success in a glamorous career, making her a boss to many men. She resists leveraging her attractiveness to snare men and refuses to look seriously at any man who's less than six feet tall because of her height. Jessie won't continue a conversation if she experiences even moderate sexism. So she refuses to flirt, play coy, or become "an easy lay instead of a complete person."

The right guy hasn't come along yet, and events have amplified Jessie's yearning for motherhood; she's painfully thinking of compromising her principles for a guy—a potential father of her child—who's "trainable."

Jessie's father, at 78, has become one of her confidants. After years of conflict, they have "rediscovered each other completely." He says he's reclaimed "the daughter of his golden years." She says she's rediscovered "the unselfish love of a wise father. It's great having him to trust." They're talking on the phone now.

FATHER: . . . And what about, what's his name—the guy with the new—

JESSIE: *(Interrupting)* Jay, his name is Jay, and he's kaput. Another faker. He got stoned at our preview party. It was bad. The next day we talked, and honest to God, I was really understanding and trying to be a friend and comforting, so he starts with some crap about how he rarely, rarely, does coke. Plus, he does a *number* on me, like I'm the cute little girl behind her man. I couldn't belive it. *God.* Dad, when you get a little close to these guys they treat you like a pet. I can't believe it. At work, I'm a whole person, but guys I see [dates] look at me like some special-function human put here for their purposes. I'd like to turn my back on every damn one. You know?

FATHER: *(Interrupting)* Jessie, it can't be all *that* bad. This hasn't—

JESSIE: *(Interrupting)* Oh, yeah?

FATHER: Look, this hasn't been a good year for you, but, honey, please don't give up. You're not an ordinary woman. And you need a *man* that's not ordinary. A one-in-a-thousand. It's gonna take patience.

JESSIE: More than patience, Dad. I'm *34*! Last month Darlene and I were talking about all this, and we figured out that I've dated about 45 men since my 20th birthday. Take out 3 years when I was with Lou and 2 with Eric and that leaves 9 years of looking and dating. Those 40-some others came at the rate of about 5 a year. So 1 out of 1,000 would take, uh, uh, 200 years! Patience isn't enough. I need *luck*.

FATHER: Maybe luck. Okay. But also maybe spotting a bad fit sooner than two months—like that spoiled, immature Michael guy. Jessie, you know as well as I do that you've had bad habits with men. Your dreams distorted all the ugliness under the charm and fake caring. It's *true*, really true. Please, dear, *please* don't push what I say aside with that stuff about me being a stubborn, old-fashioned father. You know how you were telling me I was being a possessive old worrywart about my only daughter. When we were arguing about that big selfish klutz Eric. I'm too old for that small thinking. I love you too much to mince words now. All your life I've seen your urgency with men. Even when you acted cool, there was underneath the same excitement when you were 16 and boy crazy. You were urgent to cure the loneliness or some bad memory from the last guy, and you bragged about toying with him. But *they* toyed with *you*, too. They lied to you, too. You and your men have been lying to each other for—

JESSIE: *(Interrupting) Daddy*, why are you doing this? It just makes me want to crawl out of my skin. Why dwell on those awful—

FATHER: *(Interrupting)* Only because I want to remind you to stick to your resolution and not be distracted by some passer-by looking for some incidental fun. I'm reminding you to keep looking for long-term satisfactions.

Father continues his lecture, with an occasional protest from Jessie. He claims to have put aside the typical fatherly distortions about his daughter being too good for any man. She half-believes him, and manages to make a persuasive point about her brand-new, realistic approach toward finding a father for the child she "needs." Jessie details some recent near-misses that demonstrate her reform and seems to reassure her father that she has a fair chance of finding a mate. Like the good small-town doctor that he was for 40 years in upstate New York, Father ends his lecture on a soft note.

FATHER: Well, now you're talking, Jessie. I suppose I'm not giving you enough credit. The way you used to fool yourself with men, uh, the urgency for your so-called freedom that seemed to get you nothing but that "numb despair" you talk about. Well, with you feeling like a biological clock ticking down to a place where babies are out of the picture, I figured you'd be urgent for a guy to have a baby with. And out of desperation, pick another bad apple. But that's wrong. It's not you. Now you're cooking with gas. Honest, honey, you sound so clear-headed these days that I just *know* it's gonna be good.

Facing Fear with Flooded Disclosures

She's comforted by his optimism and appears willing to face her fear more directly after he asks her just how important a baby is for her. And what if she couldn't have one? She spends her time obsessing over the possible scenarios. As she explains why it's best for her to be thinking through the most basic considerations of finding a man and having a baby at 34, Jessie slips into rumination. Her mind becomes a fish bowl as her private preoccupations become visible and suddenly color the conversation. There's a difficult problem that needs solving—soon! It floods her mind and overflows into her disclosures. She becomes lost in talk as we get an intimate revelation of her inner turmoil. It's the kind of personal turmoil familiar to many single women facing the prospect of late motherhood, or no motherhood at all.

JESSIE: That ghastly biological clock. I've been thinking about it lately, you know. It's funny, all of a sudden I'm thinking wait a minute, I'm 34, so okay if I get married at 36 and have a child at 37, uh, then I can have another one at 39, and then I start *(Laugh)* thinking about spacing—should it be *five* years apart? Should it be *two*? And then I think, wait a minute, if it's five years and I get married at 36 then I'm 41 . . . I backtrack, you know. This is how I feel about it. If I'm gonna get married at 36, I should meet the guy at 34. So then if we get married, we won't be doing it right off the bat; at least I'll have known him for a year. So I could do that, *or* I could know the guy for five, six months and then get married.

FATHER: Too quick.

JESSIE: So I'll pray that I've made the right decision and you'll examine the guy and give approval so I can get pregnant right away. *(They both laugh)*

JESSIE: *(Continuing, more soberly)* I'll just have one child, but if I just have one child, I could wait until 38.

[Facing a frightening future is the raison d'être for Jessie's obsessive computations. She's driven to detailing the possibilities in search of comfort. Maybe the details will help her predict the course of her life as a mother. She experiences a predicament about her existence that's being forced to its crisis point because time is quickly slipping away. Jessie is coping with a crisis by problem solving out loud. Life's transition points (e.g., adolescence, first love, career commitment, marriage and divorce, retirement) are commonly managed with the help of flooded disclosures. Therapy, prayer, and denial can also be present, but flooding episodes are a consistent standby for carrying us through with mental health intact. Jessie is using flooding to master her fear—to question her fate: How can my life fall into place so I can know motherhood? Can I juggle the numbers to make it better? Is it my fate to have just one child?]

JESSIE: *(Continuing)* See, I've never really *thought* about having more than one child—I always just wanted *one* child. You know 'cause I didn't want my whole *life*—I mean, I see these women who have children, like *two, three, four* children, and they're young but they're *old*. And this one lady at Rosette's, where I get my manicure, every couple weeks, ya know, and this woman there, she's the manager and she's young—she's about 28 years old. You'd never know it. And it's not because she looks old. It's her actions. Like, she's a worn-out mother, she's got two or three kids. And she's like, there's something in her mannerisms that are like, in her voice and her actions, the way she walks that says she's old. That she's been through it all, lost her zest, that she's sort of, um, blase, or sort of . . . I don't know. She's done it, ya know?

She knows *the* secret and it's no big deal. It's the kind of feeling I get from her. And I still think, *oh my God*, I still don't know the *secret*, don't know what the *big deal's* all about, and it's all out there and it's waiting for me and it's gonna be unbelievable! And she's like, I don't know—she's, she's . . . *old*! She's just old and she's a mother and she does all the tings mothers do and she's done it before and she'll do it again and that's her attitude. Sort of a resignation to the mundane things. Resignation to the mundane things in life, ya know. I mean, I've got that sort of feeling doing my wash and all of that. But *this* is the *big-time* stuff! She's *really* a mother! Oh, God, a mother. A wonderful young, old, resigned, content, tired mother who knows the secret that's hidden from *me*.

[Note how the flow of her uncensored thoughts moves from feeling to feeling without regard for grammar and with little regard to the listener's entertainment. Flooded disclosures are the epitome of self-absorption in conversation. They mimic the internal flow of private thoughts. Sometimes I see beauty in them, reminiscent of James Joyce's stream-of-consciousness writing. Remove some of the punctuation from Jessie's soliloquy, add some Welsh colloquialisms and you might fool an English major. Flooded disclosures are close approximations to the naked mind.]

JESSIE: *(Continuing)* And then the thing, I see other mothers with kids and the kids are slobbering and they're in a restaurant and they're going "Harrrryy! Bring another napkin! Missy's upchucking!" And they're *yechhh*! *(Laughs throatily)* And they're sitting there for years like that and I think, oh, God. Can you imagine? Can you imagine *that* being your life? And I *know* I would become that way, because even when I'm unattractive—well, maybe not unattractive *(Chuckles)*—but maybe, 'cause even when I'm with Skippy, this four-year-old I adore next door, when I'm with him I don't care as much about grooming myself you know because, some would say, that's wonderful, what's wrong with that? But— I see these women and their hair and everything is all messed up. They're blooming slobs. And they're just nasty, nasty, *nasty* people because they're not focused on themselves, they're focused on these kids!

And when I take care of Skippy, I just get into him so much that I become a *slob*. And I don't wanna be a *slob*. I don't wanna be a mother who's a *slob*. Who walks around and, ya know, is just a slob. And I don't know if I could take care of myself, and take care of a child—think I'd start feeling guilty, for not taking care of myself.

This has nothing to do with the tick-tocking of that clock. . . . It's just that I'm afraid that I'll become, that my child will become my whole life. *(Sighs)* But then I, so if I had more than one child, then it might happen, it might become like, oh, Sally has to go to the dentist and Billy has to go to school and I've gotta do this and I've gotta do that—there's not time to do my nails! Who has time to wash my hair? I'll wash it tomorrow. And—oh, awful! And then if there's one child—and this is gonna sound terrible . . . but then I think of that child actress—what's her name?—that died in a crash last year . . . beautiful only child. And I think, well, now her mother has *no one*. . . . *(Voice trails off)* No one . . . She doesn't have a husband 'cause he died in the crash too and she doesn't have any other children and the whole family is *gone*. Gone.

[There's a long pause. Then she continues, sounding as if she's been startled out of a deep sleep.]

JESSIE: Hey, what's going on? What am I doing to you? Poor dear, sitting there while I go off on a tangent and just dump on you. I don't know what's gotten into me, running off at the mouth while you're probably starving. My *God*, it's your lunchtime, maybe—

FATHER: *(Interrupting)* Stop it. Jessie, just stop your nonsense with the "poor dear" starving business. I want to be with you with this. It's important. Don't you remember how I talked your arm off for three whole days when Mom died? You were there every second for me—even in your own misery. So stop the stuff about dumping on me. It's good for you—we're together. Makes me feel close to hear inside your heart. Keep talking!

[Father knows best this time. This type of flooding with a willing friend can be good medicine as the flooder says things out loud that she or he may not have said internally. And when the listener isn't totally disregarded (like Jessie acknowledging possible discomfort in her father), these episodes have high probabilities of enhancing closeness. Father's wonderful phrase, "Makes me feel close to hear inside your heart," is an apt metaphor for describing the rewards of quietly accepting flooded gyrations from someone important. Jessie accepts the unaccustomed role as dutiful daughter and resumes her talking without further fretting.]

JESSIE: Yes, Dad, I'm feeling close, too. . . . I want you to hear something not too pretty about me. Something I'm just thinking about, something hard to say out loud. God. It's about having just one child. Right now, ya know, it occurs to me, uh, it occurs that having just one child at my age could . . . *(Trails off into silence, then blurts out the next sentence as if she were confessing a sin)* If I have just one child and something happens to that one child, I'll have no one and it'll be too late for me to have another child. Isn't that—I mean, that's real *selfish* 'cause what I'm saying is, I want two children for *me*. For just my sake. *(Sighs)* Ya know, I want two children so if something happens—that's terrible isn't it, Dad? If I have two children, I'll have another one, an extra, just in case. A backup. Like having extra supplies in the house. So if one is gone . . . Isn't that awful. I won't have to rush out and get another. Ya know, the store won't be closed. . . . But it's *true*. It's selfish, but it's true. So that's the kind of thing it is, it's like maybe, ya know, I'll be 45 and the store will be closed. Sorry, too late for another baby: "Call again in another life."

[Likening a closed store to the closed opportunity for fertility is wonderfully inventive. The "selfish . . . awful" metaphor of "extra supplies" for a backup second child is both bizarre and accurately descriptive of true feelings commonly held by prospective parents—but uncommonly disclosed. The poetry that pops up periodically in flooded disclosures can carry the ring of a common truth.

[To my ear, the language and spontaneous discoveries of flooded disclosures bear close resemblance to the language and discoveries of patients in psychotherapy. In both there is an obsessive, preoccupied, lost-in-thought process that provides avenues for insight and invention: going over and over the same territory, searching for missing connections, feeling into crevices for new evidence and old memories. Similar to the compulsive "repeater effect" that we use to reattach lost meaning from one mind to another (see chapter 2), the flooded disclosure seems to attach our own minds to our own creative well springs. Somehow, being dominated by an idea, memory, or problem, allowing ourselves to be possessed or bewitched can serve to create new connections and solutions.

[The process of creating something new, immediate, and unknown by focusing an obsessive spotlight of talk on an older known thought or experience reminds me of the Heisenberg Principle. Physicist Werner Heisenberg found that, ultimately, matter changes as it is observed with light—i.e., observing it changes it. Observing inner experience at length, repeatedly, with the verbal ruminations of flooded disclosures, also changes it. Maybe that's why we allow each other to blather freely in brainstorming sessions. It's no wonder that many successful comedy writers describe doing their best inventing in no-holds-barred group sessions where flooded disclosures are encouraged with a verve unmatched by any therapist. So, the half-poignant, half-silly meanderings of Jessie may be changing a major dilemma in her life. Her desperate need to create solutions is being served by a one-sided conversation. Notice how the flooding process continues to unearth discoveries.]

JESSIE: Do you remember when Lou was getting serious? The time he was always talking about marriage and made jokes about . . . Used to call you Dad?

FATHER: Sure I do.

JESSIE: Well, I was 28 then. And, say I'd married him at 28 and he wanted to have a child right away. He was about 36 or so and he'd never mentioned children before—he'd never even wanted to live together before. And then we broke up—and all of a sudden, it was, my God . . . but I remember thinking, I don't want a child right away! I'm not ready! And I remember that feeling like it was yesterday. Oh, God! It isn't distant to me at all. It's real close. In my mind, I, I can still feel that. And, ummm, it's funny 'cause that's the reverse. He said, I wanna have a child, right, and it was part of the reason I wouldn't marry him.

God, I can't believe how much I've changed in five years. It's hard to look at this. I had no *perspective* on my life. I guess I wasn't worried about it at 28. And then I went back to college. Well, I knew in college I'd be forfeiting another four years. Ya know, it's another four years I'm taking away. But I had to finish that business, so for me I sort of feel like I was gypped. There hasn't been enough *time*, not enough *time*! But believe it or not, ya know, you see me hurrying, rushing, I rush into things, I'm impulsive, you think I should be more patient, but look at my *life*—my *life*! And I haven't russsssshed into marriage, or russssshed into having a baby, just to get it off my list. *(Deep breath)* And major things *have not been rushed.* Ummm . . . ya know . . .

But I've always said, "Screw it—I'm not ready for a man and kids! Let someone else do it. I'm not ready and I'm not gonna worry about it." So I clicked that marriage-and-mother switch to the "off" position and it stayed off, undisturbed, for five—no, six years . . . or more! So why now? Why is it driving me crazy now? Why am I baby crazy now? What got into me? It's been building since spring—the urge did. It's blooming in spring. Why then? Why spring? Baby-blooming urges in spring. Oh, my Gawd. In *spring.* I think that, ya know when . . . I started, it was right after my *operation.* My *operation.* I started then. Oh, I realized, I started . . . I remember feeing God, this could be the end of me! The feeling struck me that, oh, being a mother, it could be taken away.

[Jessie's discovery of the connection between her surgery for a uterine cyst and her new drive toward motherhood was aided by her almost whimsical playing with the thought of spring and "baby-blooming urges." That discovery, along with the stream-of-consciousness talk fostered by her father, directs her toward another significant discovery.]

JESSIE: *(Continuing)* And then I see how much this means to me in terms of how I view *life*. It means . . . *(Long pause)* the view got real clear in the last minute. I mean, I view my life, really sorta *starting* when I have a child. Remarkable. Isn't that something? I couldn't, if I couldn't have a child I'd think that maybe I was missing a *beginning* in my life. Isn't that something, Dad? Maybe that's the way all women think. I, I just now realized the operation made me scared and that I wouldn't have a chance to . . . a chance to be *young*! See, *that's* being young. To have a baby. To have a baby and you're young. So, if I didn't have that baby to look forward to, I think I'd really think I was getting older for sure, instead of thinking there's this new beginning coming up.

So maybe that's why that 28-year-old girl does quick shifts on whether she's a girl, woman, or old lady, or why sometimes it feels like life's going downhill, if she gets resigned to all this mundane crap mothers do, ya know. Because she wants a baby and maybe is shifting back a bit to start to begin her life again younger. *(Laughs)* I don't know if this makes sense, but, um, anyhow . . . So I still have that to think—oh, my life is gonna be fresh, that it's gonna be fresh and new and exciting and I'll be one of those mothers with a baby and then, ya know, I don't— I feel like I don't know what I'm talking about. Then I get scared 'cause I see magazine covers of these girls with their babies and they look *older*—ya know, it's popular now to show 40-year-old cover mothers cuddling their babies. I think there's something wrong with that picture. *(Sigh)* They shouldn't look older. So I'm all screwed up. But don't give up, Dad, things are getting clearer. *(Laughs)* Hour by hour.

Emotional Housecleaning

Minute by minute is more like it, Jessie. These half-hidden feelings can come to light rapidly when talk flow freely. Jessie has babies-on-the-brain. That colloquialism for obsessive thinking fits this conversation, where going over the territory with a fine-toothed comb has recovered some lost thoughts that can be used to help solve her crisis.

Skipping ahead in the conversation several minutes, it takes a turn back to the search for a suitable father. Jessie is recalling a movie character—single, female, over 30, professional, attractive—who's reunited with a group of close college friends.

This character's obsession with having a baby before it's too late causes her to size up the guys at the reunion as prospective fathers. (Ultimately, a married friend lovingly donates her own husband for the honors.) Jessie has watched the movie over and over on videocassette and decided the female character represents the American single woman's "national anthem" of concern about finding the right man to start a family with.

JESSIE: She's talking to her old girlfriend in the kitchen; they're private, see? It's Mary Kay Place in *The Big Chill*; she's telling why a woman can't find a good man these days. And she says something like, they're either gay, or married and itching to cheat; or they've just broken up with the greatest woman in the world and they're looking for an exact replacement; or they don't believe in monogamy anymore and need more space; or they're tired of all the space in their lives but they're still afraid of intimacy, can't get close; or maybe it's the guy who's dying to get close, but he's dull and wimpy and awkward. Boy! That covers it.

She calls herself a ticking biological clock and says she can tell in the first 15 seconds if this guy is a possibility. It takes me 15 minutes now—the better ones take a few hours. See? I'm getting fast. Don't worry, Dad. Burt takes me to all those faculty club events and lunch at that lawyers' restaurant and I've even joined Great Expectations [a video dating service]. So I'm meeting guys and I absolutely don't get sidetracked anymore.

[Her freedom to mix and match topics without censure—from surgery to beginning life again with a baby to 40-year-old cover-girl mothers to a movie episode to videodating in a matter of a few minutes—allows Jessie to let her deepest feelings show the way. Her chronic unresolved condition—to be or not to be a mother—compels her to search every nook and cranny of her mind for any stray experience as she performs an emotional housecleaning. It's natural psychotherapy. Flooding helps us heal by giving the freedom to search anywhere our distress leads us, *without* much distraction and *with* the support of another person. Like soaring and being on the ground at the same time. It's self-talk with company—being mostly alone, yet attached.

[The apparent one-way of flooded disclosure is a misperception. We need the real or imagined acceptance of someone or something outside ourselves—even when there's little or no feedback. That profound need shows up in such activities as confessing to anthropomorphized diaries, confiding to uncritical pets, and even rambling into answering machines. The similarities shared by the diaries, pets, and phone machines is that they don't ask questions, criticize, interrupt, give advice, or make any of the realistic demands that come when facing another human. Things that listen without responding allow private things to be said, at will, at length, in a search for comfort without complexity, but also without empathy. Flooded disclosures offer the same benefits, with the bonus of another human in attendance, an empathic flesh-and-blood person. Jessie continues in free flight as her quiet, allowing father gives the empathy with few demands.]

JESSIE: There must be a million women like me. See, my body is ready to have that baby. . . . I feel it's sitting there, waiting. Like it's ready . . . like it just needs to be pinched. It's frustrated. All the parts are there saying, ''Jesus, I'm here, use me! I'm waiting—do it!'' It's all ready to go and I'm not using it. Then I think, oh, I could actually make a person? Me? Well, that sounds terrible, just me.

[It's often hard for Jessie to listen to her own flooding. She stops occasionally and judges herself a bit—before her father can. She does that by using disclaimers—little bits of talk about talk—that say, ''Here's

what I think about the way that I'm talking.'' Disclaimers are common
with uncensored flooding. Here's an example.]

JESSIE: *(Continuing)* It's not just me—this is gonna sound terrible, but I
still think it's meeee it's important. Because even though it
takes two, I'm the one with the ability to make it grow. And I'm
the one who—I wouldn't just let it grow; I would give it life. Not
the man. And so, it's minnnne.

Okay, I wouldn't be the only one who created it, but I'd be
the one who *really*, who reallyyyy did, did create it. I mean, um
. . . It's hard to explain. But it would be part of my body, not
part of the man's. So that's that. . . . And now when I see women
with a baby, I think, ohhhh, where's mine? Ohhhh, wait a minute—I think, oh, she's got a healthy baby! *(Long pause)* Where's
mine? *(Mumbles, trails off into long silence)* I'm sorry. That's
terrible. Just forgot you were there, uh, because it's so easy
talking to you. Daddy, I'm so sorry.

FATHER: That's okay, honey—I'm just listening.

JESSIE: I got carried away. *(Laughs)* Swept away.

FATHER: I was just listening.

JESSIE: It's so good—

FATHER: *(Interrupting)* Just listening, 'cause there's nothing I've got to
tell you that you haven't thought about. And I think you're doing
fine, just fine. I keep saying to myself, That's the ticket, Jessie.
You're figuring it out. A fine young woman that's figuring it out—
without fooling herself, either. Except maybe for thinking any
baby's only yours. Wait till the thing grows and you see the father
in it. I see me in you. And so did your mother. She used to—

Jessie interrupted to offer profuse apologies for her remarks
about the baby being more the mother's than father's. Jessie and
Dad repaired the gender breach by enumerating the many physical attributes she inherited from him. As if to balance the cred-
its, Father listed Jessie's virtues creditable to her mother. The
list led him to thoughts of his late wife (dead three years) and
their lifelong shared passion for fly-fishing. Then, in a conversational turnaround, Father began to ruminate on a memorable
fishing trip. He stopped his reexperiencing abruptly in a manner
reminiscent of someone who's about to nod off in a chair but
suddenly adjusts to a wakeful sitting position. Somehow reminded it was well past lunchtime for both of them, he joked
about needing to get off the phone before dinner and cut his
flooded disclosure short. The pair affectionately scheduled a
lunch date with implied agreement for pursuing his fishing tale.

Later, embarrassed at reading a transcript of the phone conversation, Jessie bewailed her "self-centered talking that hogged every minute with boring, silly details." I challenged her description of silly details and recounted the important self-discoveries she made by ruminating out loud: that surgery stirred up her current interest in having a baby; that deep down she feels her adult life can only begin with the onset of motherhood; how she realized regret at firmly rejecting the idea of starting a family five years earlier; how it became apparent that she feels ambivalent about becoming a jaded slob of a mother losing her life to child rearing; that she gained insight about being jealous of mothers who know "the secret"; that she found herself self-ishly thinking the terrible thought of having an extra backup child in case one died; and that she came to a decision that now is the time to schedule specific plans for meeting a man and mating.

Silly details? It would take a great conversation, a class-A therapy hour or an outstanding support group to produce all those insights. Yet Jessie trivialized them because of embarrassment from reading a transcript of her starkly self-absorbed, one-way talk. I've seen that reaction before. Maybe the shame is from taking unusual quantities of attention for purely personal needs without prior agreement. Not only does the productive flooded disclosure consume a back-breaking quantity of attention, it usually does so without entertaining the listener. Or worse, it can be just plain tedious to someone with another agenda. She did apologize for monopolizing, at one point, but hardly broke stride in her flooding after her father's command to continue.

Perhaps Jessie, like so many others, might have felt less selfish in the aftermath if she had flooded to a therapist, support group, minister, or physician. Using a paid professional or self-help group for our disclosure needs can sometimes simplify problem solving and avoid costly obligation to friends and loved ones. On the other hand, opening the dam to someone close who's capable of staying afloat against the deluge can be faster, less costly, and sometimes better. It all depends on the *safety* of the relationship and our willingness to *ask out loud* for all that attention. Even a moderately safe relationship that *explicitly* provides the occasional opportunity for a flooding episode should develop into an exceptionally safe relationship—a valuable asset in this age of guarded acquaintanceships.

Jessie's flooding was motivated by her existential crisis—her need to master a frequent dilemma of single womanhood. Mastering major predicaments by unearthing insights, creating plans, or discovering possible solutions is a task enhanced by flooded disclosures. Besides being a great aid in the mastery of personal problems, flooding also serves as a tool for reattaching to past experiences and as a conduit for coping with emotional overflow. Let me explain.

Significant Old War Stories

Reattaching to past experiences is another form of flooding that's frequently fun, even deeply gratifying at times of reliving a fond memory. Older people have a reputation for relating such lengthy, detailed "old war stories" about a variety of past events; younger people joke about getting trapped and entangled in Grandpa's 40-minute yarn about his Model-T Ford. Fascinating the first time perhaps; painfully boring the eighteenth. And even if Grandma's story about her early flirtation with George at the corner grocery store is being told for the first time, her concern for lost detail and careful recollecting of every recoverable, dear experience may well leave the listener spent. Loving listeners, courteous and dutiful listeners have all suffered in the presence of someone searching into an elusive past pleasure of a half-forgotten adventure. And the flooder doesn't have to be on Social Security. My 12-year-old son, in preadolescent rapture, shows no signs of his chronic short-attention-span disease as he floods me with details of a movie. Insensitively, he brushes aside my whining for mercy and quickly becomes oblivious to my painful boredom as I listen to his wide-eyed reliving of some vapid, child-exploiting plot.

While flooding is surely both a pleasure and a vice for every generation, our stereotype of the older addict holds some truth. For the elderly, flooded disclosures are more than pleasure; they're often an act of desperation, a medicine reducing the nostalgia for long-gone people and places. Flooding, out of misery, is an event that displays a symptom and brings some relief at the same time. It's "both a sign of disturbance and part of the restorative process," writes William Stiles, my former student, in an article titled "I Have to Talk to Somebody: A Fever Model of Disclosure."[2] Stiles uses the metaphor of fever to explore how the disclosure research ties in to both sickness (neuroticism, anxiety, depression) and health (as part of the healing process).

The comical image of a doddering old man telling meaningless tales just to hear himself talk is a disservice to our large population of mentally adept older Americans. The research of Catherine Goodman, a social gerontologist, into natural support systems for the elderly has contributed to recognition of a sad fact: National neglect of the psychological needs of older people has left them alienated from their middle-aged sons and daughters. As a result, everyone loses.

Our elders need to communicate with people who know something about the past—or just are willing to consider that parts of the past are ageless. Unlike younger people, the elderly lose opportunities for sharing past pleasures as they lose peers to death. That deprivation ranks high as a misfortune of growing old. Consider having hardly anyone, or absolutely no one, familiar with what counts in your life. Nobody who knows the familiar jokes, the tunes, the interesting social events. Nobody who's experienced the coming and going of styles, and all those familiar phrases, objects, and subtle mannerisms that make older adults feel at home in a place and time. It's a little like being in a strange country, a new culture where the subtleties of your language and humor are lost on foreigners. Being out of sync like that can mean it's no longer easy to say a lot with little effort; there's been an awful change, and now it takes a lot of effort to say a little. Deprived of such ease, such joy, old folks feel loneliness setting in. Empathy is hard to come by. Without it, we fade out, grow cold or numb or hard or desperate. When I see a very old person seek comfort by talking at length about the good old days—or just talking about anything in hopes of capturing even a reluctant listener—I think of empathy starvation. Images of a brain that isn't fully functioning take a backseat to the image of a person disconnected from the comfort of easy communication with a sincere partner.

Sure, some older people could benefit by tuning in more to current life, even learning to appreciate some of the youth culture; dwelling on their massive losses can only depress. But flowing with the times is a tough task when the past nags and nobody really can hear their message. The task could be made easier by a younger listener willing to learn the lay of the land of earlier times. There are ways of connecting with older people without condescension or boredom, and without suffering through much of the *repeater effect* (see chapters 2 and 8) that's often a part of flooded disclosures. A serious commitment to talk about the time and places that are significant to our elders can make communication more interesting, and eventually less repetitious, even in the presence of short-term memory loss. Consistently approaching the earlier life of an elderly person as an amateur historical researcher is often an effective solution. Another way is to compare parallel experiences across the younger and older set of life experiences.

My point: The bad reputation earned by flooded disclosures from the elderly is a product of our national disregard for their communication needs. The despair of losing a past world is akin to the despair of a Jessie believing her future world of motherhood will be denied. Both require some flooding and both can be eased by someone who understands that flooded disclosures are not just old war stories or self-absorbed meanderings— they're serious calls for connection.

When Feelings Spill Over

We "bubble over" with excitement, "boil over" with anger; we're "overwhelmed" by confusion, "overpowered" by love, "overcome" with joy. All of these spillovers produce flooding, which may very well "overload" the listener.

Human nature has us talking a torrent as one way of maintaining our sense of self when threatened by emotional overflow. Talk keeps us intact. It stems the tide. The need to flood from some emotional overflow is even more familiar than the older adult's need to reattach old experiences or gain mastery with unresolved problems (as Jessie did). The essential dynamics of angry, uncontrolled, disregarding, self-centered flooding during a personal argument are well known. And adolescent flooding by "boy-crazy" girls and by "girl-crazy" boys strikes me as kindred to the high-energy flooding by people overwhelmed by the good fortune of "lucking out" somewhere in life—winning a prize, getting an important contract, being promoted at work. Proverbs remind us that couples in love also never tire of talking about themselves.

Common ridicule of flooded disclosures as bothersome, boring, trivial talk distresses me. If we could only learn how to use them better—if we could "contract" for them in advance, reach an agreement that we'll spend time being a flooded discloser or listening to a flood of talk—more genuine help would be exchanged. The worst part is the callous way we turn away from both kids and elderly people when the stakes are as basic as mental health.

DISCLOSURE-MATCHING: A BUSINESS EXAMPLE

If you search your memory for pivotal conversations—talks with a friend, colleague, or lover that produced good results about an important issue—chances are they were filled with *disclosure-matching*. The phenomenon is bedrock stuff for the making of any long-term association or relationship. This positive process occurs when disclosures by one person move another to open up in return—to match openness with openness.

I have an example of disclosure-matching that was prompted by a classic office management problem: a manager keeping important information from an employee. (Unnecessary secrecy—lack of disclosure—is the sort of communication glitch that causes trouble in almost any kind of workplace, undermining morale and efficiency. But more about that later.)

This dialogue sample happened in a Hollywood studio publicity office (where meetings between the executives were often recorded for recalling decisions and details). When this conversation took place, Mark was director of the publicity promotion department at a studio that makes movies, sitcoms, and drama series for the TV networks. Valerie started as a secretary, worked up to publicist, and was promoted over others to become Mark's right-hand department manager. Together, Mark and Valerie had the high-pressure task of publicizing all the TV shows to help keep ratings up and shows on the air. Their three-year relationship had been professionally cordial, quite businesslike. Mark was a successful survivor of many TV publicity wars, while Valerie—young and ambitious—eagerly fell into the role of perfect protege. She also faced the pressure of being a rapidly rising woman at work—including jealousy from subordinates who were previously peers.

In this case, we hear how Valerie's regular pressures were exacerbated by reductions in her staff because of budget cuts by the new studio owners. She was expected to do the same job with much less help. That problem had caused her to thrash privately for months. In this slightly edited conversation, Valerie opens up to her boss because she's afraid her staff is falling apart. We pick up the conversation five minutes after it started as she describes another source of distress: upper managers expecting magic from publicity people.

VALERIE: So . . . Weiss is screaming, "Why didn't we get the *TV Times* cover!" He expects miracles from me. *TV Times* isn't going to put another "Disease of the Week" on their cover. He still doesn't believe the editors are gagging on the stuff.

MARK: Yeah, well, Weiss is always screaming about something. I just can't stand thinking about him right now. If that clown stopped being hysterical for an hour, he might produce something that isn't terminal. Listen, I just got a call from Brundage [another executive] and he needs to know about our pitch to *TV Guide* for a profile on Simpson. Hear anything?

VALERIE: No, Andy [a publicist] has checked twice.

MARK: Sure? Andy has a tendency to let things go.

VALERIE: No, he said he called twice about it.

MARK: *(Sighing)* God, we need that one. *(Pause)* Soon. Brundage is getting real antsy and I don't blame him. The damn series has been in the top 20 for a month now, and nobody is paying any attention—*nobody*.

VALERIE: Well, you know, detective shows aren't exactly a new trend—

MARK: *(Interrupting)* Yeah, yeah, but I wonder why Andy's shows keep causing us trouble—

VALERIE: *(Interrupting)* Andy's pulling his load, Mark. I know he can be inconsistent. But since the cutback, he's been hanging tough. Plus, he's got more shows to handle. He's tired. Everybody's tired. We can't just expect business as usual with about half the staff we need. Andy's been working late—all the time. He's really trying.

[Sticking up for one of her staff members and contradicting her boss's impression showed uncommon assertion for Val. When she read my typed version of their conversation, she said, "Is that *me* lecturing Mark? I must have been feeling spunky."]

MARK: *(Laughing)* Why, Valerie—it's nice to see you fighting for your people. So, I'll get off his case, but please keep in mind that Andy and the rest are lucky they've still got jobs. At all. It could've been worse. We could've *all* been canned. *Gone.* Look, Val, I've had some sleepless nights.

[Mark is saying something Valerie already knows—but he's never said it out loud. His confession peels a little layer of the impersonal veneer off their conversation. Maybe his disclosure was stimulated by her loyal defense of Andy, which seemed bold. She wasn't acting like a deferent underling; more like a peer. More like someone to whom you'd confess sleepless nights.]

VALERIE: I know. And staff knows all too well about the job insecurity. They've been worried ever since . . . I've tried to . . . It goes back to . . . And it's not easy keeping morale up when each one of 'em wonders if the ax will fall for them next. Any day.

MARK: Well, you told 'em that was the end of the cutbacks this fiscal year?

[This strikes Valerie's most sensitive nerve.]

VALERIE: Oh, yes, you and I agreed . . . I did it, I did it like you said, but it, uh, you . . . But it goes back . . . See, I had, had assured everyone before the others were cut, based on . . . *(Long pause)* Mark, there's a credibility problem I'm faced with, going back to that. I need your help on this. You know, it's not easy for 'em to forget I was telling people a couple months ago there wouldn't be any cutbacks—then, all of a sudden, four people are out the door. And a rumor is going around that all the department directors and managers knew it was for sure three months ago. They're saying, uh, *you* knew, and that *I* knew and didn't tell 'em 'cause it would've dampened enthusiasm. When I fired Colleen, she accused me of disregarding her welfare for corporate efficiency. Claimed she turned down another job she could've had if I'd told her the cuts were coming. That's what she told everyone—it was awful. And everyone was saying the business office was already secretly reshuffling the budget.

[Mark isn't ready to deal with the bleak accusation that's been cautiously placed on the table.]

MARK: Well, they ought to know by now, publicity is always the first place to get—

VALERIE: *(Interrupting)* That's something they already . . . uh, Mark . . . I'm not just trying to be contentious. You've taught me to establish trust as a top priority. It's been so important. You're right. And I *had* it, till what looked like this coverup. I did it . . . *(Mumbles)* so proud—ya know, but now I wonder if they trust me anymore. They're closing me out. It's been going on for . . . I've been losing sleep, too, because of this, and I can't figure out if I'm screwing up the, uh, way I handle things, or the cutbacks . . . I just can't . . . I've been doing the things you've . . . I've been talking to them separately, been helping out with their assignments, but there's a stiffness, or, like, you know, like they're humoring me and I've been mad 'cause things are getting screwed up, and I can't get hold of . . . I'm afraid I'm losing it. *(Long pause)* I hate to tell you this, but it's getting away from me. It's bad. I need your help.

[Confessing her failure to manage staff and asking for help is especially difficult, given Val's past performance on this job. She was promoted to revitalize a demoralized staff under Mark's guidance. Establishing credibility, opening communication and boosting morale was a proud victory for her as a new manager. She played organizational politics with an ethical hand, and won. Mark had bragged about her achievement to other department directors. When Valerie found out, it raised her self-confidence. So this disclosure is a major embarrassment. She referred to it later as "the worst mortification of my working life."]

MARK: Ah, Val. It can't be *that* bad. Of course, I'll help. It sounds awful. Like you're at the end of your rope. God, it sounds awful. *(Long pause)* You sound so down on yourself. I'm sure it's not your fault. That perfectionist streak in you causes you to exaggerate trouble. Maybe you're exaggerating.

VALERIE: I wish. It's just so obvious. Everywhere. Everywhere from Tina being afraid and hiding how bad the campaign for the series was going, to Gary giving *nobody* any warning about the party [for a miniseries] falling apart, to people finding excuses for not inviting me to lunch. It's everywhere. They're doing a "be-polite-to-Val" routine. Nobody is straight about what's going on.

MARK: Damn it! *(Long pause)* Damn! That's all we need is lousy morale and staff covering their asses. It'll hurt us. I'm sorry—you must feel terrible. Something you worked so hard for . . . in jeopardy. Well, uh, that may be strong language. We've just gotta get 'em secure again. Maybe we should call a meeting for—

[Valerie interrupts here with surprising harshness. Mark is trying to cover his executive behind instead of letting her message sink in.]

VALERIE: No, that would take it away from me if you . . . Oops, sorry, I ask for your help and cut you off when you—

MARK: *(Interrupting)* You're right. That's right. It has to come from you.

VALERIE: *(Forcefully)* I'm so glad you feel that way. I know for sure that I didn't know . . . that I wasn't trying to put anything over on . . . we've got to get it all aboveboard.

MARK: Oh, God . . . *(Long sigh)* aboveboard. That's the next step—aboveboard. *(Pause)* Let me start by being more aboveboard with you. *(Long pause)* Things here have been getting me depressed. I've got producers and vice-presidents attacking from one side and you and the staff from the other—I mean, I don't mean *you're* attacking. I don't mean—you've always been on my side. God . . . *(Laughs out of his misery)* Well, maybe *they* don't trust you, but *I* do.

VALERIE: It hurts to hear that out loud, I mean—staff not trusting me. Last week it felt like my career was crumbling around me.

MARK: Well, Val, it may be a surprise, but that's exactly how *I've* been feeling for the last month. No, no! Your career *isn't* crumbling. *(Sighs)* There's so much going for you—there's no damn reason for you to be hurting and worrying this way when it's *not your fault*. *(Long pause)* It's not. *(Long silence)* It's got nothing to do with you. You shouldn't be blaming yourself. *(Sighs)*

VALERIE: It's kind of you to take care of me, but—

MARK: *(Interrupting)* I'm not taking care of you, Val. It *really* isn't yours, it's mine. I screwed up by agreeing with Dave [Mark's boss] to keep the cuts a secret from *everyone*. Even you. You got caught in the middle. Can't you see? You're the victim of a bad decision.

Mark's self-disclosure about being the culprit and feeling stupid is necessary to rescue Valerie from her unjustified self-condemnation. He shoulders the blame. Disclosures made to correct a wrong frequently come quickly after the wrong is apparent. So hearing someone's unjustified self-criticism, misplaced sorrow, or unnecessary worry can create compassion, or, in Mark's case, the need to reduce guilt. Often, a disclosure revealing guilt, error, or other self-criticisms can "pull" a matching disclosure from someone wanting to make things right, to make the hurt feel better.

Matching as a Source of Trust

But this common psychological mechanism, where someone is quickly rescued from unfair misunderstanding by a single exchange of disclosure-matching, is not the main event in this section, or in the conversation between Mark and Valerie. The most important kind of disclosure-matching—in or out of the workplace—is created by a *series* of increasingly risky disclosures that bounce back and forth with less and less censoring and more and more trust. This ongoing exchange can be almost automatic, with personal vulnerabilities made more visible by each trade of nontactical disclosures.

A disclosure-matching episode can transform acquaintances into fledgling friends (or exceedingly good friends into lovers) in a single conversation—or more typically, a series of conversations. The reciprocity of secret-telling often seems like a contagious bout of emotional undressing.

Disclosure-matching is an event that pushes aside the urge to make negative judgments, which is an absolute requirement for establishing romance and friendship. There's safety in opening up in bits and pieces on both sides that has an alluring way of getting people closer and closer and keeping the disclosures coming. The motivation to continue peeling off layers seems to come from some of our primitive instincts to keep moving closer. It can get rather hypnotic, as in the start of a love affair or a true friendship (and sometimes warmly embarrassing afterward). So the motives in a disclosure-matching episode are mostly primitive, positive, and automatic. Briefer types of disclosure-matching—limited to one or two exchanges—are motivated by less profound emotions like manipulating someone's interest (flirtation) or inducing compliance (selling) and reducing such discomforts as anger, fear, or guilt (as Mark did in his confession of bad judgment). But a series of unmaskings that come without much contrivance is a key ingredient in the establishment of any truly trusting relationship.

Example: A friendship is being launched during a later conversation between Mark and Valerie; it occurs after their staff morale crisis has receded, thanks to an increase in the flow of disclosures between director, manager, and staff. Valerie is able to firmly promise a less concealed policy of communicating management decisions to staff members. She and Mark are becoming more informal as she feels less his student and more his colleague. The following excerpts contain their first rehash of the conversation where Mark disclosed his guilt a few weeks earlier. We enter near the beginning after Valerie jokes about feeling strange for not having any urgent items on the agenda. Mark quips that maybe they have the time to find out for sure if she's forgiven him for his costly secret.

VALERIE: There's nothing to forgive. You never wronged me on purpose.
MARK: Well, in a way, I, I . . . It was *my* choice to agree with Dave. I could've said concealing it from you was bad management. It wasn't *that* necessary. We sorta keep secrets out of habit. Been doing it for years. We do it to make our lives simple, but sometimes it does the opposite and makes a mess—like with you.

Secrecy at Work: A Disclosing Solution

Mark's observation is accurate, according to the consultants and management scholars I've known. It seems many management fashions depend on strategic interpersonal maneuvers for motivating, criticizing, fostering autonomy, etc. The subordinate doesn't know the motive behind the message. Such lack of sincerity in corporate conversations can become habitual. Secrets are kept reflexively—without function. Those unnecessary, automatic secrets can shut down the healthy flow of disclosures in an office. Habitual secrecy is an unrecognized cause of havoc in business settings. As Mark suggests, the unrequired secret is made to maintain or enhance efficiency, but in the long run it's a major cause of low innovation and low morale. Somehow, upper management secrets eventually wind their way down to middle management and staff. Bosses have a habit of overprotecting themselves at the expense of everyone. All it takes is a shadowy rumor to fan the flame of worry and speculation that can pull staff attention away from productive concerns. It's an uncommon workplace that breaches the separation between policy-maker manager and frontline worker. The barriers were erected long ago for the sake of propriety and efficiency, but the practice has proven to be overdone and inefficient. Failure to maintain a healthy flow of relevant disclosure from management to staff remains a significant problem in American business.

The healthy flow of disclosure is even an issue in the health of the individuals involved. Because the necessity for keeping secrets is so entrenched in corporate life, almost everyone withholds from everyone. Remembering what not to say to whom costs energy and increases stress. People are often on guard in business conversation. My late colleague, Sidney Jourard, argued that the almost constant requirement of guarding pertinent work information created a pattern of constant microstress.

He saw each little concealment creating a little stress and all of it adding up to chronic stress. Sid's thinking was during a period when very few women were in management, so he called his hypothesis the "lethal aspect of the male role." He even speculated on how the lack of disclosure might contribute to lower life expectancy for men. His idea is more than science fiction; the difference now is that it applies to men *and* women in careers requiring the stressful maintenance of secrets.

In the meeting between Mark and Valerie, their personal exchange pushed aside the formal agenda. The new flavor of more equality in their relationship stemming from Mark's big self-disclosure and their shared struggle to repair staff morale set the stage for a full new round of disclosure. Mark started by disclosing private thoughts on the rigidities of his fellow directors. Since disclosure begets disclosure, Valerie opened up about her secret talks with a competing studio that was recruiting her the previous year. That stimulated a "me-too" disclosure about Mark's secret offer from a group of TV stations. Their exchange of classified information was placing a certain trust—an expectation of confidentiality—on their association. They were making themselves a bit more vulnerable to each other's good will and caretaking. Then Valerie took a little psychological leap and confessed: "The only reason, the one and only reason I didn't go with [another studio] is that, uh, I had this . . . sort of professional crush on you. Don't misunderstand the way I say, uh, I, uh, sorta wanted to use you. I just wanted to pick your nifty brain. I loved working with you, more than I could ever say. I could've died if you knew."

That risky disclosure brought expressions of surprise, gratitude, and praise from Mark, and finally he rambled into a more intensely personal revelation about how work was taking too much time from his family—especially his teenage daughter, who grew up with an "always-too-busy father" and was now hanging around with a 40-year-old man and having drug problems. Telling the story brought tears to his eyes. Valerie told me the pain was contagious; her eyes also moistened.

The reciprocity of disclosure that snowballed their conversation from Mark's slightly taboo critique of his fellow directors to Valerie's confession of her professional crush to the private pain of worrying about a daughter gone astray is characteristic of a disclosure-matching episode. The reciprocity is being studied by psychologists looking for the underlying mechanism. The *Handbook of Interpersonal Communication* describes things like appropriateness of situation, sense of obligation, level of attraction, even anonymity as influencing the degree of reciprocal disclosing.[3] Whatever the cause, disclosure-matching can be experienced by anyone who has made a friend or fallen in love. Unfortunately, it's rarely recognized for what it is in corporate life—a significant step in the business of getting connected.

It's a process that can be started on purpose or stopped early before someone gets the wrong idea. Matching disclosures can even be done by mutual agreement—by conversational contract. If that sounds outlandish at first, think of someone saying (sincerely), "I'd like to get to know you more." Or: "Seems like I've been telling you all about me; how about you?" Such gambits are often the intentional instigation for a round of disclosure-matching.

Valerie wound up describing their conversations as a "milestone in our working relationship and a milestone in my *life*. Mark and I tell each other most all the motives behind important decisions—even selfish and irrational motives. And, God, we critique each other's stuff without any politeness whatsoever. It's so honest. Wonderful. I'm growing so much. He's great. Just great. You know, now we do each other all sorts of work favors, like picking up each other's leads, finalizing each other's calls.

"We do it routinely, without resentment. I love it. And the *whole damn department's* getting stronger. Honest. And it all started with that first meeting. it was opening up to each other that turned the whole thing around.''

CHAPTER 2

REFLECTIONS

"THE MISSING LINK IN COMMUNICATION."

SOMETHING'S WRONG here. The missing link in the evolution of person-to-person communication has been discovered, studied at universities like a wonder drug, and employed by a striking number of psychotherapists and other mental health professionals. Yet over 98 percent of the population doesn't even know the missing link exists. This unknown talk tool is used unwittingly on rare occasions, and people probably feel good when they do it, but they don't realize what they've done or how to do it again. If they did, they'd have in their communication repertoire the most effective talk tool that exists for demonstrating understanding and reducing misunderstanding.

I'm talking about reflection. It's called reflection because it mirrors back the heart of another's message. It *re*-presents the message, usually in a condensed version. A reflection doesn't try to understand the other person's thought or feelings better than he does. It doesn't try to solve the other's problems. It doesn't try to add new meaning or to analyze the message. Reflections simply show that meaning has been registered. They reveal an act of empathy. They tell the listener that he or she has been *heard*.

Here's a reflection that created joy for me and my son. Thinking of it fills me with love. Sasha was 18 months old. Sitting in a corner with a toy, he chanted, "Nosh, nosh, nosh." Toddling to me, he repeated, "Nosh, nosh, nosh."

Nosh? What was he trying to tell me? I tried chanting back,

"Nosh, nosh, nosh." Then he repeated it; I repeated it; we went through the same cycle a few times. But he seemed to want something more. What?

Then he grabbed his *nose*.

I grabbed *my* nose.

I repeated, "Nosh, nosh, nosh."

I mirrored back his message, becoming a reflection of his experience.

He saw I finally understood his discovery. We both sat there, noses in hands. Chanting "Nosh, nosh." Feeling intimate. And that did it—his serious face ignited with deep pleasure, he collapsed to the floor in laughter, then crawled contentedly back to his toy. Sasha had the satisfaction of knowing he'd been understood. So did I.

My son had searched for understanding by repeating his newfound word; had practically burst with the emotion of his new discovery and getting acknowledged, and when it was, his search ended, his repeating stopped, and he returned to his toy . . . relieved. A little boy, just like us bigger people, had put important feelings into a message that was repeated till someone finally demonstrated understanding. And, just like anyone with an important feeling, he felt a lot of satisfaction from the understanding, from the closeness, from the *reflection*.

When adults use reflections, the tool rarely repeats the very same words, as I did with my "nosh" reflection. A grad student of mine collected (with permission from the participants) an "adult" example of a series of effective reflections in a place I wouldn't have ever thought of looking for it—the locker room of a university basketball team. I'll call the two players Tall Guy and Buddy. Buddy will use a series of reflections ending with a big one that captures Tall Guy's experience. Notice how their slightly mocking tone distracts from the embarrassment of tenderness.

TALL GUY: Coach says I'm getting stronger on the boards.
BUDDY: Uh huh—a regular intimidator.
TALL GUY: He says my passing is semimasterful, whatever that means. Holds the offense together.
BUDDY: Yeah.
TALL GUY: Yesterday he told me I worry over the new guys like a father. They feel protected around me.
BUDDY: *(Laughing in friendly mockery)* Just a strong, semimasterful big daddy.

TALL GUY: But all I'm thinking about is Christmas and being back home
            and being told to drink all my milk and not being allowed out
            the front door without my jacket zipped up.
BUDDY: These guys here see you as a powerhouse, and all you're think-
            ing is, Momma, Momma—like a little boy.
TALL GUY: Yeah, this big powerhouse is missing his momma, like a little
            boy.

That unusually reflective dialogue demonstrates an act of understanding. It's the kind of communication that builds friendships. Tall Guy's apparent sense of being known hinged on one
of Buddy's sentences: "People here see you as a powerhouse,
and all you're thinking is, Momma, Momma—like a little boy."
A good reflection. It captured the irony, the twist, in being seen
as a masterful young man while feeling like a dependent boy. It
demonstrated compassion for the confession of loneliness. That
effective reflection gave Tall Guy comforting company. Reflections tend to do that—give company, demonstrate compassion,
capture feelings, display understanding.

PLEASURES AND PITFALLS OF FEELING INTO OTHERS' FEELINGS

All this good stuff rotates around one essential element called
empathy. The ability to harness the power of reflections is utterly dependent on it, our emotional lives are regularly salved
and strained by it, and the entertainment industry is built on
getting people to pay for the vicarious sharing of it. It's a pervasive psychological force that routinely sways our moods. It's
a required psychological condition for all forms of intimacy and
attachment. It's an everyday experience that creates most human
connections, shapes our personalities, makes social learning
possible, and stimulates orgasms. Our lives would be hollow
without any, but too much of it would literally make us crazy.

Empathy is the raw material, the necessary experience, the
required predisposition, the essential ingredient for reflection.
But empathy is also a force that nags at us every day in confusing
ways. It isn't easy to regulate—especially when we don't know
what it is or can't recognize it. So empathy can carry the potential to be embarrassing or irritating, as well as a positive experience. That's why people sometimes get confused at first about
doing reflections—about *disclosing empathy*—and why reflections haven't become a national craze. If the world were filled

with easy, tasty empathy, reflections would be as commonplace as ice cream.

The German language has a specific, everyday, nonslang word for empathy: *Einfühlung.* Translation: "feeling into someone." In English, about the closest you can get to that is the slang, "tuning in to someone." Dictionaries attempt to get at the possible meanings of empathy with words like accord, affinity, appreciation, communion, compatibility, comprehension, concord, congeniality, rapport, responsiveness, warmth. But none of those words comes close to capturing the scale of it; empathy is a lot bigger than any of them.

Psychologists have struggled sporadically during this century to map out the anatomy of empathy, but it's been a little like trying to capture a cloud and park it in the Astrodome for scrutiny. Right now empathy is an academic growth industry, with dozens of psychologists trying to tame it in scientific terms through rigorous research—a clear sign that it's a big deal.

Carl Rogers, the pioneer theorist on the role of empathy in helping people repair their lives, perhaps provided the best description of how people use it to improve: "When someone understands how it feels to be *me*, without wanting to analyze me or judge me, then I can blossom and grow in that climate. And research bears out this common observation. When the therapist can grasp the moment-to-moment experiencing occurring in the inner world of the client as the client sees it and feels it, without losing the separateness of his own identity in this empathic process, then change is likely to occur."

His emphasis on the single-minded, spontaneous entry into another inner world excludes distracting thoughts that either criticize or admire. Successful empathy is fairly free of *any* evaluation. It simply understands, "knows" the other's experience. It accepts—as is.

It can be as basic and simple as my dentist seeing my eyes narrow in pain as he works on a tooth and saying "Ow!" Or it can be as complex as a therapist getting so tuned in to a client's feelings that he can come up with precisely the right reflection out of the dozens available, almost as if he had computer assistance.

Learning to get a grip on what empathy does to your daily conversations can expand your options for exchanging love—it can add some *Einfühlung* to your life.

Contagious Moods

Anyone who has ever been influenced by someone's excitement or sadness knows about "mood-catching." As a kid, I used to feel uneasy when I got on the school bus in the morning and found myself catching some of the grumpiness of the routinely hungover bus driver. Having him grump at me, listening to him grump at others, made *me* kind of grumpy. It was embarrassing: How could I be so weak and vulnerable as to let a stranger, someone of no importance in my life, give me some of his unpleasant mood?

The contagious aspect of moods is the reason we say things like: "He made me grumpy!" or "Her happiness gave me a lift."

Anyone who walked around every day with his empathy valve stuck on "open," would become psychotic within a month. That person would absorb so many different moods in the course of a day that a normal, healthy life would be impossible. On the other hand, most genuinely crazy people feel *no* empathy—they're entirely self-absorbed. So mental health is affected by how we handle empathy, how we regulate the intake without getting sickened by the negative parts of others' thoughts and feelings. People get buffeted daily, hourly, by the unrecognized experience of feeling into others' experience.

It gets confusing. We sometimes fear being overloaded by others—that is, we fear getting close. If it's an accurate fear, discomfort is avoided. But there can also be regret. An unfounded fear of being smothered may turn us away just when it appears closeness is coming.

Fear of intimacy exists for several good reasons—a major one seems to be confusion about getting emotionally overloaded. I believe the threat of empathy overload is a common cause for aborted intimacy, for relationships that never go beyond becoming interesting strangers or cordial acquaintances. Having dinner with someone new who's feeling lousy can make *us* feel lousy enough to end the relationship. When the same thing happens between old friends, it's chalked up to part of the price paid for maintaining a good thing—in this case, the cost of the empathy is easier to pay.

The mechanism underlying empathic attachment is the same, though, whether it involves friends or strangers: feeling into feelings until they become like your own, until they make you feel a lump in your throat or make your palms perspire or increase the flow of your sex hormones. If you don't resist, it's a little like being taken on another's personal journey. And sometimes empathy rises in us so strongly that even efforts at self-control can't cancel the experience; sometimes empathy is like a state of being helplessly connected.

Part of the confusion from empathic experiences is that no sooner can you feel burned by someone's negative contagion than you can catch some extremely *nice* mood: the empathic experience of seeing an impossibly outmanned U.S. Olympic hockey team's success grow day after day with one improbable performance after another until it wins the gold medal; sharing your toddler's exhilaration at discovering the roar of the sea in a shell; empathizing so strongly with your partner's orgasm that you have one, too. (Now, *that's* major league empathy.)

So there are times when we want to jump right in and enjoy the mood contagion—the thrill of victory—and times when we want to run away before our day is ruined—by someone's agony of defeat.

Who Has Empathy, and Who Doesn't?

Some of my colleagues write in journals as if there are all sorts of people walking around who don't have any empathy. And, in particular, as if there are lots of *men* who never developed any. That's ridiculous. Any socially functioning person *has* to have the ability to empathize. People who are not functioning adequately have shut down their empathic capacity in significant ways—first by shutting down the disclosure of it, then the empathic feeling itself. These people are diagnosed as mentally ill.

Empathy researchers have found that people, given detailed instructions on imagining themselves *in the shoes of others*, were able to enhance their empathic responses.[1] When the instruction said, "Imagine yourself as being this other person—*role-play*," they were better able to empathize. But when people were simply asked to "empathize," the results were the same as from instructions asking them to *not* feel into others' emotions—another indication of how little people know about the meaning of the word *empathy*.

For a long time, women have been widely considered to be more emotional, nurturant, and absorbed with human relations, and therefore more empathic than men. But recent research on sex differences in empathy have failed to establish female superiority. In a rigorous review of dozens of studies dating back to 1923, Drs. Nancy Eisenberg and Randy Lennon at Arizona State University found the pattern of evidence did not clearly favor women. They did find a trend for women to describe themselves, on questionnaires, as more likely to feel into others' feelings. But that's expected. It seems women believe their own media image as being superior in perceiving feelings—they buy into the stereotype and rate themselves high in empathy. When more sophisticated, less obvious measures were used—facial expressions, body gestures, voice tone, palm-sweating, heart rate, and blood pressure—there were *no* differences between the sexes. As Drs. Eisenberg and Lennon figure it: "There certainly is reason to believe that males and females might differ in how empathic they would like to appear to others (and, perhaps to themselves). . . . Thus, it is highly likely that females would be more willing than males to present themselves as being empathic and/or sympathetic."[2]

So the best thinking at this time is that men are able to tune into other's feelings just as well as women. Men may not be as willing or able to *express* empathy, and years of concealment may numb some of their self-awareness, but they're probably not intrinsically blunted. Getting rid of the stereotype of the empathically dead male is important. It gets in my way when trying to demonstrate the use of reflections to both sexes. I'm wary of men who believe that they were born with less capacity for empathizing, who think they're innately inferior when it comes to recognizing, knowing, and co-experiencing the tender emotions of others. Men may be more reluctant (or fearful) to communicate their experience, but apparently they empathize as powerfully as women when confronting another person's evocative emotions.

Empathy and Vicarious Adventures

A fundamental part of the ability to empathize is the ability to fantasize—to let our imagination soar into someone's heart and head. The perennial popularity of Walter Mitty is probably due to our empathizing with his imaginative, empathic voyages into the worlds of others who achieve so much. At the same time, those who are able to fantasize vividly may tend to find themselves getting bogged down in empathizing with others' painful experiences. They can develop a resistance to feeling into feelings because it brings them too close to others' troubles.

Still, there aren't many of us—strong fantasizers or not—who don't regularly seek out the feeling of emotionally gliding into the inner lives of others. With the help of the entertainment industry, we take a vicarious adventure or receive some sensual pleasure while remaining motionless and physically untouched. We pay for that TV set and cable system that brings us fantasy for our empathy appetite. We buy tickets for that current movie and spend a couple hours in the hope the images on the big screen will be strong enough to transport us into the characters' feelings. Producers, directors, and scriptwriters are really in the business of trying to get their audiences to empathize with their creations. The more the audience empathizes, the more successful their products will be. But show biz people don't often think about their products in such terms. Instead they think of getting the right star package, finding a director with "juice," and trying to copy the formula of the latest ratings hit or blockbuster feature. Maybe there wouldn't be so many boring TV shows and unwatchable movies if the makers thought instead about stories and characters that more viewers could feel empathy for.

For entertainers who make a living doing impersonations (Rich Little comes to mind), their ability to deliver quality imitations of celebrities is strongly related to their ability to first empathize with those celebrities. If Rich Little didn't have a strong sense of feeling into, say, Johnny Carson's public persona, he wouldn't be able to do such a strong impersonation of Carson. That imitation/empathy relationship might not seem important to many people beyond impressionists, but it's a necessity for the social development of children. Growing up, kids mimic the behavior of their parents, peers, the older kids on the block, the actor they admire in their favorite movie or TV series. (Ever walk out of a theater moving with the cocky assurance of the star you've been empathizing with for the last two hours?) It's a serious way of learning about social behavior.

Empathy, Love, and Lovemaking

Back in 1923, a religious philosopher, Martin Buber, wrote a book that influenced several generations: *I and Thou*.[3] Whether Buber intended it or not, his book had to do mostly with empathy. Buber argued that the essentials of human nature could not be understood if our focus were limited to individuals, communities or societies. He helped us see that making better sense of the realities of close relationships between people unveiled the essence of humans. His work brought world attention to the psychology of "experiencing the other's side." He was fascinated with the mechanism through which you can experience an event or feeling from the standpoint of another—without forgetting that you are *you* and *not* the other person. It's not easy stuff to write about, as Buber learned in doing his book . . . and as I learned while doing this book.

Buber illuminated empathy in the context of love and lovemaking. I'll try to translate his example, taking some liberties.

A man and woman are feeling amorous out of caring. The preliminaries—dates, dinners, getting to know and prize each other—have taken place. They're together on a couch. They kiss. Kiss some more. His hand, moving as if it had a mind of its own, tentatively finds its way inside her blouse to cup a breast. As if to give permission, she moves closer, hugs him hard and makes a modest moan. Her barely audible sound has the power to send an empathic message through his body: It tells him she's also taking pleasure. That small sound signals their similarity and gives him permission to go on. His hand, no longer tentative, begins to "take" as the fingers grab and the palm presses into the softness. The breast enjoys the embracing pressure. Both hand and breast *take* and both know the other is taking. His hand knows she's taking even more now by the way she holds him and breathes, and by the trace of an enlarged nipple across its palm. (Remarkable how the palm is particularly sensitive to the light pressure of objects the size of a nipple.) And her breast knows he's taking more by the response of his body, including the concentrated embrace and the dance of his hand. So the hand and breast not only *take* pleasure but can receive messages about how they *give* pleasure. Dozens of subtle signals about their taking and giving bounce back and forth and leave sweet blurs on the participants' consciousness.

Sometimes the experiences of giving and taking become simultaneous in one person (sensing his pleasure gives her a gratification that rivals the pleasure she takes). In true lovemaking, giving and taking can easily become indistinguishable experiences. His empathy with her pleasure allows her to incorporate it into his own body. The blending gives him two-for-one.

(Whenever I think about this phenomenon where empathy doubles our experience, I also think of that Doublemint jingle: "Double your pleasure, double your fun. . . .") The boundaries between their individual senses of self are gradually melting. This is not some self-absorbed passion of recreational sex. The signs of pleasure that each reveals are like reflections for their own physical gratification; they're like mirrors for each other's experience. Then, as their interaction deepens, the mirrors reflect even more images so that she senses him sensing her sensing him . . . and so on, until the images blur. They completely include each other into each other's experience without thinking about it. A natural, unpracticed act of connecting occurs simply by letting go and doing what comes naturally. But the psychological dynamics—the messages reflecting back and forth—are so complex and rapid that my profession is at a loss to pin the process down. It humbles our science for measuring behavior, for diagramming face-to-face communication (no less hand-to-breast communication). So our science has left the empathy of lovemaking to poets and mystics like Buber, who praise it more than explain it. What we do know is that the disclosure of empathy and the reflection of empathy can blend giving and taking to a point where they become the same. And that's where love starts.

The practically automatic way we show empathy in lovemaking eliminates the need for using verbal reflections. Imagine our lovers on the couch, having become more amorous since that first tentative contact of hand and breast. They're now in fervent embrace (a romance novel phrase meaning they've "gone all the way"). Her modest moan has grown to a full-throated, immodest groan. Picture him hearing her open expression of sexual excitement, her aroused language, and then responding with a conscientious reflection: "It seems you're feeling quite passionate and want me to continue earnestly."

Fortunately, the communication of empathy in physical intimacy usually takes a mere movement, an effortless gesture, a touch, the sound of a sensitive reaction, a response to an unspoken need. But in less intimate, less loving circumstances, empathy is harder to read; there it *does* need conscientious reflections. Our successful understanding of others' feelings and thoughts can be wasted if they're not put into words that demonstrate such understanding. The experience of being known can turn into the experience of being *un*known, misunderstood, or disregarded if empathic understanding is not spoken. Without a physical connection, we need a verbal connection.

REFLECTIONS THAT WORK AT WORK

Gathering information, coming to a better understanding and establishing feelings of trust and safety are by-products of the use of reflections in the business world, as well as in the home. The dialogue example I'll use to demonstrate this phenomenon happens to come from an interview between my co-writer, Glenn Esterly, and the subject of a magazine profile, John Forsythe, but the benefit of Glenn's use of reflections should be apparent in all sorts of professional settings—from an office manager talking to her employee about his morale problem to a salesperson talking to a potential customer about exactly what the customer is looking for.

In the case of the Forsythe interview, Glenn was on assignment from *TV Guide* to do a profile of the veteran actor, an elegant, self-contained, rather private man who played oil baron Blake Carrington in the television series "Dynasty." "My approach to an interview with a public personality," Glenn says, "is that I'm there to try to find out something about what makes him tick—what's important or different about the way he thinks, feels, lives, and works. And what's there that readers could, pardon the expression, empathize with. That's not particularly easy when you're dealing with performers who, after all, tend to get used to presenting a public facade they're comfortable with, even if it doesn't have much to do with the way they are away from the cameras."

When a public figure has coped with a serious predicament or a personal tragedy, revealing private thoughts or frightening details about it can feel terribly risky. Even a seasoned celebrity is going to think twice about it (particularly if the celebrity feels he or she has been misquoted or misinterpreted in the past, which they often do). Glenn went into this interview knowing that John Forsythe had undergone quadruple heart bypass surgery a couple of years earlier and guessing that the effects on the star must have been more than just physical. As in other interviews for magazine profiles, Glenn didn't sit down to talk as a strategic manipulator; instead, he approached the conversation as an empathic partner who exercised plenty of patience and lots of reflections to allow the subject to see that important feelings and thoughts would be handled with care.

The following exchanges in the Forsythe conversation took place about 40 minutes into the interview, after they started talking about his bypass surgery.

FORSYTHE: I had noticed it on the tennis court a couple times—not feeling quite right. And when I traveled, the jet lag hit me like it never had before. But being like most red-blooded, overly macho American guys, I never did much about it.

ESTERLY: Your body was sending signals.

FORSYTHE: Right. When I finally went in for tests, lo and behold, they came up with the heart problem.

ESTERLY: There had never been a heart attack?

FORSYTHE: No, but there was a pending possibility. Turned out I had congenitally small coronary arteries, so they had to bypass some clogged arteries.

ESTERLY: Do people die in that kind of surgery?

FORSYTHE: Yes, they do. It's immensely serious surgery—six, seven hours, although they've got it down now where the risks are considerably less these days. It's not exactly a picnic, in any event. The choice was there for me to go either way, to not do it if I didn't want to. I *could* have gone without it, but it would have meant compromises in the way I lived. Just being *very* careful all the time, always cautious about any exercise and work. That wasn't appealing to me.

ESTERLY: So, even with the surgery risks, you weren't able to settle for a life of restrictions.

[Glenn boiled Forsythe's disclosure into one tightly edited sentence. Most of us would need several sentences. His writing skill, applied to talk, concentrates Forsythe's meaning into a satisfying, economical summary. Notice how that nice piece of understanding brings more emotion and increased openness.]

FORSYTHE: Oh, *that* would have been devastating for me. There was no bravado in having the surgery. There was almost no alternative. Without it, I faced the prospect of living very tentatively, always the chance that after a hard set of tennis or a hard day at work the heart could fold on me. *(Long pause)* I couldn't live under that shadow. I'm a vigorous guy. I love my tennis and my hard work. But I'm a lucky fellow—I'm functioning infinitely better now than I have in years. My stress tests look fine.

ESTERLY: The gamble paid off and now you're better than ever.

[Another one-sentence reflection that accurately reduces a 35-second message into a 5-second summary. The reflection didn't focus much on his subject's continued detailing of not wanting a restricted lifestyle; instead, it tried to steer the focus from the past ". . . gamble paid off . . ." to the present ". . . you're better than ever now. . . ." It almost worked, but John Forsythe couldn't resist turning to the past for a joke.]

FORSYTHE: *(Beaming)* Exactly. I'm getting another shot. The only thing I really worried about afterward was when the surgeon told me that one by-product of prolonged surgery could be some memory loss . . . and I said, "*What* surgery?" *(Both laugh; then Forsythe continues disclosing his past, revealing a post-operation fear)*

FORSYTHE: *(Continuing)* For someone who has to memorize lines, I really was worried about that, having seen the poignance of actors, especially older ones, who need work and can't remember their lines—God, it's *heartbreaking*. So as soon as I could, I took a role, to test myself, and fortunately I remembered every line. No problem.

[Picking up his cue about the massive biological impact of the operation, Glenn will remain with the impact, but aim for understanding more about the psychological aspects. He's interested in linking the past to the present. So now he's going to *disclose* what he wants—the interviewer's repertoire, after all, can include any talk tools appropriate to the situation.]

ESTERLY: I'm curious what a serious operation like that does to you aside from the physical aspects. I mean, here you are, looking good, feeling good, enjoying life a lot. But I'm wondering what might have changed in how you look at things on a day-to-day basis.

[Hearing Glenn's disclosure of what he's driving at—and already secure in the knowledge that this interviewer has a strong understanding of what he's been through (demonstrated by the empathic reflections)—Forsythe gives the reporter what he wants.]

FORSYTHE: *(Looking out the window at his green, lush backyard and sighing)* A day as glorious as today is an immensely moving thing to somebody who's had an operation like that. Before, I might not have taken time to look at that. It's very beneficial.

ESTERLY: You've gotta stop to smell the roses.

[A corny metaphor, but it clearly mirrors the essential lesson Forsythe has learned. Metaphors, proverbs, similes, or aphorisms that show understanding of one kind of experience in terms of another kind of experience make fine reflections. The subject of the understanding rarely cares about the corn.]

FORSYTHE: Absolutely. Sometimes you have to be *forced* to. When you come close to the edge, when you have a brush with leaving this vale of tears and are lucky enough to survive it, you should take advantage of it, get more perspective on the important things.

ESTERLY: You were confronted with your mortality and came away with a better outlook on the big stuff.

[Bullseye. This crisp, accurate *re*-presentation guides John Forsythe toward elaborating how he's changed and how the "big stuff" can come in easy-to-miss small packages.]

FORSYTHE: Oh, yes. The day I got home from the hospital, I was lying in bed and noticed these tiny hummingbirds outside the window. There's a watering place there, a piece of ironwork that hangs near the window, and I just laid there watching those hummingbirds—*miraculous* things. The way they can hover is incredible. Well, I kept putting water in that thing and kept watching those hummingbirds as I recovered. Then I started raving to my wife about them and she said, "Well, they've been around for years—didn't you notice them before?" Oh, my—well, I notice them *now*.

[Esterly remains quiet for about seven seconds as both men stop to let the message sink in. The pause allows Forsythe to touch and express a strong experience that could sound silly or trivial in another context but is unabashedly serious in this conversation.]

FORSYTHE: *(Continuing)* Hummingbirds are marvelous creatures, wondrous flying machines. I am *passionate* about hummingbirds.

ESTERLY: You're feeling very strongly about things you didn't even notice before.

[This reflection *generalizes*, goes way beyond the hummingbird but captures the essence of Forsythe's experience and steers him toward disclosing other personal changes.]

FORSYTHE: Yes. What I went through has affected my whole life. I'm not as insular as I used to be. I'm loosening up. In both my work and in my personal relationships. I come from a background where people were extremely reserved and stiff, and I've tried for a long time to break down some of my built-in restraints. The more they're broken down, the freer I am to take chances, as an actor and as a person. Since the surgery, I've been more successful at that, and I think I've gotten more sensitive about dealing with my family and other people and a lot of things.

As the interview continued, the actor talked candidly about specific changes in both his personal and professional life, his family relationships, how he had come to grips with the realization of his limitations as an actor, and his strong political views. His willingness to reveal vulnerabilities no doubt was fostered by Glenn's earlier demonstrations of empathic understanding and his continuing reflections at key points in the conversation. But the heart of the story centered around the excerpts you've read, resulting in a warm profile in which readers not only found out a good deal about what makes John Forsythe tick but were reminded of how a life-threatening predicament can paradoxically enhance life. Not a new idea, but one that easily gets forgotten, and when a public personality like Forsythe relates how he coped with it, millions of readers in similar circumstances can gain a bit of comfort.

REFLECTIONS THAT WORK AS PSYCHOLOGICAL HEALERS

Nature tends to heal by gathering scattered natural things into a concentrated medicine. Scattered white blood cells suddenly concentrate at the site of an infection. A tree rushes its protective sap to cover the wound of a cut branch. When it comes to emotional disorders—big or small—the same rule applies: Ordinary events can be harnessed and focused into concentrated remedies for preventing, repairing, relieving, and curing. Emotionally exhausted? Better concentrate some sleep or silence on your psyche. Distressed over an argument? Your mind will automatically maintain a focused concentration on the event. (Sometimes emotional pain is obsessively repeated and gets emotionally washed down a little with each runthrough. It's as if focusing our thoughts allows us to dissect distress and dissolve some of the discomfort—a form of psychological mastery.)

The natural (but uncommon and unrecognized) process of reflecting feelings in conversation can also become concentrated during moments of high emotion. Facing someone who's revealed a serious personal predicament causes people who've never heard of reflections to instinctively do a couple, rather than use quick-fix advice or a barrage of rushed questions. Hearing someone open up about deep feelings can overwhelm us. Sometimes the emotional input of others transfixes us to a point where we just naturally repeat what we hear. It's as if we're helplessly dominated by the profundity of the other's message. That sometimes causes even pushy people or "insensitive clods" to utter an exquisitely touching reflection.

I'm not saying that reflections only occur in rare, emotionally charged conversation with profoundly painful topics. You can spot them as reactions to intense joy or excitement: The parent reflects, "You found a penny!" as his child holds up her discovered treasure and exclaims the same message. I've seen an athlete running to her coach, shouting, "I did it!" and the coach repeating the same words as if announcing the sharing of a joy—and thereby prolonging the experience.

The tragedy is that reflections aren't commonly and deliberately used by laypeople to connect to either someone's good fortune (too often winners wind up celebrating alone) or misfortune. When it comes to professionals, just about all psychotherapists from every persuasion—from cognitive behavior modification to psychoanalysis (and especially, client-centered therapy)—reflect their patients' disclosures. There's some debate about how reflections help healing or when they heal, and how often to employ them, but it's unusual to find a practitioner who doesn't use them at all. A minority of therapists bring out reflections infrequently, at strategic moments; psychoanalysts sprinkle them into sessions regularly, sometimes unconsciously (yes, I mean exactly that); guidance counselors, school psychologists, pastoral counselors, and some social workers use them much of the time. Therapists who follow the client-centered approach are probably the most sophisticated practitioners of the reflection response. It's their major therapy talk tool.

I have a psychotherapy dialogue sample with a client-centered therapist, Dr. Madge Lewis. She demonstrates the uses of reflections to help a somewhat passive, overly dependent man change for the better. It has practical implications for laypeople in demonstrating exactly how the reflection can be applied to personal relationships. There's no reason to confine this safe and effective tool to therapy sessions. Reflections belong in conversations between friends, spouses, and lovers. They are desperately needed to humanize parent/child talk. The reflections used by Dr. Lewis are deceptively simple. She has years of practice in uncluttered communication. The excerpts are taken from tape recordings used in early research at the University of Chicago, with permission of patient and therapist.[4]

"Mr. Tapa" is the code name for a bright, outgoing, professional man, 27, who felt he was losing control of his life. He was dissatisfied because "things just *happened* to him." He wanted to stop just "drifting along with the tide." He felt discomfort relating to people, low self-confidence, and distress about being too dependent on others. After 35 interviews, all research criteria rated the case "highly successful." Mr. Tapa's self-esteem (measured by discrepancy between his self-concept and ideal self-concept) increased over the course of therapy.

During the first session he disclosed how his first marriage deteriorated. He was far too dependent on his wife, and she left him for another man. Now he was in love with another woman and again painfully dependent on her. His moods fluctuated too much with hers. He was also upset by the way he dumped his emotions and imposed his problems on her. "I can't tell her how this makes me feel without doing exactly what I'm trying to avoid doing," he said. Here's how it went in the initial session.

MR. TAPA: I try hard to be perfect with her—cheerful, friendly, intelligent, talkative—because I want her to love me. It's as simple as that.

DR. LEWIS: This is the way you feel you *must* be in order to be loved by her.

[Her simple, undemanding reflection points Mr. Tapa toward examining his self-deceit and insecurity—two psychological items that usually remain hidden in opening interviews, especially when therapists push for their disclosure.]

MR. TAPA: I'm not being *me*, I'm being directed by what I think she expects of me—which is probably completely wrong. I don't know what I look like from her position. I probably never will know, but it's as if all of this I *have* to know. I must make sure I won't be rejected.

[Lack of personal integrity was a major theme. He went on to describe himself as "totally artificial." Even as a boy, his lying and stealing prompted his father to insist that he seriously think about himself and then do something to change.]

MR. TAPA: How do you *do* something about yourself, a hopeless feeling. How *can* you? This is the way I *am*. So *many* things I couldn't tell people—nasty things I did . . . felt so sneaky and bad.

DR. LEWIS: You felt like a bad boy, not knowing what to do about it all by yourself and needing help.

[The last reflection amplifies his message of "hopeless feelings . . . I couldn't tell people" into ". . . not knowing what to do . . . needing help." It gently encouraged Mr. Tapa to reexamine his father's commands. He couldn't change by just thinking about it and deciding to. He needed to talk with someone, but his parents didn't know how and others scared him. Personal communication about his inner life was denied. There was nobody to talk with about sex—about how things worked in general. Furious at his parents, he entertained recurrent fantasies about tearing their limbs off. He tried to stop but couldn't control the rage until he was 14.]

These revelations made to a professional stranger during the initial hour were drawn out and managed by a series of reflections. Each time Dr. Lewis reflected, she produced an after-image of Mr. Tapa's expressed feelings, a brief extension of his emotions. Instead of describing a thought or emotion and moving onto the next issue, the reflection reiterates the message, replays the theme for 10, 20, or 30 seconds so that it remains alive in his attention. That afterglow can double the time given to think into personal matters. A therapist who gives 20 to 40 reflections an hour is producing a bunch of after-images that can add up to a significant extension of the patient's exploration of feelings.

A run of reflections can cause the receiver to dwell a little longer with each new, difficult feeling before continuing. And those extra moments repeated time and again over many months of typical therapy—or *any* helping relationship—will produce significant changes in the way a person experiences his personal exploration. It's almost like a magnification of inner life, of private memories. In addition to the after-image, there's the constant experience of getting attended to and empathically understood—without getting judged or advised. Such a combination can be irresistible, even to those who fiercely guard their private thoughts.

Reflections are like Mr. Sun in the Aesop fable who made a bet with Mr. Wind about who could get a traveler to remove his cloak. Huffing and puffing, Mr. Wind caused the traveler to tighten his grip. But that old hustler, Mr. Sun, laid some gentle, warm rays on the cloak . . . and off it came. Reflections might sound just as corny as the Aesop fable, especially out of context. But they can consistently uncloak guarded memories and emotions much better than those insinuatingly windy talk tools that diagnose, urge, and implore.

Revealing feelings about his girlfriend in the *first* session to Dr. Lewis resulted in Mr. Tapa revealing those feelings directly to his girlfriend. It was great. Instead of feeling like a fake, he "felt more like *me*." (It's easy to see the same thing happening without therapy if Mr. Tapa had a friend who could provide just an hour's worth of reflections.)

In the second session, Dr. Lewis renewed her careful, undramatic reflecting. She followed him, absorbed in his experiencing. Reacting to the steady supply of her empathy, he started exploring some basic fears about his abilities and examined his use of humor as something to hide behind.

MR. TAPA: I feel a little naked and unprotected from you. . . . Here I am, sticking out all over.

DR. LEWIS: Sort of embarrassing—and almost hating to show feelings without this curtain of safety.

MR. TAPA: It's easy to give an impression of confidence when you don't feel it—almost as easy as when you *do* feel it.

DR. LEWIS: It's easy to pretend.

[Disarmed by Dr. Lewis's unobtrusive flow of reflections, Mr. Tapa loses his facade of self-confidence, his mask of swaggering humor. This professionally successful man, who's solved professional problems with order and calm rationality, feels stripped of his defenses. After only 40 or 50 rather modest reflections, Mr. Tapa finds himself in new interpersonal territory. Unable to hide behind logic. Disoriented.]

MR. TAPA: The way I'd like this to go would be to sit down and think soberly about my problems, clearly and accurately, put my finger on them and let one thing lead to another. And there are some things where that works just fine. With others, it doesn't work at all.

DR. LEWIS: You'd like it to go honestly, simply, and logically.

MR. TAPA: I wish I were as honest as I can sound. . . . I feel sort of at a loss right now. Where was I? What was I saying? I lost my grip on something—that I've been holding myself up with!

He loses his hold on the customary ways he takes care of himself—humor and logic. Without the jokes and tight rationality, he confronts a major issue buried for years—his fear of the future, unrealized guilt about fraudulent behavior at work, submerged feelings of being a "fake."

Without strategic guidance from Dr. Lewis, Mr. Tapa began exploring his childhood experiences and discovering how early physical abuse by his parents was affecting his adult functioning. These therapeutic conversations were helping him become aware of the depth of his anger. Dr. Lewis reported that one of her reflections during the fifth session brought him face-to-face with the awful memory of being hit and complaining about it—which only resulted in even more severe physical abuse. In the seventh session, he explored a previously unexamined personal value— that it was honorable to accept punishment without complaint, wrong to object, and most of the time he somehow deserved to be punished. The experience seriously wounded his self-confidence.

MR. TAPA: I'd feel so damn helpless about it [his parents' punishment].
I felt they had complete power over me. . . . Whatever they
decided, *that* was going to happen to me, no matter what,
even if they decided to send me away.

DR. LEWIS: You felt completely in their hands and that was pretty frightening.

[The frightening memories of parental oppression were reviewed in the
safety of Dr. Lewis's reliable empathy. Her constant acceptance and the
stick-like-glue understanding of each experience allowed him the freedom to penetrate his vague childhood recollections and locate some
murderous hate. He also relived experiences of feeling powerless, dehumanized, getting treated like property.]

MR. TAPA: In high school it was, "I don't care whether you study or not,
but you're going to sit in front of that desk with a book in
front of you; maybe some of it will sink in."

DR. LEWIS: A feeling of "You're under my power whether you do anything
or not."

[Note how snugly her reflections stick to his meaning. They rapidly shift
meaning with his flow and help lead him to the awful bottom line.]

MR. TAPA: So I'd sit there and have fantasies of *murdering* everyone in
the whole family—in horrible ways.

DR. LEWIS: You had your revenge.

MR. TAPA: But the next day, everything was as usual.

DR. LEWIS: It wasn't *real* revenge.

MR. TAPA: I sure wanted revenge. . . . There were so many restrictions.
I hated them . . . felt every one of them was a direct invasion
of me. . . . There were injunctions to "love and respect"—
whatever that meant. My parents—to obey them. Every time
they said something like that meant I was their *property*. . . .
I *hated* them for it.

DR. LEWIS: Hated to feel you belonged to anybody.

MR. TAPA: Yeah. I didn't feel I belonged to *them*. I was *mine*! Every time
they treated me like property, I *became* like property.

In the next interview, he examined the pain of the process—
as if the reflections were tugging hurt out of him. That odd
sensation of reflections dragging out painful secrets is one I've
felt personally and have heard from many patients over the years.
Sort of ironic that such an unassertive talk tool—coming from
an attitude of empathy, acceptance, and following the other's
message—can make people become so undone. Taken singly,
most reflections look a little vapid, parroting, unimaginative,
even boring. But a good string of them aimed at a profound
personal experience usually proves to be unexpectedly powerful. Accurate ones are irresistibly demanding. Given enough
time, they can create an interpersonal environment with a spe-

cial drawing-out power that melts resistance and allows—even compels—us to reveal our most guarded thoughts.

MR. TAPA: Something in me is saying, "What more do I have to give up? You've taken so much from me already." This is *me* talking to me—the *me* way back in there who talks to *me*, who runs the show. It's complaining now, saying, "You're getting too close. Go away!"

DR. LEWIS: "How much more is going to be demanded? How much more am I going to hurt?"

But the hurt didn't stop Mr. Tapa as he continued exploring the bad little boy within himself and began feeling more comfortable with himself. By the 16th session, problems in relating to his girlfriend were settled and they were married. After the 20th session, he began looking at Dr. Lewis's communication style—her use of reflections. There were times when he wanted *her* to lead *him* to helpful answers, instead of the other way around. Some of her reflections made him feel she was forsaking her role as expert. Being a client and being in control, or at least a co-equal, can feel like a contradiction. Reflections force a partnership in psychological healing. Dr. Lewis's reflections brought out the independent side of Mr. Tapa as he took major responsibility for the flow of topics. Quite a feat for a patient with a chronic problem of overdependence.

Over the next couple of months, Mr. Tapa gained comfort in taking charge of improving his life. He had insights about his techniques for pushing away things he didn't want to see, his difficulty in communicating annoyances, his tendency to talk in a manner that was "stilted and artificial—striving for effect." After that, he again turned his attention to the process of therapy conversation. During the 30th session he puzzled about how the process worked. In the following excerpt, Mr. Tapa is searching for the active element that's helping him improve. It's hard for him to grasp that "just bringing up previously unknown thoughts and feelings can produce major personality changes. That's too easy." He also fails to recognize the impact of 30 sessions full of Dr. Lewis's reflections. Like so many who've received massive, long-term empathy, Mr. Tapa is at a loss to say what's happened. All he knows is that he feels better in big ways.

MR. TAPA: What's counted is sitting down and saying, "This is what's bothering me," and play around with it for a while until something gets squeezed out through some emotional crescendo, and the thing is over with—looks different. Even then I can't tell just exactly what's happened. It's just exposed something and shook it up and turned it around. And when I put it back it felt better. It's a little frustrating because I'd like to know exactly what's going on.

DR. LEWIS: That even to you, who've experienced it, it's kind of a mystery.

MR. TAPA: All I can really say is that it does work that way.

DR. LEWIS: The reasons are not obvious.

MR. TAPA: No. That's right. This is a funny thing because it feels as if I'm not doing anything at all about it. . . . The only *active* part I take is to . . . to be alert and grab a thought as it's going by.

DR. LEWIS: Just being aware of what's in your own mind and feelings.

MR. TAPA: That's right! Simply bringing it to the point where it's talkable about. But once I've done that, I always had the feeling I should *do* something with it. . . .

DR. LEWIS: That there must be some kind of action to follow the experiencing of the feeling . . . You expected to be *doing* something.

MR. TAPA: That's right. I think part of the trouble is that I don't quite trust my unconscious working yet.

DR. LEWIS: If it happens this easily and without as much of my *conscious* self functioning, then I'd better watch out because I can't trust my *unconscious*.

[The last reflection is what I call a *first-person reflection* because it appears to completely identify with the discloser's point of view—it's in the discloser's frame of reference. First-persons are used by experienced reflectors who want to stick very close or want to "fall into" the patient's inner point of view. I've seen them used in other close relationships—mother/son, lovers, or longtime business partners—where one person was tightly connected to the other. Dr. Lewis's first-person reflection didn't work well, as you'll see, because she missed his meaning. But first-persons usually work beautifully, especially after using a bunch of regular reflections.]

MR. TAPA: Well, no! The point is, I'm not sure of the quality of the readjustment because I didn't get to see it, to check on it. I don't know what happened inside me, so I don't know exactly what the results will be. All I can do is observe the fact that I . . . look at things a little differently and am less anxious—by a long shot—and a lot more active. Things are looking up in general. I'm very happy with the way things have gone. . . .

[After the 38th session, he decided to stop therapy.]

MR. TAPA: I really think it'll be a good thing for me to get out of therapy for a while. I found myself thinking Friday, as I was staring glumly at a project in front of me, not wanting to do what I had to do, Oh, gee, I wish I could go and talk to Madge and get this off my chest. When it gets to a point that the therapy hour is a pill I take twice a week, that gathers me up and carries me to the next therapy hour—it's time I quit for a while. See if I can make it on my own.

[Here comes another of those first-person reflections. This time Dr. Lewis understands accurately—and with emotion. Her response almost sounds as if it's mocking—because it mimics his emotion with a bit of drama. Instead of approving or disapproving his decision, she simply shows understanding.]

DR. LEWIS: Oh, dear! Am I getting dependent on the therapy hour?

MR. TAPA: That's right. It's a feeling of, "I shouldn't have to wait for the therapy hour to do this."

[And another first-person reflection follows.]

DR. LEWIS: I should be able to do it another way.

MR. TAPA: Therapy hour is so very convenient for this . . . pleasant sort of talk, and I feel concentrated into one package and thinking about myself. I can't be in therapy all my life.

DR. LEWIS: There must be some other way of accomplishing the same thing—something I ought to be doing myself.

[Still another first-person by her—she wants to be close and accurate here.]

MR. TAPA: There's a time, for me at least, when therapy largely turned from a helping hand to a crutch. . . . I feel I've settled to my own satisfaction what I want to do with myself. I have a feeling that I'm capable of doing more. . . . I'm getting clearer pictures of things I *don't* want to do and things I *can* do. . . .

Eight months later, in a followup interview, Mr. Tapa described how his life had changed since finishing therapy: increased productivity and creativity at work, more self-confidence in personal settings, more sensitivity in human relations, more focusing on the moment, less rigidness in his thinking, less fear of the problems of living, no longer "drifting along with the tide."

Without getting into controversial issues about how this case represents a small minority of documented therapy success stories, I want to point out that the "treatment" was almost pure reflection. My colleagues will want me to mention that some of the improvements can be attributed to Mr. Tapa's initial commitment to change, or his serious assumption of the status of "patient," or all kinds of such unspecified factors as having good luck at work or entering a new love relationship. (I'd never argue that therapy can even come close to a solid love relationship, or even a deep friendship for improving the quality of life.) But Mr. Tapa's case illustrates the power of disclosing empathy through reflections. And that the reflections need not be fancy. Almost anyone can learn how to do them. Such a waste to leave them to the pros.

ROUNDUP REFLECTIONS THAT WORK IN SMALL GROUPS

Whether it's a family or basketball team, a project staff or board of governors, the typical small group has goals that require cooperation. Cooperation requires some rapid multiperson communication, which means lots of missed assignments, turnovers, and management errors. There's no way around it— it's a major achievement to get a bunch of people to work well together, share ideas, live with individual differences, understand how each member's effort becomes either a contribution or a discard, and remember their reasons for doing the work in the first place.

Lots of people accept small-group communication breakdowns as immutable—a necessary evil that inevitably leads to varieties of tension: an argument or painful silence at the dinner table, a quiet talker's lost message in a locker room at halftime, an important feeling or fresh idea that can't be squeezed into the rushed agenda of a committee meeting.

Using *roundup reflections* won't single-handedly wipe out the waste of disordered team conversation, but it can transform small group discussions from natural calamities into tidy exchanges of opinion and feeling. Roundup reflections are attempts to recap, summarize, restate the positions of several people over long stretches of conversation.

Unlike the other reflections, they don't serve as immediate mirrors of messages from one person. Roundups can collect the diverse thoughts of a work team, the opposing opinions of a management committee, the scattered ideas from a long family discussion. They recapitulate and represent the input of group members (and also *re*-present members' input). Sometimes taking notes helps when the discussion is long or complex, but usually all it takes is a little standing back to assess what's going on and some recalling of what was said.

Done well, without much distortion or omission, recapitulations have all sorts of constructive and calming effects on groups:

They acknowledge contributions, opinions, and emotions that were neglected during the regular rush of conversation (the acknowledgment reduces frustration); they juxtapose comments by members in a fresh, condensed manner, almost like rereading subtitles to remember a chapter's content; they discourage annoying repetition of messages by group members who never felt their words were registered; they reduce conflict, speed discussion, make room for new issues, indicate how much ground has been covered, and allow misunderstandings to be corrected. (On the deficit side, roundups can also interrupt the flow of ideas or break a group's mood. And someone has to detach a bit from the interchange in order to collect messages and prepare the roundup reflection. Those disadvantages aren't minor, especially if you add the good chance that roundups will come out clumsy at first, like the first attempts at any type of reflection, but the cost is small compared to the ultimate benefits.)

I've heard roundup reflections that summarized hours of a conference or an evening's worth of family talk—even one dazzling roundup that recapitulated a whole weekend of intense work at a retreat. (It put all of the work in perspective and made our exhaustion more tolerable.) The best recorded example I have is from an unlikely source—a television show. On his programs, Phil Donahue often does roundup reflections that a corporate manager or group therapist would envy. Donahue has to juggle opposing, frequently impassioned messages from experts, victims, audience members, and callers, then summarize the meaning, recapitulating a mixture of feelings without much distortion or personal bias. And it has to come out so millions of viewers can understand. I'd recommend watching his roundup technique for summarizing 20 or 30 minutes or even a whole program's worth of intense discussion.

The example here is from a debate on disciplining children: "Are parents losing control, losing their rightful authority, afraid to believe they are natural, 'certified' experts in child rearing?" The guest is a book author who argues that modern parents are excessively permissive (Jeane Westin, author of *The Coming Parent Revolution*). As the show starts, Westin describes the rearing of her only child. Her belief is that instilling positive self-regard was essential and that understanding her daughter's stresses, offering positive strokes, and downplaying notions of wickedness and shame were good strategy. But then Westin asserts, "At 13, my daughter was bright, articulate, assertive, self-starting, ambitious, dynamic, filled with a sense of self-worth, a splendid example of successful, modern child rearing—and impossible to live with!'' The audience laughs and applauds. Members of the audience speak about curfews, parent passivity, and how expert advice can make parents feel guilty. One advocate of more discipline maintains her parents ''did a good job on me . . . and I'd like to do the same and carry out the discipline.''

Audience sentiment leans heavily toward the position that parents should exert more control and turn away from courses or books that ''professionalize'' parenting and block good natural instincts about how to handle children. When someone objects, ''I wasn't born knowing how to be a parent; I didn't grow up and learn it,'' the point seems lost.

Spanking comes up. A strong-looking woman gets a burst of applause when she declares, ''Sometimes a quick smack gets their attention and keeps it.'' And Westin continues to make points about problems with parental passivity and self-blame for children's problems. The atmosphere doesn't welcome dissent. Someone tries, with the opinion that ''the most important thing that children can learn is that parents are not perfect,'' but the dissent is again washed away.

At this point, Donahue delivers a roundup reflection summing up the audience's majority view and Westin's comments during the last 15 minutes: ''There's a certain trend she [Westin] sees in the advice—it has to do with concern about damaging the psyche of a child—that has made us almost afraid of our children and aloof from them. And that we are almost afraid to assert our own authority over them. That is her point. She also feels that there's a lot of this stuff that does sort of imply that everything is the parents' fault and there's a lot of guilt inflicted on them.''

This roundup crystallizes fragmented messages and rather evenhandedly and simply re-presents them so they need not be repeated. The simplification makes dissent easier as the scattered opinions are condensed into a clearer target. With that done, a few members of the audience disagree with the majority view and argue for more sensitive reassurance of kids. One woman accuses the majority of talking as if ''feeling guilty is some kind of crime,'' and counters that guilt is also a way of becoming more aware. Another criticizes Westin: ''You said . . . you just want to shake them and say, 'Hey, listen to me.

I'm your parent.' I can't buy that. . . . I think it's a lack of communication skills.''

Still, the audience is mostly "sick and tired of hearing kids talk back to their parents," as one woman puts it. And when a voice objects that parents "don't give enough," the audience shouts the dissenter down: "No! No!" As I see it, a talk show host with average talent would be in trouble at this point—only a few minutes left and the minority has been crowded out, even shouted down. The scattered minority comments haven't achieved any cohesiveness; the program is in serious danger of coming out badly one-sided. But Donahue has a roundup reflection in his head: "I think that in some quarters of this room is the suggestion that if we use words like 'firmness, reasserting control,' what we allow some parents to do is begin to draw lines and use absolute force without any kind of sensitivity toward the wishes of a child, who after all is still an individual. . . . Force works only for a little while. Let's take a young girl, for example. Once you get into this rigid, 'You shall do what I tell you,' it'll work till she's about 16, 17. And the fear is that you're going to look out the kitchen window and in the driveway is going to be a guy on a motorcycle with a tattoo and a helmet with a spike on it—and there goes all your power.''

The issue is powerful and probably relates to political positions and religious convictions. But if we move the passionate topic into the background and step back from any personal opinion of Donahue as a TV host, it can be seen that his last-minute verbal gymnastics have done a masterful job of getting both sides aired to millions of viewers. His two roundup reflections brought balance to the issues.

". . . Almost afraid of our own children . . . afraid to assert our own authority . . . everything is the parents' fault and there's a lot of guilt inflicted on them.''

Versus:

". . . Words like 'firmness, reasserting control' . . . [encourage parents] to use absolute force without any kind of sensitivity toward the wishes of the child. . . . Force works only for a little while. . . .''

Phil Donahue, like anyone else who does nice reflections, didn't start producing them one day out of the blue. The guy pays attention to his talk. Doing decent roundup reflections requires the deliberate, purposeful act of empathizing with a group of conversationalists and then finding the words that crystallize their views. Fortunately, few of us have the added pressure of doing it in front of TV cameras.

You can practice roundups in familiar situations: a work staff, family, social group, or classroom. The easy part is that round-ups don't need to be rushed—you can even take notes. Then, before verbalizing, practice the roundup under your breath. Many people learn roundups more quickly than other reflections simply because there's more time to rehearse.

THE REPEATER EFFECT AND CONNECTING

When the glue of empathic understanding comes unstuck in important conversations, a rush of activity begins for reattaching lost meaning from one mind to another. The person who is trying to get the message understood starts repeating the message with a little different twist, new emphasis, a new word or two, or any correction that tries to tell more accurately what's on his mind. Each repeat is aimed at getting closer to some accurate understanding.

It's one of those psychological cycles we do all the time, like reliving an event many times, mentally rehearsing a piece of communication, or repeatedly searching the same places for a lost object. The cyclic behavior in repeating a message turns out to be a practical way to do a range of mental work necessary for normal development. Kids do it to master the meaning of things (wearing down parents in the process). I call the phenomenon *the repeater effect*.

Understanding its dynamics allows the detection of some normally hidden processes in the way we think, feel, and change ourselves through conversation. And the way we penetrate each other's minds.

The repeater effect is driven by frustration at getting disconnected from another's accurate empathy. It goes on all the time—kind of like a stuck record—and particularly when the discloser feels a personal stake in getting the message delivered. Some beautiful examples of the repeater effect (and some natural mother/daughter reflections) came my way thanks to a Chicago friend, a psychologist who taught a class on communications in close relations. He emphasized early signs of disconnection between intimates and introduced the reflection as a tool for repairing rifts.

A divorced mother in the psychologist's class volunteered

some tapes (captured by her voice-activated answering machine), and later on she gave them to me. The tapes contained some strong repeater effects, plus some illuminating examples of inaccurate reflections.

The mother, Martha, has joint custody of her daughter, Denise, 16, who she said "calls at the slightest distress." We come into this conversation after a lengthy exchange in which Denise complains she doesn't get enough money from her father for clothes. Then Martha suggests Denise consider graduating from babysitting to a real weekend job, and Denise responds.

DENISE: Do you realize what a crappy life that is? Going to school five days a week, plus work on weekends, and then I wanna take this special Saturday class.

MARTHA: But you'll be doing the things you want to do. *(Pause)* Right? Taking special classes you like and buying some of your own clothes without your father's craziness.

DENISE: *(Subdued, defeated tone)* Uh huh.

MARTHA: And if you get a nice job, you'll be making money and you'll have such a feeling of freedom—you can go buy what you want without your father telling you what to do.

DENISE: Right. But the class is four hours every Saturday—they're like from 9:00 to 1:00, then go to work, like from . . . I dunno, 2:00 to 8:00? And after that, probably—*God*, do you realize what a crappy life that is? And I've been studying *five* hours every weekday without fail. I'll be totally, *totally* wiped out. It'll be a crappy life!

MARTHA: Wait a second. What's this about *five* hours? Are you serious? Two used to be enough. Are you exaggerating?

DENISE: *No*—honest, Mom. I just need to make sure—

MARTHA: *(Interrupting)* What? Make sure of what?

DENISE: Well, maybe I'm not sure. I don't understand it too much. . . . I don't wanna become some stupid woman who can't do anything but hang around the house and wait for sales. That's crappy.

MARTHA: It's not really clear, but you do know what kind of woman you don't want—

DENISE: *(Interrupting)* Well, ya . . . *(Martha stops dead in her tracks for an interruption by Denise)*

DENISE: Well, yeah, but . . . it's sorta I should be learning more. I just wanna learn.

MARTHA: Sounds like the important thing is to learn. But it confuses me 'cause your grades are good. I just don't know what's gotten into you.

DENISE: I've been wanting to tell you—

MARTHA: *(Interrupting)* What's gotten into you?

DENISE: I don't understand it. I wanna study all the time. Maybe I just wanna learn. It's a new . . . uh, new thing with me.

[The repeater effect has started. It's her second time saying, "I just wanna learn." That's not true, as will become apparent. But she's not lying. What's going on is that Denise isn't sure about what's going on. She hasn't yet come to grips with why she's on a studying binge. Note that she has also repeated that she doesn't understand why, but Martha, in her bewilderment, hasn't attended to that message. A good reflection of Denise's failure to understand could have steered this conversation into fruitful territory.]

MARTHA: *I'll* say it's new. I can't believe it! Well . . . *(Mumbles into a pause)* Maybe by now I should be getting used to sudden changes in you. You *are* growing up—in a hurry. So now you're a regular young scholar who wants to learn, huh?

[Surprised and somewhat incredulous at Denise's five-hour homework routine, Martha is trying to swallow the news about Denise's yearning for learning. She teases a bit, but her instincts are to accept that answer without pushing. She seems able to live with an incomplete picture for the moment. The truth isn't out yet. That fact shows clearly in repeat number three that follows.]

DENISE: Yeah, I *need* to . . . wanna learn . . . sorta because there's this urge in me, you know, to know more . . . I guess.

[A bit of new meaning surfaces as Denise mentions "need" as well as "want," suggesting some stronger motive for studying. She also shows doubt again with "I guess."]

MARTHA: Sorta like you need to *do it*? A strong *urge*?

[This reflection comes in the form of a question with upward inflections on the italicized words. These "reflecting questions" or "begging reflections" ask for confirmation. Sort of like Martha asking, "Am I right?" Denise's answer will indicate that maybe there's more to tell. Essentially it's another repeat that brings up a new shade of meaning.]

DENISE: It *is* an urge. I just have to do it. Feel terrible when I don't. Something got into me that I want *A*'s badly.

MARTHA: Oh, it's good grades that you're after.

DENISE: I want good grades badly. I have to get them. *(She mocks the shaky voice of an addict)* I've just *got* to get my grades. Gimme my grades!

MARTHA: So you'll get them if you—

DENISE: *(Interrupting)* It's like I've got to get them to save my life or something. Like life would be totally crappy without them. The urge to study . . . uh, like sometimes I get scared I won't get into college.

MARTHA: Oh, that's what's going on. You're scared about college.

DENISE: It's not "scared"—it's like . . . uh . . . well, maybe scared. Scared of missing my friends. Old dumb Sandra says . . . *(Mocks in sing-song voice)* "Everybody who's going to Northwestern is going to the prep class." She says Lon, Marion,

Jimmy, and Doug all signed up. It's ridiculous. I'm like a sheep following the pack. Worrying about my SAT scores. That's where I got this ridiculous urge. Yeah, that's what's got into me. . . . Yeah.

MARTHA: So . . . I see. It's not Little Miss Scholarship with an urge to learn. What's got into you is following your friends to North-western.

DENISE: Not exactly. It's for *me*, too. I'd miss Jimmy the most. He's so-o-o interesting. We could talk all night long. He's gonna be a great designer. There's really something neat about the way he—

MARTHA: *(Interrupting)* Wait a second. Are you telling me that the five hours, your new passion for learning, is also a passion for Jimmy?

DENISE: I wouldn't call it a passion, but yeah . . . I wanna be with my friends. Maybe that's what this study urge is all about.

MARTHA: Sounds like you want to be with your *friend*.

DENISE: Oh, Mom, he's not everything.

MARTHA: I didn't say "Everything." Let's just call it an urge.

[Denise was trying to come to grips with the truth that her urge for learning had more to do with an urge for Jimmy. Repeating helped her do that. That's one of the primary reasons for the repeater effect—sharpening meaning in the speaker's own mind. In making her meaning clear to her mother, Denise was forced to face reality and thereby gained a better understanding of herself. Going off alone to think about a problem can miss that kind of gain. (It helps, of course, to have a careful listener who also has some reflecting skills.)]

Repeating When a Secret Looms

The process of rethinking, revising, and reiterating messages as a way of getting to know ourselves better isn't always successful within a single conversation. The theme of a problem might pop up intermittently over several conversations. And the repeating isn't always caused by an attempt to sharpen meaning. Another cause is ambivalence about disclosing a secret. Where there's doubt about revealing, there's frequently the repeater effect. That will happen in the next dialogue sample as Denise tries to deal with confusion about changing from a "girl" to a "young woman." As a fairly sophisticated 16-year-old virgin— coping with hormones, an eager 18-year-old boy, and a headful of authentic concerns—Denise has been initiating conversations on the topic for a month without addressing it directly. There have been a dozen disclosures about how wonderful Jimmy is, how interesting, sincere, and respectful of her ideas. She's been like an airplane hovering over an airport in a holding pattern.

Martha has been profoundly patient not to break through Denise's protection of trivial talk, repeated endlessly. (Only a mother could have endured.) Now Denise calls again.

DENISE: *(On the answering machine)* Mom . . . Mom . . . pick up. . . . Are you gonna pick up?

MARTHA: Yeah, I'm here. I was outside. Let me catch my breath. *(Pause)* So, you had an important question about you and Jimmy?

DENISE: Yeah.

MARTHA: How is he?

DENISE: Oh, he's fine. . . . Then . . . then *(Speaking very rapidly, as if plunging right into it)* I was just wondering—you know, we've been going together for a long time, right?

MARTHA: Uh, months . . . several months.

DENISE: Well, I was just wondering about getting close—he wants to get closer—and that's probably not for me.

MARTHA: He wants it and you're not sure.

[Nice reflection—cogent, unobtrusive, and accurate.]

DENISE: Yeah—you know, we kiss goodnight like I told ya and he feels like wanting, more closeness . . . and it's not for me.

[Martha's nice reflection seemed to capture all of the meaning, but Denise repeats the entire message with the addition of the goodnight kiss limit. I generally suspect some hiding, some knowingly concealed fact when an accurate reflection doesn't extinguish the need to repeat.]

MARTHA: He wants more closeness than a goodnight kiss, but you don't.

[Another good one that propels Denise to a new disclosure.]

DENISE: It's not exactly that I don't want more. It might not be for me. Actually, it's confusing. Getting close can—

MARTHA: *(Interrupting)* So what you say is that you do want closeness and you don't want closeness.

[A fine example of reflecting ambivalence. Helping someone clearly see that they are of two minds on a matter can be emancipating. It unclutters emotions. It seems that experienced communicators jump on the opportunity to reflect ambivalence, while others let it pass.]

DENISE: Exactly! And it worries me. I might want to go farther. . . . But—

MARTHA: *(Interrupting)* But you're confused.

DENISE: Yeah, sometimes I want to, but don't know about the closeness. It's scary.

MARTHA: Oh—scared of more than a goodnight kiss.

[like peeling an onion, each reflection peels off an old layer of meaning about getting closer. The variations on the closeness theme started with "Not for me" and became "Might not be for me" and then "I might want to" and finally "Sometimes I want to." As the word "closeness" is repeated, we know Denise is confused about it, but we don't know what it means. It represents the untold part of what Denise is struggling to talk about. Watch how Martha's patient reflections (even the awkward ones) give Denise comfort for revealing the secret.]

DENISE: I'm not scared of a *little* more than a goodnight kiss, but a *lot* more might—uh, you know . . . It . . . *(Long pause)* A little more is okay but a lot—well, a lot is even hard to talk about. *(Choked voice)* Oh, Mom—it gets me so miserable. It's gonna be *totally* impossible not to get close.

MARTHA: Oh, baby, thinking of someday going farther makes you so miserable. Wish I could hug you now.

DENISE: It's not someday; it *was* last night.

MARTHA: Huh? What? Last night you—

DENISE: *(Interrupting)* Last night . . . *(Haltingly, starting to sob)* we . . . got closer . . . and it scared me.

[Now we know ''closeness'' means something Denise and Jimmy have actually done. Some sexual activity that's embarrassing to tell a mother, but hard to conceal when help is needed. Denise's ambivalence produced the repeated ''closeness'' theme. That active word almost drops from the conversation now that the secret is out.]

MARTHA: Ah, Dennie. I didn't know. Poor thing. What's going on?

DENISE: We've been—uh . . . It's like Jimmy's been sensitive and all that stuff. But we've sorta gotten into petting. . . . Like we care for each other—there's an attraction—and heavy petting, like that.

MARTHA: So, fine, fine. That he's sensitive and that there's caring. But I wanna help with what's frightening. If it's about how your body works, you know all that already. Or is there some—is it something you forgot?

DENISE: No. I'm just not ready . . . *(Mumbling)* to go all the way.

MARTHA: You're afraid of going all the way.

[This almost echoic reflection would sound dumb all by itself. But in context, it registers understanding and ''pulls'' elaboration from Denise.]

DENISE: Because it's getting pregnant I'm not ready to handle. *(Muffled voice)* But, anyway, at this stage of my life, I don't feel emotionally—I'd just feel strange afterward.

[Being on the receiving end of a string of reflections can make almost anyone feel self-absorbed. All of that empathic attention can induce a sense of being emotionally pampered, like receiving a skilled massage. When that happens to me, my own thoughts and feelings become shamelessly important, and my reflector becomes someone to serve my emotional exploration. In that situation I have no hesitation about interrupting at the slightest urge (even though I'm not a big interrupter). Reflections encourage a sense of self-importance and personal privilege that brings boldness in facing frightening feelings. Interrupting the reflector feels appropriate. So, anyone using reflections to help someone open up should consider becoming utterly interruptable. That means never fighting for the floor. Martha stopped fighting. She began to relinquish her talking turn whenever Denise wanted attention.]

MARTHA: Not ready—

DENISE: *(Interrupting)* Maybe I wouldn't. I don't know. Sometimes I think, Am I too young, am I too old. Or am I okay? I mean, my friends were all through it at 15.

MARTHA: You mean they're no longer virgins.

DENISE: Oh, different things happened. . . . One feels fine about it. She didn't mind it. Uh, she uses the pill. And it's no big deal. She and her guy are solid. All the others are loose. It doesn't matter to them.

MARTHA: *(Softly, with care)* But it matters to you.

Repeating When the Connection is Lost

The conversation ends, but the theme lingers. Several phone calls later, Denise is still engrossed in the classical adolescent task of starting to sort out the differences between sex, love, and intimacy. Martha has done a remarkable job of being an empathic friend with hours of fairly accurate, fairly neutral reflections. The interpersonal atmosphere has helped Denise develop the start of a personal morality about relations between the sexes. It's a lovely process to hear as mother fosters daughter's independent thought. A young woman begins to respect her body and, as a result, adds to her overall sense of self-respect.

But such processes are rarely perfect. In the next conversation slice, Martha's need to be a mother overcomes her role as a friend. Her neutrality and accurate empathy are put aside at times as she advocates a moral position. She puts the wrong words in Denise's mouth. A distorted reflection, caused by discomfort, is a subtle, unwitting act of denial. As Martha turns away from something hard to hear, she also turns away from her daughter's inner world. She disconnects—turns off her empathy valve. The lost empathy and the distorted reflections reduce Denise's experience of getting understood. And the frustration from not getting understood is a frequent cause of the repeater effect.

DENISE: Sherry sometimes goes with different guys. I met this one, and he was a nerd. She makes him use a rubber and all that, but it doesn't sound like great fun always. It doesn't sound like it would be great fun for me.

MARTHA: It's not for you. Let Sherry pop into bed with every jerk with a nice smile and come away dissatisfied. With you, it's got to be closeness and love first. The real thing or nothing.

[A moderate turning away from promiscuity as unrewarding ("It doesn't sound like it would be great fun for me") is exaggerated by Martha into an extreme rejection. ("It's not for you. . . . It's got to be closeness and love first.")]

DENISE: Well, it doesn't sound like great fun anyway. *(Pause)* She says it's not always nice for her—sometimes it is. Sometimes she learns about herself. Ya know, she's really careful about—

MARTHA: *(Interrupting)* Careful? Always going with different guys? When you lie down with dogs, you get up with fleas. Sleep with jerks, become a jerk.

[Martha's anger at promiscuous Sherry causes an exaggeration of Denise's description to a point where Denise has lost the closely following company of her friendly mother. Mom's moral imperative has quickly changed the climate from two people sharing one line of experience into one person warning the other about the pitfalls of promiscuity. It can feel awful to get guidance in the form of distorted reflections. Disguising advice as if giving empathy is a temporary ploy that can weaken trust. In this conversation, the ploy caused Denise to abandon her personal exploration. An argument followed.

[Undistorted reflections probably would have led them into a better understanding of Denise's attitudes on promiscuity. Exaggerating someone's position, even changing "sometimes" to "always" as Martha did, is a prime cause for conflict when discussing touchy topics. Doing it with a reflection is especially provoking because the talk tool essentially promises accurate understanding.

[On the other end of the scale, a series of reflections that water down meaning or weaken the intensity of someone's feelings are sure to produce frustration. Our mother/daughter pair demonstrates that later in the same conversation.]

MARTHA: You're right, it's like getting initiated into a new life—a new phase of life. You become a woman, even though you're *not* a woman. . . . Uh, you know how I mean that, Dennie?

DENISE: Uh, it's . . . yeah. It's almost like going into womanhood.

MARTHA: Almost like it . . . *(Long silent spell)*

DENISE: But it's very strange from where I am in life. It's like someone has been inside your body, where nobody else has ever been before. It's very strange to be so vulnerable. You're invaded and changed forever. This private, most private . . . place in you . . . like a private room in your home. You wouldn't want just anyone in there. It feels weird to deal with that. Just . . . very weird.

MARTHA: Kind of odd, letting someone inside you. You don't know how to feel about it. Makes you a little uncomfortable.

DENISE: *No*, it makes me feel *very* weird 'cause never in the history of the world has anyone been inside me before, invaded me. It feels very, *very* weird. A once-in-a-lifetime change. Forever!

That's telling her, Denise. You're not saying it's "kind of odd . . . a little uncomfortable"—it's much more than that; it's *extremely* hard to fathom, an awesome change.

It's uncommon to hear an incorrect reflection—in this case, one that made the meaning too soft—being immediately identified and amended. Usually an understated reflection goes unnoticed—the speaker feels frustrated or repeats himself but doesn't understand the dynamics behind his reaction. But turning the volume up or down too much is an inescapable part of learning to do reflections. It can't be consistently avoided, even after practice. The trick in doing reflections is to realize that distortion is there to stay and then to try to *reduce* it. (Chapter 8 offers methods.) The repeater effect will go on forever because of imperfect understanding, distortions in communication, unsettled secrets and our peculiar (but perfectly natural) need to talk about ourselves—even when we're not sure how to do it.

CHAPTER 3

INTERPRETATIONS

"THE PRIME CARRIERS OF NEW MEANING INTO OUR LIVES."

THE INTERPRETATION talk tool is a cousin of the reflection. These two relatives can look similar at first glance, but the things they do to people are very different. The interpretation is as aggressive as the reflection is restrained. The reflection *follows* the other's message, avoiding attempts at adding new meaning. But the interpretation can take the same message and remanufacture it, classify it, and deliver it as a piece of news.

For better or worse, interpretations *always* offer new meaning. They can be brassy generalizations about human nature or penetrating insights into a personality. Sincere or sarcastic, accurate or dead wrong, they *go for it*. When you hear problems diagnosed, dreams analyzed, insults thrown, predictions made, events explained, groups stereotyped, individuals praised, or institutions criticized, you're hearing interpretations. Given sincerely, they try to tell something that isn't known to the listener. Unfortunately, the new knowledge offered is often speculation, even though it's presented as the whole truth and nothing but the truth.

Interpretations turn up all the time in conversation because all of us have a driving, incessant need to make sense of ourselves, those around us, and the world in general. We constantly mix incoming information with things already known. Then we try to organize the new mix in ways that create some order out of what could be confusion, to bring meaningful interpretation to what could be meaningless.

THE JOYS AND SORROWS OF PERSONAL INTERPRETATIONS

Interpretations can have extremely potent impacts. They're tricky to use. They carry the potential for achieving lots of benefits—or causing all sorts of mischief. Because they're the prime carriers of new meaning into our lives, these bits of language produce more sudden joy and more instant misery than any other talk tool.

The joy and misery come mostly from interpretations aimed at us personally. *Personal interpretations* can mess with our self-image, as will become evident in the dialogue that follows. Claudette and Jean are longtime friends. They were roommates in college and have lived in the same city for several years. Both are single, in their thirties, and have careers.

As we join their phone conversation, Claudette has been lamenting for several minutes on the lack of men in her life who are "pure friends"—platonic friends. Only once as an adult has she known a man as an authentic, nonsexual buddy—and he moved to another city three years ago. Claudette and Jean agree that nonsexual one-to-one relationships between men and women aren't plentiful in their age group, but Claudette seems to stand out as especially deficient in that area.

CLAUDETTE: I've never even had those *semi*-friends that some women make out of men.

JEAN: That's been true all the years I've known you, Claude. I've always seen you that way. But it's been so easy for you to attract all sorts of lovers. You beat us all at capturing men. You're the best.

[A simple personal interpretation by Jean classifies Claudette as a successful recruiter of lovers. No deep insight or profound analysis intended, just an evaluation, a judgment of a personal characteristic. Even though the evaluation is positive (an intended compliment), the act does place Claudette's person in a category. Any interpretation that explains or classifies a person to her face is a personal interpretation.]

CLAUDETTE: Big deal—all I have to do is make myself up and catch their eye. They do the rest. A couple of little signals that say "maybe" can make any guy on the prowl come sniffing around. But why can't men see us as more than just their sexual conquest? Why does it have to be so complicated? Am I to blame 'cause I was born beautiful? *(They both laugh)*

CLAUDETTE: *(Continuing)* But really, what the hell did I do to deserve this treatment?

JEAN: *(Mock cowgirl drawl)* Not a thang, honey. Pretty little thang like you . . . *(Back to regular voice)* Uh, maybe you *can* do, you know, something about the way you talk to men. Claude, I have to tell you, over the years I've seen you contribute to the problem just the way you communicate. I mean, it's your . . . Yeah, seriously, it's not your fault you're gorgeous. But . . . it might be partly your fault that guys look at you as sexually available.

[Not hearing Jean's voice is a disadvantage here because it's wonderfully colorful, with a constant overtone of caring. That caring helps a lot in doing a personal interpretation which classifies Claudette as partly guilty. But it's more than a classification (of guilt vs. innocence) because it analyzes the *cause* for an *effect*: Claudette's inviting way of talking to men (the cause) equals being left without authentic male friends (the effect). So there are two ways of giving personal interpretations: classifying—naming, diagnosing, or pigeonholing; and analyzing—explaining, dissecting, or reordering. The same two ways apply to interpretations aimed at third parties, groups and even entire societies.]

CLAUDETTE: Awww, *Jean*, that doesn't make sense. I've tried for so long, but getting me horizontal is the only thing on their minds. . . .

[Having been confronted with a new, uncomfortable possibility—that her problem is partly her own fault—Claudette attempts denial by calling the interpretation wrong. That's not surprising. Most of us can't swallow unpleasant news about ourselves in a few seconds. Incorporating a potentially accurate but uncomfortable new view of ourselves usually occurs only after some attempts to deny it by proving the logic wrong, trivializing it, ignoring it, or questioning the interpreter's motives.]

JEAN: It may not make sense to you, but honest, the way you dress and wiggle and lower your eyes, uh, it's adorable, really, but gee . . . it's very transparent sometimes. And the way you can talk so helplessly . . . *(Southern drawl, a la Blanche Dubois)* ''Ah've always depended on the kindness of strangers.'' Sure it's a put-on, but—

CLAUDETTE: *(Interrupting)* That's right, a put-on, just for fun. A little entertainment, that's all. Why would you wanna stop me from being playful? *You* could use some playfulness in your serious life. You're plenty playful with me and the girls, but not so much with the guys. I bet you'd like to be.

[She doesn't want to hear interpretations suggesting she's the cause for the lack of men friends in her life. That results in two classical denials: trivialization (just ''a little entertainment'') and blaming Jean's motives (''I bet you'd like to be''), which suggests Jean is motivated by jealousy. Maybe Claudette's denials are reasonable, but the issue here is that these women are now debating reality with an exchange of interpretations. This interpretation tit-for-tat occurs like a natural law during arguments. Talk tools like interpretations, self-disclosures, and especially interruptions tend to beget themselves over and over again in the flow of con-

versation. Jean tries to rise above fighting back in this next response—
and fails.]

JEAN: Hey, I'm not gonna sit here and say I'm not overly serious
        with guys sometimes. I'm cautious. I've been burned. Maybe
        I *am* kinda deadly at first, but playing with strangers has
        turned me into a commodity too often to be accidental. Too
        many guys wanted *it*, instead of me. That's *worse* than deadly.
        So I'm not gonna jiggle and bat my eyes. Can't you see that
        kind of come-on turns you into a sexual object instead of a
        whole person? You *encourage* them with your teasing. Damn
        it, you're a chronic flirt!

[This angry personal interpretation sweeps all of Claudette into a single
category—as if diagnosing a disease.]

JEAN: *(Continuing)* Your dress, your moves, your talk tells men to
        pay attention to your sexual side, not your personality. You're
        crazy to be complaining all men *this* and all men *that*. It's
        you who advertises yourself as an incomplete woman—
        "Wanna ball? Give Claude a call." And you don't even have
        to be her friend. *(Long pause; then Jean continues in a slightly
        repentant, subdued voice)* I don't mean *you* are incomplete.
        You've got so much going for you. It's just this craziness
        with men . . . it's been bugging me for years. I care what
        happens to you, Claude.

CLAUDETTE: I know. I know. *(Pause)* But why can't I be sexy and still
        make friends? Does one prohibit the other? And what if a
        guy's real cute? Should I count off five dates before going to
        bed with him? Most women are hypocrites about waiting.
        And if you wait too long, they're *gone*. So where's the friend-
        ship then?

JEAN: So it doesn't always happen. Friends don't come every day,
        but you kill your chances by playing too eager. Besides,
        Sarah, Patty, even sexy Sue, have long-term friends who
        were never, ever their lovers. And they—

CLAUDETTE: *(Interrupting)* Just one little second there, Jean. What about
        Sue and Mark? Never lovers? Maybe they were just reading
        Playboy in bed? And you know damn well she had a rotten
        one-night stand with Kenny and told us they tried to figure
        out why and decided their chemistry wasn't right, so they
        discovered platonic disco dancing.

JEAN: Okay, okay, but most of her—

CLAUDETTE: *(Interrupting)* I . . . I mean, if I made it with as many guys
        as Sue, I'd be crowned Miss Promiscuity of 1984. Dammit,
        she's made it with more guys than the rest of us combined.
        God, she isn't exactly what I'd call discriminating.

[Claudette's labeling of Sue as promiscuous and indiscriminate would
be a personal interpretation—*if* it were delivered to Sue's face. Instead,
the behind-the-back labeling makes it a *third-party interpretation*. Sue

is getting classified and analyzed as the third party. She's also getting some of Claudette's immediate anger.]

CLAUDETTE: *(Continuing)* See, I think Sue cares less about making friends than "making" strangers. When a new guy offers her a seat, she lies down. *(Claudette laughs at her clever insult; Jean doesn't)* But strangers seem to make Sue come alive. They penetrate her numbness. She needs to fill up her empty feeling with the excitement of a new guy every month.

[More third-party interpretations of Sue. Right or wrong, they demonstrate that Claudette has thought seriously about the issue. They also provide fuel for speculating about *Claudette's* personal needs. That is, her interpretation could be seen as containing an inadvertent self-disclosure. Third-parties sidestep face-to-face confrontations and allow backbiting invectives with little jeopardy from counter-interpretations. Sometimes when I do one, I imagine the third party is hearing it—just to get a feeling for what might happen if it were delivered to the person's face. Years ago, I believed that I used third parties out of concern for not hurting people with my judgments, criticism, or diagnoses. Eventually, though, I had to admit I was really protecting myself from an awkward situation or even an angry confrontation. Or my interpretations might be off-base and expose my own shortcomings, fears, prejudices, and secret agendas to my victim's counterattack.

[Claudette's secret agenda right now is protecting her self-image by demonstrating that *she* isn't Miss Promiscuity. She seems so concerned about being seen as an indiscriminate woman herself that her eagerness to interpret Sue has moved the conversation away from the main issue. Now Jean will try to get back to it.]

JEAN: I know Sue can go on a binge of one guy after another when things get rough for her, but you're missing my point. I'm not saying Sue isn't easy. All I'm saying is that, aside from Mark and Kenny, she *does* have two or three guys who've been honest-to-goodness no-sex friends from the start. And one reason is that she let some of 'em know early on what her expectations were. But *you* don't really communicate that to *anyone*, Claude.

[This is another heavy-duty personal interpretation, and this time Claudette has decided to keep quiet for the moment. She's trying on Jean's interpretation to see if it fits.]

JEAN: *(Continuing)* Over the years I've never known you to directly tell a guy that you just wanted friendship. You *never* did! *(Her voice softens, pace slows, as if to show concern and affection are behind these painful interpretations)* I know you hate to think of yourself as an easy woman. The idea of being used to relieve some schmuck's biological necessity, just to keep him interested, has always galled you. It hurts to think it could happen to you, but I honestly think you're scared to let men know your body isn't automatically avail-

able. And that's because you've got it into your head that if
they can't see some sex in it for them . . . I mean, if you
don't keep 'em guessing about that part of you, the rest of
you might not be enough.

It took another 23 minutes of conversation for these friends
to pick up the pieces of that interpretation. Unlike the melodramatic conversations in soap operas, this real-life talk didn't result in Claudette gratefully, tearfully accepting Jean's critical
interpretation as a searing flash of insight to be instantly digested
and applied from that moment on to a better future. She didn't
swallow the interpretation whole; she debated it. After all, she
protested, it wasn't that she was scared *all* men would turn away
if she didn't flirt; but *some* will, and have. That's why, she acknowledged, she developed a lifetime habit of leading with her
sexual attraction. Anyway, she said, she was sexually healthy—
she finds many men attractive; staying generally unavailable isn't
in her character. She declared she had neither the convictions of
a nun nor the severe discrimination of a woman who waits for
Mr. Perfect.

It wasn't easy for her, though, to reject outright the view of
her as dangling sexual carrots, a habit formed, as Jean said,
because "the rest of you might not be enough." Claudette's
pride was hurt, but she hung up sounding preoccupied with the
possibility that she wasn't just a victim of sexist men—that the
lack of male friends in her life is a situation that could be improved by her will and behavior. Jean's personal interpretations,
drawn from years of observing her friend, created new meaning
for Claudette and may have provided an impetus for solving a
chronic problem. The long-term friendship of Jean and Claudette and Jean's sensitivity to the sting in her message saved the
transaction from disaster. Personal interpretations don't usually
fare so well; they have a tendency to blow up in the interpreter's
face.

GENERAL INTERPRETATIONS AND THE
PROLIFERATION OF HALF-TRUTHS

General interpretations don't blow up in anyone's face, but
they do frequently blow up half-truths into sweeping conclusions. They can get bigger than life and absurdly simplistic.
Even at that, they put on an air of credibility because of the

partial truths that flash from them in the ordinary rush of conversation.

Some generalizations exaggerate a trend or a tendency into a broad law of life. During the Claudette/Jean conversation we've just seen, Claudette tried to deny Jean's personal interpretations of her at one point with this sweeping diagnosis of an entire gender: "Jean, men just don't want to relate to women as friends. Grandmothers or sisters, maybe, or colleagues—but with any other women, they're at a loss. They're so busy trying to get into your pants, they don't have time to value us as friends."

That general interpretation might be true for some men in some situations. But if there is a scarcity of male/female relationships, a variety of causes might be at work—women's attitudes, cultural norms, inadequate social skills, and all sorts of factors other than men not wanting to. Claudette's goal wasn't the truth but relief from the painful possibility that her paucity of male friendship was her own fault. She shifted the blame for her limited communication style over to the entire masculine gender.

General interpretations are employed a lot to counterattack unflattering personal interpretations. When I criticized my ten-year-old as "messy" for not cleaning his room, he fought back by interpreting parents in general as hypocrites about neatness. (Parental hypocrisy was his accusation of the month.) Deflecting personal guilt or shortcomings to parents in general, men in general, teachers in general, society overall, or "people nowadays" is just one type of instant, dubious relief provided by general interpretations.

Coping with Unfamiliar Experiences

General interpretations are also employed in novel environments and new situations—especially when there's trepidation, embarrassment, confusion, or uncertainty about what's expected and concern over self-image. Dealing with strange places and new acquaintances makes most of us self-conscious, on-our-toes, and focused on the way we talk and behave. Such self-consciousness needs relief. We search for comfort by searching for sense. We want to know more about our circumstances—*fast*. Even quick and dirty generalizations can offer some sense of mastery. They make us feel less at sea. Describing foreign territory with broad guesses helps keep us from being overwhelmed. Making sudden sense of strange places and unfamiliar behavior requires some oversimplification at first—a little like whistling in the dark. Even top scientists whistle in the dark at times by privately using oversimplified hunches, wild hypotheses, to explore unknown phenomena—they have to start someplace in their search for generalizations with simple power. They're willing to settle for a speculative first approximation at truth, before testing the phenomena, just as a kid speculates about going to a new school by testing the playground. So this talk tool performs the same tasks in the hands of children or scientists: It's an approximation at truth awaiting further refinement.

The refinement eventually comes for scientists as they conduct research or sharpen theory. But it seldom comes for generalizations made in social settings. Most of us aren't in the habit of checking out assertions or reexamining comfortable conclusions. And without refinement, some simplistic first approximation of a culture, gender, or class of people can gel into a stereotype.

I have a conversation sample, starring two young men in a strange environment, coping with an almost overwhelming set of new circumstances. They're foreign athletes attending the 1984 Olympics in Los Angeles. They arrived two weeks early and are anxiously waiting to perform, while coping with the strange customs of a big, fast, frightening America.

Manuel, a volleyball player on Argentina's team, and Carlo, a member of the Italian water polo team, are resplendent in their Olympic blazers as they stroll the UCLA campus. They've managed to get lost after leaving the Olympic Village on campus, and find themselves at a favorite student hangout.

The outdoor tables at the place are a nice surprise because they're both accustomed to socializing in outdoor cafes at home. Neither has been in the United States before, but both speak English. They seem excited by the large, complicated campus, and talk rapidly at their table (which has a view of the neighborhood), while eating American junk food and eyeing young women at other tables. One, Naomi, smiles at them. In traditional Italian style, Carlo smiles and strides boldly to her table and asks, "Would the signorina be so kind to join two unfortunate, lost athletes for a coffee?" She accepts, and after the usual introductory exchange of demographic data, tells the men about her project to tape-record dialogues with foreign athletes and publish excerpts in the *UCLA Daily Bruin*. Carlo quickly tells her he's just the ticket for her project, and is followed immediately by Manuel, who starts describing his studies at the Catholic University of Buenos Aires.

Pleased, Naomi pulls out a tape recorder and starts asking questions. It becomes apparent the athletes are anxious about performing well "in front of the world." They haven't slept well on "those soft American mattresses." Small asides and offhand remarks reveal these guys are having a hard time relaxing; they're drained by coping with new customs, yet they don't confess to stress directly. They try to humorously explain how they failed to mentally prepare for the fast, loud, large American ways, but the humor gets lost. They're unable to bring the subtleties of their thoughts into their language with Naomi. The poor guys are tired, nervous, unable to express themselves well, and unwilling to let this friendly, interested American know they're feeling miserable. So the interview progresses politely until it's interrupted by the screech of tires. Looking over the railing, they see an ultralong Cadillac limousine joined at the fender to a small foreign car. The drivers get out to gauge the extent of the crunch. Carlo laughs, points at Naomi and feigns anger.

CARLO: What are we to do when you invite us here and then you drive big cars as if we with small cars are not existing?

[Even in the early warmth of acquaintanceship, Naomi is instantly classified as a representative of the American national character: an arrogant big-car driver.]

NAOMI: *(Shrugging)* Why are you so sure it's the big car's fault?

MANUEL: *(Answering for Carlo)* But there *is* truth to this thing of these people who love the cars *grandissimos*—uh, *mal gusto*—how do you say, ostentatious. They think that theirs is the road. We have a few grande uglies in Buenos Aires, but you have so *many*.

NAOMI: Don't look at me. I've got an old Fiat that me and my boyfriend keep together with bent clothes hangers, and I wouldn't trade it for one of those gas-guzzling Cadillacs.

CARLO: *Benissimo (Reaches over to kiss her hand with a flourish)* . . . that you honor my country by being Fiat owner, but maybe for you it should have been a Ferrari . . . or a Maserati.

NAOMI: Strange you should say that. I was just about to buy one of each, but they looked too *grandissimo. (Looking down her nose at him, acting stuck-up)* Us Americans don't enjoy the ostentation of $50,000 exotic cars, so I've selected a tastefully dented '76 Fiat with five forward speeds.

CARLO: Ah, I see! *Una donna intelligente.* You don't depend on the automatic. They're an insult to—

NAOMI: *(Interrupting)* Automatic transmissions.

CARLO: Yes. You people love them. Big, long automatic Cadillacs that look like, how do you say, uh, a living room inside. Americans don't *drive* the cars, they live in them. Houses on wheels.

[These garden variety general interpretations pepper conversation between people of different cultures or social classes. Carlo's complaint about American cars may be inspired by a more diffuse discomfort at dealing with unfamiliar surroundings, habits, food, traffic, and language. All these odd things are adding up to drain energy from concentrating on the upcoming athletic task. I'm not making any long-distance, exotic psychological interpretation here—just observing that this guy is under some stress and could be irritable enough to expand on his distaste for U.S. cars.]

NAOMI: I've noticed how visitors from other countries put Americans down for being preoccupied with bigger-is-better, and you make fun of our cars, dishwashers, and technology. It seems as if, ah, maybe there's a jealousy. Do ya think?

[She's fighting back with her own generalization, one that analyzes—it interprets a cause (the visitors' jealousy) for their behavior (a put-down of Americans). Note that she didn't interpret them directly, but referred to "visitors from other countries." And the analytic style of her interpretation makes it harder to brush off as a little light name-calling. Unlike interpretations that classify, the analytic ones dig in with seriousness and evidence. So Manuel is stuck because formally she's not strictly talking about him, but she's psychoanalyzing him. Nothing much he can do except grab her point and counter with an analytic interpretation of his own. Interpretations beget interpretations, just like a law of nature.]

MANUEL: Is true. We envy sometimes your technology, but your reputation is also deserving. This car's business . . . we have . . . how do you say, curvy roads and the gas costs much, so we learn to negotiate corners, like skiing, like art is driving. A skill requiring the shifting and a nimble car. We are proud of how good is the handling of our cars. But you people are rich and have freeways and drive in straight lines—no art. Your cars are clumsy and you think first about how they look. In other countries, they think first about how they handle. Sad to say, Americans with their freeways and money are superficial with cars, because they only know the surface of them.

Manuel's just delivered a counteranalysis to Naomi's interpretation that foreigners' criticism of American abundance is usually caused by jealousy. Naomi went on to meet the challenge—and the conversation escalated into a full-fledged international debate on the national character of put-down in the form of negative stereotypes that kept them from trading direct, personal information about themselves; it kept Naomi from her task of uncovering the private experiences of athletes in an Olympic village; and it kept these acquaintances from becoming friendly.

Worse, the stereotypes grew nasty. Naomi told me that she started feeling rather guilty about not finding a way to break the cycle of stereotype-swapping, but she "couldn't turn away from these guys' outrageous interpretations about Americans." At least it felt that way to her. When Manuel classified American women as emancipated to the point of "losing their femininity," Naomi came back with a lengthy indictment of Latin men oppressing their women "like animals." And for good measure, she added observations of Italian males as a "depraved bunch of mommas' boys" who "*act* gallant, but it's cute to pinch the bottoms of women pedestrians." Carlo said some things about "superficial Californians," and it became plain that they were using general interpretations as indirect insults.

At no time during the conversation did anyone call anyone a name—directly. Ostensibly, they were talking about whole nations, states, genders—not each other. They were playing a mischievous language game that most of us learn on grade school playgrounds. It's a transparent game that masquerades personal interpretation as general interpretations. The game is to pretend that criticism is actually an impersonal picture of a distant, large group. We use it to avoid *open* conflict. We also use it to maintain a conversation that would surely be disrupted by making the insults explicit. It buffers the expression of anger and keeps the communication process intact. Pretty clever. While the platitudes are bouncing back and forth on the surface, we're kicking each other under the table.

Early Signals of Personal Attraction

General interpretations are the escape clauses of conversation. They allow us to express important emotions and thoughts obliquely, so that we can escape from the pain or trouble that comes from direct expression. That goes for positive expressions, too—not just the sort of negative stuff that came out of the Naomi/Carlo/Manuel conversation. In the same way that the trio of students disguised their early signs of disagreement, disapproval, and dislike, our early signs of agreement, approval, and *liking* can also be transmitted indirectly through general interpretations. If a man sincerely tells the appropriate woman, "Blue eyes are especially attractive with dark skin," he's not nearly as committed as if he said, "I love your eyes." That general opinion about blue eyes and dark skin shields the guy from directly confessing his admiration for a woman who's right in front of him.

The strategic hiding of risky self-disclosures behind interpretations is a commonly accepted act because interpretations are so handy for shielding our vulnerabilities. Telling too much too soon is a genuine worry, and not just for shy people. Getting emotionally undressed prematurely can put a crimp in the development of relationships—especially romantic relationships (see chapter 1).

Romance resists rapid honesty, quick sex, flat-out self-disclosures, or the unnerving spotlight of severe scrutiny. Many people use cautious, roundabout ways to reveal interest—especially when strong attraction comes early. This point was well illustrated by the meticulous notes of a film editor, Angie, who helped me piece together her first face-to-face conversation with a man she met through the Great Expectations dating service (referred to by members as G.E.) in Portland, Oregon. She occasionally described important events in her diary with the detailed care learned as a professional observer of film dialogue. In this important event, her date is Larry, a public relations executive. They've previously watched each other on videotape in five-minute interviews conducted by the service and then talked briefly by phone. So they were still basically strangers as they arrived at the restaurant. They were also both quite new to the dating service experience and clearly felt self-conscious about it. The evening started out quite typically for a first date—light bantering, small compliments, and tactical questions to avoid awkward silences.

ANGIE: Well . . . how do you feel so far about G.E.?

LARRY: *(Smiling)* Good. *(Pause)* At this moment . . . actually, I've been so busy with work the last few months, I don't think I've dated more than two or three times.

ANGIE: Oh, that's all? I thought probably people would use it like a candy store—so many goodies to choose from.

LARRY: One date told me she went out almost every night for weeks and turned into a detached sleepwalker. All those guys started blurring together. Great Expectations turned into Burnout City. *(They both laugh)*

ANGIE: Yeah, the fantasy and reality are two different things when it comes to seeing new men every night. It's not good to be with strangers so much. How can you be discriminating? It's shallow. Doing candy store selection with a dating service is worse for a woman than making herself an easy pickup.

LARRY: *(Sighing)* It's bad for men, too.

[This is the start of an "agreeing" stage and the end of using questions as crutches for drawing each other out. Angie's general interpretations about the frequent shallowness of the acquaintanceship process between men and women are going to be matched by Larry's general interpretations on the subject.]

LARRY: *(Continuing)* Really, using women as toys can make you feel like hot stuff. *Whoopee*—look at me with all these women tumbling over for me. But when you find out they're using you as a toy, too, you're not such hot stuff. And so many of 'em are depressed. The whole quick pickup scene is so depressing.

ANGIE: That's how I see it. A lot of desperate people scared of getting close enough to really know anyone. And blaming it on just not being able to find the right one.

LARRY: Hey, that makes sense: "Sorry, you're not perfect, goodbye." That's what they say, but they're actually scared of what would happen if somebody really got to know them. I bet if you lined up all the fast-action people for a mental exam, they'd be diagnosed as having "intimacy phobia" or something.

[Two people who agree. They're being alike, at least in their opinion—their interpretation—of singles bar people. And being alike can be the start of liking. Their generalizations serve to indirectly communicate that both disdain rapid turnover and are candidates for getting close. Even if both suspected their characterization of more active people were distorted, it probably wouldn't change their tune. In a case like this, the display of similarity—and indirect disclosure of laudable personal attributes—is more important than accuracy.]

ANGIE: That's a good one: intimacy phobia. It's not only in fast-action people. Half the guys I know find all sorts of cool excuses for not getting close 'cause they're scared. They just won't—

LARRY: *(Interrupting)* Ah, come on. You can't believe men sit around *scared* of getting close. That's just a rumor. Maybe weary or discouraged, but not many are scared. It's rough meeting women and playing games with so many while you're looking for the right one, uh, a good one. No joke. Men may be less afraid of actually *being* close than doing whatever is necessary for *getting* close.

ANGIE: Interesting . . . very interesting, because that's really true for women, too. The dating and rating game can be murder. Blind dating isn't only a miserable event between unlikely people but a waste of time—oh-h, so discouraging. So we're full of second thoughts about getting close, too. We'd rather just *be* close. Getting there is the problem. That's why I joined G.E.

LARRY: Me too.

ANGIE: So why don't others do it? They'd rather be miserable and alone all their lives than admit their loneliness and solve it by getting assertive.

LARRY: Exactly. They'd rather be safe and miserable than take a chance. And people even look down on me for joining a thing so "mechanical, unnatural"—like I should just flow with fate and wait to be stopped on the streets of downtown Portland by a woman born to be my mate. You know, I'm walking along one day and here she comes, like in a dream, the gorgeous corporation head who immediately sees all of my attributes and starts unbuttoning her blouse on the spot. *(They laugh)*

Later, Angie reported she felt attracted to Larry at this point. Her notes on the conversation said, "He's not what you'd call great looking, but all of a sudden he seemed so cute. Maybe his image of getting stopped on the street did something to me. Something was clicking."

The clicks came as their general interpretations showed a similarity in their distaste for promiscuity, reasons for joining G.E., views on getting close being harder than staying close, and their amusement at the public's negative opinion of dating services. This pattern of using general interpretations to explore similarities and differences can be predicted to occur with great regularity whenever two people with romantic intentions first talk. Sometimes the testing is ended abruptly when a single general interpretation reveals a critical difference in values, expectations, or personal style. The end of testing ends the need for more general interpretations. Platitudes are put aside—and so is the relationship. But Angie and Larry are still going strong as they disclose private thoughts in the guise of general attitudes.

ANGIE: Wonderful image. You two standing there in downtown Portland, love at first sight. Like a silver screen romance. Send the idea to Erich Segal.

LARRY: *(Laughing)* How about a Harlequin romance novel?

ANGIE: Well, uh, instant love for a woman executive would work—even passion on a downtown sidewalk might work. But you'd need something exotic—Rio . . . Madrid . . . even New Orleans. Portland won't make it.

LARRY: Portland won't make it for a lot of reasons.

[Larry is starting to take on the whole city with some general interpretations. Can Portland native Angie handle *this* kind of private thought masked as a general attitude?]

ANGIE: Sounds like this place is getting you down.

[Her reflection offers a touch of empathy, which is all Larry needs to open up more.]

LARRY: It's got me down this week. I don't know why. Some things bug me a lot and other things are great. My job is great. The white-water rafting is great, especially the Salmon River run. Most of the rafters, men and women from here, will do anything to help you. But they're so uptight about anything that's not socially on the straight and narrow. You'd think that people who seem on the surface so unpretentious would try to be a little more tolerant about things different from them. I never knew anyone like 'em in Chicago.

ANGIE: What kinds of things do they say?

LARRY: After I told one guy I was in G.E. and it got around, they'd say stupid things like, "What's a nice-looking guy like you gotta do that for?" or "I'm gonna fix you up so you don't have to settle for those dating service dogs."

ANGIE: Unbelievable!

LARRY: Really. And river-rafters aren't the only grim people in this town. The women at work found out and *they* started making cracks. So I got mean and shut 'em up. They hated what I was doing. They'd rather sit home getting fat and watching reruns of "Gilligan's Island." I dated a couple of 'em when I got here in '86, and they were envious and disapproving of someone from the outside world. They were *courteously* cold to black people. They ridiculed gays. These women are more concerned with social pretentions than basic human contact. You get some people like that in Chicago, but I keep running into them all over the place here—incredible. I was out with a private school teacher who actually got mad at this couple in a restaurant because a white guy was with an Oriental girl.

ANGIE: *What?* Oh, no.

LARRY: She accused them of just wanting attention, trying to rebel against society—a schoolteacher! This dumb bitch would probably jail us for belonging to G.E.

[This guy has slandered all of the young women of Portland. As we say in the trade, he's probably overgeneralizing from a small, unrepresentative sample. Putting Larry's pejoratives aside, the interesting action is in Angie's response as a Portland woman.]

ANGIE: I must admit some women in this town *can* be kinda backward at times. I've got some straightlaced people in my family, but I don't know people quite as prejudiced and deliberately mean as the women you know. There's really a lotta good folks here. But I guess there's also a lotta old-fashioned ideas about the deport-

ment of men and women—so my life would probably be complicated if everyone knew Sweet Angie was in G.E.

LARRY: Do your friends know?

ANGIE: Yeah, the people who know think I'm misguided. They want me
to meet men through the usual slapdash methods—same thing the
rafters said to you.

LARRY: Yeah, maybe it happens a lot. I bet most G.E. members sneak in
the back door. *(They laugh)*

ANGIE: Or disguise themselves.

LARRY: It's true; this town can get so uptight.

ANGIE: Unfortunately.

The vilification of poor Portland seems to be getting out of
hand. Chances are both of them would say nice things about
their city to a stranger in Europe—and mean it. Nothing like a
common enemy for bringing two people together. And nothing
like general interpretations for creating common enemies. These
newly acquainted people (who are still together at the time of
this writing, ten months after meeting) collaborated in charac-
terizing the fears, prejudices, and other psychological dynamics
of Portland, which allowed them to indirectly disclose their initial attraction for each other. It's an oblique verbal dance that
says, ''I like you. Let's be alike.'' The dance is universal and
usually unwitting, although I suppose it will always be a planned
part of the seducer's tool kit.

The thing is, there's no reason to be sneaky about playing
with general interpretations for getting a little closer or testing
the intimacy waters (see chapter 9). There are ways to do it
without maligning cities or other humans. Looking back, Larry
and Angie were embarrassed at their sweeping, all-inclusive,
indiscriminate interpretations, even though they came from a
base of sincerity. Their distortions weren't evident in the heat of
their collusion. They did remember feeling like a minority, hud-
dled together against so many who didn't understand them. But
they understood each other—like two special people linked by
a common view (or a common fantasy) of a disapproving city.
Their mutual admiration escalated. A romance started. And once
again, Cupid's arrows were those ubiquitous, unheralded general interpretations.

OLD PROVERBS NEVER DIE; THEY DON'T EVEN FADE AWAY

Most proverbs are nothing more than general interpretations claiming to carry the wisdom of our ancestors, although sometimes they only carry the cliches of our ancestors. Sometimes proverbs can tease fixed ideas and warn us about our foolishness. But they can also serve our prejudices and disguise lazy thinking with an easy one-liner.

Modern-day aphorisms and pop proverbs appear with surprising frequency in conversation, doing the same work as spontaneous homemade generalizations. Even when they're simplistic and trite, these pithy sayings appeal to our interpersonal needs. It's not so much what they say, but *how* they shape conversation. Proverbs are used to come to grips with unfamiliar situations, reveal private thoughts obliquely, insult others indirectly, and indicate romantic attraction with no commitment.

In the busy flow of conversation, a well-placed proverb (also known as motto, aphorism, maxim, or slogan[1]) is hard to quarrel with. That's because even when it obviously doesn't hold true for most circumstances, the popular generalization can offer insight into a particular circumstance, a particular human condition, at a special place, during a specific time. So it's easy in the rush of talk to let the polished proverb, the well-worn "truth" pass by unchallenged. But at times it pays to quarrel a bit with the merits, exceptions, and weaknesses of some of these proverbial truths. Such examinations can change the course of discussions. The incompleteness of the thought is easy to spot. Take a moment to think about these as robust truths or half-truths.

"All things come to those who wait." (Passivity always better than assertion?)

"Attack is the best form of defense." (Battles were lost and people have died believing this one.)

"The family that prays together stays together." (This hypothesis should be researched.)

"A bad workman blames his tools." (I use this one on my graduate students.)

"The grass is always greener on the other side." (Seems like an experience common to children.)

"Bullies are often cowards." (And research suggests they learn not to empathize from their parents.)

"Fools rush in where angels fear to tread." (Thank God for the angels that have rushed in where fools feared to tread.)

"Lovers never tire of talking to each other because it's always about themselves." (Probably true, until they have a baby.)

Sometimes there's a choice of which half of the truth you recite.

"Absence makes the heart grow fonder" versus "Out of sight, out of mind."

"Many hands make light work" versus "Too many cooks spoil the broth."

"Confession is good for the soul" versus "Only children and fools tell the truth."

I'm convinced that some proverbs, perpetuated across the centuries, can have serious impacts on human behavior, for better or worse, because they're a way of dealing with our fears, jealousies, values, and ignorance. They partially mask personal contempt and concealed prejudice for a nationality, a physical deformity, a personality trait, a race, or a gender. Medieval attitudes about male/female relations in England, for example, could be interpreted from a popular proverb: "A woman, a dog, and a walnut tree—the more you beat them, the better they be." Variations on that wife-beating theme seem to have been handed down at least into the 1930s. Now, anybody knowing their walnut trees would agree with the wisdom of beating the long shoots until they break into short, fruiting spurs that increase the harvest. But linking that truth with the beating of women and dogs into obedience may have encouraged many men toward cruelty and given others some social permission, some public legitimacy for turning angry impulses into angry behavior.

Other proverbs and aphorisms dating from second-century Greece to current America reveal cultural prejudices by interpreting the character of women with demeaning language.

"A man is as old as he feels, and a woman as old as she looks."

"Six hours sleep for a man, seven for a woman, and eight for a fool."

"A whistling woman and a crowing hen are neither fit for God nor men."

"A man never knows how to say goodbye; a woman never knows when to say it."

"A woman and a ship always need mending."

"Women are never stronger than when they arm themselves with their weaknesses."

"Never choose your women or your linen by candlelight."

"A woman's place is in the home."

Personally, I've been wary of the sweeping generalizations in proverbs since age eight, when a well-meaning man next door, wishing to soothe my fear of his yapping Boston bulldog, intoned, "A barking dog never bites." Believing *that* time-honored interpretation of animal behavior cost me two stitches. My misfortune was a precise playing out of the old joke, "You believe the proverb and I believe it—but has the dog heard it?"

GROUP INTERPRETATIONS—FOR CONTEMPLATION, INSPIRATION . . . AND PERSPIRATION

Here's an entire family—father, mother, three children—coming home from a long car trip, pulling a trailer behind. Everyone is exhausted and irritable. The father, at the wheel, keeps telling the kids to be quiet. The youngest daughter, 6, is whining. The oldest daughter, 15, and the middle son, 11, keep up an ongoing verbal sniping contest. Finally, the mother calls for a cease-fire, announcing: "All right, so we're all grumpy 'cause we didn't sleep much last night. There was no way of knowing the trailer park would be so noisy, okay? It wasn't the fault of any of us. So we're all getting on each other's nerves 'cause we're all pooped. *That's* what's been going on for the past couple of hours."

Mother just delivered a group interpretation. She classified and analyzed her family in 15 seconds. Group interpretations are similar to personal interpretations in naming and explaining face-to-face—except the group variety do it face-to-faces.

Group interpretations tend to be more superficial than the personal, general, and third-party kind—it's hard, after all, to characterize the psychology of five or ten people as if they were one, unless you stick with easy-to-defend assertions, such as, "Everyone's hungry because they skipped lunch," or "The first staff meeting was a little tense and the new people were reluctant to talk because they were being sized up." It's also tough to offer deep or painful interpretations of a group with all those eyes looking at you (unlike the safety of third-party interpretations).

So good group interpretations aren't easy, but they can be very valuable in pulling a bunch of people together, and good communicators almost instinctively employ them to diagnose such standard group problems as miscommunication, unexpressed issues, hostility, loss of confidence in a task, and poor morale. Sometimes the tone is a combination of criticism and encouragement. Our traveling mother, for instance, obliquely criticized her family for failing to recognize the causes of the grumpy atmosphere on the way home. She also tried to absolve them of blame, so they wouldn't hold each other accountable. Her group interpretation probably came from the constructive impulse to raise her family's morale and reduce hostilities by analyzing the causes for stressful behavior.

The majority of group interpretations, I'd guess, are for correcting on-the-spot, immediate problems. To offer a critical insight for improving things *right now*. Here's one from a self-help group: "We've been tiptoeing around each other all session. Walking on eggs. We're afraid to say what's on our minds." This straight diagnosis describes the cause for the tiptoeing without analysis. Sometimes just naming behavior stimulates correction.

Teachers often interpret their classes as if they were a single organism: "You've been so noisy during study period that recess will be short today" or "Class was very good about cleanup. You're getting neater every week."

A former student of mine, now a consultant to corporations, believes skillful group interpretations are a key to strong communication for top management. He tells of how an entire corporate team was drawn out of a tailspin in morale with two powerful interpretations by a manager who knew exactly what her group interpretations could do. The first was an analysis linking an unexpected failure on a minor project to a contagious defensive reaction that lowered team pride and enthusiasm. The second was a positive evaluation explaining why the team shouldn't be apologizing to anyone. She convincingly called their performance outstanding and analyzed their despondency as a typical reaction for a fairly new team with no previous experience at coping with project failures. She added that their real failure was in letting the loss get them down so badly. Her interpretations had the effect of creating new meaning for the team—"We're better than we thought"—and that raised group morale in a manner worthy of an outstanding football coach.

Win One for the Grouper

A real football coach provided me with a wonderful string of group interpretations aimed at prodding his scared, outmanned, small-town Missouri team into an extraordinary effort. His classical pregame pep talk was faithfully transcribed by a former high school English teacher who volunteered to assist the overworked coach. Today, the ex-teacher's a somewhat jaded sportswriter for a big city daily, but he admits to still getting a lump in his throat recalling the chemistry back in 1976 between a coach and his team.

This school bus address may sound as corny as a 1930s locker-room melodrama to anyone who hasn't played a team sport, but it was delivered at an opportune moment: a Friday night game for a town I'll call Beaver Creek against a much bigger school, Slayton. Beaver Creek has traveled 30 miles by bus to face undefeated Slayton, which won last season's game by four touchdowns. To everyone's surprise, Beaver Creek is still undefeated, too. Bigtime Slayton actually has bleachers—gaudy aluminum bleachers—for fans, as opposed to the Beaver Creek field, where people stand along the sidelines or sit in their cars at the end of the field. The teams have just finished their warmups and Slayton runs off to its locker room for the pregame prep. Beaver Creek has to settle for returning to its bus because the visitors' dressing room was swamped by an overnight plumbing leak. The coach waits for his tense, anxious, strangely subdued team to settle in their seats, then boards the bus very calmly, closes the door, and slowly sweeps his eyes across everyone. The volunteer assistant is in the bus driver's seat, wondering what the veteran coach can tell these teenagers to help them overcome a heavily favored opponent. The coach begins.

"Well, here we are in lovely Slayton. They like to think they have a big-time athletic operation here. But we know about Slayton. Their staff somehow manages to have the visiting dressing room unusable. They just *happen* to have a little john flood last night so that we have to dress at home and ride over here in our uniforms. Somehow, their coaches always manage to have some unforeseen little problem that *somehow* manages to make it a little rougher on us. And *somehow* it all happens just before the game. It seems to happen almost every year I've brought a team here. You know, you'd think if they have such a big-time operation here—we all keep *hearing* about how good they are—that they'd *act* like a big-time operation instead of always trying to find some halfass edge. . . ."

[The coach has unearthed and analyzed a conspiracy against Beaver Creek. His interpretation creates a picture of a dishonorable enemy oppressing his innocent team. Interpretations are customary in competitive sports. They occur whenever someone describes an entire team with a single emotion (discouraged, vengeful, overconfident), or a single virtue (strong when the chips are down, making the most of their skills), or any singular interpretation that treats a varied group of individuals as if they were clones of each other. These interpretations allow us to identify with a team's fortunes or misfortunes. Faithful fans want each player—the whole team—to experience the thrill and agony. Who wants to hear about athletes dispassionate about a victory or loss? That's why group interpretations are enjoyed every day in newspaper sports pages and television interviews.]

"It's ri-goddamn-diculous, but we aren't gonna let it bother us. Nope. This team's been overcoming edges and odds all year and I don't think it's gonna stop now. To tell the truth, I never expected you guys to get this far. I never expected ya to be unbeaten at this point in the season." He motions to Beaver Creek's fans outside, then continues. "I don't think many people out there did either. And those fans are wondering: 'Can our team see Slayton as ordinary players? Can we concentrate on fundamentals and come up with one more win? Are we exceptional?' "

[If you'll excuse my tinkering with the coach's ritual, I'd guess he doesn't actually wonder about anyone concentrating on fundamentals and not overrating Slayton. The interpretation here is a piece of romantic language that joins a group of kids into a single fantasy about passionate fans and overwhelming odds.]

"Well, let me tell ya, *I* believe. This team has made a believer out of me. I look around this bus and I see people who have done exceptional things all season and I have to believe they're gonna do it again tonight." He begins walking down the aisle, popping players on the shoulder pads as he names them.

[He's about to do some personal interpretations that effectively set up rousing group interpretations.]

"Abbott here, with his bad knees and all, just keeps hanging in there at center—*exceptional*! *(Pop!)* Ericksen here, never played a game before this season—*exceptional*! *(Pop!)* Goeppert here couldn't walk and chew gum at the same time last year; now he's as tough a tackle as there is in this state—*exceptional*! *(Pop!)* Truitt, Truitt can hardly see through those goggles he's got, but he can damn sure find the holes—*exceptional*! *(Pop!)* Byrnes is too damn small and too damn slow, but he's one helluva linebacker anyway—*exceptional*! *(Pop!)* Martley, well, Martley, here could have hung it up when he got hurt the first part of the season, but he's back and he's tougher than ever—*exceptional*!'' He turns and starts walking back to the front of the bus. Many of the players have tears in their eyes. The players have been individualized, then brought together with an "exceptional" and a popped shoulder pad.

[Now the coach is ready for a crescendo of group interpretations, leading up to a rousing finish, where the team acts as if one, as the individuals interpret themselves.]

"Now, you know about Slayton. Those guys have three times the students to draw a team from—they've got blocking sleds and all kindsa fancy equipment and they get new uniforms every couple years. Hell, we're lucky if we've got enough *helmets* to go around. They get more press, they get more glory, they get people on the all-state team every year. But you know what they *don't* have—they don't have the *guts* you guys do, 'cause they haven't faced and overcome the adversity you have. And they don't have the *cohesiveness* you guys do, 'cause they haven't been through so much together. And they don't have the *desire* to win you guys do, 'cause you're hungrier and leaner and meaner.'' He turns and faces them at the front of the bus. "You guys have more guts. You have more cohesiveness. You have more desire. And all of that makes you *exceptional*! What are you?''

The team shouts in unison: *"Exceptional!"*

"What are you?''

"Exceptional!"

"All right! All right! Beaver Creek, let's *kick ass*!''

The coach jerks the door open, and the players—roaring—go charging off the bus.

Note: The Beaver Creek players—interpreting themselves as "exceptional"—won, 14–13.

CHAPTER 4

ADVISEMENTS

"A KEY DEVICE FOR ENACTING LOVE."

ASK THE TALK DOCTOR

Dealing with a Know-It-All

Dear Talk Doctor: Boy, am I aggravated! I'm a mature 32-year-old loving mother of two, a loyal wife, and I work as a substitute schoolteacher. But despite all of that my mother persists in treating me like a kid. I mean, she maternalizes me. Her motto: Mother knows best—*about everything*. She's constantly telling me how to live my life, how to raise the kids, how to treat my husband—everything from the best laundry detergent to how to conduct myself in the bedroom. I know she means well, but it's really gotten out of hand, and there's no way out because she only lives a block away, so she's always over here telling me how to live and breathe. I've sat down with her several times and talked to her about being less bossy, but the next day she's right back at it. So I try to protect myself by giving her advice about the way she gives advice, but it hasn't helped yet. And now she's deputized my son and daughter as her advice agents—''Grandma would do it like this'' and ''Grandma would do it like that.'' Good grief, Talk Doctor, her bossiness is catching! What can I do?—*Maternalized Mother, Barnwell, South Carolina*

Dear Maternalized Mother: Last year I received over 8,000 letters about advice-happy mothers (and mothers-in-law) who ''mean well'' but fail to notice that their little daughters have grown up. It's a national epidemic, and sitting down to talk just doesn't help. Why don't you try some self-protection techniques for quieting your exasperation with Mother's ardent advice-giving? Something safer than popping a Valium or muffling Mom with a gag. I know your kind of suffering because *my* mom behaved like a walking how-to manual, but I found a defense: I would smile gratefully, nod agreeably—then promptly forget what she said. That little technique made us both happy.

Now if you can't pretend without getting caught, or if you're not skilled at letting it go in one ear and out the other, perhaps giving her an overdose of her own medicine would help—you might read a back issue of *Consumer Reports* on detergents or find a guide on bedroom relations and give a fully documented lecture showing *her* who knows best. If those steps fail, you'd better lay down the law about limiting her visits, because that'll limit your aggravation. As for your copycat kids, flat-out tell them it's time to stop using Grandma's advice against you. Embroider this motto on their pillows: "*Your* Mother Knows Best."

What do you think? Even though the language of the hypothetical reply was breezy, her problem was taken seriously. And many maternalized mothers would take the advice seriously. An advice column like this could propel thousands of sane women into pretending gratitude as a form of self-defense against nonstop motherly advisement. Just a little bit of harmless verbal maneuvering. Nobody's going to get hurt, right?

Personally, I wouldn't even begin to advise Maternalized Mother if she were a real person. The presentation of her problem in the letter isn't remotely close to giving me what I need to provide some help. If she were seriously distressed about the conflict with her mother and desperate enough to follow the quick guidance offered, there'd be some chance for a psychologically nasty repercussion. I believe many major advice columnists feel the same and wouldn't offer such specific types of guiding information. But even generalizations on the nature of human relations aimed at a specific letter can be debatable: "Sitting down to talk just doesn't help." Sometimes it does help if the talk is careful.

My primary reason for packing the above response with so

many specifics is to illustrate the five major kinds of advisement in the order of their assertiveness: their tendency to insist on a course of action; press for a preference; or firmly, assuredly urge the listener to comply.

- "Why don't you try some self-protection techniques for quieting your exasperation with Mother's ardent advice-giving?" That's an "advising question." It has a question mark at the end, but it's really a piece of advice masquerading as a question. (Much of the next chapter illustrates how questions masquerade to carry even more important baggage than advisement.) Advising questions are gentle devices for telling people what to do. They're not very assertive.
- "I know your kind of suffering because *my* mom behaved like a walking how-to manual, but I found a defense: I would smile gratefully, nod agreeably—then promptly forget what she said. That little technique made us both happy." That's a "me-too" piece of advice. It's almost as low on assertion as the advising question, but me-too's are a little more direct. Done empathically, they have the big value of offering a personal story, a self-disclosure about something similar that happened to the adviser. That's why, for me, they're often the most convincing form of advising. In this particular case, I believe the actual content of the me-too advice is awful, but it still has the power to convince because it's a supposedly successful verbal demonstration.
- ". . . perhaps giving her an overdose of her own medicine would help. . . ." A suggestion. On the advice assertion scale, suggestions are middle-of-the-road. They give direct hints, "tips." They offer possibilities with a mild to medium nudge of intensity. They soft-sell ideas. Suggestions say, in effect, "You really should consider trying this."
- ". . . lay down the law about limiting her visits, because that'll limit your aggravation." A "soft command." It does two things: (1) It gives the *reason* for telling you what to do, and (2) it directly tells you what to do. The soft command is much more assertive than the suggestion, but some of the authoritarianism in it is cushioned by the courtesy of including a rationale, in contrast to:
- The "hard command": ". . . tell them to stop using Grandma's advice against you." An order, crisp and efficient. It simply insists on compliance without telling why. The bold-

est, baldest form of advice. Hard commands top the scale on insistence.

I include these five forms of advising under the umbrella term *advisement*—a term that many people have advised me sounds pretentious, ponderous, and overly formidable. Fair enough. But I'm still using the term to cover the advising waterfront because I've simply never been able to come up with a better label. The fact is, there's a lot more to this set of talk tools than can be covered by the common meaning of "advice." So I'll use advisement much of the time to remind you to think in new ways about this stuff.

The examples I wrote for the Talk Doctor's reply serve as introductory snapshots of the advisement family. But actual conversation is needed to show how these talk tools attempt to influence behavior in many vital ways. They're principal go-betweens in our attempts at persuading others to reshape their thinking, change habits, reduce interpersonal conflict, or become pawns to our sneaky manipulations. Advisements are also key devices for enacting love feelings, articulating empathy, or disregarding someone else's discomfort.

ADVISING QUESTIONS

Look for advising questions in the following poignant disclosure.

JEANETTE: So, it's Christmas, and where's my Mary? I, uh, felt *weird*, ya know. When this time of year rolls around, I keep expecting my daughter and everybody together, and I get so down. Keep having to tell myself she is . . . not *here*. Not here. It's not, I can't *cope* with it sometimes. I want my little girl so much. Can't get rid of wanting it so bad. It won't block out.

NAN: Don't you think it's time to stop fighting the feelings and sorta let 'em happen? Wouldn't it be better during Chris—uh, during the holidays, to tell yourself the feelings are gonna come and make pain, and ya know, uh, they're gonna go, too?

[Both advising questions offer serious possibilities for how to feel and think about an overpowering situation. Strong advice here is made respectful and less pushy because it's couched in the form of questions that give the illusion of asking opinion more than providing advice. Advising questions are less aggressive than unadulterated advice-giving. These women are peers in a self-help group for mothers without custody of their children (because the fathers either kidnapped the children or obtained legal custody). The women were strangers seven sessions ago, and now they're so close that Nan can challenge Jeanette's entire manner of coping with grief. That challenge is made gentle by the advising question's ability to practically ask permission for giving the advice it carries. Any kind of advisement, by nature, appears assertive, but when it's loaded into a question, a certain deference occurs.]

JEANETTE: Well, I tried saying to myself, Hey, it's only a holiday; just a tradition I'm hooked on. So it'll feel terrible and pass over. But then when it actually comes down on me, the pain drops me to my knees. I forget it'll . . . like stop; that the pain will end.

[Jeanette already tried Nan's advice. Advice-givers rarely ask if their plan, solution, or cure has already been tried. Maybe that's why people who are very close have a better chance of advising wisely; they have more information about what's been tried. I believe advising questions can take a little annoyance out of being offered problem-solving methods we've already used and discarded.]

NAN: Yeah, that's true. *(Pause)* It's easy to *say* you're gonna talk yourself out of it, then *really* talk yourself out of a bad place—sorta when ya—

JEANETTE: *(Interrupting)* I just have to let it happen; tell myself that's just the way it's gonna be and wait till March, uh . . . March is, it's our month together 'cause Carl goes, uh, to . . . Oh, God, it's so unfair. (She starts crying softly.) Why did he, why—so, she's *my own* baby, just because he's clever, and, uh, lawyers . . . *(Long pause)* Ya know, there's this poet who wrote this book of poems about losing custody of his little girl and called it *Heart's Needle*. And in the front it has this old Irish poem, about a man who's worked himself into a frenzy 'cause he's lost just everything. See, a messenger is telling him about how his house burned and his wife is dead . . . and everything almost is gone; he's sorta, um, reeling when the messenger finally tells him that his only daughter is gone. The guy says, "Ay! That's the needle in the heart." Well, this thing is the needle in my heart and it's gonna kill me if I can't cut the pain. . . . Gotta figure some way to take away *some* of the pain.

RITA: *(Another group member)* Couldn't you take some of the pain away by making your own tradition, and doing your own damn Christmas in March? Your Mary won't care. Why can't you turn December 25 into any day you please?

These advising questions take Jeanette by surprise. After some resistance, she seriously considers Rita's plan, for a March

Christmas and decides to try it. The group comforts her and discusses prospects for the plan reducing at least part of her pain.

Besides showing respect for the advisee's judgment, or covering the possibility that the advice is stale, advising questions work as shock absorbers for guidance that might be heard as presumptuous if given directly. The indirect quality of questions loaded with guidance works as a signal that says, "I know this advice may be too much, unwanted, stale, or ill-informed—but couldn't, shouldn't, wouldn't you consider it anyway?"

"Shouldn't you be drinking decaffeinated coffee?" "Wouldn't you be better off investing in money markets than real estate?" These advisements are somewhat uncertain about the chances for acceptance. "Wouldn't it be smart to get a maintenance policy instead of waiting for the washer to break?"

They're cautious talk tools, especially when trying to guide someone we don't know well. If the acquaintance accuses us of meddling inappropriately, we might make a weak claim of innocence: "I was *only* asking a question." It's become a famous defense.

Like many basic talk tools, advising questions are multipurpose. They can be sneaky, respectful, *and* respectfully sneaky. In moderation, they're fine as part of a talk repertoire, but like other things that frequently bring a little reliable comfort, they tend to be overused. By my quasi-casual but earnest observation, the advising question ranks as one of the most popular talk tools in the history of the English language. Some people get addicted, using them to the exclusion of more sensitive, more convincing advisements such as me-too's or more assertive varieties such as suggestions and soft or hard commands. When the addiction takes over, advising questions can even inhibit the conversational utility of honest-to-goodness questions. As a heavy habit, advising questions can detract from your self-presentation, create distance between people, and start damaging communication. So if you've got a strong advising question habit, uh . . . wouldn't it be wise to consider using other types of advisement?

ME-TOO ADVISEMENTS

Compared to advising questions, these are less popular and more difficult to use well. The Talk Doctor's me-too was frivolous, but me-too's are artful bits of talk capable of performing heavy-duty guidance. Employed with a little forethought, they become great ways to give advice as serious help. The following example comes from the same group of mothers without custody. They've been learning how to use me-too's and other talk tools from my audiotape communication training program (SASHAtapes). By now the mothers are getting good at using me-too's, so what you read isn't exactly everyday conversation.

PHYLLIS: I don't want to tell my kids that their father did me dirty. The macho bastard absolutely believes women are the second sex—deep in his heart, we're inferior beings. And he puts me down with so much insane distortion that I, I kinda space out and actually start believing that I'm some sort of abandoning villain, a selfish mother. Someday they'll know I'm okay. They'll know. Truth will come out.

[The group members talk all over each other with a rush of support for her hope: "You bet." "They sure will." "When they're older and can understand . . ."]

PHYLLIS: Yeah . . . So I've been learning to live with that. But something else has been buggin' me bad. Last weekend—God. A cold chill hit me in the shoulders and creeped down to my toes. *(Long pause as she stares hard at the floor with fists clenched)* They called her "Mom"! Can you imagine? They call this Wicked Stepmother of the West "Mom"! *(Group laughs)* She's all sweetness and light to them, I get the full dose of her true bitchiness. I'm damned *furious*, but didn't say anything to the kids; but they must've known something was—

JANE: *(Interrupting)* It's wrong to keep quiet about these things because it's gonna—

PHYLLIS: *(Interrupting)* What am I gonna do? Tell 'em never to use that name in my house? That'll make things worse. Maybe make 'em call her—what? Artificial Mom? *(The group laughs and someone says: ". . . and call you 'Authentic Mom.' ")*

PHYLLIS: *(Laughing along)* So what do ya do? Forcing 'em will push 'em toward her.

[Jane is going to change the course of things here with a convincing me-too advisement.]

JANE: Wait a second, Phyllis. You're not the only one of us who got slapped in the face by our kids' new attachment. I want ya to know that last year Sandy did a "Mom thing" with me. But I couldn't hide my anger. I said, "She's not *your* mom—she's got a real name. Call her that." I had a tantrum. At first I wished I'd clammed up, like you, but now I'm glad it spilled 'cause we talked openly and got closer for it. I told all about why it bugged me so much and he *really* understood. And I even admitted she was doing a good job helping him with his asthma medication, and always driving him to basketball and all that. We agreed, *really* agreed to call her "stepmom" in public and *he* decided—honest, he thought of it—that it was time to call her Marge. My little young man cared that it bothered me and it was easy for him to change. It was great, but, uh, what I'm saying is, that you, that nothing would have happened, like I'd still be carrying that crap around if I didn't let him know how import—if I'd just shut up or *made* him not say it, it'd be worse now. Maybe it isn't exactly the same for you, but maybe your kids would want to know what you . . . what's really going on.

Some of these me-too's can get long. Why not? They do provide a detailed verbal demonstration with evidence and personal reaction. When done with a little skill, they spell out and endorse a plan for action—without being pushy or self-righteous.

True, they can become too evangelical: There's a fair amount of healthy assertion in telling a whole story in an effort to get across guiding information. But me-too's usually don't insist much that the guidance be followed; all they ask is that we give attention to the detailed enthusiasm of the testimonial: "I used to make fun of vitamin junkies, but to pacify Katherine I took some B complex for a week. My afternoon fadeouts disappeared. That converted me—I started taking 'em daily and they affected me kinda like caffeine. The stuff works. Katherine discovered the same thing. It works for both of us."

Me-too's do their best work with hard-to-give advice—personal matters and psychological advice. Essentially, they're self-disclosures that say, "I, too, have felt, thought, or acted like you, and here's what I did about it, and here's how it came out." They're more convincing than other advising talk tools because they're a bit like a research report, a how-to manual and a guidance counselor rolled into one. Me-too's often describe the results (maybe the results for a third party) and then spell out each step of the process, like a manual. They frequently demonstrate that the advice-giver is empathic or especially informed about what the advisee has already tried—just as Jane was with Phyllis. Sharing a common bond stimulates the use of me-too's. That's why they're a major therapeutic tool within most effective self-help mutual support groups. By demonstrating the personal experience of the adviser, me-too's take on more credibility and are more apt to be taken seriously than advising questions. My examples may have sounded familiar because me-too's do occur "naturally" in daily conversation. But not often enough. When used deliberately, they can become as skilled as advisements get. Using them on purpose (with a few tips from the advisement how-to chapter) goes a long way to persuade, to protect the advisee from your errors, and to make the advice-giving more comfortable for everyone.

SUGGESTIONS

These are the most familiar forms of advisement but, along with the less familiar me-too's, they are the least used. The few suggestions we *do* use stand out because they tend to actually announce themselves: "Here's my suggestion about . . ." "You may not like this suggestion, but . . ." "I'd like to suggest . . ." "Hold it—may I suggest that we all . . ." "If you want *my* suggestion, try . . ." "Might I suggest the onion soup this evening?"

We make a habit of using the word "suggest" in many ways that connote a soft or indirect intention to recommend a preference, make an implication, show a hint, or offer just a tinge of advice. The word can introduce a subtlety, an elegance, and sometimes an ostentatious strain toward elegance: "What would *you* suggest?" "She had the nerve to suggest that I actually . . ." "We tried it at her suggestion." "His voice gave a faint suggestion of urgency." "Are you suggesting? . . ." "It seems the solution almost suggests itself."

No other talk tool besides the question has its name mentioned so frequently in general discourse. And a favorite claim is that our forceful advisements are mere hints, gentle promptings: "It was *only* a suggestion, just a suggestion." But a closer look reveals many suggestions are commands made less assertive by a courteous, tentative tone.

More forceful than advising questions, more eager and bold than me-too's, suggestions modestly offer orders *on approval*—like trying an appliance on a ten-day home trial. Used with reserve, suggestions offer an idea to be (or not to be) acted upon, an idea to be bought or refused. They propose how someone *might* think, feel, or behave. Their offerings are meant to be used at the pleasure of the listener. With modesty (but not as much as advising questions or me-too's), they prefer to prompt rather than to push. The promptings are of eager proposals for *action*, but the tone is almost always courteous.

HOWARD: I'd suggest that you consider practicing even when it's embarrassing. . . . Perhaps practice will make it perfect. You might try just getting more experience to help your confidence talking to girls.

ANTHONY: It's so uncomfortable. It's not only backing off of girls, but other, uh, new things. My way has been to stick to things I know well, so it's always—I always fall back on talking about things I know very well. New things make me, like, uh, so I hardly talk to anyone besides a friend—

[These are seniors in a communication training group at a Catholic high school. Howard's suggestions are deferent, respectful, but nevertheless are a direct call for behavior change: more practice talking to girls. They make a distinct proposal for Anthony's *approval*. The fact that the proposal may be simplistic is beside the point—it's a clear piece of advice, a counsel for cure, a specific opinion offered for Anthony's consideration. The suggestions aren't softened by a question mark in Howard's voice, and they don't offer testimonials, yet they remain respectful of the listener's right of refusal. Note Howard's use of the word "suggest" as he defines his advisement as only a suggestion and nothing more. It helps to make sure that Anthony will not mistakenly hear the suggestion as a command.]

ANTHONY: *(Continuing)*—and my friends are guys, so, uh, I'm afraid of saying, well, to tell the honest-to-God truth, I blame it partially on being in an all-boys' school. That's my honest-to-God thinking. And now I'm afraid of situations, ya know . . . ya can't predict. Like I've never worked anyplace but the Bell Tower and the library—mostly library.

HOWARD: What did you do there?

ANTHONY: Stack books. Do notices. Mostly stack. I'm still there.

HOWARD: Oh, I see. I see . . . Hey . . . *(Long pause)* I'm not, uh, suggesting you quit your job or anything, but I'm thinking it *might* be a good idea if you did a little other work where you *had* to come into contact with other people more than stacking books. That's just my opinion. But you might wanna consider it, Anthony.

Howard's suggestion even carries the caveat "That's just my *opinion*." He also shows the idea's force and tentativeness when saying ". . . but I'm thinking it *might* be a good idea if you .." Such care isn't a requirement for creating suggestions; some are phrased as commands offered on approval: "Think about stopping work now and coming to my house." The force of the suggestion says: "Consider putting my idea in your mind and changing your behavior." The command is: "Change your behavior," but the authoritarian tone is removed by "Consider putting . . ." This speech act gives an order *after* it requests compliance. It transforms the command into a proposal for action, into a directive on approval—into a suggestion.

I once called them "simple suggestions," before learning that using them crisply and simply is rather an art. Maybe that's why suggestions aren't used nearly as often as advising questions.

Warning: Some talk-tool imposters use disclaimers that try to falsely present themselves as suggestions: "I suggest you finish cleaning your room before asking for this week's allowance." That's a threat, not a suggestion. It's a command that can sometimes ridicule the listener by pretending respect for his freedom of choice. Such imposters try to con their way through: "I seriously suggest you pay me back before tomorrow." These plainly assertive advisements mock the courtesy of suggestions. Real suggestions always pay honor to the listener's self-governance. They use some respect to get their business done.

SOFT COMMANDS

Here are some commands from public signs and notices that tell *why* they command.

"Don't touch handrail—wet paint."

"Have exact change ready—it saves everyone's time."

First, they tell us what to do, with some sense of authority, then they provide a reason for obeying.

"Don't send cash—it's unsafe."

"Do not talk in this reading room. People are studying."

These inanimate, impersonal messages order us around rather reasonably. Giving a rationale for a command can make it more effective. In a way, the rationale gives a metamessage (a message about a message) that says we deserve to be told why we should comply. It's considerate. That extra feature, telling us why to comply, single-handedly erases most of the harshness from getting ordered around. It allows us to oblige a command without blind obedience.

On the other side, *giving* soft commands allows us to respectfully manage others with gentle authority. That's why I call them "soft" commands. (By coincidence, while writing this section, I was compelled to write a personally relevant soft command: "Sasha, don't slam the front door—it's ruining both my concentration and the door latch." When exuberant, my young son could perform a slam that rattled china and damaged unprotected eardrums. My simple, soft command affixed to the door gave evidence for the effectiveness of this bit of language. After only a week (!), the slams were significantly reduced from four to a mere two a day—a powerful effect in preadolescent psychology.)

Spoken soft commands also tell why to comply: "Don't smoke here 'cause Alan has an allergy." "Show Dad your report card; it'll put him in a mood for taking us to a movie."

Because these advisements are face-to-face and verbal, they tend to be taken as cordial orders. Unlike the practice of simply adding "please" as a courtesy ("Don't smoke here, please"), soft commands take courtesy further. The mostly automatic "please" is more an *emblem* of courtesy, often used indiscriminately and often heard that way. It carries some sense of "If you please, at your pleasure," but essentially it rounds off the sharp corners of the demanding command: "Hurry up, please."

In contrast, "Hurry up or we'll miss the beginning" creates a soft command that gives us the formal authority of "Hurry up, please" with logic added. It almost asks for the listener's approval, like the suggestion. Soft commands assume the listener will agree with the logic before complying. They don't require unquestioned obedience. They don't say, "Do it"; they say, "Do it for this good reason." It usually makes mandates more acceptable.

HARD COMMANDS

"Keep off the grass."

"Deposit 35 cents and press selection."

"Guests must wear jacket and tie after six."

"Reenter last input."

No explanations offered. Sometimes the reason for compliance is evident, sometimes it's avoided or simply disregarded. Obedience is expected because of the context where authority is traditional (the military, church, work settings, public facilities) or anyplace where giving orders is situationally appropriate: "Get off my foot!" These talk tools are not negotiable. Ask any preacher or rabbi about holy commands, and you'll hear that what Moses brought down from the mountain were not the Ten Suggestions.

The most universal use of hard commands occurs in parent/child communication: "Don't put that in your mouth." "Put gas in the car before you come home." Since these are mostly parental prohibitions that limit freedom and pleasure, hard commands often remain aversive, even in appropriate adult-to-adult communication: "Do the Jacobs letter before calling Brophy and then pick up our mail."

It's not only the hidden memories of parental commands but the act of compliance—to be at another's disposal for a minute or a day—that interferes with the efficient use of this talk tool. Commands pick up feelings associated with master/servant, being ruled, compelled, dominated, even oppressed. So it becomes a troublesome message in any cross-age, cross-gender, or boss/staff communication. The potential trouble is one good reason we avoid hard commands in ordinary social settings. They're rarely found in polite conversation, because they *insist*.

These potentially explosive, severe, assertive, troublesome hard commands show a strange flip-flop when viewed over a wide range of human relations: They occur with greater frequency during both very formal, very authoritarian interchange *and* very informal, very nonauthoritarian interchange, but are rarely found in middle-of-the-road interchange. So we use them more in places where we put ourselves in someone's power or, on the other side, ask someone to do *our* bidding. Ironically, that includes communications ranging all the way from military operations to lovemaking. It doesn't include cocktail parties or casual chats with our neighbors. These hard commands, then, show up in both the strictest and the most intimate aspects of civilized life. The drill sergeant shouts at his subordinate, "Move those feet, soldier!" And the lover whispers, "Move your foot, babe." But in standard polite conversation, the shoe salesman softens a command to a customer: "Move your foot onto the measuring stick, ma'am, so I can check your size." Hard commands are hard to find among peers in courteous social situations that lack the privileged control of intimacy or the contractual control of authoritarian relations. It's a paradox that these bits of language—designed to control others in both small and large ways—are used so often in such extremely opposite circumstances.

The key to commands between people who are close is that there's little pretense. That's when hard commands become uncomplicated ways for intimately moving each other around. Those of us who don't like to be told what to do might become more tolerant by realizing that when someone close insists, "Stop working and get some sleep," it's nothing but the loving familiarity of a hard command.

ANOTHER IRRESISTIBLE URGE

Sometimes our appetite to advise takes the shape of a hunger, like the hunger to help someone, to reduce their discomfort or steer them toward pleasure. All sane adults experience occasional urges to make that little useful suggestion, that wise command, that lifesaving me-too advisement. I've seen so much of it, given with such unquenchable desire, that I've come to imagine that act of advisement as a reflex, a basic drive, some primitive instinct that functioned way back at the beginning of human relations. It had to. Prehistoric survival techniques must have been transmitted across generations, using advisement as a primary talk tool. Did it all start with demonstrations (a basic form of me-too's)? . . . Maybe hard commands came first. . . . When did the act of suggesting come into the human communication repertoire? . . .

My intrigue with this stuff about advising as an ancient urge spilled into my communication classes. I remember making lame jokes about Eve advising a reluctant Adam that apple-sharing might spice up a lazy afternoon. The classroom entertainment improved a bit when I tried archaeological fantasy humor about how the early australopithecine (who gave us the famous Lucy skeleton) used advisement to keep alive. Imagine one of the ancestral families roaming the Tanzanian plain 3.2 million years ago. Dad recognizes a distant moving blur as a pack of hungry saber-toothed tigers. He screeches fear and demonstrates a few frenzied climbs up a nearby tree for his family to imitate. Or imagine their communication having developed to a point where he simply screeches and points to the distant tigers, then to the tree as an order to his family to climb—a superb soft command conveying something like, "Get the hell up the tree *now* or you'll be hors d'oeuvres for those hungry tigers!"

There was no room for cheap or show-off advice or careless communication among the australopithecine. Can you imagine our modern rate of communication failure combined with their schedule of hourly survival crises? The poor australopithecine would have been wiped out in a week. You could even go so far as to say that good advice once saved the human race.

Today, advising too often deteriorates into a bad habit, used for the wrong reason at the wrong time—a perfectly good talk tool corrupted by an irresistible urge. The first time the power of that urge hit home for me as a communication researcher was in 1967 when I found myself leading a seminar for several scholars and grad students. The scholars were developmental psychologists, curious about my (then) unusual speciality and willing to partake in talk experiments (at the Institute of Human Development, University of California, Berkeley). One of the experiments I had these keen observers of behavior try went like this:

The scholars were told to form talking pairs, with one person disclosing and exploring feelings about a long-standing unresolved problem for 20 minutes. The other in the pair, the "helper," was instructed to try to help clarify those feelings but *not* to offer problem-solving ideas—simply, no advisements. The result: Every helper forgot my admonitions. Some even insisted that the disclosers take their prescriptions for changing some basic way of behaving.

When the first part of the experiment ended and we reviewed the conversations, none of the participants noted the breaching of the verbal contract to avoid advising. So I started the second part by emphasizing the violations, playing taped excerpts as proof. And the scientists laughed at themselves for getting "caught" and then pledged that during *this* session, having clearly learned a lesson, they'd absolutely resist the urge to offer solutions of any kind.

Here's one example of what typically happened during the second session. It contains one advisement after another from a brilliant researcher, Lou, who'd pledged advisement abstinence. The discloser is Marie, an academic mother-figure nearing retirement, crusty but idolized by many professors and grad students. Lou is the helper and a respected senior scientist who's known Marie for years. After ten minutes of interchange, Marie starts to rekindle her long-standing disgust over the publish-or-perish world of her graduate student proteges.

MARIE: Their damn ladder-climbing is a nuisance to everybody. That burning ambition fills their lives and they simply stop thinking creatively. I get bored with these kids always worrying about getting ahead. Every one of 'em is boring, even—

LOU: *(Interrupting)* Why don't you tell 'em that they're hurting their careers by trying to be inventive on a rushed, ambitious schedule?

[Lou is falling off the wagon after only ten minutes. In fairness, he did offer a reflection or two before succumbing to this advising question.]

MARIE: Tell 'em? Listen, Lou, I spend half my time nagging 'em to put scientific curiosity up, uh, ahead of publishing. When I talk about science over job security, they say it's like committing academic suicide. God, they must think I'm old-fashioned. Oh, I know they don't say it, but it's obvious they think I'm living in the '50s and don't appreciate the pressure they're under. I really do. But both of my post-docs and most of my grad students just want to publish prematurely—they just . . . They even want to do it with half-assed data. . . . They're not driven to get to the bottom of things.

LOU: Maybe they need to watch you work more closely and learn the pitfalls, Marie. I've been taking Laurie through all my struggles with the adolescent study. I showed her my false starts, the dead-ends and how some spurious correlations got me barking up the wrong tree. She says that's helped her comb her data more carefully before she writes.

[A pretty good me-too advisement, but it's still advice. Maybe Lou thought he was simply disclosing.]

MARIE: Every Thursday morning last quarter I took the whole bunch of 'em through every lost battle we had on the coping styles project. God, they still came to me with crap. I don't know what's going on. How can I help them? Am I too demanding? Are these kids scared and I don't see it? Have they lost their curiosity? They're *supposed* to be gifted researchers and all they think about is quick publications to get promotions. Career development *über alles*. Honest, I'm getting so sick of the whole thing.

LOU: Listen, Marie, you've just gotta see that they can't survive being like you. They all can't be as meticulous as you. They don't have your security, your tenure, your talent. They don't have your experience yet. And it's time for you to stop aggravating yourself and getting all exhausted and everything over the fact that these kids don't have the leisure or whatever. . . . They don't have to turn out impeccable, inventive articles. You've got to accept the fact that only, uh, maybe, one of 20 will end up doing something really useful.

[Hard commands are frequently used to express soft emotions. Here Lou's caring imperatives express worry and insist Marie stop upsetting herself. We give others the privilege of commanding us when they do it with affection.]

MARIE: You're right, Lou. They're still green and scared, but it, it tears me apart to see, uh, what's happening in the journals. Our field is getting so self-absorbed, so political, and proliferated with this useless, ritualistic research, everyone wanting to do their version of every damn thing. It's a hell of a time to have to retire. *(There's a long pause, Marie seems embarrassed as her eyes moisten, she wipes them quickly, looks out the window and continues, more slowly)* I was hoping to get just a *few*, just a *couple* of young people around me who'd have what it takes to buck the trend. That's all. It's an awful situation. *(She looks directly at Lou)* This is the first time I've been teary since Edward died.

Lou, who'd never seen Marie distraught, became upset. He reached over and put his arm around her shoulders for a moment. It seemed he wanted to stop her hurting quickly and was half-desperate in his helplessness to provide fast relief. It was poignant for me to see someone care so much and not know what to do besides offering unusable advice. That's what he did. While feeling distressed, Marie had to sidestep his inappropriate, top-of-the-head advice. She had to take care of *him*. Lou couldn't see what she really wanted from the conversation—simply to complain for a while to a caring person, get this ongoing complaint off her chest. Her thinking was way beyond Lou's easy prescriptions, and he seemed to almost know that—but his primitive urge to make it all better, to rescue her from modern life's saber-toothed tigers, wouldn't let him stop. It was awkward. For these two friends, it took weeks to clear up the debris. If two people in the same business who enjoy and respect each other can get into *that* much trouble in a 20-minute talk experiment, imagine how many problems are created in day-to-day conversation between people who don't even know each other very well by the irresistible temptation to advise, advise, advise. . . .

Behind the Urge to Advise

The question here is how we get so terribly entangled in the exchange of advisements. Why do we continue telling others how to think, feel, and behave, when they resist our guidance? For centuries it's been common knowledge that "advice is seldom welcome, and those who need it most like it least" (Samuel Johnson). Unless those who need it are paying specialists for it; income tax advisers, lawyers, astrologers, counselors, therapists, interior decorators, nutritionists, palm readers, tutors, political consultants, fitness instructors (and even communication scholars) get rewarded for advising. And professional advisers usually enjoy telling strangers what to do. They love their work. It doesn't have to be dear friend Lou advising colleague Marie. For many, the urge is practically promiscuous. Easing someone's, anyone's, *everyone's* discomfort, making their booboo better, their soul stronger, or swaying their attitude toward ours can be pure pleasure.

A penchant for helping unknown folks appears to tie into our basic human nature. That's one big reason we read advice columnists. They provide a vicarious connection with the adviser. I know newspapers claim their columns are for helping the public with sound guidance on human relations, but my own little survey of college students suggests that many readers fantasize *giving* guidance instead of getting it. A large proportion of readers seem to identify with the columnist. I suspect the perpetuation of both good and sleazy advice columns is supported by our fascination with figuring out how we might answer the poor, confused, unsophisticated, helpless, or foolish letter writer. We readers may heed some suggestion (or soft command) that hits close to home, perhaps a familiar predicament in someone else's letter, but it's also feeling on top by pretending to be the adviser that keeps many readers coming back. We even forgive an occasional touch of ridicule or the trivializing of what may be someone's serious plea for help because it's only amusement. Many columnists seem to care. Most claim to be in contact with mental health professionals and justify their work by sidestepping issues about the paucity of information for the letter writers or the obvious difficulty of translating something like, "Stop doing that . . ." into the reality of complex human relations. And maybe private woe *is* close to public comedy. But I'm not always able to shake off that sense of exploitation—a residue of creepy feelings that something kind of sinister is going on here. Despite the claims of harmless fun and beyond the thousands of letters with oblique cries for help, there is some inevitable dehumanization involved.

We go for it, though. Sometimes we might even compete with the columnist. Some people I know regularly try to outdo printed counsel by vicariously being brighter or more sincere or more psychologically sound. They go at it as if it were a crossword puzzle. There's pure pleasure in figuring out how to give advice better than the next guy, but that's a minor motive in a long list.

Here are some everyday advisements with parenthetical motives.

- Detailing the good points of a movie, book, or restaurant as evidence for why someone should see it, read it, or eat there (shared pleasure is a basic experience in any intimacy).
- Convincing a friend that the bad engine idle is from the fuel pump, not the carburetor (the simple sense of power in giving knowledge).
- Recommending your dentist as the best around (only fools see second-rate dentists).
- Giving wisdom on how to buy fresh halibut or the best bet in video recorders (revealing sophistication while making life better for others can be a tonic for our self-esteem).
- "Suggesting" that your class of students read chapter ten before the final exam or commanding a nine-year-old to clean up her mess (the sweet efficiency of giving orders that bring accomplishment and resist chaos).
- Lecturing the back spasm sufferer on the ins and outs of visiting a chiropractor (a willing patient could bring a sympathetic adviser instant relief).
- Offering some wise advice and tested home remedies for curing a serious love affair problem (doing "therapy" free of charge is a favorite American pastime, because instead of being the lowly patient, we become healthy helpers, village priests, and insightful gurus to our friends).
- Convincing a bewildered parent that his teenager has all the symptoms of drug abuse (the mixed gratification of translating a magazine story into critical help).
- Ordering a sexual partner to do it *that* way just once in a while (giving sexual commands is more than a privilege exchanged

by lovers—it's a primitive necessity for survival of the species).

- Instructing a sun worshipper on the latest research linking skin cancer to ultraviolet light (many strangers have met at the beach over a friendly health hint).

These seemingly trivial acts of influencing, selling, insisting, hinting, and urging serve the not-so-trivial function of connecting lives with advisements. Unfortunately, much of the advising ends up with the adviser on top. Maybe the instinct or habit of getting on top makes people (mostly men, according to recent research) give more than minimum advisement. Or maybe our current concerns with passivity create a distaste for being on the bottom, which can be compensated by a few aggressive, haughty commands or suggestions. Either way, the urge prevails.

SHAPING OTHERS OUT OF LOVE AND NECESSITY

It's handy to think of just one motive behind each act of advising, but it's also simplistic. To relieve some of my professorial guilt for oversimplifying, please hear my disclaimer: Each piece of advice springs from several motives. One motive always found in the mix is the desire to shape someone's thoughts, behavior, or feelings. Shaping is intrinsic to advising. It's the common denominator among all motives, behind each act of guiding. At first, the idea of "shaping" a person was an unattractive image to me, with its connotations of controlled training, or sculpting something inanimate like a statue, or training a pet.

Maybe remaking someone has such appeal because it touches our parental instincts, child-rearing fantasies, or the dangerous desire to reshape imperfect mates into romantic ideals. The disappointments between real and ideal in romance are often dealt with by a lifelong campaign of advisements aimed at changing our mate's traits. Often such guidance is given unwittingly, but when psychologists "shape" behavior, it's deliberate. Behavioral shaping usually involves an ongoing program of negative and positive reinforcements (punishments and rewards) that can create some preferred new behavior. It's usually no secret. The maneuvering psychologist is clear about his or her interventions for making someone's life better. But, if the maneuvering becomes secret and the motives for shaping remain hidden, society smells something sinister and becomes fearful. Then the shaping is called sneaky manipulation. The popular book and movie *A Clockwork Orange* illustrated secret behavioral shaping as the sinister element in its science fiction plot. Lives were changed without permission by menacing behavior modifiers. Frightening stuff. It gave all those decent up-front behavior modifiers a bad reputation. We hate the thought of being remanufactured, even for our own good, without permission. And we would violently resist anyone planning to redo us to their own preferences (except when we fall into a heavy adolescent infatuation or come under the power of a successfully seductive manipulator). But most of us try to influence others with little forethought or planning. Sometimes, of course, there's deliberate manipulation, but my guess is that the vast majority of our attempts to shape each other are made spontaneously, unconsciously, casually, without much tactic.

Long-term bad habits, so easy to see in others and so hard to accept in people we like or love, are prime targets for our shaping campaigns. We really do tend to mount an interpersonal campaign when an admired friend puts herself down or won't stop smoking or is wasting her time through procrastination or never gets out of the house or never stays home. Our persistent desire to change a friend for the "better" translates into some form of shaping behavior—advising usually is the first means that comes to mind and mouth. And when blunt, direct advising fails, we can get carried away into very indirect, somewhat sneaky behavior-changing gambits with *A Clockwork Orange* overtones. It can be a dilemma, because backing away from shaping to a strict live-and-let-live attitude is nearly impossible *if* we want durable intimacy. A bald fact of human relations is that getting close forces us into a continuing series of adjustments. To keep life balanced, we work at shaping others into adjustments with us. And when our shaping is successful—even on minor habits or personality traits—it can bring us more than relief and more than simple satisfaction. It seems almost a fundamental rule that our effective attempts at influencing others, at changing behavior for the "better," bring a special, deep pleasure. That pleasure encourages us to get closer and give even more guidance. Successful shaping leads to rewards, like reducing conflict, sustaining love, even exploiting, which in turn stimulates further shaping. This vital cycle slowly serves to make changes in people around us—it changes our interpersonal environment. So there's a chain of events linking advisements, the shaping of others, and the shaping of the quality of our own human environment. It's one way we control our destinies.

A CAUSE AND CURE FOR CONFLICT IN COUPLES

Anyone claiming that he or she can cut down a verbal conflict with a dose of advice would appear absurd, as far as I'm concerned. It strains my imagination to picture a feuding couple quitting their argument and talking peacefully because one produces, say, a nifty advising question or a stirring soft command. My replays of arguments show the chain of events are the other way around: Advisement often *creates* debate and fuels it as in, for example, "You shouldn't have another drink because you've had enough." That familiar soft command has been known to stimulate a hard command: "Don't tell *me* what to do."

Soft commands and advising questions seem to be, in particular, common generators of conflict. "You shouldn't be dreaming of vacations when you need a new car." "Wouldn't it be wise for you to? . . ." Almost any form of advisement does a fine job of keeping fights alive, e.g., "Why don't you take a good look at the way *you* do it instead of criticizing me?"

Advising *reduces* conflict by slowly reshaping people between their fights, not during them. The advising has to be done repeatedly between battles. Say, for example, a wife believes nothing can be done about her miserable premenstrual syndrome crankiness. The husband advises her that some PMS symptoms might be eliminated by taking vitamin B_6. Later he hears about a TV special on the subject and urges her to watch. He's mounting an advising campaign to improve the way they cope with the problem—not with a deliberate blueprint, but out of an attitude that moves her thinking closer to his when it comes to coping with PMS. Sometimes his advice strikes her as old, one-sided, or just plain dumb, but sometimes it helps a little. She may believe he's on her side, even when his guidance is rejected. In this consistently spontaneous manner, he slowly influences her behavior and thinking. The enduring pattern of advising comes out of caring. Their closeness sensitizes his antennae to any knowledge of her problem. He becomes very familiar with PMS—largely because of his own advice campaign. Secondarily, the shaping of her has altered him, too. He may start changing his behavior and attitudes. Now the couple is more alike in awareness of a pertinent area.

"Natural" advising campaigns between spouses, friends, and close colleagues may seem chaotically disorganized, until we understand the power of *accumulated* influence—the hundreds of times the wife's suggestions kept the husband away from cholesterol or kept him moving toward buying a station wagon or watching modern dance on TV, going to church, taking weekend vacations, believing that blue is a great bathroom color. The more they see eye to eye, the less they quarrel. Years of mutual advising makes couples, partners, families, and workers more symmetrical—even when half of the advice is rejected. Maybe that's why members of Japanese-style work teams called "quality circles," with their policy of frequent group meetings filled with reciprocal advisements, become so similar in attitude that the individuals frequently become lifetime friends. The interpersonal symmetry created by effective advising is a major component required for intimacy.

All of us have struggled to arrive at some beliefs about right and wrong and the good life, and we want those beliefs acknowledged, confirmed, and respected—even fully embraced personally by those around us. We want some company for our big inner experiences. If the wife can advise the husband, guide him, for instance, into her deep and private religious commitment, then he'll know much more of what she experiences. A symmetry is created. They become closer. There's more harmony. Maybe that's one motive behind the evangelizing of religious doctrine and the proselytizing of political issues or social ideas. It secures us some company in our leaps of faith and our commitment to causes. It bridges personal distance, defusing potential differences and turning strangers into acquaintances and acquaintances into friends.

The big myth about the way advisements work in bringing us closer and reducing conflict is that a single, searing piece of advice can suddenly turn a life around. Advisements sometimes have dramatic effects, but I'm convinced that almost all of the influence happens in uneventful, unexciting little pieces. Each small successful persuasion or obeyed command can become a nudge in the direction of greater similarity. Advisements serve our pervasive urge to diminish differences—differences that detract from smooth interaction, prohibit intimacy, ruin projects, cause tension, and erode love.

MACHIAVELLIAN MANIPULATION

In those unkind situations where one person takes advantage of another, advisements are crucial. Using deceit or guile while guiding or persuading is a popular pastime first publicized in 1582, when Machiavelli published *The Prince*—the first do-it-yourself manual for tricking others to do it *your* way. Four centuries later, Richard Christie and Florence Geis wrote *Studies in Machiavellianism*, describing research that examined the quality of manipulative thinking in children and adults.[1] They found that the Machiavellian-type personality believes that others don't know what's best for them, that it's a good idea to put pressure on others if you want them to do something, that breaking promises and using white lies are often useful, and "it's smart to think about what will happen if your advice backfires."

The research suggests there are plenty of people who specialize in looking for the soft touch, who enjoy the company of gullible folks. Back in 1970, Christie and Geis believed that the proportion of tactical-tongued people becomes larger each generation: "American life seems to be getting more manipulative. . . ." Even if you doubt that pessimistic outlook has come to pass, it's clear that, as a society, we have mixed feelings about our rogues. Famous ones like Svengali, Elmer Gantry, and Don Juan are regarded as fascinating, sinister, artful, and despicable—all at once. It's the same with famous female manipulators like Cleopatra, Evita, and Scarlett O'Hara—they're portrayed as part villainess, part victim, part heroine. Silver-tongued tacticians, specialists in slick advice have their admirers as well as critics. Even professors Christie and Geis, after their years of studying manipulation in communication, couldn't help but admire Machiavellian talk skills: "Initially, our image of the high MACH [a person receiving high Machiavellian scores] was a negative one, associated with shadowy and unsavory manipulations. After watching subjects in laboratory experiments, however, we found ourselves having a perverse admiration for the high MACH's ability to outdo others in experimental situations. Their greater willingness to admit socially undesirable traits compared to low MACHs hinted at a possibly greater insight into an honesty about themselves. . . . This doesn't mean that our admiration was unqualified: It might better be described as selective.''

The scientist's ambivalent attitude toward such verbal ''operators'' seems universal. Our fascination for those who excel at persuasion and manipulation becomes entangled with distaste when the combination is used for locating a vulnerable need and betraying trust. Big MACHs (I couldn't resist that one) are adept at influencing others while disguising their motives. Maybe their sinister abilities are more effective at producing quick short-run attitude changes than less calculating skills. In that way, we might admire their abilities while deploring their motives, their easy treachery, and their assaults on the innocent. Openly trying to guide someone toward a new attitude is slower than the Machiavellian's tactics.

Talented talkers, good at deceptive advising and able to remain emotionally disengaged, can receive considerable payoff for some slippery suggestions, tactical me-too's, and a seductive soft command or two. Con games can also be played for smaller stakes with lesser skills in regular relationships. The risk-to-gain ratio for fooling people may look so good that some part-time, minor-league manipulators give it a shot. Second-string Machiavellians are all over the place and are easy to spot—you've heard them relentlessly advising why doing it *their* way was for *your* own good.

I'm not suggesting that Machiavellian types have exclusive rights to sneaky advisements. All of us, at least once in a while, have offered some selfish advice without disclosing our motives, without a ''buyer beware'' notification. If you listen carefully, you may learn that even children occasionally employ a piece of self-serving advice to peers or parents.

MAINTAINING LOVE

People who love the person they're advising—unlike the dispassionate Machiavellian—can still secretly manipulate with advice. Parents, spouses, lovers, and friends often give tactical guidance riddled with white lies on the rationale that it's for the others' ''own good.'' In effect, we deceive those we love for ''altruistic'' motives. And that kind of advice, flowing from love, is far more influential than the guidance of outside experts like therapists. It must be, because others sense that maintaining our love requires changing their ways—significantly and often.

Whether it's romantic, parental, humanitarian, or some other variety, caring for another human means wanting to move him or her toward a better experience, a stronger idea, a less painful condition, toward more shared tastes and attitudes, or an easier way to do things. Advising out of love is often aimed at shaping the other's existence closer to our own.

Since it's difficult to clearly separate the loving, altruistic motives from the more selfish ones, we become confused about advising those we care about. Giving and taking are so blended in authentic love that the line between self-serving and generous advice is blurred. (The sexual aspect of such blending is explored in chapter 2.) In addition, the temptation to use white lies a lot—for the other person's own good—can backfire and generate guilt, ultimately bleeding through the cover and damaging intimacy.

I believe that realistic two-way loving requires a flow of unmasked and generous mutual influencing—mutual advising. And that requires some skill in using advisements, combined with the knowledge that the advice sometimes is more for the adviser's needs. "Love, honor, and obey" might work better as "Love, honor, and advise"—provided the advising is directed at the gentle influencing of each other.

THE SECRET WISH OF THE PURE COMPLAINER

Our capacity for empathy regulates our capacity to love. Empathically feeling into another's experience is a trait that varies markedly among individuals. Full-blown Machiavellians have less capacity for it, which is handy for them as they remain emotionally disengaged from their victims. But a little less empathy can also be handy for people who plunge easily into others' miseries—compassionate people often suffer from empathy overload.

Consider an occasion where a strongly empathic person listens as someone close relates an unresolved problem. Maybe the problem is being aired to vent painful feelings, to merely complain a bit. There's no solution in sight, but some of the discomfort is shaved off by disclosing. The empathic listener soaks up the discomfort rapidly, feels into the pain and the sense that there's no quick solution at hand. But loaded with the other's predicament, it can be hard for the listener to understand that simply hearing out the other's complaint can give relief. The complainer's discomfort could sound almost . . . *unbearable*. (Did you ever grimace or tense up with empathy watching someone scrape a knee or cut himself, only to realize when the same thing happened to you that it didn't hurt *that much*? I believe the same things happen to strong empathizers observing emotional pain.)

Confronting such apparent emotional agony, the supersensitive listener wants to *do* something. The mind searches for a way to relieve the other's distress. It becomes almost unthinkable to take in the predicament you're hearing with only concern and quiet acceptance. We've come to believe that caring means making it all better—like Mom kissing the hurt away. Providing a solution to quell the pain becomes imperative. Advice must be given: "You've got to do *something* soon!" "Why don'tcha try not thinking about it for a couple days?" "Get out of town—you can't just sit there and suffer."

In such cases, the adviser is usually verbalizing some self-talk: "I can't just sit here and let you suffer—*I've* got to do *something* soon!" The urge to advise about someone's disclosed discomfort, rather than taking it in and absorbing it, seems a way to discharge an overload of empathy. The interpersonal formula goes something like this: "Your discomfort brings me discomfort, so here's a quick solution that'll bring *me* relief." The poor complainer searching for some empathic company has to cope with the burden of cheap advice. The wish to simply unload a pure complaint hasn't been realized, and distress is amplified. It would have been better to unburden to a pet. Too often, our capacity to connect causes us to disconnect by delivering bad advice. So, when your empathy is strong, it's sometimes best to steer clear of advising at all.

BUMPER STICKER BRUSHOFFS

Sometimes the primary motive behind advising is to quickly dismiss a complaint, to brush off the self-disclosing person. It could be that we're rushed, or can't tolerate a painful story at the moment because of empathy overload or lack of empathy. We may also give advice or a brushoff because we don't care and want to disconnect. "Bumper sticker" refers to those one-line slogans: Save the Whales; Let Go and Let God; Question

Authority. So "bumper sticker brushoff" is my name for rapid-fire advice used for pushing aside complaints. No shaping is involved, unless it occurs repeatedly between the same people so that the dismissed complainer gets the message and quits disclosing.

These ritualistic brushoffs are a customary tool for everyday acts of alienation at the workplace, campus, playground, and home. And they have much more impact than just giving the *adviser* quick relief. Dismissing serious complaints with dumb advice may relieve our distress at being a helpless witness to another's discomfort, but it's at a heavy cost in close relationships. Offering some simplistic, one-line, bumper sticker brushoff to a discontented mate, resentful teenager, or an intimate friend seeking understanding is belittling. The habit of turning complaints into trivialities is a crude, almost primitive defense, even though it's rarely motivated by a desire to make someone feel disregarded. The motive is usually to just get away or show that we're "caring," or at least "courteous."

Bumper sticker brushoffs persist not only because they dismiss the discomfort but because they're easy to get *away* with. They often *appear* thoughtful, even considerate, and are hard to challenge on the spot. Imagine feeling rotten and disclosing your distress, then hearing someone respond, "Time heals all wounds," or "Just laugh last and you'll laugh loudest." Such things are actually said in response to distress. It's hard to argue with such brushoffs. These quick little mottos help people sidestep the burden of compassion. They seem to carry the concern and proverbial wisdom of generations as they get rid of unwelcome complaints with a disengaged courtesy: "Give her a dose of her own medicine." "You'll feel better after a little rest." "It's better to forgive and forget." "Suffering small annoyances might get great results." "No use crying over spilled milk." "See it as God's will." "Keep your chin up and things will get better." "Well, at least you still have your health." "You're just trying too hard."

Such flip little haiku-like advisements render some bland guidance—a vapid dose of mock help to deflect the complainer off course while the semi-sincere adviser makes an escape. I'm not saying these brushoffs should never be used. After all, spending careful attention on careless complaining is a waste. But I'm convinced that it's useful to know when you're giving or getting brushoffs. That's my point here. If you're derailing the important disclosing complaints of a friend without really wanting to, you may have vague guilt feelings later about having poisoned something significant. And learning to recognize brushoffs for what they are might ease the pain as you walk away from a conversation with a shallow proverb still stuck awkwardly in your sincere self-disclosure.

CHAPTER 5

QUESTIONS

"THE MOST POPULAR PIECE OF LANGUAGE."

WE USE questions all over the place. We use them for reasons that are plain and veiled, innocent and wicked, protective and generous, loving and spiteful . . . and for other reasons known only to a few super-specialized linguists. The spoken question is used for a wider range of motives than any other talk tool. That's why it's the most popular piece of language for adults, and by far the favorite with kids.

I estimate about 25 percent of everything we utter is followed by a question mark. My students accuse me of exaggerating when I mention that figure. They find it hard to imagine people trying to find out something during every fourth utterance.

It *is* hard to believe that such a huge amount of our talk is motivated by curiosity. The typical person in a typical conversation doesn't seem *that* eager to gather information.

But gathering information isn't the issue here. The issue is question use—and questions are used for much more than gathering information. Many of our questions aren't the least bit aimed at "finding out." I'm not just referring to those colloquial questions like, "How ya doin'?" (a friendly, familiar way to say, "Hello"), but to an entire family of talk tools that are loaded with the potential to perform dozens of important psychological functions. The biggest news about questions is that much of the "asking" in our lives is, in fact, "telling."

LOADED QUESTIONS

"Loaded" questions are typically described as somewhat sinister things, with hidden agendas. They're viewed as questions that require much thought about the motives behind them or that are scheming in a way that won't let you win, no matter how you might answer. People I've questioned over the years feel these talk tools range all the way from slightly sneaky to downright menacing. Dictionaries agree to the extent of labeling loaded questions as being worded "unfairly." Still . . .

I think loaded questions are unappreciated, misunderstood, underestimated, and simply not recognized as bits of language that allow us to be bolder and more verbally involved with each other without sacrificing respect. Of course, they can be indirect, threatening, demanding, and even carry the answer to the alleged question they ask. But they also carry—and often enhance—important advisements, interpretations, and self-disclosures. I'm saying these mischievous talk tools that "tell" have their good points, too. And spotting them in action expands our conversational perspective because loaded questions both carry and attenuate messages. They serve a surprising variety of our daily needs, particularly controlling the degree of directness in our conversation.

My best reckless guess is that about half of our questions are loaded with extra meaning. Their messages are more important than the questions they ostensibly ask. We maneuver verbally every day with them—for better or worse. Getting to know what they are and what they can do is useful for spotting subtle coercion, noticing signs of respect, diagnosing some discomfort, and even watching how early signs of personal attraction are veiled.

Here's an example of how questions become loaded with advisements and interpretations (disclosing questions are in a later section).

Two women are finishing lunch and talking. June, eating an ample slice of cheesecake, says to Stacy, her sister: "If Ted [her skinny husband] walked in and saw me eating this, I'd crawl under the table."

Stacy asks, "Isn't it about time you gave up that dumb cheesecake habit?"

If humans were equipped with a reflex for detecting any loaded question, it would go off at this point: advisement alert!

Stacy uses a question loaded with advice—an "advising question" that carries a rather insistent, commanding piece of advice. June can't answer because her mouth is full, but even if she could, a yes or no would not be forthcoming. The formal grammar of Stacy's loaded question calls for simple agreement or disagreement. But the embedded rules of the talk game say, "Change your reading of this question into a piece of commanding advice: 'Cease and desist with the cheesecake.' " So Stacy's question isn't really motivated by curiosity or an urge to find out. She's irritated or frustrated or worried, and she's advising June to change her habit. There's no need to answer.

As June chews, Stacy speaks again with a question mark in her voice: "Why don't you try counting to ten while you picture a fresh, low calorie, juicy orange?"

Advisement alert!

That talk tool is loaded with a prescription for performing self-care in the area of cheesecake addiction. Stacy has delivered an explicit diagnosis, a command for action, and a therapy treatment plan with two quick advising questions. If June seriously attempted to answer her sister's second advising question as if it were a genuine inquiry, she'd be performing sarcasm: "Because I believe a cheesecake a day keeps the doctor away." Or if she habitually went around answering all loaded questions as if they were innocent inquiries, she'd be diagnosed as nothing less than mentally disturbed. Inability to follow all of the implicit rules for using questions is an emblem for pathology in thinking. Most of us just obey this language law automatically. Even nursery school children know how to play a few subtle games with questions. Some three- and four-year olds use loaded questions, observes Professor Mathilda Holvman, who found that "at this early period in language development, children already use the interrogative form [questions] analogously to their mothers for making suggestions [a form of advisement]. . . ."[1] These kids used advising questions such as, "Where's my tapioca?" to commandingly advise, "Get me some tapioca." There's no doubt—literally "no question"—in the kids' minds that the tapioca will be delivered.

As children grow into adults, they use social commands with less insistence. When they begin to learn that others have wills of their own, the advising question serves to soften the presumptuousness of hard advisements that directly suggest or command. As kids mature, the self-absorbed "Where's my tapioca?'' will eventually become, ''Could you bring me some tapioca?'' And later, when adult decorum arrives, ''If it's not too much trouble, could you bring me some tapioca next time you're at the fridge.''

The ability of questions to soften advisement, to make us sound less presumptuous and more deferent, explains why they're so popular. It's the main reason one out of four utterances has a question mark at the end. The almost ritualistic ''asking'' that's performed by couching advice in the question format offers a moment of respect, or some attenuation for our pushy commands. At minimum, our use of questions for *telling* offers some recognition of the other person's will. That fact is worth remembering. Loaded questions often soften telling—''Don't you think it might be useful to remember the previous five words?''

The same kind of recognition occurs with ''interpretive'' questions. I'll illustrate by having June defend her diet: ''Stacy, aren't you being a hypocrite about my cheesecake when you always eat three eggs for breakfast?''

Interpretation alert!

Here's a loaded question that classifies Stacy as a hypocrite. June's diagnosis is nothing more than grown up name-calling, made more presentable—and less hostile—because it's cradled in a loaded question. Drop the question and you have, ''Stacy, you're a hypocrite.''

Now let's have Stacy resist the interpretation: ''Well, that's not fair. I haven't had a three-egg breakfast all month. I cut down; I only eat two now.''

June replies, ''Only two! But doesn't 14 eggs a week dump enough cholesterol into your system to harden arteries on the spot?''

Interpretation alert!

This time, instead of classifying Stacy, June uses the interpretive question to explain a cause (14 eggs' worth of cholesterol) for an effect (heart disease candidate).

Loaded questions aren't difficult to spot in conversations. They often start with a mild opposition and words like wouldn't, couldn't, aren't, doesn't, and shouldn't. ''Wouldn't it be better if? . . .'' ''Why don't you? . . .'' ''Shouldn't we try to? . . .'' ''Aren't you being? . . .'' ''Doesn't that make you? . . .''

They render us incapable of responding with a simple rejection. You can easily find one by remaining quiet while people within earshot engage in earnest discourse. Later in this book, I'll describe methods for managing loaded questions so that they cause less mischief.

SEMI-INNOCENT QUESTIONS

I've located an unusual conversation in my tape collection that not only contains popular loaded questions but also illuminates most of the other question varieties. After all, there are questions that *do* want to find out and willingly accept answers—decent, straightforward, simple questions like, "Can I have some ice cream after dinner, Mommy?" I put these in a category called "semi-innocent" as a reminder that they aren't always perfectly innocent questions. Even though semi-innocents differ significantly from loaded questions—because they can be appropriately answered—they can serve some scheming purposes.

"Can I have some ice cream after dinner, Mommy?" asked by a six-year-old with a hidden agenda transforms the child's language into mock innocence—into a semi-innocent question. If you're puzzled as to what could possibly constitute a hidden agenda for a six-year-old, you may have forgotten your own early gift for perceiving language behavior in adults (especially parents) and how it helped you get what you wanted from them. An early drive toward necessities like ice cream quickly teaches kids that parents produce a fairly predictable proportion of yes's. A six-year-old can learn, for example, that her health-minded mother rejects after-dinner ice cream pleas about half the time. From that, it's easy to sense the advantage of making many bids, even if a sizable percentage of them fail. Thus, the semi-innocent question gets used as a mother-management device in hundreds of situations.

Sometimes kids use questions to resist demands: "Why do I have to do the dishes?" Or in calling for justice: "Is Shirley gonna stay up later than me again?"

Semi-innocents in the hands of adults serve a panoply of daily needs, from getting a bit of approval ("What do ya think of this new sweater?") to a trite pickup gambit ("Haven't I seen you around here before?"). For both adults and kids, these semi-innocent questions—with their motives and ability to extract answers—are major managers in social exchange.

The variety of their managerial skills is displayed in the following phone conversation between 16-year-old Denise (the girl who talked to her mother about being in midjourney between childhood and womanhood in chapter 2) and her stepbrother, 18-year-old Greg, who lives across town with his father. You may recall that Denise's conversation with Martha, her mother, was an attempt to sort out her ambivalent sexual feelings about "going all the way." Now it's three months later and Denise is still "in a *totally* committed relationship with Jimmy" and still trying to decide if she will remain a virgin much longer. Martha remains a caring listener (and reflector), according to Denise, but the girl also wanted "to get into a man's view, a young guy's view of being with a girl and sharing her first *total* sex." This is another answering machine capture, used with their approval. Names and a few details have been changed.

GREG: I dunno what to tell ya. It was really dumb, 'cause it didn't even feel weird 'cause I was just 14, like just past my birthday, and she was almost 17! Gawd, I was really dumb doing it at that age. She knew, uh, she wanted me to take over and, uh . . . When you're young, you don't even know what you're doing.

DENISE: Well, but did you know what you were doing when you two—

GREG: *(Interrupting)* I sorta knew what I was doing, but it wasn't something that—

DENISE: *(Interrupting)* I know you knew what it was, but did you know what to *do*?

[Denise's questions so far are innocent enough; she really wants to find out. She wants a quick, pinpointed answer.]

GREG: I . . . *(Laughs)* She's the one that turned down the lights and went right on her back—took her panties off. I remember thinking that she just wanted to give up. She just *gave* up.

DENISE: What's so earthshaking, what's so awful about people in love giving up to each other?

[Beyond simply gathering information, this question scolds and asserts opinion, but it also contains some curiosity—some intention to really find out why Greg is so impressed with a girl giving up. The question, in part, is innocently asking and, in part, is guilty of complaining. That's why I call it semi-innocent.]

GREG: Uh, it's not so awful, but it's . . . Like, she just gave—ya know, like some dogs, they—look . . . us guys, when we wrestle, we never wanna get on our backs, ya know? And besides, we *weren't* in love, the girl and me. You girls are different, giving in to us before we do to you.

DENISE: Okay, okay, so we're different. Big deal. But I wanna know—tell me, please, did ya know what to do?

[The third repeat of this innocent request for a yes or no. The perseverance shows Denise's almost urgent eagerness. Repeats in language often reveal the condition of the speaker.]

GREG: *(Laughs)* Well, since *she* did all the preparation by getting on her back and giving up without a fight, I got on top out of courtesy . . . *(Starts laughing, out of control for 30 seconds)* and I stuck it in her . . . ear.
(They both laugh at length)

DENISE: But really, Greg, did ya know what to do?

Closed Questions for Short Answers

Denise's persistence in repeating her question four times tells the tale of her serious need for information and Greg's understandable resistance to disclose. She urgently wants to gather information on his sexual competence when he was an inexperienced 14-year-old, probably because it parallels her condition at 16. Whatever the reason, Denise is starting a question barrage. She genuinely wants answers. No loaded questions here.

At this point, her little interrogation has employed only "closed" questions. Closed questions want brief answers like yes or no or maybe. Brief doesn't always mean trivial. Answers to closed questions can be vital. We recognize these oftdemanding talk tools by their context—and especially by their music: an upward inflection at the end. They often slide to a higher note on the last syllable. We sing closed questions with a voice that sounds eager or impatient, wanting a speedy, cogent, short answer: "Can I use your *phone*?" "Will you marry *me*?" "Are you *ready*?" "Do you under*stand*?" "Did ya know what *to do*?"

Greg will finally oblige Denise's closed question with an appropriately brief response.

GREG: Yeah, I knew what to do. Knew where it went. Maybe I wasn't gentle enough or something.

DENISE: Right. Right. Did she scream a lot?
[Another closed question wanting a rapid answer, especially from a virgin worrying about pain.]

GREG: No, she was 17; she probably got laid a lot of times.

DENISE: Probably. Oh, my God, I don't know. The way you view girls is . . . *(Trails off)* See, you're such a—

GREG: *(Interrupting)* See, that's the bad thing about being a virgin.

DENISE: What?

GREG: The first time you do it *(Mocking sing-song voice)* it hurts so bad. *(He laughs, Denise doesn't)*

DENISE: That's so gross! Are you taking a course on crudeness [at Pierce
          his junior college]?

[Her loaded question interprets Greg as insensitive. In this case, the
interpretive question doesn't soften the name-calling but transforms it
into sarcasm. The question's absurdity, along with its mock softening,
work to sharpen her insult. It's loaded with a verbal slap.]

GREG: Aw, c'mon, Denny. Quit taking everything I say so seriously.
          You're so sensitive.

DENISE: Uh, I *am*. It's scary. Damn it! You'd be scared too, Mr. Macho.
          Just like you get petrified by the dentist. Hey, maybe I could go
          to Dr. Haljun and get some novocaine, just before doing it with
          Jimmy. *(Both laugh)*

GREG: Uh huh. If you could numb out that way, it wouldn't be scary.

[An excellent untutored reflection from Greg. Her sisterly counterattack
steered him into some empathy. His kind, understanding reflection provides safety for her to dip into more personal memories.]

DENISE: *(Wistfully)* Yeah, yeah. If I could only overcome the fear. It could
          hurt bad—and to be so open and vulnerable and pinned down
          and there's no turning back. Ugh. And it's hard for guys to be
          gentle—right?

[A peculiar closed question that's willing to hear "right" or "wrong"
but prefers "right." It wants confirmation for a hunch, so it's only semi-
innocent.]

GREG: I guess so.

DENISE: If I could only be there and not feel pain—just feel the hugging.
          Maybe if I took Tylenol. Maybe drinking. Hey, Mom—Mom told
          me that she was 17 and the guy she was with, 25, and she didn't
          even know she'd lost it. Could you believe she never even? . . .
          Did she ever tell you about it?

[An innocent closed question. It's simply trying to find out. It's free of
hidden agendas.]

GREG: No.

DENISE: Okay, she got a little drunk before. She numbed out. I asked her
          what happened. She never knew! She missed her own first *total*
          sex experience.

GREG: Probably 'cause the guy filled her full of—

DENISE: No, this guy loved her. She went out with him a long time. She
          really cared for him. Right?

[An innocent closed question with the force of, "Do you follow?"]

DENISE: *(Continuing)* And he was 25 and she'd admired him a long, long
          time, and after they knew each other good, she felt she was ready
          to lose her virginity. And he took her to his apartment and she
          knew, yeah, she went to his place, yeah. And he's living by him-
          self and you know what's gonna happen. So she knew what was
          gonna happen and she asked him for two brandies or something.
          And she told me that the next day, when she woke up, she didn't
          even know what had happened, like she never lived it. Erased it

from her life. God. And when he told her, she was in shock. So—

GREG: *(Interrupting)* I was just thinking, she didn't even know what happened. Probably the guy's dick was soft or small or something. *(Laughs)* Sorry, I shouldn't say dick. You've always hated that word. When you were little, you never even liked it when Mom said penis. And I think it's ridiculous to call it a p-e-n-i—

DENISE: *(Interrupting)* No, penis is better than dick.

GREG: *(With a big-brotherish tone)* Oh? Is it?

[This semi-innocent closed question carries the force of contention, resistance through mock information-gathering. The mild sarcasm says, "Since you're the expert here with the final word, I'll just assume the role of a questioning student." The question is much more "semi-" than "innocent."]

DENISE: Yes, well, *of course* it is, 'cause that's the real term. I mean, dick is slang, like slang for boobs. It's not facing the plain truth of the thing.

GREG: Well-l-l-l, oh-h-h, well-l then. *(Laughs, pauses)* I just don't like the word penis, but I'll use it if you want. How would that be?

[An innocent open question. He could have asked "Is that okay?" for a quick closed answer. The open quality allows her—*invites* her—into further discussion if needed. A courtesy.]

DENISE: You don't like the word. That's funny.

GREG: Ah, Denny, who cares? What I keep thinking is, that was dumb doing it that young. I did it to her dumb.

DENISE: *(Eagerly)* You think so?

[Apparently, she wants to know a lot more about the dumb things inexperienced boys do as sexual partners. Her closed question seems intended to draw out Greg; she wants him to talk more about it. But she asked a closed question when she wanted an open-ended answer.]

GREG: Yeah.

[And she gets what anyone deserves who asks the wrong question: disappointment. So she tries again.]

DENISE: You think you treated her dumb?

[Another closed question. Somehow, she won't ask the open question: "What kinds of dumb things did you do?" So Greg gives her another "Yeah," almost as if a detailed answer would be too much. Denise follows with a third closed question. But this time it's semi-innocent. I believe she's becoming seriously curious for details and wants to get him to produce a lurid narration. Wary of pushing hard, she unskillfully uses a semi-innocent to persuade.]

DENISE: Do you think it'd be good to tell me about the dumb sexual things you did to her?

GREG: I dunno. I just treated her like a sucker. She thought she knew what it was all about—acted cool—but, God, she actually believed . . . Hey, the doorbell. Hold on, Denny.

[Greg interrupts to go to the door. When he returns, they discuss the visitor, a mutual friend, and then wander back to the topic of Greg's first sexual intimacy. Not using open questions costs Denise the information she wants so badly. A common error.]

GREG: Let's see, it's been about four years since that first time.

DENISE: How many times have you done it since then?

[Purely innocent questions like that one can be hard to find. In many settings, the innocent question is swamped by the occurrence of the loaded and semi-innocent varieties. Greg rewards Denise's honest-to-goodness, direct query with some real information that encourages her to use more innocents, which will pay off.]

GREG: Maybe 10 times, 10, 12 times, I dunno.

DENISE: Not how many different times, but with different girls. How many different girls?

GREG: I did it with Gloria and Cindy, Eleanor and Bev, Christine, Julie . . . uh, let's see . . . and, um . . .

DENISE: Six or seven?

GREG: Yeah.

DENISE: What kinda things did they feel? I mean, how do ya think they really felt about doing it with your hearts beating against each other and naked and then it's over, and seeing each other in school, and acting like it never happened? What did they feel like?

Open Questions for Longer Answers

Denise's success in obtaining Greg's list of lovers with innocent closed questions has moved this talk into a new conversational episode. She has a skeletal outline of his love life and can now work at fleshing out the details. The three inquiries in her last response are good examples of "open" questions. In this case, the open questions want bigger answers about the girls' big emotions. Clearly, Denise identifies with them and wants some inkling about what might be in store for her.

Her open questions have no upward inflection at the end. Open questions rarely do. They don't perch at the end of a high note like most impatiently eager closed innocents. Open-ended questions invite long, unrushed, rambling answers. ("What did ya do in the war, Daddy?") In the hands of a skilled talker, leisurely open questions get to the heart of things faster than those fast-paced, closed inquiries. That's why open questions are illegal in 20 Questions. The distinct shapes and sounds associated with open and closed questions signal the listener as to the type of answer wanted. Obviously, Denise is wanting some vivid views inside the minds of early adolescent girls who've loved and lost. She'd sit still for a dissertation on this topic. This time she's using the proper kind of question for her need. She's not committing the error of asking a closed question when looking for an open-ended answer.

Errors in asking open questions for closed questions and vice versa are one significant source of frustration in conversation. The errors consistently waste time and truncate information. These tiny communication breakdowns where people need to know more than their closed questions can find out, or find themselves swamped with unwanted long answers from open questions, produce minor irritations, little stresses at having to try again. For some, it may happen dozens of times a week, or thousands of times a year. Using open and closed questions with some awareness is basic to effective information-gathering—not only in social exchange but in the workplace (especially in the workplace). These talk tools are so easy to learn that we could teach them in third grade. Learning and using them as adults won't guarantee results, but getting accustomed to using the right tool can make stunning improvements in effective information-gathering. Denise used the right tool but didn't get as much as she wanted. It's a touchy topic for Greg.

GREG: I dunno what they *all* thought. It was different. Maybe some felt we should of known each other more. Maybe a couple regretted being easy and decided not to, uh . . . Julie moved her seat away from mine in math class and wouldn't even say hello for a long time, and, uh, well, I can't, uh . . . Eleanor . . . you see, I didn't feel like doing it again with, uh, Eleanor; she was mad 'cause she said I used her like her body was . . . meat. God, I didn't do that. . . . *(Long pause)*

DENISE: So, she—so they wanted more than you did?

[An innocent closed that does more to summarize her understanding and get confirmation than it does to expand Greg's story.]

GREG: Yeah.

DENISE: But later, how was it between you and the others in school? Besides Julie and Eleanor, what do ya know about the others' feelings? What went on between you and them?

[Her eagerness generates a cluster of related open questions in a form resembling the multiple-choice question (a type you'll hear about later in this chapter). Such excitement can swamp a listener, but in this case Greg opens up more. The sharp focus and innocent, open tone of her inquiry probably help him answer.]

GREG: Well-l-l, uh, like almost it didn't happen for some girls. Never happened. Like, sort of a canceled . . . the memory. Not like

Mom getting juiced to block things out, but like, uh, it never happ—like they weren't turn-ons anymore. They were just ordinary girls and we were finished with each other. It was best when they were cool, or pretended cool. . . . But when they acted like they didn't like it, or hated it, it was bad. Like they hated *me*. Maybe I pushed them too hard. Maybe I didn't respect them enough—but I *did* try to be . . . to feel the same toward *all* of them.

DENISE: Greg, but didn't you just kinda feel that when you find that one girl, you really, really love, didn't you feel like, by the time you found that girl, you'd have had to have done it with 20 girls? And then they all feel the same, I mean, I don't know—are they all different?

[When a question starts with "But," or any other contrarily flavored word, look for some extra meaning, like persuasion. Her complex, semi-innocent query isn't clear in content, but it's clearly biased. It started open, became greedy, then judiciously turned closed. In my thinking, it isn't fully loaded because it's partially asking and semi-innocently wants some answer.]

GREG: Not really. It depends what you think. Sure, probably they're different, much different; they're the same, too.

DENISE: How could it be the same when you talk to each one and you undress and the bodies and the privacy and specialness? And if it's all the same, why do you go from one to another? What's the purpose? How could it be really the same? Really?

[Poor Denise. So much she wants to know, but her long list of semi-innocent open questions are just too demanding and too prejudiced. She started this episode by asking a barrage of closed questions and received short, orienting answers. Then her queries became more open and the answers richer. She's asked about 15 questions in a few minutes; she's way over the 25 percent ratio of questions versus other verbal responses—more like 90 percent. Now she wants broad information and has switched to innocent and semi-innocent open questions with heavy demands. The last batch were difficult to answer—self-defeating semi-innocents. She would have learned more using open, unbiased innocents. Greg can only respond to the central idea about girls being the same.]

GREG: Well, afterward it is.

DENISE: Whattaya mean, afterward?

GREG: Afterward, you think about the same thing. I dunno, okay—girls are different, they're not all gonna be the same. I dunno. It's basically the same release you feel.

DENISE: Oh, it's like relief?

GREG: Not a release, like it's taken care of, I can't even express it. It's mostly relief . . . and getting back to other things, other friends.

DENISE: I know what you're saying. I understand.

GREG: If you don't like a girl a lot, if she's just okay and can turn you

on, it's basically the same thing you're looking for—getting satisfaction. But it's hard to keep getting release from the same girl.
[Greg's struggle to differentiate biological tension release from establishing intimacy is teaching Denise something more than her questions
call for. The rewards probably reinforce her interrogation. She's been
doing what I call a full-scale question barrage.]

DENISE: So it's just getting the lay, and it's over?

GREG: No, no, it's like you like the girl at first, then you don't like her
anymore. You just wanna drop her off nicely. Or, on the other
hand, you don't like the girl, but you did it with her and you say
you're gonna drop her off, but it's not because you first liked her,
and now you don't, ya know?

DENISE: You like her after?

[A closed innocent question.]

GREG: No, that's not what I meant, but if you like her after, it's different.

DENISE: But don't you really feel guilty when you just dump—

[Closed semi-innocent.]

GREG: Well, I—*(Laughs awkwardly)*

DENISE: —drop a girl off right after?

[I'd guess there's hardly any innocence left in this one. It sounds like a
fully loaded question advising Greg he ought to feel guilty.]

GREG: Uh, not really.

DENISE: But you know that it's just—

GREG: Maybe she doesn't feel, ya know, it's like—

DENISE: Okay, then doesn't it—

GREG: —see, I'm not experienced, okay? *(Haltingly, laughing nervously)*

DENISE: No, but let me explain something to you, okay?

GREG: Uh hm-m.

DENISE: Okay, would it help to put yourself in a girl's position for even a
minute sometimes?

[An advising question with the force of, "I suggest you put. . . ." This
softens the question slightly.]

GREG: I know what you mean. If you go with this guy and you think
he's gonna like you and everything—

DENISE: No! It isn't just—

GREG: —and you have sex and everything, you still like him and he
dumps you and you feel real—

DENISE: *No*, it wasn't just dispensing this female body after use. Ha!
"Dispensable" girls. Like dispensable cigarette lighters.

GREG: *(Laughing)* Well, yeah, Denny. Lotta guys, most guys, are like
that. Not to be mean, they act nice, but it's . . . uh, it's like
natural to seek new territory, like going to a new movie every
time. Sometimes you see a good one more. But it's usually boring. Guys can be polite and show interest not to hurt a girl, but
it can be like going to a movie. Entertainment. I dunno why
we're that way. It's not so good for girls sometimes.

DENISE: Yeah. I know. Isn't it awful? But it's worse if you think a girl, a woman, when she gives herself, ya know, takes a man right up *inside* her private body! So-o-o-o-o think if you have one place in the world only you knew about. A secret place in the wilderness. Or a private spot in a house, or somewhere where you could always be perfectly by yourself. And then wouldn't you want a person you let into that place, whether it's the wilderness or a house, or whatever, to be special, and very, very honest, and loving of you, as if your body were theirs, so they could respect it rather than see you as some pussy to masturbate in for getting bodily relief?

[Her loaded question carries a set of values that reveals some of Denise's character, intelligence, and perhaps the books she's read on relations between the sexes. Her question is a cogent little lecture on morality. Her intention is to persuade with rhetoric, and so she asks a "rhetorical" (or leading) question (one of the few types of loaded questions, incidentally, to enjoy wide public recognition). Greg, who agreed to be an older brother/consultant, has become a pupil receiving a lesson from Denise's question/lecture—and he seems overwhelmed.]

GREG: I dunno. Gawd. I . . . *(Long pause)*

DENISE: How does that, could you think, what does that do to your thinking?

[At this point, Greg confessed that his thinking wasn't producing ideas on her previous lecture, but maybe, if he had some solitude . . . So he deflects into a lecture on thinking drawn from his junior college psychology text. Poor Denise was only asking him to think about her idea. Please note that she made the mistake of asking an open question when she apparently wanted a brief answer. After Greg completed his seven-minute psychology discourse, Denise asked the closed question she should have used earlier.]

DENISE: Okay, okay, so would ya think about what I said?

GREG: Okay, okay, but I already know that I can think a little bit like you've been saying at first; yeah, but not, uh . . .

DENISE: So that means you're able to think a little that she's an entire person at first?

[A loaded interpretive question. She organizes his confusion and explains what he's thinking. I can't tell if she's accurate or asserting her own position as his. Either way, she's loaded that question way beyond its capacity for clarity.]

DENISE: *(Continuing)* I'm just saying, think about it—about someone entering into *your* body. A stranger into your flesh, ya know?

GREG: Okay, okay, the first time, *yeah*, but not after she's given into . . .

DENISE: Right. After you've done it 10 or 12 times, I guess it doesn't matter. Right?

[A semi-innocent closed question that could use the label "semi-guilty." It's used for light sarcasm.]

GREG: Right.

   [He missed the sarcasm.]

DENISE: That's a man's way of being, I dunno, would ya wanna marry a
         girl who's a virgin or not?

   [Sounds like an innocent closed question—but . . .]

GREG: *(After a pause)* That doesn't have anything to do with it.

DENISE: Well, would it make you feel better as a husband, knowing your
         wife has never been with anybody else?

   [An authentic semi-innocent. Sincerely innocent questions can be hard
   to find.]

GREG: No, it wouldn't. Actually, it wouldn't.

DENISE: It wouldn't matter?

GREG: No, I wouldn't like it.

DENISE: You wouldn't like it knowing that she slept with someone else?

GREG: Yeah.

DENISE: So then you would rather marry a virgin?

GREG: What? I would rather marry . . . not a virgin.

DENISE: Not a virgin?

GREG: Yeah.

   [I can't figure out if there's authentic misunderstanding here, or if Greg
   is maneuvering. Maybe the indirectness of these semi-innocents has
   caused the confusion. I leave it for you to analyze. I *can* figure that
   Denise's question barrage isn't ending; after all, she's still voracious for
   information. She's also been using strings of closed questions that serve
   her rhetoric. They make *general* interpretations about human nature as
   they attempt to influence Greg toward considering her values on decent
   relations between the sexes.]

DENISE: But that would mean she's been with other men.

GREG: Uh, wait I can't hear you.

DENISE: Wouldn't that mean she's been with other men then?

   [Innocent closed.]

GREG: Yeah.

DENISE: And you wouldn't mind that?

   [Semi-innocent closed.]

GREG: No.

DENISE: And you don't feel funny when you do it with a girl, and you
         know she's been in other cars whispering in other ears, just like
         she did with *you*?

   [Only a hint of innocence is left in this one.]

GREG: *No* . . . 'cause it's . . . *(Laughs)* cause when they get to a certain
         age, there's a certain understanding going in—she wants some-
         thing from you, and you want something from her. And it's, uh,
         always like that.

DENISE: So, you think it's an equal thing? But no. Joyce Brothers once
         said that in sex a guy penetrates more than her vagina—he pen-
         etrates her mind, too, and if they're, uh . . . they're closer, he

penetrates her heart. And you think all there's to it is trading pleasure? Right? Shallow as trading pleasure?

[You can't get much farther from innocence in a question. This one is loaded with the rhetoric of a general interpretation and the diagnosis of a personal interpretation.]

GREG: *No-o-o.* There's like . . . psychological, and there's like what you think about the girl, and what you think about yourself being with that girl. Lotta things—

DENISE: *(Interrupting)* So you mean—

GREG: *(Interrupting)* It's not just a guilty, when you have sex with a girl, if she wants to, then she wants to, you know. Why should she feel guilty, you know?

[He can ask loaded ones, too.]

DENISE: Okay, now, out of all the girls, six or seven, right?

[Innocent closed.]

GREG: *(Pauses)* Ha-a-a-a—you're not supposed to ask me this question, you know? Ha.

DENISE: No, no, no.

GREG: I'm not experienced. I dunno. I don't wanna have a big mouth about it, you know, it's stupid—

DENISE: *(Interrupting)* Wait, no, no. Out of those, has there been one— I'm sure there has—you've liked more than the others?

[Innocent closed.]

GREG: *(Laughing)* Of course, whattaya think?

DENISE: Of course, okay.

GREG: They're not all equal.

DENISE: Okay. So, the one you liked more than the others, shouldn't it feel better doing it with her, more than the others?

[This one just about advises Greg how he should feel. Strip the question from its load, its baggage (an advisement) and it has the force of, "You should be sexually better with a girl you like more."]

DENISE: *(Continuing after pause of 25 seconds)* And do you get more pleasure with one you really like and understand than doing it with someone, with a stranger you just sort of meet and do—

GREG: *(Interrupting)* Sometimes when you look back, you know, you look back on it—

DENISE: *(Interrupting)* When you look back, what?

GREG: When you look back, they're almost the same. Some are easy, some are choosy and want to know you a lot. They're not, they're not . . . When you look back, there's no one you liked a *lot* better. . . .

[Denise's insistent attempts to persuade—to align values and become closer—are failing here.]

DENISE: Yeah, but is it gonna mean something to you when you do find a girl, when you fall in love with a girl? I'm just saying, don't ya think it'll mean a lot more to you when—

[An example of how Denise unwittingly labels her question as "saying" rather than asking. All of us often do the same.]

GREG: *(Interrupting)* Yeah, of course it will.

DENISE: When?

[It's starting to sound like a moral inquisition.]

GREG: Yeah, of course it will.

DENISE: Yeah . . . See, I think it's different if a guy loses his virginity at 14, it's no big deal, but if a girl does, it's like, ah-h-h, she's a little slut.

[No loaded or semi-innocent for a change. Just a flat-out general interpretation of social standards.]

GREG: I know. I know. It is for a girl, I think.

DENISE: I know, it's way too young. I mean, if a boy does it at 14, it's like he's like a, he's a big boy.

[Again, no question to soften this interpretation. She's becoming bolder.]

GREG: Yeah, I think that's true.

DENISE: Double standard.

GREG: It's like getting stoned real young, ya know. Or even smoking.

DENISE: Oh, yeah, but if a girl smokes at 12, it's better than losing her virginity.

[Three times in a row, Denise has asserted strong opinions. Without the protection of the question, her ideas are more vulnerable targets for rejection.]

GREG: I don't think so.

DENISE: No?

GREG: Well, I dunno. It's like smoking at 12 means she doesn't have any respect for herself. Doesn't respect the value of her one and only body. She doesn't know what she's doing.

DENISE: Oh? Oh, well? If a girl goes off with this unknown guy as soon as she meets him, and does it with someone she doesn't understand, does she have any respect for herself and for the value of her *one* and *only* body?

[Her loaded question challenges and mocks.]

GREG: *(Laughing)* What, you're making the front page of the *National Enquirer* with this?

[It sounds as if Greg is being forced to face some unexamined issues asked by his kid stepsister. She's getting pushy. His voice tone is a bit sharp, annoyed.]

DENISE: *No, no.*

GREG: *(Suddenly louder)* Well, it doesn't mean a damn thing. If she likes the guy and thinks she should make it with him, and the guy wants to make it with her, and . . . I mean, she's—

DENISE: *(Interrupting to ask a loaded question)* But how does that have any respect? I mean, for a guy, it's no big deal, if a guy does it with a hundred-seven girls, it's no big deal. But if a girl does it with a hundred-seven guys, it's like she's a *prostitute*, right?

GREG: Yeah, so what? But with *that* many, she'd have to be a real prostitute. You always have easy girls like that.'Cause they're insecure or crazy, maybe, and dumb about how guys operate.

DENISE: I know, but then don't ya think, when she lets so many enter her, uh—when she opens herself up, like her personality is . . . maybe something's wrong?

[Loaded closed question.]

DENISE: *(Continuing)* If *I* opened myself up before taking the time, would you—

GREG: *(Interrupting)* I don't know. . . . I guess I wouldn't think you were too healthy of a sister.

DENISE: Right. But then if a guy does it, it's no big deal.

GREG: Well, a guy has strong needs, okay? And a normal girl, I don't think has so strong needs.

DENISE: Then that's true, you're right. A girl doesn't feel—

GREG: *(Interrupting)*—as much like doing it, ya know?

Rhetorical Questions to Soften Interpretations

Denise is about to continue by giving her general interpretation of female feelings on the issue to Greg and asking for his concurrence at the same time. The tool she'll use is the rhetorical (or "leading") question, calculated to persuade and amplify her point. Just like true interpretations, rhetoricals try to create new meaning about human nature or society for the listener. Sometimes they just about demand capitulation and strain to make the listener think the same as the questioner. They can be mini-lectures.

DENISE: [A girl doesn't need sex]—as much as a guy . . . That's for sure. But her needs are to get into her feelings. I think a big part of the reason—the difference between guys and us is, it's like, that is, the boy goes *inside* the girl: that makes it kinda worse. But do you know when some guy goes right up inside the flesh that it's you—it's *you*, the only *you* you have? Can you imagine that it's your only vagina, your only organ, brain, mouth—and he wants in for no reason, except that he needs relief? And he wants to use you only 'cause it feels better than masturbating? No big personal, special reason. Would you believe it's like they wanna get in you almost for the hell of it? And when you're a girl, what happens when someone wants the real *you*, all of you?

[Denise is almost begging for understanding with her loaded rhetorical questions. She wants to pull acquiescence out of Greg. Instinctively, she isn't using bald, outright general interpretations on the nature of sexual relations to try to get him on her side. Instead, she's carrying interpretative cargo inside rhetoricals in an attempt to cushion their force. Rhetorical questions are less arrogant as they attempt to explain, classify, and persuade (lead). Someone, more than 100 years ago, described them as questions that don't want answers but are only put as questions in order to produce greater effect (*C. Bradley's Aids to Latin Prose*, 1884). The book proudly promises 150 examples and makes it easy to assert that these talk tools have served humankind for centuries as engaging purveyors of political and religious opinions. More recently, they served Denise's moral opinions.]

DENISE: *(Continuing)* And it's the *real* them you want, not their penis—not just that. That's great. Isn't that great? But some girls don't know the difference between a penis and . . . uh, a penis and a person. I've read how so many girls fool themselves into believing guys see them as a person. Joyce Brothers was telling about this psychologist who found girls who were emotionally damaged—uh, I think it was her . . . Anyway, she said this guy studied how these neurotic young girls that look for cheap thrills actually *believed* these guys respect 'em, or actually like 'em after a one-night stand. Can't you see they lie to themselves for sex thrills that end up hurting their egos? That kinda line is bad for you for, uh, 'cause if you get your kicks like—kicks easy as dogs in the street, it's gonna be harder on the girl in the next . . . in the future. Doesn't all that say that girls pay a big price for loose sex?

GREG: Well, uh, but . . . yeah . . . but I never thought . . . Girls are sure complicated.

[Rhetoricals are often successful interpreters of large ideas, but Denise's big message carried in her rhetoricals escapes Greg. He's grappling with mixed feelings and confused thoughts. Denise seems frustrated and lonely in her continuing search for truth.]

DENISE: It's like . . . It's hard to explain. . . . It's like if you go in and . . . into someone's house, okay? And, um-m-m, just looking around, let's say—*(Greg interprets her as he breaks up in laughter; halfheartedly, Denise joins in)*

DENISE: *(Continuing, plaintively)* I'm just trying to put this into—

GREG: You're trying to put me down. Huh-h-h?

[He's never been so far inside a girl's mind. It's difficult to grasp and seems to be a devaluation to his gender.]

DENISE: *No!* You go into somebody's—*(Greg laughs insincerely over her words)*

DENISE: *(Continuing, sounding a bit hurt)*—house out of curiosity. You're just there for the hell of it, okay? Isn't it better that *you* do that to somebody than to have somebody go into *your* house just for the hell of it? Do you see?

GREG: *(Quietly, thoughtfully)* No.

DENISE: No? *(Greg laughs, a little uneasily)*

Multiple-Choice Questions for Multiple-Choice Feelings

Denise is going to keep trying and will eventually succeed in getting Greg to run multiple possibilities through his head.

DENISE: Oh, Greg—this is totally . . . Please see it's the girl's only *body* that a man goes inside of. That makes it worse for a girl—being entered. It's her one and only lovin' body he enters, just for the hell of it. It's her . . . it's so precious 'cause shouldn't someone be selective as to who they let *inside* of them?

[Closed semi-innocent trying to persuade.]

GREG: Yeah, of course. Otherwise, you have self-disgust.

DENISE: Right! Otherwise, you have self-disgust 'cause there's no place for a girl to go inside a boy. That's why . . .

GREG: Yeah, there is.

DENISE: All right, stop right there.

GREG: I didn't mean it that way. *(Laughs)* Like other sentimental values and being nice to the guy and going into his feelings and his once-in-a-lifetime thoughts, his personal . . .

DENISE: Right, but I'm talking about *literally* going into the body.

GREG: I don't think it makes that big of a difference.

DENISE: Oh, you don't?

[Semi-innocent, challenging, "questioning" his opinion.]

GREG: No.

DENISE: But isn't going deep into another human being kind of a sacred thing?

GREG: *(After a pause)* Never thought of it that way. But it is so powerful . . . and natural power that maybe if anything's sacred, it, uh—

[Now that choices are poised in Greg's mind, Denise will attempt to sort them out and maybe reduce his confusion, with a "multiple-choice" question.]

DENISE: Right! Now, honestly, if you just met a girl, and you didn't understand each other well yet, would you rather wait to see if she was really worth getting into, or just stick it in her for bodily relief, or get close so you could enter both her, uh, all of her, or just get in for the hell of it? Honestly, don'tcha—which is the best way to be as a human being?

Multiple-choice questions—a series of closely connected closed questions—can help sort out confusion and choose the "correct" answer. They tend to control information: "Did she say anything about liking it? Did she smile? Or couldn't you tell?" As we leave Greg and Denise, his multiple feelings about the mystery of the sexes are still too jumbled to sort out a clear answer. Overall, however, Denise's lengthy question barrage allowed the exploration of her sexuality, gave her further insight into the mentality of boys, and helped her feel a lot less lonely with her new thoughts and feelings. It also stimulated Greg to think much further into a young woman's private attitudes about intimacy and sexuality. I suspect he will bring some new awareness to *his* intimacies with girls. Not bad gains for 26 minutes of conversation. And all those good things might not have been possible without those special questions that carry, and soften, and slant, instead of just innocently ask.

I think youthfully idealistic Denise was wishing for another world, where all boys see all girls as whole persons—more than seduceable bodies that bring relief and a sense of accomplishment. Her lonely yearning for Greg's brotherly understanding of the female experience was a bit too embarrassing for her to make direct self-disclosures. Disclosing loneliness is very risky business, so she tried a less dramatic, more conventional route: manipulating his thinking in a rather obvious way. It became clear that she changed some of his opinions using the soft filter of loaded and semi-innocent questions. (Later on, Greg appeared less resistant as he admitted the conversation brought out his "sometimes kind of dumb thinking about girls.")

Denise's multiple-choice question near the end of their conversation was dangerously close to being hard-sell persuasion. Ostensibly, the question was asked to clear up his confusion—one major generous function of multiple-choice questions—but, in truth, her intention was less altruistic. Denise had a stake in how Greg resolved his ambivalence. She wanted to guide him toward *her* choice: "The best way to be a human being with a girl you don't understand well is to (a) wait to see if she is really worth getting into, (b) just stick it in for bodily relief, (c) get emotionally close and enter all [mind, heart, and body] of her, (d) have sex for the hell of it."

Professor Denise's correct answers: (a) and (c).

The way we all fall victim to the multiple-choice as a rhetorical device amazes me. In the fast flow of conversation, we rarely stop the process to address the half-masked, fully loaded piece of persuasion carried by the question. Some skilled salespeople use the device as a deliberate (and sometimes sinister) tactic, but most of us conduct ourselves like Denise and Greg in giving and getting a softened pitch without thinking of the process. There's no need to know what's happening most of the time. But when the conversation becomes uneasy *and* polite at the same time, and you're feeling subtly coerced by some indirect aggression, look around for one of those loaded multiple-choice questions as the culprit.

Now for an example of a generous, sensitive multiple-choice to counter any thoughts that this talk tool only sells opinion.

During an intense conversation within a self-help group for recently divorced older women, one woman discloses a confused message about her emotional hurt and psychological numbness. One of her peers carefully responds: "Are you saying it's hurting a little bit less, or that you were just getting used to the pain, or that you can't tell the difference anymore?" These choices disentangled a confusion of feelings into three likely possibilities. The empathic question helped the woman sort out her condition, showed that someone was listening seriously, and set the stage for moving out of her doldrums. So the multiple-choice can also be a sensitive caretaker. Even more than some other omnibus talk tools, multiple-choices have multiple personalities.

DISCLOSING QUESTIONS

Still another side of multiple-choice questions is that they can disclose. One way the multiple choice does that is to display knowledge, even to brag.

A teenage boy talks to a mechanic about a problem with his car. The boy says: "Ya think the carburetor's too lean, or does the fuel pump sound weak, or could it be a clogged gas line?" Pretty smart. The boy's disclosing his sophistication about engines and demonstrating he's not just a know-nothing. That can be self-protective if the message to the mechanic is also, "Don't try to sell me parts I don't need." More often, multiple choices that disclose knowledge are simply semi-innocent ways to show off and enhance self-esteem.

But self-disclosing questions, of any type, are less common than advising or interpreting questions. Maybe it's because we do less disclosing in general than advising or interpreting. In any case, disclosing questions work well for diluting embarrassment when they're used to reveal our imperfections, to blunt the directness of a negative emotion, or to veil the nakedness of a tender feeling.

They can be loaded with high-risk confessions or minor revelations. Disclosures invite immediate feedback. The difference between disclosing with loaded or semi-innocent questions isn't as important as the fact they both *intentionally* reveal private thoughts or feelings. Innocent questions frequently disclose *un*-intentionally. They give away privacy when a perceptive listener interprets varied meaning. Please don't confuse the "taking" of meaning behind the innocent question with the deliberate, intentional giving of disclosure done by loaded questions and semi-innocents. Many talk tools inadvertently reveal the talker's motives, but loaded and semi-innocent questions are spoken *precisely* to disclose.

Grandma on the phone to her four-year-old grandson can get away with, "Do you know how much I missed getting a good-bye kiss yesterday?" But the same loaded message won't work for a young man communicating with an elegant woman he's recently met (unless it's done with a great sense of humor).

Out of context, disclosing questions can look like advising or interpreting questions. For example, I watched my neighbor's nine-year-old waiting for one of her two teenage brothers to break away from a TV football game and drive her to the local video rental store. She plaintively, sincerely asked: "Are you guys gonna be watching *all* afternoon?" Translation: "I'm so bored, but I don't dare try to push you guys around now 'cause Mom isn't home and if I complain harder, you'll pretend to be more annoyed than you are as an excuse for not driving me, which will get you uninterrupted viewing. So please have mercy on your nice little sister." I'm not kidding. Ordinary nine-year-olds can think and feel that way. The girl in this case leveled with me when I asked about it. (Unfortunately, her disclosing question didn't work; her brothers sat glued to the set through the game. But since she gave me a fine talk specimen, *I* drove her to the video store.)

Imagine now the girl's question being asked by a strong, no-nonsense mother, annoyed at waiting for her boys to help with a task: "Are *you* guys gonna be watching all *afternoon*?" Some disclosure of frustration is carried, of course, but the force of the question is mostly a command. And, unlike the previous example, these guys aren't given an invitation to answer. In no uncertain terms, the loaded question advises the boys to comply—soon. Her question uses the same words as the girl's disclosing question, but the different contexts create separate meanings. Asking someone "Shouldn't your poison ivy be healed already?" can disclose different emotions when asked by a caring mother (worry), a formal colleague (courteous concern), and a dermatologist (bewilderment).

Some disclosing questions disguise negative emotions, such as disbelief, semicleverly: "You mean you finished reading the entire chapter in 20 minutes?" Here's one that is partly effective in describing childish braggadocio: "Have you any idea what that car cost me?"—as if asking about a serious fact instead of boasting about conspicuous consumption.

The melodic Yiddish language, which specializes in loaded questions, brings the disclosing question to the level of art. I can demystify some of that subtlety with a classic Yiddish question that discloses nine different messages, from surprise to insult, depending on which word is emphasized. Try it first with a lightly mocking (tongue-in-cheek) feeling and overemphasized first word. "*You* want me to buy two tickets for your daughter's recital?"

Now try it with the same tone overemphasizing the second word: "You *want* me to buy two tickets for your daughter's recital?"

See how the quality of disclosure changes?

You can create seven more messages by emphasizing the words "me," "buy," "two," "tickets," "your," "daughter's," or "recital." Emphasizing "me" adds the meaning: "Of all people, you chose *me*?" Or perhaps: "You have the nerve to ask *me* after you failed to show up at my son's Bar Mitzvah?" Emphasizing "buy" could connote that the tickets should be given as a gift . . . and so on, as each emphasized word loads the question with a newly revealed feeling until the final outrageous insult from accentuating "recital." I can almost hear a Yiddish father from a past generation affectionately roughhousing with another that his beloved daughter's piano performance wasn't even worth the prestigeful word "recital"—both men then dissolving in laughter.

Ordinary disclosing questions don't demand that the listener answer. The Yiddish variety tries to leave the listener speechless.

THE BIG QUESTION ABOUT QUESTIONS

On her deathbed, a whimsical Gertrude Stein asked her intimates, "What's the answer?" Getting no response, she characteristically flipped her meaning upside-down to reveal something essential. Laughing, she asked, "In that case, what's the question?"

Her cryptic playfulness symbolized a profound search, both in her life and over the history of civilized arts and sciences—the search for important questions. Even before Socrates used the Socratic question, wise teachers struggled to steer students away from easy answers and toward the discovery of capable questions. Ironically, capable questions about the ways humans use everyday verbal questions are rather rare. We academics haven't come up with a strong set of questions for illuminating the spoken question's essential character. As a result, we know little about the psycholinguistic laws governing one of our most frequently used talk tools.

I believe our failure to capture a clear picture of the question's character is a result of its chameleon-like quality—its penchant for quick change allows it to perform dozens of psychological tasks, from flirting to rejecting. And it's not only those message-carrying members of the loaded question family that advise, interpret and disclose; it's also those semi-innocent creatures that work as quick-change artists instantly ready to serve our momentary motives. More than any member of the question family, semi-innocents illustrate why it's so hard to establish a simple picture for these pieces of language that psycholinguists fondly call "interrogative forms with an elocutionary force of questioning." Here are some representative, everyday motives, along with the semi-innocents that do their work.

Complaining. "Isn't it hot in here?" "Have you any idea how long it's been since we went to a movie?"

These questions disclose a complaint and leave room for the listener to add his or her opinion—to "correct" the complaint: "It's actually not very hot in here right now. Maybe your heavy sweater . . ." Or: "You're right, it's been six months since we've been out to a movie; seems we've fallen into the tube."

It's much harder to answer fully loaded questions that disclose complaints unless the answer is a bit absurd—e.g., a latecomer finally arrives and is greeted by an annoyed friend: "Do *you* know what time it is!" Answer: "Let's see, it's 8:15." The annoyed friend could insist, "You know perfectly well what I mean," but the absurdity of pretending to miss the loading of complaint usually does the job of creating humor or contentiously dismissing the complaint. A loaded question is divorced from inquiry. The semi-innocents remain married, but are cheating with some attractive extra meaning.

Requesting approval. "Do you like my haircut?" "Did I do all right?" "Did I do it faster than you even hoped?"

These press for positive confirmation while watering down the message: "Please agree that I'm good."

Resisting demands. "Why do I hafta do everything?" "Are ya sure you need it?" "Could you write me a memo so I can see if it's feasible?"

These devices help say an indirect "no." They resist advising; they're great for stalling: "Why do ya wanna know?"

Softening surprise. "And you did that all by yourself?" "Are you trying to tell me we're washed up?" "Are you kidding?" "Would you believe he ate the whole thing?"

Initiating flirtation. (The pickup question) "Haven't we met someplace before?" "Do people come and tell you that you look like Linda Gray?" "Would you happen to know if this store carries chutney?" "Is that a good book you're reading?"

Pickup lines are so loaded with trepidation, humor, posing, and straining for originality that they must be placed in context. "Haven't we met someplace before?" is such an archaic cliche that it makes occasional comebacks on campus as a satirical, yet serious, gambit. A semi-innocent about a specific item, like chutney in a store, usually comes from a semisincere, semi-helpless male. If the woman takes his bait, he may push his luck with something like, "Do you live in the neighborhood?"

Semi-innocents that intend to initiate contact seem to originate mostly with men. Topics are often broad and bland: "Where do ya work out?" "Are ya satisfied with that Buick?" Here's a male to a soaking wet female sitting on a beach: "Been in swimming yet?" Women who respond as if the question is innocent are complying with the minifraud, acquiescing to the flirting ritual. Discarding the fraud and exposing basic intentions can be a bit startling and funny: Chevy Chase, in a movie, not so innocently asks Goldie Hawn at a party, "Wanna take a shower together?" If the humor is shared, reciprocal contact is established. (Goldie's character, in this case, found it rude.)

Bragging. (The show-off question) "Do you think it's fair for me to play chess with him?" "Did I ever show you the snapshots of me and Kenny Rogers?" "Will we see your team at the championships?"

They can become ridiculous mockeries of leisure-class/jet-set conspicuous consumption. "Did you see that garish display at Gucci's last week?" "What colors are your Mercedes this season?" "Don't you love the Riviera in spring?"

This type of semi-innocent (actually 95 percent guilty) question may look fictional in print, but reasonable facsimiles appear in real life with regularity—especially when the real life is preoccupied with status or wealth.

Demonstrating a common bond. "Don't we make a great team?" "Isn't it strange we both crave Chicago-style pizza?" "Can ya believe the coincidence—both of us having been in Marvin Diskin's communications course?" "So you're involved in saving whales, too?"

These semi-innocents take some of the bluntness from the intention to become more attached, to "share," to be similar, symmetrical. They're employed frequently (and frequently tritely) by novelists and screenwriters.

Reducing anxiety. (The ice-breaker question) Two strangers alone, moving slowly to the 37th floor: "Isn't this the slowest elevator?" Two strangers alone in a classroom: "Do you think we're the only ones enrolled in this course?"

Awkward silences are broken by semi-innocents. They usually ask the listener to say *something . . . anything*. They even work on painful pauses between friends: "Do you think we should finish this some other time?"

Semi-innocents are frequently used, with blatant insincerity, for melting interpersonal tension by changing uncomfortable topics: "Hey, by the way, who won the game?" "How 'bout us getting some coffee?" They also break painful silence: "Hot enough for ya?" "Think it's gonna rain?" (I think Mickey Rooney said that last one to Judy Garland when the scene called for a nervous moment.)

Softening persuasion. "Does the idea of working a year before starting college sound appealing to you?"

A gentle inquiry with a mild suggestion and room for an answer. Say the reply were, "Mom, please don't worry about me being ready for college now. I can make it." Then Mom could get away with saying, "I was just asking a question, Son." She lamely claims her innocence, but anyone within earshot knows she's only semi-innocent.

All of these semi-innocent questions that water down persuasion, reduce anxiety, show a common bond, mask flirtation, seek approval, resist demands, attenuate surprise, and declaw complaints make face-to-face relationships more comfortable. We customize them to fit each situation. Linguists would call them contextualized.

They also soften the often bumpy ride of conversation by blunting the impact of insults, sales pitches, early affection (infatuation), intense personal needs for connection, excitement, anger, rejection, depression, joy—almost any emotion than can hurt, confuse or embarrass. They're shock absorbers. In that sense, they dilute the raw exchange of feelings. The moment we drop an innocent question in a context that allows it to attract extra meaning and serve our psychological needs to be less than direct, it becomes a sophisticated semi-innocent talk tool. It becomes a marvelous manager of detours, deflections, and even double-talk. It melts the potency of language, often for good reason. It helps create interpersonal rituals where deep feelings aren't so intense and opinions are merely inquiries. That's why adults get hooked on questions. As these devices move beyond the simple open-and-closed innocence of pure information-gathering, they take on a new identity as heavy-duty, multipurpose, always-ready talk tools that both carry and regulate the power of our meaning. We're starting to understand some of the ways they work, but there's a long way to go before the picture is complete—Gertrude Stein's last words are still appropriate.

CHAPTER 6

SILENCES

"THEY SHAPE THE QUALITY OF OUR CONVERSATION."

THE UNTRAINED eye underestimates the importance of spaces surrounding objects. It fails to recognize how solids take their shape from voids, from the spaces between things. Good architects and artists don't make that mistake—they pay attention to the ways spaces shape our visual world; they understand the connection between spaces and objects. Skilled talkers also understand the connection between spaces and objects— between silences and words. And that's what this chapter is all about.

I'm using "silences" to mean those spaces between talking turns, pauses in midsentence, and long silent spells during conversation. When there's a series of recognizable, longer-than-usual silences between talking turns, it becomes a special event that I call "conversational allowing." When there's a recognizable, shorter-than-usual crack of silence between talking turns, it becomes "response-rushing." Allowing and rushing are major shapers of the quality of connection between people. Science supports that view.

Silences establish and maintain order between talking people. They constantly regulate the atmosphere of our conversations by controlling the exchange of every thought and feeling. In fractions of seconds, they can change our sense of being allowed or being rushed.

Silences regulate the flow of listening and talking—and the rhythm of our listening and talking regulates the flow of our

159

thinking and feeling. Our conversations are full of these almost automatic regulators, these talk traffic signals. We rarely recognize them as they control the give-and-take of attention. To understand that silences govern our attention is to know that they shape the quality of our conversation and, ultimately, our relationships. Pretty big effects for such small bits of rushing and allowing. Almost as if a bunch of little unrecognized nothings add up to an important something. Silences are to conversations what zeros are to mathematics—nothings, yes, but crucial nothings without which communication can't work.

I want you to see that these little slivers of quiet in conversation—where someone pauses, where people switch turns talking, or when talk stops while thoughts are collected—are not trivial. When they're not there in the appropriate places, conversation loses its easy flow, and when those small silent allowings become short in supply, conversation begins a vaguely felt turn toward the worse. Depending how long that continues, people walk away from the conversation feeling either a bit uneasy, mildly upset, or emotionally sickened. And most folks don't know what's hit them. Those puzzling, uneasy, leftover feelings are easy to diagnose—and easier to avoid—once you pay proper honor to the significance of silences.

This is something much bigger than just "better listening," which has been blessed with a great press in recent years but badly misses the target. The pitch usually advises people to "listen better," which in turn will repair relationships, boost sales, or get you the man/woman you want. It's deteriorated into bumper sticker thinking: Good Listening Equals Good Communication. That's simplistic, and if I haven't made a convincing case against it before this chapter ends, I'll have failed in *my* attempt to communicate.

APPRECIATING THOSE SWEET NOTHINGS

Silences, especially the lack of them, have been a big enough deal to fascinate writers and philosophers over the ages—as they walked away from crowded conversations wondering what had gone wrong. Author Edwin Newman complains of the modern public's ignorance of conversational allowing. "People seem to think there's something wrong with silence," Newman says. "If someone asks you a question and you stop to think before answering, he thinks there's something wrong with you."

James McNeill Whistler, in the nineteenth century, had a different, more self-absorbed view: "If other people are going to talk, conversation is simply impossible." (Whistler's mother presumably learned to shut up when he was around.)

Centuries earlier, Benedict Spinoza's penetrating mind was discovering something about interpersonal prowess: "Surely human affairs would be far happier if the power in men to be silent were the same as to speak."

With the advent of tape recorders and stopwatches, it's easier to figure out why silences inspire such strong opinions. Here's a statistic I believe has more impact on our daily lives than any figures about the gross national product, the latest election returns or Dow Jones averages: The typical amount of time between when one person in a conversation stops talking and the other person starts is about nine-tenths of a second. About the amount of time it takes to say, "Silence."

PAYING ATTENTION TO ATTENTION

It boils down to getting and giving attention. The moment-to-moment activity of human attachment. Frequent small, fragile activities that can add up over the years to being connected or isolated. Failure to get attention is a major and sometimes tragically underestimated phenomenon that figures into making infants cry, children whine, wives fume, husbands pout, bosses fret, employees complain, and teachers nag. Attention does much to determine our sense of self-worth. We value it more than we like to admit. Attention is such a precious commodity that people will attempt suicide for it. People have killed because attention was denied them too long.

Some even run for president because they want attention. A cousin of Lyndon Johnson recalled that the late president ran away from home more than once as a kid because "he wanted attention" and then spent his adult life running for public office—"It was his way of making sure he never lacked for attention." Some people starve for attention, literally: Right now some one million American teenagers are suffering from a serious eating disorder—anorexia nervosa—because they feel more worthy of loving attention when they look like hollow-cheeked fashion models. (In her autobiography, Cherry Boone, first-born daughter of Pat Boone, described how she developed anorexia nervosa as a teenager and attributed part of the problem to competing with her younger sisters for her parents' attention.) And some grown-ups simply shell out money for attention—going to psychotherapists, who usually spend much of their time giving mute attention. Therapists pay attention . . . and patients pay $80 an hour.

Our lifelong search for effective attention-getting techniques starts in the crib. What could be better than that shrill, staccato, persistent cry? It's perfect. It's an attention-grabber that's served the whole human race for a millenium. But parents, who are genetically programmed for attending to shrieking, utterly dependent infants, may turn away from the complex, more subtle demands of toddlers and young talkers. Some eventually betray their growing children as cries for survival become cries for comfort or pleasure; parents then spell out some variant on how kids should be seen but not heard and turn their attention elsewhere.

The weaning of parental attention during early childhood seems the time that most of us began to develop techniques to recapture it: melodramatic pouts, cuteness routines, reckless stunts, clever discoveries, running-away-forever tantrums, the good-little-kid act. Adolescents gain attention with a long list of independence maneuvers that can abrasively capture the eyes and ears of the world with deviant dress, strange slang, and other familiar, wild behavior.

Our skill for getting attention grows remarkably between adolescence and adulthood. We want attention for our good work. We develop methods for attracting friends and lovers. We learn how to capture the attention of our superiors and customers. Sometimes we even look for attention when giving kindness or being generous. And when we're lonely and won't admit it, what better way of finding company than an attention-getting tactic that draws some company without revealing neediness. Even when clever tactics are dropped for the openly expressed need of getting closer to someone we love, the instinct to draw attention is still there.

To really make a case for the critical nature of getting attention as an essential human activity, I can point to the ways we work at attracting sexual attention: our styles of flirtation, the way we present ourselves as sexual creatures with unabashedly erotic clothing, grooming, and posing. Our methods for attracting mates—including those ''effortless,'' innocently ''natural'' mannerisms aimed at seduction—are usually scrupulously honed, time-honored techniques for arousing the lustful attention of a potential lover. Study the romantic attention-getting patterns of adolescents and young adults, and you'll find some pretty systematic methods.

I'm elaborating this matter of attention-getting as one of life's essential activities from crib to college to corporation because most of us don't find the notion flattering. It's as if seeking attention is for children or weaklings. Maybe the unpleasant forms of attention-seeking that we see in others cause us to be less direct when wanting the eyes or ears of someone. Maybe that's why attention-seeking has become subtle and camouflaged and entertaining. We still need it—but we hide that need and get into all kinds of trouble because of our deception.

Attention-gathering techniques are so important that they're now seen as basic to social relations, person-to-person attraction, and business. They're so important that few people are satisfied with the effectiveness of their attention-getting skills, their ability to get enough, to get it at the right time, with the right person, in a graceful way, with a sincere attitude. When the dissatisfaction occurs in a specific situation with a specific person, after the familiar procedures and techniques have been tried, we might resort to earlier methods or crude devices. We might get clumsy in the face of being disregarded (sort of like jumping up and down, waving our arms, and shouting). We might get desperate for attention. And the desperation usually makes things worse. It makes people withhold attention, divide attention, or turn away completely.

A sad fact of human relations is the inverse correlation between desperate attention-seeking and *satisfying* attention-getting. An unusually basic example of desperate attention-seeking by a mother from her infant daughter is described by researcher Daniel Stern in his book, *First Relationship: Mother and Infant*. "Whenever a moment of mutual gaze occurred," Stern noted, "the mother went immediately into high gear, producing a profusion of fully displayed, high-intensity facial and vocal behavior. Jenny (the infant) invariably broke gaze rapidly. Her mother never interpreted this as a cue to lower her level of behavior (her extreme attention-seeking), nor would she let Jenny control the level by gaining distance."[1]

The mother trying so desperately for the baby's attention caused Jenny to withhold it. And not getting the attention made the mother more desperate. Result: a cycle of desperation.

In less dramatic ways, people contract millions of times every day for the exchange of attention. When a colleague at work suggests, "Let's have coffee," it's really a way of saying, "Let's have a cup's worth of conversation—we'll pay some close attention to each other for that long." Of course, people don't come right out and announce, "I want your attention" when seeking ordinary social conversation, but that's what it's all about.

The Scientific Mystery of Turn-Taking in Conversations

Telling someone when you're ready to relinquish their attention and then give yours is an automatic activity done over and over again every day, but it's done below the surface of talk. The phenomenon has the almost breezy scientific label of *turn-taking*. We suspect turn-taking to be a key to someday understanding the basics of power in person-to-person talk—like who has control. If these events were consciously verbalized in broad daylight, they might sound something like, "I'm just about finished with my turn at paying attention, so now you listen and I'll respond to your message for a while." Researchers and theorists are still puzzling over how humans manage any semblance of orderly give-and-take in conversation. Many of us specialists believe people use embedded cues and signals, like changing the slight song in their voices (raising or lowering their pitch), slowing the speed of their talk (easing the pace), or by gesturing, gazing, and using other body language.

A pioneering set of observations by Starkey Duncan (a classmate of mine back at the University of Chicago) set the tone for studying this stuff. He found that we yield our speaking turns with a very complex set of signals, including paralanguage cues like pitch and loudness, body language, phrases such as "you know" and syntax cues such as an open-ended grammatical clause. He also studied "attempt-suppressing signals," in which we use hand gestures to hold our turn.[2] This type of meticulous work may eventually shed light on the fundamental nature of those mysterious rules that govern interaction in any culture.

Another pioneer in exploring the essential ways we give and take attention is Emanuel Schegloff, a UCLA sociologist. Schegloff believes the kernels of interpersonal power can be seen in our reflexes for starting and stopping talk, overlapping (I call it "overtalk" in this chapter), and turn-taking. Those elements are prime targets for an entire field of talk scholarship that Schegloff helped to start 20 years ago. It's plainly labeled as "conversational analysis," and involves some 30 full-time scholars. It uses a meticulous, elaborate system for transcribing natural talk and searching for fundamental "rules" of conversation (like Starkey Duncan and his colleagues). The findings are described in an academic style that would strike the lay reader as arcane.[3]

Conversational analysis researchers want to uncover rules of talk that are basic enough to be used by all societies. They suspect that many rules exist simply to avoid unpleasantness. They put a powerful microscope to conversation by listening to recordings repeatedly for nuances of sound, pauses, stutters, breathing, laughing, mispronunciations, and dozens of other tiny details. This painstaking care is needed, they believe, to understand critical features of interchange that transcend situational factors like the gender or the status of the speakers. Focusing on contextual things like sexism may be important, argues Schegloff, but it's even more important to know precisely what happens from moment to moment that causes turn-taking or interruptions. Schegloff also wants to elevate the study of talk to a basic science like physics or chemistry without being distracted by applied matters. His position is that we just don't know enough to get practical yet; thus, it's too early to demonstrate how to improve turn-taking skills.

I agree that communication specialists are a long way— perhaps 20 or 50 years away—from getting to the bottom of turn-taking phenomena. I don't agree that withholding information on what's already been observed from research is in the public interest. We know right now that a profoundly essential, deeply primitive need for exchanging attention exists between people—and that leaving our "natural" exchange styles unexamined diminishes our capacity for great communication.

CROWDING CASUALTIES

You've experienced verbal crowding. When someone's talk presses up against yours or cuts off the tails of your sentences or just flops right on top of what you're saying, you've been crowded. Chances are that verbal crowding has caused you some lost thoughts, squashed feelings, and other vague discomforts. It has a sneaky hit-and-run quality that can slip into a conversation, push you around, rob your talking space, and race off with the attention you'd been holding before you can recognize it, confront it, or catch it. It's just like being jostled in a crowd by a conversational pickpocket. And it's done almost automatically by almost everyone, even by the kindest of people.

I'm not worried much about crowding when it comes to small talk. In fact, small talk lives off of short silences, not to mention some rushing and interrupting and fast-paced repartee. Small talk turns lame when there are long pauses between talking turns. And, obviously, there are many occasions when quick and lively small talk is required to avoid social or professional uneasiness or avoid the appearance of being aloof, unfriendly, or disrespectful. My point here is that bigger talk needs bigger silences, more empty spaces where larger emotions can find room for expression. Big feelings rarely fit into crowded conversations.

The typical talker crowds only when defending against others' interruptions, or when bored or excited or anxious. Conversational crowding and interpersonal anxiety often sprint along hand in hand. Even a mild tension—when wanting to say the right thing, feeling intimidated, fretting about appearing foolish—can cause crowding.

Some people stimulate rapid turn-taking with or without interpersonal tension. *Chronic* crowders are compulsive stealers of conversational space. They take premature talking turns in most conversations; they knock the pins from under others' paragraphs whenever they want attention. It's rarely done with forethought or malice. Typically, chronic crowders aren't calculating people; they aren't trying to be rude; most honestly don't realize that they're cutting off others' thoughts. Some don't even know they are habitual crowders. If they happen to hear themselves pushing someone around, they're shocked by the discovery. They don't even know why they continually steal attention. Psychologists don't really know either. I suspect it has something to do with clawing for attention from parents and friends while growing up, or having an ongoing case of the worries about saying the right things, about just plain talking well. Chronic crowding can also come from a lifetime of struggling with people who talk in long paragraphs or switch topics in midsentence without skipping a beat and without letting anyone respond to their first topic. And, of course, some fast-talking crowders are doing what they have learned from their families, their neighborhood, or even their region. It's normal and comfortable and even affectionate. (See Deborah Tannen's book in the "People Who Write about Talk" section on page 353.)

Usually the crowding addiction isn't too serious. It may cost the chronic crowder an occasional friendship on one hand, yet save him or her from boring talk on the other hand. By hogging attention from a less assertive talker, the crowder is robbing some of the richness from conversations. But sometimes it goes beyond that. Sometimes unilateral crowding becomes serious enough to contribute to the breakup of a marriage or to the insidious disconnection of parent and child. And sometimes, under severe circumstances, it can contribute to serious mental illness. A growing body of research links some patterns of parental attention management to the unfolding of schizophrenic behavior. (Schizophrenia is the most widespread major mental disorder, hitting two million Americans, taking up 40 percent of mental-hospital beds and costing the economy $20 billion annually.)

What's involved is the repeated deflection of parents' affection from their children's talk topics. Summing up research on causes of schizophrenia at a scientific conference, Dr. Margaret Singer of the University of California, San Francisco, observed that good parental attention was one of the fundamental, ongoing properties of conversation necessary to prevent youngsters from learning "to become disassociated, alienated, withdrawn, or autistic. . . . A sharing of a focus of attention . . . and the acknowledgment by parents of what has been said by each of them and by offspring produce a sense of continuity, worth, and commitment to others involved."

So, a healthy exchange of attention, along with talk that demonstrates a message has been received, are conversational events in families that contribute to growing up mentally healthy. The role of crowding and allowing in human development is obviously significant.

How Crowding Builds

Whether it's the occasional milder kind most of us do, or the more serious, habitual kind, crowding comes in three basic forms: "response-rushing," "interruption," and "overtalk."

Response-rushing occurs when the usual silences between talking turns dwindle from maybe a second to a half second to a tenth of a second . . . and less—so that before your last word has even echoed in your listener's ear, he or she is squeezing in a response. It can feel like someone can't wait for you to stop talking—as if they knew ahead of time what you had to say, or as if what they're saying is more important than anything you could say. Worst of all, you're denied time to think about what you've said, or to pause and collect thoughts. The basic sensation is that someone needs your attention quickly, and the sensation is felt over and over again—a sense of being rushed. Ironically, you're forced to spend the bulk of your attention recapturing lost ideas and trying to get a word in edgewise. It's a messy way to communicate, leaving leftovers of unexpressed thoughts and feelings. Response-rushing in large quantities can disconnect the best of friends (unless both of them do it as a way of life).

Response-rushing is usually the start of major crowding cycles. In conversations, a single rusher will cause rushing in others. It's contagious. Rushing begets rushing. Two or more people doing a lot of response-rushing will accelerate the jostling to a point where the space between talking turns becomes the incredible shrinking silence: a quarter of a second, a tenth of a second, zero seconds—and then beyond the barrier of tiny silences into negative half-seconds, into actually stepping all over each other's talk. Disrupting someone's talk in midsentence or at the slightest pause has officially been designated by talk scientists as the *interruption* (one of the few words language specialists have managed to put in plain language; perhaps the sheer magnitude of the response's impact sobered my colleagues into an awed simplicity).

Take a man and a woman. If the man jumps in before her last word is finished, she is more likely to clip off his last word. A chain reaction starts. As the escalation continues, the interruptions dig deeper into sentences. Interruption begets interruption. And the more interruptions there are, the more incomplete messages there are, which builds frustration.

There are some understandable reasons for interrupting. Confusion is one. The interrupter is really feeling, ''Wait a minute, I want to clear this up.'' Or the urge to express freshly stimulated thoughts leads to the attitude, ''Let me squeeze this idea in before I forget.''

We also interrupt as a reaction to repetition: ''Yeah, you said that before, now what about? . . .'' or downright boredom, thinking to yourself, ''I really don't care.'' And then there's eager impatience: "I've just *got* to get this in now, can't wait a second longer."

Another motive—and one of the most damaging attitudes behind interruption—is a feeling of dominance or some inner sense of superiority, as if the interrupter felt, "My talk is more important than yours, so I'm taking control." It's surprising how that inner message gets through from bosses and parents, and far too often from men to women and from young adults to the elderly. Frequent interruptions done for dominance over long stretches of time are hard to deal with—hard to confront because few people realize what's happening to them. But they do realize a rotten feeling. And in the case of those who can't escape easily (kids, employees, oldsters, some women), the costs can involve a little lowering of self-worth, somehow learning to believe that they're worth less than the interrupter. (Research continues to show that men interrupt women a lot more often than they interrupt other men and more often than women interrupt other women.)

As interruptions increase during a conversation, there is frequent midsentence disruption—sometimes entire sentences are shoved aside. When the stage is set for both talkers to interrupt *at once*—"overtalk." Both talk at the same time, neither yielding attention to the other. It may go on for a couple of sentences or more. It may even become fierce crowding: two or more people hurling talk at each other simultaneously for several sentences, delivering, in effect, this message: "I know this is a verbal fight and I'm not backing away; I'm going to outlast you, so you may as well give up." It's an extreme form of interruption. If this description of "overtalk" sounds exaggerated, like my fantasy of a Wild West shootout, just step back and listen carefully next time two crowders go at each other. You'll discover an authentic duel.

Overtalk is a form of verbal crowding. And it's surprising how much we accept such aggression without complaint. It's a little like the acceptance of New Yorkers nudging each other on a crowded subway. No outright fights result, but it's definitely uncomfortable.

To get an idea of how overtalk, interruptions, response-rushing and conversational allowing work, let's look at a conversation between Phil and Charlie, friends who work together. Every Sunday morning during the football season, like clockwork, they banter on the phone over a bet on a game. Their playful routine (aimed at outfoxing each other with communication maneuvers like bargaining and mock outrage) is a common form of verbal roughhousing among American men. Like the physical roughhousing of male adolescents, the grown-up verbal version is a ritual for expressing affection.

The following verbatim examples happened to get caught in Phil's voice-actuated answering machine and were later retrieved for my collection. I'm especially grateful to them for donating their tape for research because their conversation beautifully illustrates classical patterns of crowding and allowing. I've twisted a meaning or two, changed names and places, and skipped some overdetailed and irrelevant sections of dialogue (like a three-minute search for a restaurant number). But what you read is essentially the real thing—unself-conscious conversation. The "wait-times"—the pauses between talking turns that add to or subtract from conversational allowing—are noted in parentheses. The overtalks—when both are talking at once—are also indicated in parentheses.

PHIL: *(Recorded message on phone answering machine)* I can't get to the phone right now because I'm at my yodeling class. But if you leave your name and number, I'll give you—

PHIL: *(Picking up receiver and overtalking with his message)* Hold on, I'm here. Sort of—

PHIL'S MESSAGE: —a holler. If not a yodel. *(Overtalk, 2 seconds)*

CHARLIE: Are you awake? *(Silence, 1.9 seconds)*

[Almost two seconds of silence is twice as long as the typical wait-time between talking turns. But we often delay another second when answering questions—or when half-asleep like Phil.]

PHIL: Well, just about. *(0.8 second)*

CHARLIE: Good. Then you can hear how you've lucked out this morning. *(Pause)* Just because I like you and want to avoid your usual sob story, I'm offering you the Giants plus six points for three dollars. *(1.1 seconds)*

[Like regular people in regular conversations, these friends allow a bit under or a bit over a second before responding, but the regularity ends as their bargaining begins. The next two rushed responses set the stage for a burst of interruptions.]

PHIL: Only a touchdown? You must think I'm completely asleep. They'll lose by two touchdowns—maybe more— but I wanna give you a bet just to make the game interesting. I'll take the Giants with 11 points.

CHARLIE: Eleven points! You must still be sleeping. And *dream-*

ing. They're playing at home. They're healthy. And this week the Rams are the walking wounded. *(0.4 second)*

[Note how silences are mostly a little less than a second so far. That's like most conversations.]

PHIL: You mean wounded grizzly bears—it hurts seeing you trying to take advantage of a friend for money. It's about time you—*(Interruption, less than 0.1 second)*

[Charlie anticipates the scolding and in the spirit of mock fighting pushes Phil offstage and makes a counteroffer.]

CHARLIE: Okay, okay, just to stop your crying I'll donate seven points to—*(Interruption, less than 0.1 second)*

[An example of interruption begetting interruption. It usually takes several interruptions from one person to get one in return. Phil did it early, probably because they're playing their familiar roughhousing talk game.]

PHIL: Seven points will *start* me crying, especially if I think about the Rams' front line. Offer me ten and see if— *(Interruption)*

[They're not just stepping on each other's lines now, they're censoring each other's ideas. It's real roughhousing. In serious conversations, such deep interruptions usually appear after a much longer period of response-rushing—maybe dozens of half-second or quarter-second wait-times between talking turns before the first interruption.]

CHARLIE: You don't wanna bet, you—*(Interruption)*

[This is the fourth consecutive interruption. Play is getting rough. It would be rougher if the conversation were earnest—disastrous if they were discussing important feelings.]

PHIL: —I'm crazy enough to give my money to Charlie's charity—

CHARLIE: —want a sure thing. *(Overtalk, 1.5 seconds, then silence, 0.3 second)*

[They're talking simultaneously in the previous section, each finishing sentences started earlier, as if trying to make their point by bullying through. It's like a shouting match without the shouting.]

CHARLIE: Okay, if stealing is what you want, I'll offer you eight points for four dollars. But only if your conscience can handle—*(Interruption)*

PHIL: Now it comes out. Now it's clear. Your bet's so good it's worth an extra dollar—

CHARLIE: —abusing someone who's always been kind to you. *(Overtalk, 2.3 seconds, then laughter by both, 4.5 seconds)*

[Charlie's offer to increase the bet shows his hand. He's obviously convinced his team will win big. That revelation gives Phil the bargaining position of someone taken advantage of. His excitement can't be contained. Excitement creates interruption.]

PHIL: *(With a smile in his voice)* You gave yourself away, Buddy. You should've waited. Getting greedy for that

> extra buck's gonna kill you. Now I want nine and a half
> points.

[The banter continues with frequent overtalking and interrupting, along with a few slivers of silence *totaling* less than a second. We join them about three minutes later.]

CHARLIE: Nine's the limit. I'm just a generous fool who should've—
           (Interruption, then silence, less than 0.1 second)

PHIL: You'll see who's generous in the fourth quarter. I'll take
           your nine even though my Giants are really two-touch-
           down underdogs. Next time it's your turn to bend a little.
           (0.5 second)

CHARLIE: Okay, okay, it's a bet. Four dollars? *(0.3 second)*

PHIL: Okay, okay. *(0.5 second)*

PHIL: *(Continuing)* No way I'd back them if they weren't going
           to be my home team next year. *(2.4 seconds)*

[The longest silence in six minutes. There's huge news in Phil's almost incidental disclosure about "my home team." Charlie takes the extra second to swallow it. Phil's aware of the impact of his "incidental" disclosure. He waits, allows.]

CHARLIE: What! . . . You mean . . . the offer came through? The
           New York job? *(0.6 second)*

PHIL: Yeah—but I'm not 100 percent sure yet, because—
           (Interruption)

[Apparently, the possibility that New York isn't a certainty is important to Charlie. He jumps on the phrase "not 100 percent sure." He wants to know *now*.]

CHARLIE: Well, well, how sure are you? *(1.6 seconds)*

[Another long silence as both men want to talk carefully now about an emotional matter—the separation of friends. Their conversational climate will change from mock debate into sincere debate. Charlie and Phil are entering the second episode of their conversation, a second mood, with a second set of rules for crowding and allowing. The conversation takes on a new rhythm as they cease their wild interruptions and overtalk. Their interruptions will become precise, emotionally charged, as they begin to allow more thinking time for the other. I use the term "episode" for these distinct and separate moods, rules, and topics within a conversation. Most conversations have a couple of episodes or more. The first episode for Charlie and Phil was full of crowded, playful, verbal roughhousing about the bet. Their second episode is a little less crowded. It's a serious, tense debate about the job decision.]

PHIL: Well, *almost* sure. Haggerty's doing some good work.
           She thinks I'll fit in, and she says—*(Interruption)*

[Unwillingness to hear unpleasant truths stirs people to interrupt. Charlie challenges Phil's leaving, debates Phil's decision.]

CHARLIE: But Phil, how about her rigidity? You're the—*(Attempt
           at interruption)*

PHIL: Well, yeah—*(Interruption)*

[Interrupted interruptions are common. I've seen men, in particular, do it to women and children a lot. At this moment, Phil yielded because he sensed Charlie's hurt feelings. I know because that's what Phil recalled when he read this transcript. Charlie also read it and remembered "feeling pained."]

CHARLIE: You're the one who worried about her rigidity. *You* told me she's stubborn and all caught up with being the Iron Lady. *(0.4 second)*

PHIL: Yeah, I know. I see her overdoing the Joan of Arc number, but she's good, terrifically inventive. *(0.7 second)*

CHARLIE: But what good does that do ya when she suddenly decides the whole damn department has to change course, and when—*(Attempt at interruption)*

PHIL: She promised me—*(Interruption)*

CHARLIE: —she plays her nasty power games with that— *(Interruption)*

PHIL: Ah, come on, Charlie, we've got the same crap here. Our department has the same share of double-dealers and morons—present company excluded, Buddy. *(0.8 second)*

CHARLIE: *(Sardonically)* So what do ya need New York double-dealers for when we have some perfectly good ones right here? *(Phil laughs, 3 seconds)*

CHARLIE: *(Continuing)* Well, seriously, hell, why transplant yourself to work with New York's morons?

[The debate continues without great change in pattern as each takes a turn to support his position. Compared to their earlier verbal rough-housing loaded with overtalk, interruptions, and response-rushing, the job debate has no overtalks, not as many interruptions, and more silences of more than a half second. These subtle changes in conversational rhythm reshape the conversation's climate. It's less stormy. Each talking turn is longer; the men allow each other to say more during each turn because the content now is more important. Both feel the tone change from fun to tension, not only by what they say but by the many small changes in response-rushing, overtalk, and interruptions. The talking turns are longer, but I'd still classify the conversation as crowded, terse, propelled by unexpressed feelings. We resume the transcribed dialogue about eight minutes later as an emotion is about to be disclosed by Phil. That self-disclosure will change the rhythm again—a few seconds will be added to the spaces between talking turns in their exchange. You'll see how those few seconds reshape the conversational tone. The change is radical. A third conversational episode is about to begin.]

PHIL: No, wait a minute, Charlie. You're making everything about the place sound rotten. Rotten boss, rotten staff, crummy weather, terrible parking, exorbitant living. Even a rotten football team to lose money on. *(Laugh-*

ter, 1.9 seconds, as Phil starts chuckling and Charlie joins in)

CHARLIE: Well, it's sorta . . . uh, some of it's true. You've heard the stories. New York has . . . uh, some serious drawbacks for peaceful living. *(0.9 second)*

[The conversational pace is more regular here: longer talking turns, and occasional interruptions and silences of about one second. This looks a lot like everyday talk, except for the very low incidence of response-rushing—the wait-time between their talking turns is rarely less than a half second.]

PHIL: Yeah, you're right. But I'm not looking for peace right now; I'm looking to change my tune, to take a chance, to examine my life. My job's a dead-end here. I feel like a robot with habits I can't shake off. New York might get me in touch with my real choices. I have no love for the place. Your arguments make sense. I don't even know why we're arguing. *(1.8 seconds)*

CHARLIE: I know. Just, uh . . . uh . . . *(2.8 seconds)*

[Both men have capitulated a bit; they've rather abruptly stopped pushing each other and cut down their crowding, providing a safer climate during this third episode for disclosure of important personal feelings and thoughts.]

PHIL: The decision's been rough on me. Leaving this place is scary. And sad. The friends. The weather. The sailing. Crazy Freddy's bar. I'm gonna miss you guys—especially you, Charlie. You've been there whenever I've needed a friend. When I've felt knocked down. I guess that stuff is right about friends being good medicine. . . . *(3.1 seconds)*

[This isn't like everyday talk, not only because Phil's self-disclosures are unusually revealing but also because the wait-times before responding are unusually long (two and three times the typical 0.9 second). There's no hint of the ubiquitous response-rushing. The climate is dominated by conversational allowing. These men are *waiting* for each other. A common way of describing such allowing, when someone relinquishes his talking turn as Charlie is doing, would be to call Charlie "speechless." For many men, it's not easy to hear such sincere warmth from a male friend.]

PHIL: *(Continuing)* I'm also gonna miss the easy gambling money each week. *(Laughter by both, 2 seconds, then silence, 4.3 seconds)*

[This long moment of mutual allowing is for collecting feelings, for inner editing before more talk, for being careful with each other. A far cry from their football banter. Charlie's about to reflect the sincere message contained in Phil's affectionate comment about missing "easy gambling money." He's also going to touch on the way they've been talking, which brings a bit of "here-'n'-now" immediacy to the conversation.]

CHARLIE: I'll miss you, too. Maybe that's why I'm knocking New York and that Haggerty. I know you can protect yourself. And maybe New York can get you the freedom to deprogram your thinking. But I'm gonna miss ya. You're one of the main reasons I've had a good time at work. *(2.7 seconds)*

[This careful exchange of sincere feelings was difficult—both men told me so. Imagine this dialogue between women, and it takes on a more relaxed, normal tone.]

PHIL: You know, I'm getting old enough to know that good friends are the biggest part of living in any city. If it weren't for you and Erica and Jim, I'd have gone to New York without any fuss. *(4.2 seconds.)*

[This much silence in a conversation without important emotional exchanges would feel strange, awkward, puzzling.]

CHARLIE: *(Sigh)* Well . . . *(1.2 seconds)*

CHARLIE: *(Continuing)* We never talked about the roughest part. . . . *(0.4 second)*

PHIL: Huh? *(0.9 second)*

CHARLIE: The gambling—who's gonna pay the long-distance phone bill?

The not-so-funny joke about the phone bill allows a polite escape, a deflection, from the emotional, almost confessional self-disclosing between the men. It ends the third episode. Their work is done for now. The fact of separating has been revealed, and the pain of separation is evident. The episode rendered them vulnerable. And that made it more valuable. After Charlie's little joke, they switched to arranging dinner after the game, and the long silences and long talking turns disappeared as the need for allowing to exchange personal feelings faded. And as the talk got more relaxed, the standard rhythms of rushed responses measured out their trivial talk. The fourth and final episode of the conversation became one of those familiar routines about scheduling time and place, the kind of talk where crowding and allowing have little importance.

Most conversations contain a couple of episodes; a substantial personal talk can easily contain three, four, or more. The Charlie/Phil conversation progressed through four moods, four rhythms, four topics—from playful, recklessly crowded football banter to a tense, somewhat crowded why-move-to-New York debate to a warm, very allowing mutual affection confessional to a trivial, slightly rushed scheduling of dinner. Admittedly, their talk was a bit unusual in its range of moods, rhythms, and topics, but it was a splendid way to display how crowding and allowing shape interpersonal moods. Can you imagine the two parting friends disclosing their mutual respect during that warm third episode if they had interrupted and overtalked each other? The human relations that needed doing between Phil and Charlie couldn't have happened without conversational allowing. That fact, unfortunately, is not known to many who choose to discuss important feelings in an interpersonally crowded environment. It's a reckless venture. Tender talk is easily wounded by the common clumsiness of ordinary crowding.

The Damaging Effects of Crowding

As a therapist, I heard a hundred horror stories from patients who initiated emotionally charged conversations with children and other vulnerable people in interpersonally crowded atmospheres. The cruelty caused by a few little overtalks and interruptions is so elusive, so quick to flash in and out of human interchange, that the cause and effect is missed. But after it's observed just once, the damage done by crowding is rarely forgotten. Such observations must be made in real-life circumstances (or the experiments in chapter 12), but I've got a story that can enhance your awareness—make it easier for you to spot the real thing when it happens. It's not about serious psychological damage (which takes repeated crowding) but only a single ruined conversation between a young man and young woman planning to be professional conversationalists. They were graduate students in clinical psychology who were not yet aware of crowding's impact. Both had studied psychology as star undergrads and came to me as third-year grad students, well-read in all the major theories of therapy. They were eager to learn about "interpersonal process" (moment-to-moment talk phenomena). So I had them record some of their off-campus personal conversations for later analysis.

One recorded sample they brought me bewildered them. Listening to the tape stimulated recall of unexpressed thoughts and feelings that occurred beneath the conversation. By agreement, they dropped their defenses and told me everything they remembered. It took courage. This is a running account of what happened. It's a pure picture of talk process that doesn't display actual dialogue or even describe the topic of conversation. I'll just describe the *way* they talked.

Imagine that this conversation started about ten minutes ago. My student, Jim, has just finished describing his feelings about a complicated personal problem to his classmate, Carla. Carla takes a little more than four seconds to let the end of Jim's message sink in. Her silence response seems to have a strong impact on him. Jim closes his eyes and clasps his hands.

He feels comfortable with her silence; he has a hunch she's using the time to quietly dwell on his problem. His hunch is confirmed as Carla reflects his problem in a few slow sentences, and he feels so well understood that he's eager to disclose another feeling—he starts to talk a half second after she finishes her reflection. He reveals another important feeling and, again, she gives a silence response—six seconds—before reflecting his feelings. She has started a pattern of conversational allowing combined with the communication of empathy through reflections. Then Jim rushes in after a tenth of a second with more about his problem.

There are a few more exchanges in a similar manner as she waits three, four, five seconds before responding. And he leaps in a tenth of a second later or almost simultaneously with her last syllable (response-rushing). Carla senses Jim's anxiety as he describes things he's never told anyone before. She isn't paying specific attention to the crowding behavior because she's never really thought about it. She just knows that she's feeling *very* crowded and figures it's because she's talking too much, maybe making her reflections too long. Actually, he's experiencing relief—almost excitement—and thinks she's great. Carla doesn't know that and decides she'd better squeeze everything in quickly and get out of his way so he doesn't have to hit-and-run her sentences. She stops giving silence responses and starts talking very rapidly. The allowing pattern turns to crowding. Result: Now *Jim* feels crowded and can't wait for his turn to begin. He starts clipping the last word or two off of her talking turn (interruption).

Tense times in this alleged helping conversation. Carla's anxiety increases because she believes it's important for her reflecting messages to get registered. She hasn't had much experience with allowing. At the same time, Jim rushes in at every opportunity. Even when she's saying, "Ahhhh . . ." or "I mean . . ." while searching for the right word, he cuts her off. She's frustrated as her well-intentioned communication can't get out. Jim is preoccupied with his self-exploration. Her kind words are brushed aside as if they didn't matter, as if *she* didn't matter. She's feeling alone, a little dehumanized, a little tearful. He doesn't notice and continues nonstop. (Afterward, as the three of us listened and Carla described her feelings, Jim became angry at himself—embarrassed at his crowding.)

Distracted by her frustration and sense of belittlement, Carla disengages. Distress pushes her recently learned reflection and allowing skills aside. She listens superficially. She makes an occasional response and garbles his meaning. Jim's earlier experience of being known is shrinking. His sense of connection is leaving. He reacts with a common reflex to feeling misunderstood—repeating the lost message, trying to fix the broken connection by saying it again. The repeater effect is operating. She interrupts his repeated messages, but he won't yield the floor. Then they overtalk each other. A mess.

This episode lasted about eight minutes, followed by a half hour of interruption and overtalk. The three of us listened to every powerfully crowded minute of their verbal shoving match. We witnessed a beautifully empathic conversation deteriorate into a fight for attention. It was difficult for Jim and Carla to hear themselves—they moaned and writhed in half-mock agony (a common reaction I've observed for years when people hear themselves talk on tape in ways they don't like; it's similar to rereading an old love letter . . . but worse). There's something about scrutinizing crowding behavior—our own or others'—that seems to make an unalterable impression. Months after listening to their conversation, my students described their new awareness and said it was sharply present whenever crowding crept into their exchanges. (Such learning is one of the great pleasures that make professoring worthwhile.) I've heard the same from others, but I've also observed that simply reading about the problem without watching it or practicing some allowing exercises won't reduce the habit. Chronic crowders can carefully read this chapter and sincerely decide to stop their habit, only to fail in their very next conversation. It's a tough, ingrained addiction that takes weeks or months of practice to be broken. (Some of the methods described in chapter 12 have been useful to crowders who are interested in curbing their habit.)

Breaking the habit is especially difficult in the company of other crowders. The stuff is contagious. Reformed crowders often suffer relapses after receiving a barrage of rushed responses. I can testify to that. Crowding can be fun. My own control is

gone after getting hit with three or four interruptions and engaging in an overtalk or two with anyone close (and then I'm
fair game for criticism as a hypocrite—just another occupational
hazard for a talk specialist).

WOMEN, MEN, AND WAITING

The familiar image of a waiting woman haunts song lyrics,
drama, poetry, and traditional views of the female role—the
patient, attending, homemaking woman. She waited for her body
to grow fertile, waited for her lover to appear, waited to be
asked, waited for her sailor to return, waited for her unborn
child, waited for the kids to come home from school, and waited
for her social rights. She has waited through the centuries. It
seems her occupation has been waiting. Much of that is changing now; women are tired of waiting. But I have a feeling they
understand the nature of waiting better than men. They seem to
have a larger capacity for utilizing patience with intimacy. Maybe
that's why some theorists see the psychotherapist as woman—a
professional wanting to have compassion, caretaking, empathy,
and openness packed into a waiting presence. A woman's role.
That's why I usually prefer taking my emotional hurt to a woman. I think, deep down, most people would. And that's not just
a sentimental thought.

So the waiting woman is more than an old image. When it
comes to waiting in conversation, women do a better job than
men. That's partially true because of an awful tendency for men
to unwittingly crowd women's talk. Research supports that view.
(See "People Who Write about Talk" on page 353.) But it's also
possible that biology, child rearing, and the more sensual female
sexual response have shaped some preference for patience and
waiting. Regardless of cause, my observations lead me to suspect that women are better equipped to *deliberately* enhance
closeness or provide help by waiting.

All too often, the word "wait" in modern times has come to
mean a passive holding action, a boring experience that goes on
until an event occurs. Back in the sixteenth and seventeenth
centuries, though, the genteel act of waiting was rich in interpersonal meaning. Sometimes it meant to give some company,
to escort. ("She smiled and bid him wait [accompany] her to
her room.") The giving of *company* eventually came to mean
the giving of *care*, and the word "wait" grew to mean the ren-

dering of service with respect, protecting with honor. ("As a squire I wait my knight to his battle and wait him home again.")

The meaning of attending someone with honor, to assist with a care akin to love, was behind the title "ladies in waiting" in the sixteenth and seventeenth centuries. Another meaning of the word "wait" had to do with paying a respectful visit, moving toward someone with deference. ("I went to wait [visit], but he had gone ahunting.")

Over the centuries of English-speaking history, people didn't always passively wait for someone; they actively waited *to* someone (consider those ancient roles of waitress and waiter). Waiting was *doing* something, *giving* something—company, respect, food, care, protection, close attention. These old meanings crop up now when, for instance, a parent waits for a child to learn a skill, a teacher waits for a student to grasp a concept, or a lover waits for a mate's orgasm. I believe the old meanings of waiting become reattached, in our fast-paced society, whenever people do their waiting with affection or respect. That kind of waiting isn't passive.

WAITING IS NO GAME

Of all the places where people can wait for each other—either with care or boredom, with protection or impatience—none occurs more frequently than when conversing. Every time we allow another second before responding or resist the urge to crowd, we wait—in the old sense of the word.

The effectiveness of deliberate, active waiting shows vividly in the act of teaching—informally in the home or in the formal setting of a classroom. I don't know of any studies exploring waiting differences between men and women teachers, but there is evidence that any teacher who doesn't wait long enough for students to think about questions can rush the curiosity and creativeness right out of those students. Many teachers allow only a second or less for students to start answering (the average wait time in the bustle of normal conversation), according to research by Professor Mary Budd Rowe at Columbia University. "After a child makes a response," Rowe reported in *Science and Children* magazine, "you [teachers] apparently are still in a hurry because you generally wait slightly less than a second to repeat what he said or to rephrase it or ask another question."[4]

The impact of short wait-times on classroom atmosphere?

Very short student answers, many thoughtless responses unsupported by evidence, a gradual lowering of student self-confidence, and virtually no child-to-child exchange of ideas.

On the other hand, when teachers purposely allowed five or more seconds for responses, as Professor Rowe asked, good things started to happen: Kids gave longer, more thoughtful answers using many complete sentences; they expressed themselves with greater confidence; they started disclosing their speculations, supported by evidence. There was also a significant exchange of ideas between children in open discussions. (Insidiously, before the admonition to allow more time for answers, some teachers rushed children they considered inferior students even more than others. "Giving longer wait-times can change your expectations about what some children can do," said Professor Rowe. "Teachers who have learned to use longer silences report that children who do not ordinarily say much start talking and usually have exciting ideas. . . . Response by 'slow' students increased gradually at first, and then rapidly.")

The striking set of improvements in the process of classroom learning was produced by changing a small talk habit, by adding just a few seconds of waiting to each student/teacher interaction. It would be a mistake to think those teachers could permanently alter their talk styles just by remembering to mechanically count to five after a question, but the experiment underlines the fact that longer wait-times are a necessary luxury for learning.

The Power of Positive Waiting

Longer wait-times are also a necessity for other forms of interaction aimed at creating personal change. That's why waiting has been a significant element in several denominations of psychoanalytic therapy. There's a lesson in the fact that dozens of therapies with radically differing ideas for producing personality change share a common belief in the power of waiting. Some lawyers, managers, journalists, even a few detectives understand the utility of giving people long silence responses.

One of our generation's most influential psychologists was a firm believer in waiting for people who need to talk about their troubles. The late Carl Rogers rarely rushed or interrupted his clients or students. Conversational allowing, which he did masterfully, is an essential ingredient of his therapy system. He influenced several thousands of psychotherapists (and probably a million or more other people around the world) to patiently wait for each message, to wait with as much empathy, positive regard, and integrity as they can muster before responding. His work advocated active waiting filled with energetic attention and a willingness to respond that eventually creates an unusual bond between people. Rogers's penetrating style of vigilant waiting has become a form of high conversational art.

I have a favorite example of Rogers attending to a severely disturbed schizophrenic man (pseudonym: Jim Brown). It's the kind of waiting with care that even best friends or lovers rarely give each other. I know it *can* occur in personal conversations when someone almost instinctively allows minutes of attentive silence for a friend or loved one to search his or her mind before disclosing difficult thoughts or profound feelings or partially recognized emotions. Such constructive allowing doesn't happen enough. Typical conversations, even in close relations, are so fast paced and filled with interruptions that people become comfortable with speed and fearful of giving or receiving long wait-times. Too bad. The wide-open spaces of a conversation in which minutes of thinking time are allowed can help heal wounds and foster creative, searching expression. Chances are you've never enjoyed the sheer luxury of having someone just sit there patiently while you let your mind roam about important personal feelings . . . minute after minute without feeling pressed to say a thing till you're ready.

You may have a hard time believing the length of some of the waiting spells Dr. Rogers gives in the excerpt that follows. Please don't disregard the wait-times between the dialogue—their length is the key to this unfolding drama.

ROGERS: I see there are some cigarettes here in the drawer. Hm? Yeah, it is hot out. *(Silence, 25 seconds)*

ROGERS: Do you look kind of angry this morning, or is that my imagination? *(Jim shakes his head slightly)*

ROGERS: Not angry, huh? *(1 minute, 26 seconds)*

ROGERS: Feel like letting me in on whatever is going on? *(12 minutes, 52 seconds)*

[Most mortals never give or receive such conversational allowing.]

ROGERS: *(Softly)* I kind of feel like saying that if it would be of any help at all, I'd like to come in. On the other hand, if it's something you'd rather—if you just feel more like being within yourself, feeling whatever you're feeling within yourself, why that's okay, too. I guess another thing I'm saying, really, is, I do care. I'm not just sitting here like a stick. *(1 minute, 11 seconds)*

ROGERS: And I guess your silence is saying to me that either you don't want to or can't come out right now and that's okay. So I won't pester you, but I just want you to know I'm here. *(17 minutes, 41 seconds)*

[A busy professional could have eaten lunch and made a decision as Rogers waits upon the troubled man.]

ROGERS: I see I'm going to have to stop [for another client] in a few minutes. *(20 seconds)*

ROGERS: It's hard for me to know how you've been feeling, but it looks as though part of the time maybe you'd rather I didn't know how you were feeling. Anyway, it looks as though part of the time it just feels very good to let down and . . . relax the tension. But as I say, I don't really know how you feel. It's just the way it looks to me. Have things been pretty bad lately? *(45 seconds)*

ROGERS: Maybe this morning you just wish I'd shut up—and maybe I should, but I just keep feeling I'd like to, I don't know, be in touch with you in some way. *(2 minutes, 21 seconds; Jim yawns)*

ROGERS: Sounds discouraged or tired. *(41 seconds)*

[Skilled helpers reflect any bit of salient communication, like body language, excuses, hesitation—even yawns, as Rogers just did. Chapter 2 illustrates a talk phenomenon where people correct even slightly inaccurate reflections given to them. The correction is often an attempt to be known even better after receiving a comforting dose of empathy. Maybe that was the motive for Jim's next response. If so, it signals a wish for better connection. Rogers's research demonstrated that reflections in the context of conversational allowing can eventually penetrate the protective wall of the schizophrenic.]

JIM: No. Just lousy.
ROGERS: Everything's lousy, huh? You feel lousy?

Reading the interchange has bewildered some of my students. "*Seventeen* minutes of silence!" one restless undergraduate told me. "Seventeen *seconds* would make me tense and a minute would make my skin crawl."

After a few more heroically long wait-times punctuated by few reflections, Rogers's patient attention finally started Jim talking. He said, "I just ain't no good to nobody, never was and never will be," and that he was "beyond help." It seemed his own underlying feelings of worthlessness had been exacerbated that week by the comments of an acquaintance who accused Jim of being "no good." After relating that, and defiantly declaring, "I don't care, though," Jim started weeping quietly—the first crack in his detached facade.

Three days later, Jim met with Rogers again and the facade began to melt even more. This time Jim started detailing his sense of worthlessness: "I just want to run away and die. . . . All day yesterday and all morning I wished I were dead. I even prayed last night that I could die." Rogers, in addition to his reflections and self-disclosures continued giving long silences. Toward the end of the session, Jim burst into tears and unintelligible sobs. The crying went on for several minutes as Rogers waited in silence and reflected Jim's sobbing. ("I do get a sense of how awful you feel inside—you just sob and sob.")

Afterward, Rogers noted that in his relationship with Jim, "There was a moment of real and, I believe, irreversible change. Jim Brown, who sees himself as stubborn, bitter, mistreated, worthless, useless, hopeless, unloved, unlovable, *experiences* my caring. In that moment his defensive shell cracks wide open and can never again be quite the same. When someone *cares* for him, and when he feels and experiences this caring, he becomes a softer person whose years of stored-up hurt come pouring out in anguished sobs." As Rogers observed, "Many events are necessary to lead up to such a moment," but a crucial event, performed over and over for long periods, was the therapist's extraordinary waiting, which epitomizes the art of unrushed caring, of giving respect without pity.

The conversations did change Jim Brown's life—"little by little he became willing to risk himself in a positive approach to life." He ultimately left the hospital, developed friends on the outside, found a part-time job on his own and began to live his own life, apart from any hospital or therapy influence. A special way of talking made the difference. The mystique of this particular therapy was little more than an allowing, attached attitude and the sincere application of silences, reflections and self-disclosures. It doesn't require a Ph.D. or an M.D. Carl Rogers wanted the world to know that fact. He wanted to demystify this therapeutic force of talk.

SLOW TALK/FAST TALK

All of the scientific data aren't in about what factors influence our different rates of speech, but my guess is that environment plays a significant role in the fast-paced, crowded conversations. Crowded rooms, busy buildings, and tightly packed cities do have an impact on us. You'll probably find, then, that a typical citizen of Chugwater, Wyoming (population 187), talks slower than most long-time Manhattan residents. If a verbally facile New York City couple goes camping for a week in the wilderness, they're very likely to experience some mild environmental culture shock and drive home talking at a more deliberate clip. I've heard of two city dwellers who taped some of their conversations during a week of sailing on the Atlantic. When they listened to the tapes later, they were stunned by their utterly uncrowded, languorous ocean talk. They were amazed by the serenity. Unrushed environments can make unrushed talk.

In an *Esquire* column on politics, Richard Reeves noted how rapid speaking habits can contribute to a reputation for insensitive disregard. Observing a visit by New York Mayor Edward Koch and other city officials to Washington, D.C., in search of federal loans, Reeves reported that the New Yorkers were "talking so fast" that some members of a Senate committee "had trouble keeping up with them. . . . New Yorkers, I would estimate, hustle at about twice the words-per-minute of other Americans. . . . Usually Koch or [City Comptroller] Goldin were in with their answers before the senators could finish their questions."

The result? "The style, the hustle, was on display at the Washington hearing—'pushy' was a word heard in the corridors after the New Yorkers left."

Maybe senators recovering from the rushed responses felt a little like down-home former football coach Bum Phillips who, after an encounter with a rapid-speaking colleague, observed, "He talks faster than I can listen."

Satirists Bob and Ray had an amusing go at the fast/slow phenomenon, with Bob playing the painfully slow-talking president of the STOA (Slow Talkers of America), appearing on a talk show hosted by fast-speaking Ray.

BOB: We . . . believe . . .
RAY: In speaking slowly.
BOB: . . . in . . . forming . . . our ideas . . . and opinions . . . clearly . . . before speaking . . . We are here . . .
RAY: *(Impatiently)* In New York City.
BOB: . . . in the . . . city of New York . . . attending . . .
RAY: A convention.
BOB: *(Blissfully unaware)* . . . our . . . annual . . .
RAY: *(Almost screaming)* Convention!
BOB: . . . membership . . .

RAY: CONVENTION!
BOB: . . . convention . . .

Some fast talkers would insist that skit wasn't too exaggerated. Taking lots of time for stating the routine or obvious is one of the major complaints fasts have about careful, cautious, self-editing slows. Slow talkers, meanwhile, grouse that they go through life having their sentences finished for them—usually incorrectly—by fasts who aren't even paying attention in their own ratchet-tongued rush.

What I believe is that slow talkers hate fast talkers. And fast talkers hate slow talkers. And slow talkers and fast talkers are attracted to each other. Hate each other/attract each other—another great paradox of human behavior. They prefer each other's company, pair off as kids and tend to wind up as work colleagues. I wouldn't be surprised if the large majority of marriages are mixed—one spouse speaks distinctively slower, one faster. Each lacks, and somehow wants, what the other possesses. They create a complementary pairing. They're similar in wanting a relationship containing such talk-style differences. After all, the crowding between two fast talkers can get fierce. A double fast-talker marriage (two fast talkers) can be one long, ongoing battle for the verbal floor. Double-slows struggle, too. They've been known to bore each other silly or even resent each other for lack of stimulation and spontaneity. After studying double-slow pairings years ago, I nicknamed these relationships "resentment factories."

Slow talkers and fast talkers of the world, face it—you need each other.

"SHE WASN'T LISTENING TO ME, EVEN"

Time: Late 1940s.
Place: A hotel bar in a large city.
Situation: A teenage boy is looking for excitement. Drinking a Coke, he starts chatting with three women at the next table and finally persuades one of them to dance. She's several years older than he is. He tries to carry on a conversation as they dance.

"You really can dance," I told the blonde one. "You oughta be a pro. I mean it. I danced with a pro once, and you're twice as good as she was. Did you ever hear of Marco and Miranda?''

"What?" she said. She wasn't even listening to me. She was looking all around the place.

"I said, did you ever hear of Marco and Miranda?"

"I don't know. No. I don't know."

"Well, they're dancers, she's a dancer. She's not too hot, though. She does everything she's *supposed* to, but she's not so hot anyway. You know when a girl's really a terrific dancer?"

"Wudga say?" she said. She wasn't listening to me, even. Her mind was wandering all over the place.

"I said, do you know when a girl's really a terrific dancer?"

"Uh-huh."

"Well—where I have my hand on your back. If I think there isn't anything underneath my hand—no can, no legs, no feet, no *any*thing—then the girl's really a terrific dancer."

She wasn't listening, though. So I ignored her for a while. We just danced.

Holden Caulfield in *The Catcher in the Rye* had an ongoing problem: People didn't listen to what he was saying. He couldn't capture much attention. Like most of us faced with an inattentive audience, he felt a mixture of frustration, rejection and to-hell-with-it detachment (while pretending that having his talk disregarded wasn't a big deal.)

Listening is, indeed, a big deal. It must be, based on how many people talk about *listening* better. Corporations shell out good money to advertise how their employees *listen* better. And they hire consultants who teach employees little gimmicks about eye contact and message memorizing under the guise of *listening* better. When characters in movies and sitcoms have communication breakdowns, it's usually attributed to someone who didn't, for crying out loud, *listen*.

Listen, I'm not going to fight a national tide. I hereby declare myself in favor of better listening. . . . I just have to add that good communication isn't that simple. Mutual listening is to good conversations what mutual attraction is to good love affairs—important, but only one element in a larger event.

For most people, simply learning to listen better will make little difference in their talk. Even if they listen like a bulldog, if they don't know what to do *after* listening, they're in trouble.

Listening gets so much publicity because a short supply is an easily recognizable cause of talk trouble. Everyone has been on both ends of bad listening—as a discomfited talker or as an unwilling attention-giver. It's easy to diagnose the symptoms of bad listening or to sense the satisfaction of good listening; it's a lot tougher to know what makes them happen. Or how to change bad to good. Simplistic resolutions to listen better by trying to tame a wandering mind or trying to beat unfocused attention into shape with pep talks won't last beyond a conversation or two. Changing bad listening habits takes more than willingness and resolve.

So the campaigns to make Americans more aware of how good listening makes for better customer relations and office efficiency give me both pleasure and a touch of indigestion. Pleasure because the efforts should help put many in touch with how listening affects not only professional but personal lives; a touch of indigestion because any one-minute recipe for good communication is bound to fail. And that failure can discourage further attempts to understand and repair chronic communication problems or to add luster to already adequate communication. Not only that, but many attempts at all-out better listening are misguided. Listening to careless, self-absorbed, confused, or selfish talk should be a matter of choice. I might *choose* to give my attention, my allowing, my waiting to someone close whose talk is disordered, overdetailed, or self-concerned due to distress, but I might not choose to listen to someone in the habit of flooding others with trivial and redundant disclosures designed to entertain only themselves. Sometimes "good listening" can be hazardous to your communication health.

When people need to get serious about listening better, superficial solutions aren't the answer. A grown-up effort demands familiarity with turn-taking, wait-times, allowing, interrupting, overtalking, response-rushing—all of those factors we've covered that regulate attention between people. And attention—in the form of slivers of silence, conversational allowing and waiting for others' feelings—is basic for state-of-the-art listening.

I believe that improvement in attention-giving and attention-getting starts after we gain increased awareness of how rushed responses, interruptions, and overtalk contribute to verbal crowding. The improvement usually continues after observing how longer wait-times make others feel more allowed. No gimmicks, no resolutions, no mechanical counting after your talking turns—just trying to stay aware of what's covered in this chapter and trying to observe these elements in conversations for a few days. And, if you're really serious about this vital business of attention, try one or two of the practice routines in chapter 12. The practice routines have been tested for effectiveness and will sharpen your awareness; they'll also probably make you self-conscious for a while (you'll get over it), as well as providing some entertainment. Most important, the methods might change the way you wait for others, which is almost guaranteed to change the way others wait for you.

Note found under a rose on a breakfast tray:

Good morning, Darling,

Thank you for a wonderful and wondrous 25 years. Thanks for letting me confide in you. Thanks for hearing my endless complaints when others tired of listening. Thanks for hearing those harebrained ideas of mine that left others hopelessly confused. Thanks for sitting there silently for reruns of my childhood history and remaining still with a faraway look in your eyes at the eleventh installment of my old war story.

I'm thanking you for 25 years of listening. Even when the world turned its back on my long-winded tales, my feeble jokes, my complicated plans, my amateur psychology, my self-pity, my elaborate confessions, my juvenile poetry, and my armchair philosophizing, you remained loyal, stood beside me, and listened over and over again. You hardly complained. And, thank God, more than a friend and a mate, you were my kids' chauffeur, my therapist, my mother, my sister, my housekeeper, and my buddy—all rolled into one great listener.

So, my dear, remember this: You will *always* be my one and only special listener.

Note found under a tuna sandwich on a luncheon plate:

Good afternoon, Dear,
So, who listened?

PART II

THE INTIMATE SCIENCE: MASTERED

CHAPTER 7

MASTERING
DISCLOSURES

ELLIE WAS an honest-to-goodness, blue-and-gold UCLA cheerleader, with wonderful flying hair and an infectious flash of smile that roused the crowd during basketball games. She was sitting in my office, crying. During my office hours with students, I had heard similar stories time and again: Her boyfriend had left.

There were the usual arguments about trivial things, the string of communication breakdowns—and, finally those awful "silent treatments" where he'd clam up his feelings for weeks. It was puzzling at first, but Ellie was realizing the damage to their relationship was done that night she confessed "everything" about the Bruins ski trip she'd taken two years earlier as a sophomore. Now she had a severe case of "discloser's remorse," a condition caused by premature (or promiscuous) opening of the inner life. "I was a damn fool for telling the truth," she said, "because men are big babies—they can't handle honesty."

The trouble started when her former boyfriend discovered he was getting serious and decided to share his romantic history with Ellie by laying bare the facts of the two "loves" (and four fleeting encounters) of his 22 years.

He revealed all—even the embarrassment at realizing that both of his passionate love affairs were nothing but adolescent infatuations, unlike the "mature" and "committed" involvement he had with Ellie, which was grown-up love by his standards, without the need for games and secrets.

She was touched to tears and remembered every word. He wanted them to "always share everything," "share the beautiful and the ugly," "share their hidden hopes and dreams," and "share their pasts, the good and the bad." Ellie recalled that the "sharing" started immediately as he admitted some "incredibly empty, quick encounters with loose girls, sordid little events." But now he was done "sharing my body with women who give theirs to all kinds of guys." (There wasn't worry about catching some awful disease; this was the pre-AIDS era. His professed allegiance was inspired by romance, not fear.)

Although some of his confessions stung Ellie, it didn't really matter because she'd been taken inside his private world now—a trusted friend. He honored her with his secrets. She loved it and wanted to repay the new trust by trusting him with a similar secret. She wanted to *match* his trust by making herself just as vulnerable with a risky disclosure. She, like him, wanted an *honest* relationship for a change. It would be a rare and beautiful thing—a "completely open togetherness." At first, there was trepidation at telling of her "brief encounters," an uneasy feeling about how he'd take it. She remembered worrying that it wasn't quite the same for women and men; she had a vague feeling she might be more at risk revealing a similar past. Her intuition said, "No, not now—maybe later." Her *heart* said, "Well, maybe just one little confession to get closer. At least undress some slightly shocking secret to match his big revelation." Her *mind* said, "Quit being so scared; he's a modern man, free of that sexist stuff and double standards. Give him what he gave you—the whole story. He can handle it."

A couple of days later, she listened to her mind and confessed some wild times with strangers during that Bruins ski escapade. Two new guys had entered and exited her life in seven fun-filled days. She disclosed all the details at his request, "because he seemed to need a complete picture. . . ."

He grew more quiet as the unexpurgated vision of her adventures on the slopes, in the sauna, by the fireplace, and under the comforter filled his head. During the next week, she had an uneasy feeling that he was a bit more distant, perhaps a shade more formal. Was it just her inexperience at being so emotionally unveiled in front of him that made her imagine him stepping back? Do men take longer to digest such emotional stuff? Could he be secretly upset by her confession?

She was confused but decided to conceal her concerns—an

early breakdown in their "*completely* open togetherness." After a few weeks, she became certain something was wrong. He was hiding his feelings—acting odd. She kept questioning him. He continued to claim everything was okay, but she never disclosed fears about his reaction to her past. They avoided the topic and continued to pretend it didn't matter. At that point, she felt helpless about repairing the rift because she couldn't figure out what was happening. They began telling each other "little white lies." That did it. The relationship never recovered.

And now she was staring me in the eye, asking, *Why?* as I offered her tissues for her tears. I couldn't give her a good answer, although I'd heard similar stories many times. She wanted to know if men and women are really different in the way they handle sexual histories. I had vague recollections of fuzzy studies suggesting males have more difficulty than females with jealousy over their mates' past love lives. I remembered something about how a majority of men couldn't tolerate details of their women's past relationships, while women were able to hear all and forgive much. And, of course, there was the social double standard that ranked indiscriminate sex for men as a necessary evil of growing up but viewed indiscriminate sex for women as self-destructive. That made her wonder if even modern men who give lip service to emancipation still carry double standards in their hearts.

We also talked about how males are more visual, sexually, and Ellie remembered how this guy wanted to know the whole story. "It was like he was putting the pieces of a puzzle together" so he could really know her, she said. "He wanted to know how things looked. He must have been picturing me in bed, embracing one guy after the other. At first I got scared that the images would make him feel that I was with them the same way I am with him. But then I thought how his telling *me* hurt for a while and then turned into okay feelings. And then good ones. So I figured it would be the same with him. He heard about everything. *Boy*, was I dense. Because now, looking back, there was evidence that my one-night stands were affecting him more than his affected me."

Then she had an insight that stuck in my mind. She connected her broken romance to an idea I'd lectured on in class: "Something went terribly wrong with our daydreams about sharing and sharing and sharing every last scrap. We wanted honest-to-God honesty, but we didn't know how to handle it or make it work right. His honesty opened me up—but my honesty closed him tight. Maybe it's not the same for men and women, like you say. If that's so, then maybe like you said in class, there was an imbalance in our disclosing. We never knew to avoid that imbalance. Or to make things better. And it's not knowing that kept us cockeyed and threw us off balance forever.''

THE INTIMACY INDEX

When Ellie said that ''it's not knowing that . . . threw us off balance forever,'' she gave me the boost I needed back then for rethinking my academic ideas on intimacy into a practical form. We ended our discussion by applying some scholarly notions to understanding her broken heart. Using my ''Intimacy Index'' scheme, which was stimulated by social psychology and psycholinguistic research, we began to see how their relationship started, faltered, and died. Weeks later, Ellie and I had coffee, and she was feeling much better. She said our talk started her on a thinking jag that clarified what happened and gave her more confidence in being able to manage future relationships. I was feeling good, too, because she showed me that some abstract notions about human relations could be brought down to earth. Ellie's application of the Intimacy Index to the healing of her broken heart changed my career. I decided to make my work more practical, in this case by working up a rule-of-thumb guide for making some sense of how intimacy comes into—and falls out of—our lives.

The Intimacy Index triangle blends three basic ingredients that can demystify the coming or going of intimacy in any relationship.

- Symmetry
- Self-disclosure
- Empathy

Symmetry refers to the matching of desires that bring people together and the psychological balancing act that maintains intimacy. So it's about similarities that attract and the matching of opposing parts that maintain connections. Think of a good or bad fit between personalities, the interpersonal harmony of a group, an equilibrium of give and take, a common bond or a fragile connection, and you have my notion of symmetry.

Self-disclosure involves the giving or withholding of private experience. In particular, it's about the telling of secrets or the foisting of lies, and all those other ambivalent behaviors attached to psychological vulnerability described in chapter 1.

Empathy is mostly about feeling into another person's experience.

In ongoing relationships, the three parts blend, enhance each other, depend on each other, or weaken each other.

I put symmetry at the triangle's base because it's the cause for connecting. Disclosure usually follows, rising from symmetry's foundation, followed by empathy, which completes the structure. Think of the three sides as representing the behaviors and experiences of people in pairs or small groups—cycling from symmetry to disclosure to empathy. Knowing even a little about how they mingle, for better or worse, is knowing about how intimacy flourishes or perishes.

(I need to make an observation about the common fear of examining intimacy. There's an awful idea prevalent in our culture that when it comes to deep feelings between mates, lovers, friends, family, and colleagues, ignorance is bliss. Obviously, some people overanalyze their relationships, scrutinize every move, spend too many years in therapy, obsess over what to say to him or her. But most people seem to live on the other side of such excess, feeling even moderate analysis could ruin romance, undermine a friendship, weaken family ties, or make a work relationship too manipulative. Figuring out our face-to-face living is entering territory where angels fear to tread, because it can make us self-conscious and awkward. But the self-consciousness usually fades away into a comfortable self-awareness. As with applying any new skill to old customers, things can get a little worse before getting better.)

The first *practical* necessity for getting better at relating to others is for people to let their guards down and become more interested in the process of human connecting and disconnecting. (I'd be happy to see soap opera fanatics spend one-tenth of their fascination on their *own* ways of communicating.)

The common practice of entering, maintaining, and exiting our close relationships on a blindly emotional, haphazard basis is absurd. Sometimes we're scared of ruining spontaneity unless we operate on gut feelings. My argument is that things get better with more cognition—with just a little more of our minds informing our hearts. Maybe just 10 percent more. I'm talking about occasional thoughts about symmetry, self-disclosure, and empathy, some stock-taking that can often be entertaining as well as educational.

The Intimacy Index can help prevent discloser's remorse (as with Ellie)—or its opposite, concealer's regret (for a lost opportunity). So, if you habitually avoid analysis of your interactions in order to preserve the "naturalness," consider the triangle of ingredients in the Index as a simple working scheme for removing a little of the troublesome mystery from your style of getting closer.

Symmetry and Intimacy

Symmetry is especially useful for clarifying what happens when people first connect. It helps make sense of early attraction or dislike. It also brings to light the primitive, unwitting, instinctual, and sometimes embarrassing ways we "attach" to each other.

Interpersonal symmetry between people means a lot more than similarity here. It means a balance of needs, a matching of temperaments (or the attraction of opposites), a good fit between opposing skills, and some evenness in the exchange of psychological resources such as caretaking, giving pleasure, being trustable, or accepting the burden of each other's secrets. Symmetry for the Index, then, is not only a similarity of values or beliefs about existence, politics, art, and the good life but also a harmony of proportion, a kind of equality in the way a pair or a group gives and takes.

For a couple, it's handy to see symmetry as a complementary pair of different yet matched preferences. He likes to get things started and she handles the details. She enjoys his dry-witted slow talk, and he's entertained by her rapid-fire verbal facility. They're symmetrical in wanting different and complementary qualities in each other. They're similar in what they want from the relationship. Couples continually and automatically check out symmetry between themselves. Sometimes coping with the checks and balances encourages spending years—even a lifetime—together.

Put a little too simply, symmetry is a common view of the external world outside the couple and a complementary, balanced pattern of inter-action within the couple. As an ideal image of the way humans attach and relate, it can never be achieved, only approached. Our unwitting, partly instinctual need for symmetry parallels our need for intimacy and love and puts us in a lifelong balancing act called relating to people. In my view, symmetry is the foundation of intimacy. But it can't create a durable relationship without some risky self-disclosure and empathic understanding. The continual, automatic symmetry-check built into us is nature's way of reducing errors of attachment. Still, it's only a partial safeguard, one that we often disregard foolishly as we override danger signals in the search for connection. The temptation to ignore warning signs on one hand, or mistakenly reject promising partners on the other, occurs with awful regularity. Putting a little thought into our emotions can serve to save "the real thing" while braking headlong dashes toward impossible involvements or superficial affairs.

Our automatic symmetry-check comes into play in the first minutes after meeting. The prospect for an encounter or relationship is first judged by context, appearance, and manner of talking. More serious appraisals of romantic potential are usually made after just a few revealing discussions in which couples deliberately, or unwittingly, size each other up for a "good fit" on dimensions of intelligence, sense of humor, honor, courage, kindness, perceptiveness, loyalty, patience, and all sorts of virtues or faults.

The symmetry-check has been a functional rule-of-thumb tool even for those who are limited to brief encounters. A quick symmetry-check comes into play even when a couple's only ground of attachment is impersonal sex. Before the onset of herpes and AIDS, the classical pickup in public places was prevalent. Initial similarities between strangers could be discerned from context clues ranging from the fact that someone is patronizing a singles bar or has chosen to dress in a provocative manner to the ostensible sharing of interests by attending public events (e.g., art shows, yoga classes, dances, exercise clubs).

Most of the signals are first made by the woman. For example, she could "present" herself as a stable target in a public place by just being alone and looking around frequently. Even men who aren't hunting might interpret her isolation, searching eyes, posture, and clothing as irresistible signs of presentation—signs of potential availability. If she responds to a guy's pickup gambit, they're both one step nearer to knowing their desires are matched. The resulting conversation is used variously to confirm their impressions of attraction or to discover some "red flags" for rejection.

Underneath the standard pickup ritual and mutual search for fun, there's an assessment of symmetry—maybe superficial, but still symmetry. And the ritual also serves as an interpersonal device for establishing some sort of subtle sexual contract before going on. She may be sizing him up for safety, or the possibility that they both might want more than one evening. He could be hoping for the opposite: a transition-minded woman who'll allow his expedient getaway without too many awkward moments. Between jokes and feigned aloofness, they may surreptitiously glance at each other's bodies to see if minimal standards of acceptance are met. Her laughter at his jokes and his agreement with her affirmations and stated values are signs of contracting. Their willingness to engage in implicit contracting is another form of similarity. Of course, these elements are rarely overt. The entire ritual is designed to blunt the embarrassment of hard bargaining for a balanced one-night stand. The pretending can also serve to cloak any desperation, fear, or pain in the guise of light-hearted excitement. Typically, both people only have a rough idea of what they're doing and what they want. Empathic understanding is not an issue. Neither is the validity of their self-disclosures. Generosity is matched, but limited to etiquette. Bilateral self-absorption is their common bond (usually unrecognized). Pretending is the common commodity. It allows excitement and novelty to exist undampened by the sometimes brutal paucity of caring. So symmetry alone can take strangers to a one-night stand or a two-week liaison. Empathy and risky disclosure are not needed.

Sometimes symmetry can be sensed by the talk tools used. A person who tends toward the passive may show early signs of receptivity by "pulling" advice from a more aggressive acquaintance. In extreme situations, a very passive person may give helpless signals with "I don't know . . ." "I wonder how I could . . ." "How do you do this? . . ." These questions draw advisements and show a willingness to follow guidance—to comply. They may display a will that can be bent and taken. Such a person might be attracted to an aggressive, take-charge, advice-giving, interpreting, even dominant personality. It happened often in old-time movies that caricatured breathy, helpless, advice-seeking, Southern leisure-class women submitting to those gallant, commanding, strutting males. (The complementarity of sex roles was a major theme in the work of Tennessee Williams.) Symmetry of that sort is rare today. But vivid images of the good fit between male and female stereotypes of that time serve to illustrate how communication style can quickly tell two people if they're a possible match.

Sometimes that early sense of symmetry is called "love at first sight." A lucky couple could parlay that into a lasting love, if the early symmetry served as a springboard for some durable disclosing and empathic understanding.

Strangers who are superficially attracted, or couples in an early state of infatuation, may even need to *create* some symmetry by trying to fit each other's interests, attitudes, and beliefs. She may learn the rules of football and watch games with him. She loves her meditation, so he tries it. When the strain toward symmetry gets out of hand and overrides complementarity, it produces those cloned couples who seem to think, act, feel, and dress alike.

A good illustration of how symmetry creates romantic attraction comes from cheerleader Ellie describing the start of her ill-fated relationship. She met her ex-boyfriend during a break in a comparative religions class at UCLA and discovered he was also from a strict Protestant home. Then they discovered their common bond of being soul-searchers in the area of religious commitment. I suppose a fair number of college students who elect comparative religion courses are soul-searching, and maybe many are Protestant, but even such expected similarities are usually enough to stir mutual interest. Ellie would be classified as particularly attractive by impartial observers, and she described her one-time boyfriend as "looking like Paul McCartney with big biceps." Thus it seems they were both physically attractive, soul-searching, Protestant students taking the same course—easily enough similarity for agreeing to a cup of coffee's worth of conversation.

Scanning her memory, Ellie searched for and found points of common ground that most new couples connect on—liking the same movies, books, campus events, music, food, travel, ideas, political prejudices, basketball, and "unbelievably, we hardly ever missed a Sunday watching '60 Minutes.' "

Some couples actually go through a sort of verbal search, looking for some odd point of similarity as confirmation of their special connection. (A couple I know delights in the fact that they independently discovered and loved an English peppermint called Altoids.) Big things like religious development, world view, and ethical position can bring people together at first—but so can small things like popping an Altoid in public places. Common ground on some sublime or ridiculous matter can create a link that provokes acquaintance. Then there is the similarity in what both want out of their connection. For Ellie and her ex, there was agreement that couples should be totally open at all times, strictly equal in every way, super-monogamous in thought and deed, well-groomed, and always earnestly respectful to each other. (In reviewing her relationship, we were amused at her unrealistic set of expectations but knew they were a standard condition of young love.)

Even older, more mature people make critical mistakes repeatedly because they lack the tools for thinking about the management of intimacy. (Management sounds so *efficient* next to intimacy, but it's better than the all-too-frequent mismanagement or, sometimes, myth-management.) So Ellie's ruined romance would have been hard to avoid without something like the Intimacy Index at hand. Even then, she might have overlooked the hazards because the relationship was so exciting for her. They had a strong common bond made of similar religious beliefs and struggles; their tastes, values, and aspirations were so alike. Their separate dreams of marriage were marvelously symmetrical. They even had a complementary balance of interpersonal styles. She was outgoing, while he was a bit shy. The contrast was obvious to them and to friends, who joked that their match was made in heaven. During those first few months, it felt so right that she was sure they'd lucked out and would be together for the rest of their lives. If I had been there to view all that good symmetry, I would have had high hopes, too—but symmetry in itself isn't enough.

Self-Disclosure and Intimacy

Symmetry can initiate and even propel a relationship out of first gear, but a pair cannot attain even moderate intimacy without some risky disclosing. The popular meaning of intimacy is so linked with "sharing secrets," "being private together," "letting it all hang out," and "opening up" that for some people risky disclosing *is* intimacy. I like to think of self-disclosure as the vital second element—the second gear in the acceleration of intimacy. It's an element that looks for balance. If one member of a pair or a group consistently accelerates faster, the intimacy is jeopardized. Unilateral disclosure will create a one-way intimacy, which is no intimacy at all in social relations. In nonprofessional close relationships, when only one person is vulnerable to the other over an extended period, the relationship loses its balance of power, its equality of access. The symmetry that gives intimacy its start must extend into the giving and taking of openness. If not, the human connection becomes unstable. Access to each other's inner lives is not only a matter of fairness, it's a psychological necessity for successful couples, families, and intimate assemblages such as self-help groups.

Intimacy shrinks when there's a prolonged imbalance in emotional risk-taking. It also shrinks when there's an imbalance in who carries the psychological burden of the other's disclosed secret. "Burden" refers to carrying the psychological weight of hearing what has been disclosed. It's just the opposite of disregarding the other's experience or making some of it disappear from mind. Accepting the burden of the other's secret and all its uncomfortable consequences can bring people together fast. When there's a sense of potential balance, the expectation is that the discloser would reciprocate. Such acceptance might mean hearing without judging (Ellie could have used some of that), or immediately disclosing in return any discomfort (she could have used that, too), or even some empathy. The key here is that there is a long-term equilibrium in the way each takes on the full impact of each other's serious disclosures with honesty. It's hard to do. It's hard to shoulder big secrets without distorting or rejecting them.

The character of Edwina (from *All of Me*, in chapter 1), for example, is brutally honest in explaining why no one showed up at her funeral: "I don't have any friends." Instead of watering down her blunt confessions with some vapid balm, like "Lots of people don't have friends," her listener takes it in, accepts the depressing burden as she documents the painful details. Some risky disclosures may change our entire conception of the discloser's personality or force a different reality on us that's hard to digest quickly. Ellie's ex-boyfriend may have been overwhelmed by her disclosures. His burden probably felt heavier than hers, and the imbalance killed their relationship. The point is, intimacy not only needs symmetry in emotional risk-taking but in carrying the uncomfortable burden dumped on us by a partner's heavy secrets.

Opening up to each other and then absorbing what was heard is an ongoing balancing act we all do. (I'll illustrate that with dialogue later.) Disclosures tend to get matched—in couples and groups. The same is true for accepting the burden of disclosures—people usually want to carry their fair share of the load. Most adults intuit the need for symmetry of disclosure. Those who don't end up without intimacy.

Empathy and Intimacy

Empathy, the third side of the Intimacy Index triangle, feeds on self-disclosure. Risky disclosures can bring empathic understanding. Since being well understood creates psychological safety for vulnerable feelings, empathy for minor confessions usually invites more risky disclosures. The new, private information unearthed by risky disclosures allows greater opportunity for seeing and confirming new similarities, new connections between people. Empathy is a critical link between symmetry and disclosure. If it's felt but not clearly communicated, trouble will come. If the communication of empathy diminishes in just one person, it can reduce the safety in self-disclosing and increase vulnerability, starting a chain of breakdowns in a couple (or in an entire intimate group).

Some of my social psychology colleagues might want me to make the three-sided Index more complex, but experience teaching the Index tells me it can go a long way toward helping people figure out their interpersonal strengths and weaknesses. I've watched people find ways of repairing damaged intimacy, understand their own style of becoming close, make better sense of what went wrong, make plans for doing it better next time, and just enjoy more about knowing how their successful relationships work. It also helps with seeing problems and strengthening parent/child relationships, friendships, and important job relationships.

That afternoon in my office, the Intimacy Index helped Ellie organize her bewilderment. She was already halfway there—she had already observed that the secrets she and her boyfriend traded seemed alike but were actually very different and that this difference ultimately upset the relationship's symmetry. Her warmly intentioned mismanagement of disclosing disturbed the delicate balancing act required for the growth of intimacy. Maybe "mismanagement" is excessive; after all, it's so easy to over-disclose or underdisclose and mess up the blending of hearts, minds, and bodies. In fact, I suspect disclosure disasters help account for much of the bad success-to-failure ratio in building relationships.

Empathy disasters—when empathy is weak, absent, or isn't *expressed* in reflections—also contribute to the failure of relationships. Malfunctions in empathy and disclosure elements of the Index are *the* major causes for couples breaking up. Disclosure and empathy screwups are often the unrecognized villains behind the naive explanation: "We just didn't have the right chemistry."

Using the Intimacy Index, Ellie figured out that her disclosure disaster created a situation in which her boyfriend wasn't able to empathize. She blamed herself for not listening to her intuition that wanted to conceal, or maybe reveal just a little. Why didn't she put two and two together after he referred to his brief encounters as "sordid" little affairs? Why couldn't she see that he might regard her as a loose woman? She believed it was her "too much, too soon" disclosure that started the whole mess. Then she blamed him, because now she was sure he was so profoundly upset by her vivid disclosure that it caused him to shut up while denying anything was wrong. He lied. And his failure to disclose made it impossible to fix the disconnection; the relationship veered into imbalance. He couldn't carry the heavy burden of her disclosure without judging. A lack of symmetry of openness or understanding on this critical matter left them without symmetry of purpose. As their disclosure/empathy/symmetry cycle deteriorated, so did their intimacy.

Disclosing Sexual Pasts

A key cause of the breakup of Ellie and her ex was his discomfort at handling the psychological burden of her disclosed sexual past. Her discomfort at hearing *his* past did not seem as severe. The large difference in how the burden was accepted worked as a wedge to separate them. He seemed so hurt by her brief, indiscriminate escapades. Maybe he was ashamed at reacting so much more strongly than she did and was confused by the entire event. Maybe he wanted to talk about it but didn't know how. The misery rendered him unable to value the gift of her honesty. They were out of balance and didn't discuss the terrible tilt in their relationship. She was scared and couldn't help because of his concealment. He couldn't empathize with her fear or disclose his confusion. They were disconnected. And it all started with an imbalance in his ability to accept the weight of her secrets.

If their mutual disclosures were about some other area besides sexual history—if it were about an alcohol problem, gambling, bouts of depression—their relationship might have remained intact. But sexual self-disclosure is a notorious troublemaker because it impacts differently on men than on women. Such self-disclosures, or the lack of them, tend to be of huge importance to romantic couples. Some people are fervent about never telling anything about their pasts because "what they don't know won't hurt them." Some argue that maintaining such lies drains energy off intimacy, but my guess is that most people would opt not to disclose. I believe most feel that telling the truth is more dangerous than lying or agreeing to protect each other from the difficult truths. Obviously, both men and women are pained at the reality of their nonexclusivity, but women tend to believe that men can't handle it at all, especially when it comes to infidelity. This popular psychology is evidenced by the advice columnists and influential media psychologists who endorse keeping men in the dark on this issue. In *What Every Woman Should Know about Men*, for example, Dr. Joyce Brothers concludes that it's best to conceal: "If a woman is unfaithful, it's wiser and kinder not to let her husband know. He may not be able to handle it."

I don't agree that it's usually wiser to conceal. The white lie is rarely the benevolent verbal instrument we want it to be; it's often self-serving and manipulative instead of generous, and it eventually peeks through the curtain of concealment. Even at that, Dr. Brother's colorful description of gender differences in disclosing sexual history does have the ring of truth: "After the initial shock, a woman usually comes to terms with her husband's infidelity. She does not like it, but there it is. It happened. In time, she forgives, although she may never be able to forget. But let a woman be unfaithful and watch her husband's righteous indignation, his angry outrage, his horror."

Understanding these differences has practical importance for keeping relationships healthy. It's hard to keep a fair balance of disclosure without some idea why men are so confused and have trouble absorbing the truth about their women's other lovers. The pain of hearing about old lovers sometimes rivals the jealousy over recent lovers. I have some ideas collected over the years from the experiences of my male therapy patients, along with a group of ten men in a workshop who happened to be in relationships where their women disclosed substantial portions of their sexual histories. I'd disclaim that these collected experiences comprise a sample worthy of serious generalization. But the two dozen men reported some strikingly similar experiences that bring me to some intriguing hypotheses about why men seem to struggle so much more in facing the reality of their mates' pasts. Maybe my hunches can serve the thinking of men who are ambivalent about knowing, women who are ambivalent about disclosing, or couples now coping with the long-term residuals from *her* telling the whole truth—or even a potent part of it.

Less than a quarter of the men I've worked with in therapy brought up issues of jealousy. When they did, the most pain was created by the image of her "giving" herself, "allowing" herself to be used, submitting herself to another's selfish lust, "melting" for a stranger's come-on, and "yielding" to his advances. Imagining the woman as giving up so much control to another man sometimes caused outright anguish. The image could be almost unbearable. Even when the women was described as the initiator, the seeker of a liaison, my patients continued to see her as the docile one, the sexually accepting one, the succumbing one. And the man she succumbed to was rarely judged good enough or respectful enough for her. Oftentimes, the other men were seen as careless, exploiting, demeaning. So, to simplify a bit, it appeared that the women were seen as succumbing to an exploiting other man who asserted himself on her. It was the classical image of the sexually aggressive male selfishly sweeping a succumbing woman off her feet. Not an easy way for a man to visualize his beloved mate—especially if he ever bragged to his buddies about his sexual conquests or heard other men demean women as notches on their belt.

Please hold that idea as I describe what I learned from the ten men at the workshop. They were part of a larger group of mental health professionals attending a weekend on self-disclosure that I did with my friend, the late Sidney Jourard (the nation's major self-disclosure theorist). The men volunteered to break away for two hours and explore gender differences in accepting the burden of sexual secrets. All of them had heard such disclosures from women close to them. We went around the group describing the impact. Just like my patients, these professionals tended to view their woman as deferring, succumbing, surrendering, abandoning her body (at least), and maybe her will, to an assertive man who wasn't worthy of her. I told them what I learned from my patients, suggested that many modern women don't see themselves as "taken" or "succumbing," presented some conceptual tools, and asked them to help me organize some hunches about why women's sexual pasts cause men so much grief. There was talk about women being the stronger sex in handling *psychological* discomfort. And about women having perhaps a greater capacity for abandoning themselves to lust in the context of love. Then I asked if the men actually visualized their women in the sexual activity revealed to them. Did they create pictures in their minds? To some degree, *every* man saw his woman in a sexual embrace with "that worthless scoundrel," as one guy only half-jokingly described it.

That concordance surprised me, and the surprise enlarged a month later when, in response to my query, over 30 of my undergraduate women students anonymously said in writing that they tended *not* to visualize their boyfriends' sexual embraces with old girlfriends. (About one in ten reported visualizing, picturing, imagining details.) If it's true that men run movies in their minds of such scenes much more than women, we have one clue why they're hit harder by unveiled sexual secrets: Their sexual imaging is simply more vivid, more impactful. The discovery of a common tendency toward being sexually visual set the ten men to thinking about other male-specific traits that made their burden of acceptance heavier than the women's. What they came up with during the next 90 minutes may be a fair composite of how sophisticated men think (when pushed) about gender differences and managing their partners' disclosures. A summary of their thoughts:

Most men, by nature or nurture, feel like hunters, wanting to "conquer" a woman, sweep over her, take her in ways somewhat reminiscent of how other male mammals "take" or aggress or capture the interests or wills of female mammals. Women are the opposite in feeling like "an attraction," a "walking aphrodisiac" to males. They essentially want to be swept away, to be prized by the right guy. They want to succumb to the experience created when connected to the right man who really cares.

At some level, both sexes intuitively know the above is true.

That means women might think of their men capturing the wills of other women. That's easier to live with than men actually visualizing their women being captured, which means relinquishing not only their bodies but their wills. It's easier for women to imagine a partner helping melt someone else's will than for men to imagine a partner succumbing to someone else.

I believe the thoughts of the ten men reflect some true gender differences. If the truth were known, it would surely show a more complex picture of gender differences reflecting the greater importance of affection and love in sex for women. Men may bring their self-esteem into sex more, as well as the need for control. Chances are, they may also bring their overdeveloped fear of succumbing and the standard list of mischievous, manly, and machismo virtues into intimacy. Someday the research of social and developmental psychologists may give us a practical picture of the range of differences between the way men and women handle the knowledge of each other's past intimacies. Right now, it seems useful to regard the man as more visual, more pained at the woman's surrender, and possibly more disparaging of her past lovers. So when Dr. Joyce Brothers implies that we guys just can't handle the *same* kind of disclosure, she's being unfair. It's *not* the same—because men see their special companion succumbing to a sexually dominant person, and what's worse is that they probably see it vividly. That doesn't necessarily mean that disclosing to us means big, long-lasting destructive trouble. It means that women ought to slowly test the reception before overloading a man with images that bewilder, hurt, and make him feel guilty because he can't accept what a woman can. It may be useful to try a *general* talk or two about the differences between the way men and women attach before even considering minor disclosures. A solid sense of each other's attitudes can be achieved by asking each to imagine the other in sexual intimacy with another. That could show if one or both prefer concealment because disclosure seems unbearable or too emotionally costly, as in: ''What's past is past and should be forgotten.'' ''Let sleeping dogs lie.'' ''I don't care and don't wanna know what she did before she met me.''

On the other hand, it's quite clear that knowing *can* be tolerated, disclosure *can* be rewarding. Opening up often brings deeper connections. That principle is broadly true for so many secrets between couples. The big exception is with sexual pasts. If you think the risk is worth the reward in your relationship, I urge you to go slow in your testing. A miscalculation could create an imbalance and ruin a relationship—like it did for Ellie.

The reveal/conceal ordeal is among the costliest conflicts in human relations. Most of the time, the solution simply involves learning how and when to move toward the reveal side.

MANAGING DISCLOSURES

Whether it be sexual pasts or minor broken promises, the balancing act of managing self-disclosure is a daily activity for all of us. Some people become very stressed-out from needing to regulate what to reveal or conceal with many people on many topics. The practical task of regulating disclosure is limited not just to our own opening and closing; it also involves what we want from others. Knowing something about how it all works can reduce problems and allow more control of the interpersonal environment. We really do walk around wishing for changes in our own or others' disclosures. Young men and women like Ellie want to disclose enough to be close, but not enough to lose their lovers and friends—discloser's remorse. And parents want their young kids to disclose more about school, their adolescent children to disclose more about their aspirations and dates, and their grown-up offspring to say frankly what's in their hearts.

Shy people want to disclose a little bit more with a lot more comfort. Men and women who habitually cannot get romantic relationships out of first gear would surely like to learn more about how disclosure works. Almost everyone wants to shut down the endless flooded disclosing of those lonely, disconnected "compulsive" talkers. And the best known, most popular cliche about disclosure reform is heard in the woman's complaint that her man "should open up more"—be more expressive about romantic feelings.

Even beyond romance, men could use lessons in making a few more minor disclosures that could prevent major communication maladies. I've got a story that should persuade the strong, silent types to do some more revealing for the sake of their women and kids. It's a down-to-earth demonstration of how *under*disclosing can create unnecessary stress and mental heath problems. Disclosing too little in close relations or maintaining heavy secrets over the years dilutes intimacy—which dilutes our mental healthiness.

Among the considerable recent research linking patterns of

underdisclosing to stress-induced physical and mental problems, the work of psychologist James Pennebaker (Southern Methodist University) shows the danger clearly. In a series of studies, he found that widows had more illness if they underdisclosed their grief to others; wido*wers* suffered even more illness because they underdisclosed more; widowers who remarried and thought they shouldn't talk about their previous wife to their new spouse underdisclosed the most and had the most disease; people who were repeatedly induced to disclose their serious emotional upsets showed drops in blood pressure and anxiety and made fewer visits to their physicians.

In another study, immunologist Janice Kiecolt Glaser (Ohio State University) observed that disclosing stressful memories at length brought a healthy increase in people's immune system activity for six weeks afterward. These facts about the way we talk can be hard to believe, since the cause and effect between concealment and the cost to health is usually separated by months and sometimes years. The connection between a habit of underdisclosing and mental health is rarely obvious, but a growing body of research provides evidence that habitual concealment can create grave, long-term consequences. I want to make that fact vivid by showing a real-life example of how the impulse to conceal can weaken intimacy. As you read the story that follows, please consider using it as a practical device, a demonstration that can be read by someone who prefers a stingy communication style. If someone close to you is a resolute underdiscloser, this story might start to soften a hard attitude.

The Closed-Mouth Spouse

Allan resents anyone thinking he became an orthodontist just to make money. His wife, Michelle, a department store buyer, claims that anyone watching her husband work with children or listening to his private thoughts on inexpensive ways to help low-income kids feel better about themselves through simplified orthodontia would know he's driven by a grand affection for children. That affection was apparent in the emotionally charged way he told me of an unfortunate incident between him and his son. It was difficult for him to talk about his failure to disclose because Allan believes that most people "talk too damn much, for their own sake, just to hear themselves."

As a farm boy in Pennsylvania, Allan grew up seen and not

heard and fiercely believes in looking carefully before he leaps into talk. He communicates lovingly with his children patients through pantomime much of the time. He said, "Kids can't talk much in my chair because they're scared and their mouths are filled with fingers and drills. They gesture and make faces. So it only seems fair I do the same." (I'd say he's practicing some effective interpersonal symmetry.) With his help, I've put his story into a dramatized format that allows me to highlight some issues.

Allan is having a fitful sleep. His wife, Michelle, has been jostled to wakefulness and turns on the light.

MICHELLE: Allan, Allan—please get up. I can't sleep with your tossing and grunting. (*Allan grunts and finally sits up, half-asleep*) You've been thrashing a lot, and you know why. So let's talk about it. (*Allan grunts*) Come on.

ALLAN: Whattaya *want* from me. I'm still asleep. (*Long pause*) Look, we've already talked.

MICHELLE: That wasn't talk, that was shouting.

ALLAN: (*With weary resignation*) Oh, God—so *talk*.

MICHELLE: I just don't understand why you didn't care about my promotion. I mean, I come home with this great news, and you act like it was *nothing*.

ALLAN: I did care—uh, I *do* care.

MICHELLE: Oh, do you? Do you really care about *my* work? (*Sarcastically*) The "little woman's" work?

ALLAN: Don't pull that feminist crap on me! You know damn well—

MICHELLE: (*Interrupting*) Okay, okay. That's true. But why didn't you care?

ALLAN: For God's sake, I told you I do—ah-h-h, hell. Please stop. I need some peace—some sleep for tomorrow. Have pity and stop *grilling* me.

MICHELLE: Grilling you! Grilling? The poor mute little man can't stand a simple question about feelings? (*Fuming, she jumps out of bed and stomps out of the room, pillow in hand, aiming to sleep on the couch*)

A simple communication breakdown caused by a delayed disclosure is at the root of the trouble between Michelle and Allan. It involves their six-year-old son, Eric. We're going back to the situation several hours earlier to see how it all started.

Allan is tussling with Eric on the living room floor, play-wrestling. There's laughter as they partake in the familiar routine where Allan pretends mightily to pin his wiry boy, only to lose like a surprised giant in defeat to a mere child.

ALLAN: *(Puffing in exaggeration)* You little twerp—Godzilla knows what to do with pushy little kids like Eric.

ERIC: *(Giggling)* Oh-h-h, no-o-o!

They play-wrestle a while, roughhousing with Allan's mock sounds of effort and the boy's furiously wild struggle. Eric frees himself with delight and throws himself violently toward his father's chest, but carelessly crashes the back of his head into his father's lips—hard.

ALLAN: *Ow-w-w-w*—jeez, damn it!

Without thinking, reacting reflexively to the pain with the flash of anger, Allan raps the boy's head with his knuckles. The automatic hit is harder than intended. Eric and his father both freeze in shock. They stare at each other for a moment as Eric's eyes begin to moisten. One tear rolls down his cheek as he turns and, tight-lipped and with deliberation, walks away—stopping to stare at his father one more time before leaving the room.

Allan will never forget the strange, almost adult expression on his boy's slightly wet face as he stopped to stare. Allan's intense love for his only child, his sensitivity about needing to tame children as a dentist, and his vow to never spank his boy, even lightly, for punishment came to this moment and made it bitterly painful. He was ashamed. Mortified. He heard Eric's bedroom door slam and felt that even a sincere apology couldn't wipe out this ugly, impulsive strike. The poor guy told me he was practically paralyzed with regret. He sat motionless in a chair for 15 minutes before Michelle came home from her job, bounding into the bedroom in a burst of joyful energy. Michelle reached over the chair and mussed his hair, with exclamations about how good it was to be alive. That brought him halfway out of his reverie. Being accustomed to his quiet ways, outgoing Michelle thought nothing of his silence. The scenario played out like this.

MICHELLE: Babe, I *got* it!

ALLAN: Uh huh . . . Got what?

MICHELLE: The promotion! I got it! It came through!

ALLAN: Oh, that's good, Michelle—very good.

MICHELLE: Wait till you hear about the money. The raise is even bigger than I thought. Isn't that wonderful? *(She's practically floating off the floor)*

ALLAN: Yeah. Wonderful.

MICHELLE: *(Now noticing he's even more subdued than usual)* Hello? Someone home in there? Are you feeling okay? *(Allan looks like he's on another planet—or would like to be)* Anything wrong? Got a headache?

ALLAN: Um-m-m, no . . . I'm okay."

MICHELLE: Deep in thought?

ALLAN: Uh huh.

MICHELLE: Well, come on out of the think tank for a minute and give your old lady a hug.

He lies and she believes him. Telling the truth about not being okay would surely draw further questions and cause Allan to self-disclose when he wants to remain silent and ruminate. So the little lie creates the little secret that protects Allan from the discomfort of disclosing at the moment. A common pattern. Also an interpersonal error. I'm not sure why so many of us lie instead of simply telling others we need time to back off before disclosing some trouble. Disclosing on the double can mean disclosing that you're not ready to disclose. The problem with Allan's "little" lie is that it cuts off Michelle's empathic understanding at the pass—misleading her into behavior that can crash into his mood, eventually making her feel "manipulated" when the truth comes out, and contributes a bit to her future sense of doubt when Allan claims "no problem." Failure to disclose creates an imbalance in their interpersonal symmetry. It interrupts the flow of their disclosure/empathy/symmetry cycle. Frequent interruptions of the cycle will erode intimacy. These minor breakdowns in disclosure will sabotage the empathic process and, if done consistently, reduce symmetry to such a low point that it can serious affect the quality of life for a couple or social group. I've witnessed such breakdowns vividly in my study of self-help group audiotapes. Failure to disclose important immediate experiences invariably leads to frustrations, costly misunderstandings, and "off-track" discussions that drain the groups' energies and effectiveness. Underdisclosing is used as self-protection but ends up causing more trouble than it saves. Allan will pay *his* price for underdisclosing as Michelle strains and fails to open a communication channel.

Michelle, in the wake of his life, sits on his lap and hugs him tightly. But he's still feeling the ache of Eric's stare.

MICHELLE: (*Still hugging*) It's been 18 months of hard work and I had to beat out five good people. I still can't believe it. (*Allan continues to ruminate; Michelle stands up and begins to heedlessly waltz around the room in excitement*)

MICHELLE: (*Happily chanting*) I did it, I did it, I did it. . . . Come on, Allan, I'm getting lonesome dancing by myself. Please get out of your brain and into my good fortune. I got the *promotion!*

ALLAN: (*Absent-mindedly*) Yeah . . .

MICHELLE: (*Dancing in earnest now*) One . . . two . . . I'll give you ten seconds—three . . . four . . . five . . . six . . . seven . . . eight . . . (*She dances by Allan and playfully tousles his hair; he pulls his head away, and she stops dancing; in her familiar role as outgoing agitator, complementing his sometimes reticent flatness, Michelle laughingly grabs both his hands and starts to pull him up*)

ALLAN: Can't you see I don't *feel* like it? Quit screwing around, Michelle.

[He'd prefer more empathic understanding, some "sensitivity," even though he refused to disclose his unhappiness. The lie about feeling okay meant to save trouble will now *give* trouble.]

MICHELLE: Can you believe this? Thanks for sharing my victory, *partner.* (*She wheels and starts to leave the room, turns back for a second*) Thanks a *lot.*

She exits. Allan slumps back into his chair, feeling even worse now that he's alienated his wife. He stares at his knuckles, pounding them into his open hand, and feels a tear tickle his cheek as he thinks of Eric's tear. The man is temporarily disconnected from his wife and son. When Michelle asked Allan if anything was wrong, he was feeling too disgusted and confused to respond. He asks himself why—why did all this happen? Was he just exhausted and without patience for Eric's wild playful fury? He *did* warn Eric in previous tussles several times not to get out of control while they roughhoused, but why did he strike back? Was it a commonplace reflex that many parents had? Was it because his father spanked him? Was this the way child abuse starts? But that could never be for him—he could never justify hitting someone so small. Allan wanted to make sense out of it, like he and Michelle often did when potential trouble arose. Instead though, he succumbed to another reflex—clamming up. Being mute is his instinctive way of dealing with emotional overload: feelings of love, anger, confusion, even pride—but especially shame.

"When in Trouble, Disclose on the Double"

Allan *did* have options that could have made a big difference. I've rewritten the scene in a way that allows Allan to use one of those options. He's going to use a critical principle when facing sudden distress with someone close: "When in trouble, disclose on the double."

My rewrite starts where Michelle bursts into the room while Allan is numbly staring into space. She tells him about the promotion, he acknowledges it absent-mindedly. What changes is his response when she notices that he's even more subdued than usual and says: "Hello? Someone home in there? Are you feeling okay?" The first choices to go through his mind are: (1) lie to her and say he's okay, then feel even more rotten at having deceived her; (2) tell her what happened and get into an immediate, overblown discussion about it. Miserable choices. He's in trouble. The first thing he needs to do is recognize his predicament and do something about it. So when she asks whether he feels okay, I want him answering something like this:

ALLAN: Uh, well, actually, I'm *not* okay.

[Now he's using the first half of my guideline—"When in trouble . . ."]

MICHELLE: *(Concerned)* What's wrong, Allan?

ALLAN: I'm feeling rotten about rapping Eric on the head—

MICHELLE: *(Interrupting)* Huh?

ALLAN: —while we were wrestling.

[Allan delivers the second half—". . . disclose on the double." At this point I'd have Michelle show some simple compassion, some loving empathy.]

MICHELLE: Oh, my. I can imagine you feeling rotten. Especially you.

[Allan is experiencing a touch of comfort, and perhaps relief, from her understanding.]

ALLAN: You know, the way that kid looked at me afterward killed me. He wasn't really crying—sorta proud and betrayed. Besides the pain on his head, he had pain from me breaking my solemn promise to never ever hit him in anger or for punishment. Aw, damn it, Michelle, he's been so proud telling everyone that his dad would never hit *him* for anything, *never*. You know, more than anyone. *(She nods in empathy)* I've been sitting here, disgusted at myself.

As the scene continues, I imagine Michelle putting her hand on his and saying something caring. It needn't be a gorgeous reflection that gives profound emotional company. I don't see her giving a terrific me-too disclosure that quickly gets into his heart and melts much of his misery. All that I want is for her to stay away from any instant advice, hotshot interpretations, or distracting questions. Maybe a simple disclosure of worry: "Allan, you love him so much, I'm afraid you'll overdo it." Or an expression of empathy: "Oh, Allan, seeing that little betrayed face must have really hurt." Any ordinary, compassionate response would do to illustrate that his disclosing on the double could bring *some* instant relief by showing caring. The scene could conclude by both of them going to Eric's room and having a long talk. Allan, after receiving some forgiveness might even forgive himself and give some attention to Michelle's promotion.

Even without such a fine happy ending, disclosing on the double has a high probability for making things at least a little better when emotional overload clogs the connection between mates or close friends. Allan's story is meant for underdisclosers—people who disclose too late or too little for their own good. They wait so long that either the undisclosed fact or feeling causes irreparable mischief, or the incomplete information and the partial picture distort meaning and create a misunderstanding. Sure, *over*disclosing causes many problems in relationships, too—by boring or by making all sorts of demands on the listeners' empathy, time, and patience. But I'm convinced that underdisclosing is by far the most prevalent troublemaker for two-person relationships and small groups, including families and support groups. We simply don't tell enough, fast enough, either out of habit or because we're scared the truth will be too costly. That may be true for disclosing our sexual histories to a sexual partner, but it hardly fits any other area of human conduct. The irony here is that we keep secrets and tell lies to protect our vulnerability and preserve intimacy, yet the long-term effect is usually an increase in vulnerability and the deterioration of intimacy. Too often, long-term concealment makes the other person feel duped, disrespected, and disenfranchised.

Of course, the issue of when and how much to disclose depends on each situation. It can get complicated, but I'm afraid our habits move us most toward unnecessary concealment. We tell self-serving lies in the name of serving others. We fail to disclose because of potential embarrassment. We habitually lapse into silences that fit some "role" as unimpeachable boss, selfless parent, discriminating woman, strong man, or independent child. Sometimes it's simply a matter of laziness, lack of social skills, or the ongoing national illiteracy in the area of face-to-face talk. Allan told me that his thought in this area was so limited that all he could think of was to make an apology to Eric later when the embarrassment subsided. He was part of a majority, including intelligent, caring, curious people who haven't had the opportunities to learn talk skills that provide freedom to have communication options. Even Allan, a bright, well-read, extremely paternal man who devours psychology books looked at me in disbelief as I described other choices he had to help his son, his wife, and *himself* achieve a wholesome resolution. Those choices about *when* and *how much* to disclose are somewhat cryptically packed into my hokey but often valid maxim: "When in trouble, disclose on the double." It's an admittedly crass attention-getting device, but it's easy to remember and it's amply endorsed by hundreds of users. To expand:

"Trouble" here means interpersonal trouble with people who care. Allan's distress and mortification are good examples of that. The maxim is *not* applicable to interpersonal problems with strangers or enemies. So a more compulsive version, perhaps done by a committee, would start: "When in trouble with someone who's essentially trusted and caring . . ."

The practical guidance in this is to grow more aware about the times you're in minor or major interpersonal talk trouble. Often we sense it in our tension levels, but it's so easy to turn off our biofeedback, override the discomfort, and deny trouble even exists. My hope is to demonstrate that solutions to talk trouble are easier to execute than paying the price of disregarding the problem.

"On the double" uses an old military term referring to a rapid, double-time marching pace. I mean it as a reminder to self-disclose at the first opportunity that allows decent communication—before concealment compounds the problem.

Here-'n'-Nows to the Rescue

"On the double" also means opening up immediately when possible—*here and now*. For instance, "Eric, the way you looked at me just now made me regret what I did." Or, "Telling you about this is making me feel awkward." Unmasking without delay builds trust. Disclosures about disclosures are great ways to untangle trouble with minimal mess: "I'm feeling so rotten about rapping Eric on the head that talking about it now is hard.''

These immediate, ''on the double'' messages fall into a category of talk tools that I call ''here-'n'-now'' disclosures. They're on-the-spot private reports that occur instantly in mid-conversation between two people or within small groups. Sometimes they're spoken spontaneously without much forethought: ''Did you get my point?'' ''This isn't coming out right—let me say it better.''

Here-'n'-nows can also be deliberate, thought-out messages about what's occurring at the moment: ''I was worried about us getting into another argument today, and it seems to be happening now, so can we get some coffee and cool down?'' ''Oh, don't mind me—I just get a little embarrassed when you talk that way. It'll pass in a minute.''

Whether spontaneous or thought out, the prime characteristic of here-'n'-nows is their way of immediately disclosing a current thought or feeling. What you experience *now* is what they get. If what you experience now happens to be a long-forgotten event, the here-'n'-now disclosure would describe the event along with the fact that it was just recalled: ''I haven't thought about it in years, but I just remembered . . .''

Frequently, here-'n'-nows disclose something about the conversation at hand: ''The way you're going on about cream soda made me think back to the first time I tasted it.''

So here-'n'-nows often refer to something just said or about to be said. They often talk about talk: ''You're not gonna believe this, but . . .'' ''Wait a second—I've got one more thing to say!''

And sometimes here-'n'-nows talk about nonverbal communication: ''The way you looked at me just then . . .''

Here-'n'-nows are instant windows to the mind's personal moments. They can bring fresh immediacy to a stale conversation. The immediacy comes from refocusing the listener's attention from an ongoing topic to some aspect of the immediate relationship between the talkers—a misunderstanding, embarrassment, or momentary emotion about what was said or heard. They sort of say, ''This is how I see you and me talking to each other.''

After hearing about disclosing on the double with here-'n'-nows, Allan and I discussed the alternatives to merely apologizing to Eric later, when the mood allowed. Allan's eyes widened as he examined the unused option of walking to Eric's room in the middle of his stunned confusion and telling the boy the truth and nothing but the truth. Allan wondered at first if harm wouldn't come from telling Eric as quickly as that—after all, Eric would then witness his father's confusion, remorse, and self-criticism. After serious thought, he concluded the only possible harm was to his own manly vanity. In fact, it would be much more "cleansing," Allan thought, than a semiformal apology. So why did he limit himself? Why did he fail to give his son the truth? Was he concerned about his six-year-old seeing a bewildered, contrite, imperfect father? Yes. And, in retrospect, he was angry with himself. Like some vestige of the unflinching, powerful, confident adult male warrior-mammal who makes no mistakes in judgment and shows no loss of control, Allan discovered his macho pride kept him from rushing upstairs to care for his emotionally wounded child. Nursing his wounded pride took precedence over nursing his wounded son. An eye-opener.

Later on, he wrote me about how that strong, silent image of manhood crept into his personality, but that "it wasn't 'strong' at all. It was a weakness of character to fear showing my human confusion. Maybe sometimes that strong, silent stuff can be a coward's way out of facing the truth with someone you love." His insight led to exploring how he might have disclosed on the double: "Eric, I should have told you this right away, but I felt so confused and rotten about hitting you that I froze. I'm still feeling so bad about hurting you that my mind is filled with that look on your face when you were leaving the front room."

This "might-have-been" message goes beyond a simple apology. It approaches a state-of-the-art act of parenting. Did you notice that it contains a fine here-'n'-now disclosure near the start? Telling Eric as soon as possible was the *best* option for disclosing on the double. After that, his next option (a second choice because it keeps Eric in the dark too long) was telling the newly arrived Michelle without delay. I know his impulse was to put a lid on his miserable confusion, to prevent any chance of a lengthy discussion while he was bewildered. That's often true for many of us during such distress. But disclosing that very fact is another useful option. Disclosing the here-'n'-now can be a terrific troublesaver. So when Michelle asked, "Hello? Someone home in there? Are you feeling okay?" Allan could have answered, "Yeah, I'm here, but I'm not okay. I'm all caught up with trying to figure out what just happened between Eric and me. It's hard to talk right now; I need to be quiet a while.''

I'd guess the typical person hearing that here-'n'-now disclosure would probably accept that situation and leave or negotiate a time to talk later. For example:

MICHELLE: Okay. Did you guys have a bad argument or something?
ALLAN: Something like that.
MICHELLE: Do you want a drink or dinner?
ALLAN: No thanks, nothing right now.
MICHELLE: Okay, I'll make dinner and you can eat it when you're ready and we can talk then.
ALLAN: Yeah. Thanks, Michelle.

The scenario would grow more complicated if she insisted that they talk with Eric right away. There again, Allan could disclose on the double with another here-'n'-now repeating his need for time.

In the regular rush of conversation, here-'n'-now disclosures are superb, underused tools for preventing and repairing misunderstanding, bringing perspective to arguments, and overcoming all sorts of emotional predicaments.

Here's another situation where here-'n'-nows will come to the rescue: A young man, Steven, is at a party, sitting with a pretty impressive young woman. She's bright, self-assured, witty, and talented enough to have raised two young brothers through high school. She's at least mildly interested in him (or maybe she had too much wine), Steven thinks; she's behaving warmly and is self-disclosing about her family and her work designing mail-order catalogs for a department store chain. Her name is Dana.

Because he's suffered from years of shyness, Steven has an unusual attitude about interpersonal attraction. To him, sex appeal means being able to communicate easily—to skillfully say what's on your mind and in your heart. He's a slow-talking, reticent communicator. Saying exactly what he means has been difficult, so talking well is *really* something that appeals to him. He knows most men and women walk around getting turned on primarily by physical appearances like slim bodies, good facial bones, stylish clothes, fashionable haircuts, and even straight teeth. He hates to think some women are attracted to men by their income and ridicules the image of teenage girls being made breathless by the make of a guy's car. As a teenager, he both detested and tried to imitate flashy talkers who tell clever jokes by the minute. The imitation failed—often and painfully. He's no longer trying to talk cleverly. All he wants is to say it without getting awkward or feeling like a fool afterward—especially with a woman. Right now, he's hardly talking at all because Dana is expressing herself beautifully, so gracefully. He's attracted—and hiding his fear behind that slow smile he has used so effectively all his life—he's showing his straight teeth because he's scared to talk much. She's about to switch the conversational spotlight from herself to him, and Steven is about to try some here-'n'-now disclosures. (I loaned him an early draft of this book while he was doing electrical work at my house.)

DANA: What do you do?
STEVEN: I'm an electrician.
DANA: Do you like your work?
STEVEN: Yeah, pretty much.
DANA: What brings you to Julie's party?
STEVEN: I work with Corbin, her boyfriend.
DANA: Is Corbin an electrician, too?
STEVEN: Uh huh. He's a master electrician.
DANA: Are you a master, too?
STEVEN: Almost. Maybe next year. It's hard . . . *(Pause)* real hard. *(Silence)*

[And not a comfortable silence by any means. At this point, Dana is starting to feel uncomfortable at carrying the conversation. Her discomfort shows as she starts to take the lead again. He responds with a bit more depth, but it's obviously one-sided. She has become the reluctant sole source of conversational assertion. The poor guy's smile is becoming an aching grin. He's feeling *pain*—and more than that, he's becoming annoyed at himself for not seizing the chance to start what might be a nice relationship. Steven is on the verge of blowing it. But—even though things look bleak—he refuses to give up. Even though he's been "faking it"—getting by with a grin while she filled in the silences—the guy is going to try some of those here-'n'-now disclosures he's been reading about. Straightening in his seat, he takes a deep breath.]

STEVEN: I've got a confession to make. . . . *(Long, dramatic pause)* The way I'm talking to you . . . or not talking to you . . . *(Nervous laugh)* is because I tend to get kinda, um, awkward when I meet someone like you, ya know, who's appealing to me.
DANA: Oh . . .
STEVEN: Yeah, really. I generally keep quiet when I feel awkward in this kinda situation. And people get the idea I'm sorta standoffish.

[Another here-'n'-now disclosure.]

DANA: Oh, no, I didn't get that idea.

STEVEN: No? Well, anyway, I'm glad I told you—I really want to talk to you some more. And it's a relief to let you know how I'm feeling.
[Another here-'n'-now disclosure.]

STEVEN: *(Continuing)* I mean, it didn't seem fair for you to carry the ball, ya know, and that was very kind of you, but you seem, you honestly seem like a neat person. And it's so crazy to sit there and let myself be shy. Because, uh—

DANA: *(Interrupting)* Sure, I'm glad you told me. My little brother, Andreas, is real shy. He's a great kid, gifted long-distance runner, but people give him a hard time 'cause everyone's in a rush nowadays—they keep cutting him off. That bugs me.

STEVEN: It bugs me too. Uh, the way you can think about your kid brother is, uh—just great.

DANA: Well, I just see what people can do to him when he's shy, and it gets to me 'cause I love him.

STEVEN: That's obvious. Right now I'm wishing I had a friend like you, maybe, well, uh . . . maybe not exactly a *sister*—a friend. Yeah, a friend. Like you. *(They laugh.)*

[That last here-'n'-now disclosure of admiration by Steven is worthy of any good talker.]

Here-'n'-nows can be snapshots of immediate inner experiences of discomfort like Steven's shyness or Allan's confused shame. They can also be about comfortable inner experiences like Steven's admiration. They are effective when they focus on the talk itself—on the immediate give and take of conversation: "The way I'm talking to you . . . or *not* talking to you . . . is because I tend to get kinda, um, awkward when I meet someone like you. . . ."

For Steven *and* Dana, here-'n'-nows came to the rescue in the nick of time (at last report they were still seeing each other).

Here-'n'-nows are a marvel. They fix communication. They work on the spot to end awkward silences and to clear up confusion. They can be effective for large or small matters—especially when done very simply: "I feel confused." "Maybe we ought to finish tomorrow—I'm tired and grumpy." "There's something I need to tell you, but it'll take 20 minutes." "I hate to make you go to sleep every night like this, but I'm worried about your math test in the morning."

Here-'n'-nows are simply the best tool for correcting communication breakdowns—or avoiding breakdowns in the first place. They ward off negative undercurrents and rout boredom. They live for the moment—saying, in effect, "Here's the way I feel about how we are right now; here's what I'm experiencing *this moment.''* Or when they reveal feelings about the communication itself: "Oh, *now* I see. I'm glad you told me." "It's getting hard for me to follow you. I need some time to let it sink in." "I'm getting annoyed by you saying that I 'never help you.' " "I think you're getting into a long story that I'll have to interrupt 'cause I have to be there by five." "It seems like we're both having a hard time saying good night."

Here-'n'-nows are a safety valve—psychological safety in relationships grows in their presence.

The next time you face a predicament or get caught in awkward talk and remember, "When in trouble, disclose on the double," please be sure to consider a courageous here-'n'-now to make things better. I realize my advice can be emotionally paradoxical—telling you when under threat to make yourself even more vulnerable with disclosure. It's counterintuitive. It goes against the grain of habitual concealment. And that's exactly why it works so well.

PRACTICING

I think it's women who are most concerned about their men underdisclosing. Many are frustrated at not knowing how men feel when it comes to relationship matters, according to a survey of 2,000 adults by Professor Michael McGill at Southern Methodist University. Over 90 percent of the men in the survey said they don't fully disclose significant feelings to their mate. A cynic might say the remaining 10 percent were liars.

Even though survey questions on self-disclosure are prone to be unreliable, Professor McGill's study does create a rough picture of how men hide feelings. I'd say that a clear view of how American men and women disclose to each other is a long way off, but that men have been reared to reveal less. We want to get closer, but we haven't had the practice. Or we're weary of being prodded to open up just a little more by our mothers, girlfriends, and wives, who can cause trouble when they actually hear what they've been asking for.

There are all sorts of strong, silent type images in fiction and real life for men to model themselves after. Our culture, in gender terms, finds Clint Eastwood easier to understand than Woody Allen. Many guys couldn't tell why women find Allen sexy. His character dialogue puzzles a lot of men and intrigues most women. That's why I like to use him as an example. His characters display many traits women wouldn't seem to want: indecisiveness, instability, immaturity, phobias, obsessive fretfulness, and all sorts of unmanly characteristics.

At rare moments, we see his self-esteem rise off the floor as he becomes a semiswaggering, in-charge, take-over kind of guy. Yet Allen's characters consistently contain a trait that some want badly: emotional openness. His men are often as self-disclosed as a girlfriend can be. They offer on the screen what real women often miss in their real men—an exposed picture of the masculine inner life. Allen's filmed inner lives may be exaggerated cartoons of what typical men feel, but all we need to do is tone them down to see the normal secrets of the average man. So the sustained national attraction to Woody Allen's untraditional heroes suggests that women want their men more accessible, more willing to disclose those "normal" secrets. Women's magazines have tried helping with thousands of articles over decades about making males more expressive to females. Alas, tricks, interviews with eminent psychologists, questionnaires, case histories, and tips from film stars haven't seemed to stamp out male reticence.

The problem remains—and so do the articles. And here I am with a book section on the practicalities of self-disclosure. I won't join the crowd and claim a simple solution, because the difficulties are monumental. But I can offer some thoughts on how to spend energy toward inducing a man (or an emotionally concealed woman) to open up a little more. That is, I have some not-so-simple procedures that should help in the hands of someone willing to start a serious campaign for changing an underdiscloser.

First, study chapter 1 with an eye toward selecting sections that might make interesting reading for your underdiscloser. Don't get ambitious about him or her reading all of it. My barber had her husband read the brief introduction about my race car and then the section about opening up at the office (because he's a businessman). A week later, they discussed disclosure in general and had a long, interesting conversation, according to her. Months later, he picked up the chapter again and read it all, and they talked again—this time about the way *they* opened and closed to each other. It was a little tense, but useful. He didn't complain much, and he began examining his hiding habits. I gave her a draft copy of this chapter and suggested they read it together in a low-pressure atmosphere. The story about Michelle, Allan, and Eric started them talking about how they were communicating with their own three daughters. Every month at my haircutting, I receive a briefing now on how the self-disclosure issue has entered my barber's household. They've played, as a family, with one of the exercises, and the father has experimented with a disclosure gimmick to uncork a long-standing problem he had with one daughter. Solving the father/daughter problem brought a willingness to reveal a couple of "normal" secrets to his wife.

At last report, the father was using here-'n'-nows with wry humor. No roaring extrovert, but no longer a clam. It took more than a year and a very patient mate, but reading the chapters, discussing them, trying an exercise and experiment, made a difference in an underdiscloser's talk style.

Changing the disclosure style of someone close has been the number one priority of those who've asked me for practical ideas. Opening up an underdiscloser is the most frequent request, followed by the desire to close down an overdiscloser (a flooder). Only a few students or patients have ever approached me to help with *their* reticence or excess. That pattern makes me wonder if it's particularly hard to spot troublesome disclosure habits in ourselves. It's probable when I think of "compulsive talkers" (like flooders, promiscuous disclosers, and premature disclosers) who complain of others' long-windedness with a full knowledge that they also sometimes "talk someone's ear off" or "blather too long." Faced with the fact that most are interested in changing others, the following experiments, games and exercises emphasize effective inventions for helping others modify their disclosure style. (But take warning: They just might change you, too.)

"Immodesty Tag"

PURPOSES
1. Serves as a low-threat consciousness-raiser for underdis-closed people willing to briefly play with the experience of deliberately self-disclosing.
2. Acts as a balancing device for the self-disclosure equilibrium of an established self-help group or work team. It's been known to restore some positive morale to a self-critical depressed support group or work team unbalanced in its praise between members.

3. Can provide a small boost to those (especially adolescents) who struggle with self-esteem. Though the purpose is not for specifically practicing disclosure, some fairly regular effects on the participants' sense of self-worth have been found, especially when using Immodesty Tag with families.

METHOD

1. Form a small group for at least half an hour or try it with one other person who can remain private and undistracted for 15 minutes. Warn participants they'll be required to publicly admit something good about themselves—*seriously*.

2. Read these steps out loud. Do one step at a time. Do not read them all at once.

3. Allow plenty of thinking time for participants to search for an admirable trait in themselves: a good feature of personality, a decent attitude, a satisfying habit, a good long-term deed, or a special talent. It *must* be something positive and expressed without many disclaimers, backtracking, or dutiful modesty. The goal is to go clearly beyond modesty. It helps to write down the good quality boldly on paper so that it won't be watered down when disclosing. Be *im*modest.

4. This game works well when someone feeling good at the moment makes the first disclosure. Watching someone's courage to openly like himself or herself can inspire the overly modest to try a little positive self-praise. Most of us need permission to produce an honestly positive disclosure on our self-worth.

   If you're in a pair, for fun try saying it with eyes cast downward at first—without eye contact. If you're in a group, make sure your disclosure is addressed directly to a specific person, so that he or she is "tagged." In a pair, the partner is automatically tagged. Say your immodest disclosure twice, very slowly. Avoid the self-mockery of outrageous bragging.

5. After the volunteer has finished, responsibility shifts to the person in the group whom the volunteer has tagged. (If it's a pair, the rule is simply to take turns.) The tagged person's first duty is to search for any confirming evidence that supports the previous immodest disclosure. Think of examples that give truth to the good quality, or ask questions that can expand the good picture. No teasing, because self-praise is seriously embarrassing for some, and even painful for a few. If it's a group, other members must join in, and even inter-

rupt to bolster, boost, and add evidence demonstrating that there's some real goodness there.

6. Before support for the immodest disclosure dwindles, stop the procedure so that the tagged person can reveal one of his or her own better qualities. Then repeat as before: say it twice, without self-mockery; tag someone to start confirming; give supporting opinion or add evidence without teasing. Make sure the group gives support, too.

7. Continue until each person has made two or three immodest disclosures and finish with an open discussion on who took the biggest risks, whose set of disclosures is most varied, and how it feels to be forced to brag out loud.

VARIATION

Do the game by role-playing another participant's disclosure—that is Person *A* pretends to be Person *B* and discloses something *very good* about Person *B*. Then Person *B* must help confirm that with evidence—a terrific twist that needs a committed, imaginative group of people or an established couple who previously has been too busy or too hardened for mutual admiration.

I've seen Immodesty Tag become a screwy, funny mess when some clever participants "immodestly" admitted some good thing about another participant, such as: "An impressive thing about you is the relentless way you went about getting me to fall in love with you for months after I'd already fallen." The playful possibilities are hard to resist, but I have to be the worrywart and warn you to first attend to the feelings of those whose self-esteem might, at the moment, be at half-staff. Save the mischief for the second round.

"Secret Pooling"

This unusual small-group procedure was born in a Berkeley think tank during the mid-1960s. I was getting restless thinking about the academic side of self-disclosure and decided to make some practical gadgets for professional use. My colleague, Dr. Bill Smelser, and I developed an early version of Secret Pooling that we tried out on a group of social scientists attending a workshop. The thing worked better than we expected. It was refined over the next year, used in several skill-training programs for group leaders, police officers, therapists, paraprofessionals—

even lawyers. Then it got out of my hands and popped up in various psychology books, audiotape training programs, and family therapy systems.

The procedures seemed to jump from one professional circle to another over the next decade, and then I heard of its use in Europe and Australia. It was translated into Japanese and God knows what other languages. A remarkable proliferation for a small group exercise. I can't figure out why Secret Pooling disseminated so widely—it's not that it's simple to do. Maybe it gets around because of what it accomplishes for group atmosphere, or what it teaches timid disclosers. Professionals tell me that it saves them time in moving their groups toward openness. It can do the same for families, social gatherings, children's camps, self-help groups, and business offices—but somehow the routine has remained in professionally supervised (fee-paid) hands. I hope that will change now.

PURPOSES

1. To quickly help a group learn about its inner life in a non-threatening way, without exposing anyone emotionally and without connecting disclosed secrets to their individual owners. To tell secrets anonymously and see how others react.
2. To teach reticent disclosers how well their group can respect, understand, and accept risky disclosers.
3. To explore how the basic urge of using self-disclosure is used for (1) connecting with others, (2) securing the sense of "being known" by others, and (3) gaining some relief from carrying a psychological burden alone.

METHOD

1. The group coordinator locates and distributes matched sets of paper and pen for each participant. (I'm not kidding about matched sets.) File cards, notepaper, letterhead stationery will all work. Don't allow anyone to be singled out through some distinctively colored ink or irregular paper. The similarity maintains anonymity.
2. Spread the group out around the room or house or office so they can have five minutes of quiet and privacy to write a *nonidentifiable* risky secret. Nobody should identify themselves by mentioning gender, occupation, physical characteristics, or recognizable problems. Demonstrate how all the written secrets can be folded the same way—preferably twice

or three times. Toss the secrets into a paper bag or bowl or in a pile on the floor and mix thoroughly.

3. Pass around the pool of anonymous secrets so that everybody randomly selects one and reads it—*silently*. Allow each person to silently read the secret they picked before the next person selects one. If by chance someone picks out their own secret, stop the process immediately. Toss all the secrets back into the pool and start over.

4. After everyone has picked an anonymous secret, allow time for each to empathize with it, get the feel, and seriously pretend that the secret belongs to them. After that, one person reads their selected secret aloud and slowly, still pretending it comes from him or her. The group also pretends that the secret is from the life of the reader and *respectfully* tries to help. Using me-too disclosures or reflections works well if participants know how. Avoid advice-giving. The idea is to let the anonymous secret-writer *safely* hear how well the group can vicariously care for his or her private life.

5. Stop at five minutes (or up to eight minutes if participants know each other well) and move to the next secret-reader. Destroy each written secret after its use. Do no start this exercise before reading the sections ''Variations'' and ''Unexpected Aftereffects.''

VARIATIONS

1. If it's important for the group to be very orderly or operate consistently across classrooms or self-help support groups, it will be necessary to spell out details. Just before people write their secrets, read them the following Secret Pooling instructions that have proven reliable in thousands of groups using my SASHAtape program.

Secret Pooling creates an unusual situation—one where some great learning can come out of hearing your secrets discussed by others. Research shows that all sorts of good things can occur if most participants take the risk of writing things that would *not* ordinarily be revealed. If you play by the rules, this procedure can create an interpersonal environment—a group circumstance—so unique that it happens rarely, if ever, in most lifetimes.

Please start getting in the mood to stop and write something the group doesn't know about your personal life or the way you've been feeling lately or the way you feel toward this group, good or bad. From past experience, some participants have mixed feelings about contributing a secret and end up writing something that disguises the message through vague, fuzzy wording. Putting down some important feeling—a feeling that may not sound dignified, honorable, or strong—can feel like a big risk. If the risk seems *too* big, don't write something cute or clever that belittles this routine and the sincerity of other participants. Just write a small but honest secret. If you are mildly fearful or feel threatened and want to overcome it, try a plain, bold, genuine, direct inner secret—and then write a less bold one for the group. Seeing both on paper may help you decide which one to give to the group. You'll have plenty of time to decide. When writing, follow these ground rules:

A. The sentence should *not* reveal your age, sex, physical features, or anything else that can identify you.

B. No pretending. No jokes. The secret *must* be real.

C. Try using your writing skills to create one strong, clear sentence for the secret. Unvarnished truth makes better writing, and it saves the group from the frustration of trying to decipher what you *really* mean. Too much detail clutters.

D. Everyone should fold papers the same way.

E. Hold on to your secret till everyone is finished writing. Do not talk. Someone may be struggling silently about taking a risk. If this procedure is easy for you, please don't assume that others are also comfortable taking chances with their private or frightening thoughts.

2. If you're in a setting where the group runs itself without outside leadership, you can use my programmed SASHA-tape combination of audiotapes and workbooks that automatically guides groups through Secret Pooling. It's available from the Talking Tools Project, c/o Gerald Goodman, Department of Psychology, UCLA, Los Angeles, CA 90024. The disadvantage is that you must buy an expensive six-session communications program for a single exercise.

3. Instead of risky secrets, this exercise can be done with immodest disclosures, revealing personal qualities that are held with pride. See Immodesty Tag earlier in this section.

4. Secret Pooling has been used as a periodic (monthly, semi-annual) group cohesion device in self-help support groups, project teams, and therapy groups. Secrets can be limited to current unexpressed experiences or work issues. When used

repeatedly, special care must be taken to respect any low-risk secret. This exercise requires the absence of even mild coercion toward a reluctant participator.

UNEXPECTED AFTERAFFECTS

Feedback from participants and leaders over the years can predict some of the longer-term impact from Secret Pooling. (If you discover something not mentioned in the following, please write me at UCLA.)

- Secret connections can be developed between participants when someone views his or her secret as empathically ''owned'' by the reader but cannot express direct appreciation without revealing everything. Some people feel their secret parallels the experience of another secret read in the group and feel frustrated at not being able to talk with the anonymous owner. Your group may wish to discuss these afteraffects.
- Hearing your secret receive understanding and respect and watching others openly admit to having similar secrets can make the group very safe. If that sense of a psychological safety net is combined with the frequently found mild frustration at the reader's inability to express every nuance or angle of the secret, a peculiar urge takes over the writer of the secret. He or she feels tempted to tell the truth. This exercise can open up groups with remarkable rapidity, but there's a hitch. If everyone but one or two open up and ''own'' their secrets, the reluctant holdout could be entrapped and discovered by the process of elimination. It's best to agree *not* to confess ownership of secrets unless *all*, without ambivalence, contract to go public. I'd suggest that, in most cases, such contracts be delayed to avoid ''disclosure's remorse'' for a hasty confession.

"Disclosure Bank"

PURPOSES

1. To enhance the flow of spontaneous disclosures within a family, athletic team, military unit, or any small group.
2. To rescue momentary messages and solitary thoughts from oblivion.
3. To increase the frequency of occasions where someone's dis-

closure is (1) heard without rush or the need for quick reply, or (2) discussed as needed *after* the message has sunk in.

METHOD

Disclosure Bank is more a system or a regular routine than an exercise or experiment. It requires the use of an audio tape recorder that can be dedicated solely to the collection of disclosures. (I bought a simple $25 microcassette recorder that has served our family fine for two years.)

1. After your group or partner has read this description, find a convenient, permanent location for the recorder. If necessary, tape instructions to the machine.
2. Agree to deposit disclosures in the recorder for joint discussion at a later date. Disclosures can be made whenever they come to mind, whenever others aren't around or are preoccupied, whenever the present situation is too tense, hectic, or otherwise a not fair hearing. You also have the option to "withdraw" your "deposit" later.
3. Set up a regular time for a meeting to hear and discuss each disclosure deposit. In my three-person family, the weekly meetings last from 15 minutes to an hour. We rewind and listen to disclosures in sequence with the depositor elaborating first and eventually announcing when he or she is satisfied (sometimes that means satisfied for the moment). Weekly discussions may be too frequent for you. Whatever the schedule, make sure that the disclosures deposited are not in need or rapid reply and can wait for your scheduled review.

TESTIMONIAL

Disclosure Bank has simplified my busy family's communication. And it hasn't dehumanized us one bit. Just the opposite. Now we talk about things that used to fall between the cracks. My son deposits thoughts on increasing his allowance or reducing his swim workouts for his parents' leisurely, hopefully more agreeable perusal. (My breakthrough idea for partitioning the bread supply in our refrigerator/freezer might not have come to life without Disclosure Bank.) Our spontaneous thoughts on vacation plans and household organization never need to be put in writing. We routinely deposit a laundry list of complaints to each other, from minor to chronic. Sometimes the system falters and even breaks down for weeks, but overall it's a plus.

Two years ago I suggested this procedure to a local college basketball coach. She used it to collect minor grievances, conditioning reports, workout ideas, post-mortems on past games, and ideas for strategies. The recorder was placed on a bleacher during team practices for use at any time by any player. The agreement was that any deposit would be heard by the team during their weekly open discussion session. It worked so well that the procedure was picked up by other basketball and volleyball coaches around the country. One called the tape recorder a "confession box" because his athletes frequently disclosed their workout lapses, finding the machine more comfortable to talk to than their coach's direct (disapproving) presence.

"Sidney's Yoga Disclosure Game"

Sidney Jourard believed that underdisclosing contributed to the shorter life expectancy of males. I argued about that with my late colleague at the time (mid-1960s) and—lacking the imagination then to grasp the importance of his idea—almost convinced him the assertion was overstated. His belief that the added stress of underdisclosing on an already stressed male would bring an earlier death might still strike many as farfetched. But the evidence linking emotional concealment to chronic stress and illness is building.

Sidney's search for ways to help people disclose more inspired him to invent all sorts of games. Many didn't work, but interpersonal yoga proved successful. It's loosely inspired by the basic concept of personal, momentary limits in bending and stretching the body—found in Hatha-yoga exercises. That is, certain body positions extended in time will reach a point of discomfort, a limit. Some positions can only be attained partially before the biofeedback of discomfort signals the limits. The yoga practitioner, feeling the muscles protest, will respect the signal to stop. To force beyond the limit is to cheat and hamper chances of going farther next time. So going as far as you can and pressing gently is pressing against your limits. It's complete. It's all that your body has earned at the moment.

Sidney transposed that idea into the realm of interpersonal self-disclosure with this particular exercise. I've revised it to fit within my communication framework.

PURPOSES

1. To safely move a couple into increasing openness over a period of weeks or months.
2. To mutually learn precisely how much each partner can comfortably expose on a given day.
3. To practice a healthy respect for not pushing each other's self-disclosure limits (while allowing each to push on his or her own current limits).

METHOD

1. It is best done with a pair or a self-help support group. Newly acquainted people should start slowly. It requires a series of brief sessions (perhaps three to ten or more) with absolute privacy. Couples can meet for 15 to 20 minutes, groups much longer.
2. Using the following list, the pair or group selects a *single* topic—starting with the easiest, top-of-the-list subject that everyone can handle. People who are just getting acquainted are safest starting at the top.

Someone starts by disclosing on the topic, being scrupulously honest, until a personal limit is reached. It's okay to encourage and support the discloser, but *don't* probe or push. The rule: *Respect the limits*—and then push on the limits gently. Avoid discloser's remorse. Try to limit each turn to five minutes unless there's agreement to disclose longer. Testing courage is not the idea here. Machismo will ruin the exercise and hinder future progress. And women competitively showing off their capacity for doing risky disclosures better than men can destroy the effort.

After five minutes, or sensing a limit, the partner or other group volunteer discloses in a similar manner.

Here are some topics inspired by Jourard's list from his book, *Self-Disclosure.*[1]

1. Hobbies, interests, and favorite leisure pursuits.
2. Likes and dislikes about body, appearance, health, etc.
3. Work: satisfactions and frustrations.
4. Financial situation: income, savings, debts, investments, etc.
5. Parents: joys and sorrows, family problems while growing up.

6. Religious views, philosophy of life, meaningful perspectives and ideas.
7. Close relationships in the past. (Warning: See earlier section, "Disclosing Sexual Pasts.")
8. Things to learn about intimacy; current or past dissatisfaction about getting close to others.
9. Likes or dislikes about the others in the room now. Agree on the dimensions of this before disclosing: personality, appearance, values—and go *slowly*.
10. Add your own dimensions. Or see Jourard's book for a hundred other topics.

VARIATIONS
1. For a very close pair. After several sessions, the couple may want to disclose the wish for physical contact, using the following list from Jourard as a guide.[2] If the disclosure is received with approval, the wish can be made real in the following manner:
   A. Massage shoulder of partner.
   B. Massage neck or head of partner.
   C. Massage back.
   D. Massage calves.
   E. Massage feet.
   F. Message thighs.
   Once again, it's critical to sense the limits. Please respond to the slightest "no" and see if the limits expand in future sessions.
2. Intimate couples could, of course, have more advanced touching or connecting lists in their heads. Consider disclosing sexual wishes slowly, one item at a time.

IDEAS FOR TAILORING YOUR OWN OPENING-UP PROCEDURES

A quick review of this chapter's procedures for enhancing disclosure (along with other interpersonal recipes in the remaining chapters) will provide a variety of mechanisms for creating tailor-made exercises, games, and gimmicks to fit your needs. I'll briefly suggest some of the most effective procedures that can be readily shaped into working methods.

"Mental Striptease"

This can be used in a variety of ways for helping lovers bring new thoughts, feelings, and even behaviors into their sexual lives. It's an odd striptease that turns things around and asks a couple that is already physically naked to slowly become more *emotionally* naked. The task is for intimate couples—in a very good mood—to disclose just a *little* bit more of a previously unexpressed thought of feeling. It should be done in a light mood, teasingly, with deliberate slowness in an attempt to titillate the partner. Look at it as an undressing of the mind limited to a single issue, like a secret urge or an old feeling of affection, a good thought about the partnership, an attribute admired in the other, an unspoken fantasy—something true and positive and slightly risky. Negative disclosures won't work here.

This one needs a very strict warning: Mental Striptease is *not* designed for people engaging in casual sex or for clothed couples.

You can put the idea into any exercise, experiment, or game format, such as 20 Questions or Disclosure Tag, etc., as long as the *pleasant* disclosure is revealed slowly or tantalizingly in a lovemaking context. The couple's minds should not be undressed quickly. Several of my clinical psychology graduate students "implemented" the idea and all reported success. One told me it took her and her husband into an experience never attained during their conventional lovemaking.

Mental Striptease can be varied by limiting the revelations to here-'n'-now disclosures revealed frugally to a partner who must only respond verbally with reflections—no judgments or disclosures in return. Here-'n'-nows are riskier and make the event more of an adventure best suited to very close couples or to those who have tried the standard Mental Striptease first.

"Flooded Disclosure Insurance"

This is a form of conversational contracting that can: (1) protect a caring person from the random, entrapping onslaught of a long-winded, self-indulgent burst of disclosure about problems or nostalgia; (2) provide habitual flooders who are lonely, troubled, or elderly (or all of those) with an *occasional* but reliable and substantial human contact; (3) allow any two people who know and like each other special times for venting feelings, exploring issues, reviewing the past, and locating insights.

Basically, the conversational contract calls for scheduling when, where, and how long the flooding will last. It's usually best to use terms like free talk, free-flooding, listening sessions, disclosing sessions—something positive. The contact can save you from those frequent, random demands for attention. It's best, and sometimes crucial, to reciprocate, but not necessarily within the same occasion. Sometimes, with confused or emotionally handicapped people, reciprocation is difficult. Central to the contract is the full permission for the flooder to speak on anything that comes up with absolute freedom to change subject at will and without any interruptions.

Contracts usually range between 30 and 90 minutes. Two-hour contracts have been much less successful in my experience.

The listener never gives advice or makes judgments or interpretations—only gives reflections during pauses. The listener essentially waits, accepts, keeps time, and announces when five minutes are left. This routine can be worse than nothing if the listener has unrealistic expectations about the burden of keeping close emotional company with the flooder. It's work. On the other hand, contracting with a friend or family member can be nice work. It can be a wonderful way to use time during a car ride or trip. I know couples who alternate roles weekly and schedule special sessions whenever one person needs support for a matter outside the relationship.

Consider, too, that the Flooded Disclosure Insurance structure can be organized to work on the phone between friends or acquaintances facing a similar predicament. You can make this format work like a mutual support group for two. Start phone contracting for no longer than 20 minutes and increasing the time slowly. This routine is *not* suggested for back-to-back flooding. Switching roles from listener to flooder is too hard to handle all at once.

Each pairing requires its own rules, but I'd suggest a firm rule for protecting both from additional discussion soon after the flooding has ended. Before setting up a flooding agreement, make sure both participants read the section "Flooded Disclosures: Exceedingly Private Personal Talk" in chapter 1.

Pay attention to the fact that serious self-disclosing in human relations can be both a symptom of discomfort and a psychological cure. Making a pact for free-flooding sessions can do more than reduce annoyance; it can foster some permanent improvement.

"Me-Too Disclosure Games"

These experiments and exercises are safely shaped by the peculiar empathic property of powerful me-too disclosures—the most efficient conveyors of empathy in all of language. This infrequently used talk tool is described in chapter 1.

Me-too's are disclosures stimulated by disclosures—analogous to the way we might yawn after witnessing another's yawn. For example, I hear you describe a vivid romantic event from your teens that contains a basic experience such as infatuation, self-consciousness, embarrassment, growth, or naivete. That jogs my memory to unearth a distant experience that must be expressed right now through a disclosure—a me-too. And perhaps, in the same way, my disclosure invites your memory to unstore more material for another disclosure, one that's analogous to mine—another me-too disclosure. The two-way stimulation could easily start a meaningful personal exchange.

No talk tool works better to provide emotional company with evidence that demonstrate sincerity and accuracy. (Unfortunately, therapists can't use them because me-too's become unbelievable when used repeatedly. They become condescending and artificial coming frequently from a professional.) Reflections are best for repeated use in most context, but me-too's *do* work great in self-help mutual support groups, providing profound feedback of empathic understanding among people with a common concern. They also work nicely in social settings when there's conversational contracting. Here's an idea that can be tailored for a pair, a family, a newly acquainted couple, kids at camp, or a staff on a retreat.

The pair or group members face each other without having selected a starter topic. In round-robin fashion, everyone takes a deep breath and discloses their immediate here-'n'-now feelings in one breathful. Any honest expression from "I feel silly doing this dumb game" to "I'm scared." Give examples and maybe set an example by starting it yourself. Make it okay to be awkward and don't allow two breathsful of disclosure, even at the cost of someone's incomplete expression.

Then, as a group, decide on a starter topic for the first *sub-*

stantial disclosure. Three or four breathsful are enough. This is an important decision because the first disclosure usually determines the lightness or heaviness of the couple's or group's mood. My habit is to start new conversational contracts on the light, pleasant side. Dealing with a new talk format and a serious, absorbing issue simultaneously is bad policy. After a volunteer breaks the ice by telling a true story about his or her life, the group remains silent for as long as it takes for another person to speak out with a me-too disclosure.

Remind the group that anything brought to mind will do. The disclosure need only be linked with a common experience like confusion, surprise, irony, coincidence, absurdity, love—any major feelings.

The arbitrary time limit measured by breathsful of talk not only protects the pair or group from flooding but can also comfort the nervous disclosure by providing a limited demand. The breathful twist on timing also adds a touch of novelty and a bit of distraction when facing more difficult topics. It's a bit silly, but the gimmick has proved itself useful. Give it a chance. On a couple of occasions, I've encountered a group member unable to take a normal breath. The problem was solved by simply allowing 45 seconds for each allotted breathful.

Here's an example of three breathsful of me-too talk by a couple. She started: "I picked up a few things at the market this morning and went to the express lane and started to write a check, and this bitch of a checkout woman says, 'Can't you *read*?' I hadn't noticed the 'No Checks' sign. So, like an ass, I apologized and slunk away like a meek little girl. I felt like a child. But later I got mad and wished I'd spoken up. It bothered my mood all day."

After a minute of silence, he comes up with a me-too: "When I was a kid, I used to pick up the newspaper for my dad at the corner liquor store. I was rushing one day, so I just dropped the change on the counter while this new clerk waited on someone else. I was running out the door when this guy bellows, 'Hey, did you leave enough money, kid?' I go back and it's enough, but my ears are hot 'cause I'm feeling so untrusted—so crappy. This guy treated me like I'd stolen his wallet. I ran home crying, but dried my eyes before Dad could see. I wanted to tell Ma the next day, but it felt silly by then. I hated that clerk for years. Wow—never, ever told anybody till right now!"

On my honor, that last me-too was uttered rapidly and in only three breathsful. Try it.

If someone doesn't come up with a me-too, you could make a rule that he or she simply do any disclosure that fits the mood. For familiar couples, you might want to expand the timing to four or more breathsful. Or simply remove limits and encourage flooding. (Please see the section on flooding in chapter 1 before contracting for such a demanding empathy task.) You may wish to read some of this section out loud, especially the examples, *before* starting. Fix a limit for how many me-too's each person does *before* you begin. Usually five or six is a good limit for couples, and fewer for a group, especially if it's more than eight people.

Building me-too exercises into a self-help group has worked beautifully. The exercise enhances what the group already wants to do; it can also serve as a booster shot for groups going through a communication slump.

Examples of me-too advisements are in chapter 4. Me-too advisements are somewhat similar to me-too disclosures, but differ markedly in their intention, which is to show "a better way to do it," a new way to think, feel, or behave. Me-too disclosures have little interest in trying to guide; they simply want to show, share, and connect.

If you're thinking of making some changes in self-disclosure habits for yourself or another person, please remember that you're getting involved with a major personality trait that connects to basic beliefs, long-term habits, gender behavior, and psychological vulnerability. So expect resistance and backsliding. Also know that deliberately using self-disclosure as a *primary* talk tool for *helping* is the most difficult skill to master. That's because it takes much practice to repeatedly disclose while keeping most of the attention on the person you're trying to aid. But it's worth the trouble. Practice gets easier when you mix in reflections (see chapter 8).

Here's another fact to remember when trying to open up someone quickly: Eliciting extremely high-risk disclosures can cause some bad aftereffects. Professor Irving Janis at Yale found that women in a weight-reduction group were somewhat demoralized and overdependent on their counselor after being induced to give risky disclosures.[3] Such things are less likely to happen among close friends, but discloser's remorse can be a problem with any method, whether it's one of my tested procedures or something you create. The warning here is simple: Take it easy when drawing someone out in a new way. Risky disclosures are powerful—they can both harm and enhance.

CHAPTER 8

MASTERING REFLECTIONS

COUNTERINTUITIVE.

That's the best word for describing why reflections aren't put to practical use by the public. Show someone how to do reflections and ask him to do one for real and you'll probably hear a complaint: "It feels unnatural." Using reflections in ordinary, helpful conversations is contrary to our immediate instincts. To *give* them is counterintuitive, but to *get* them in the flow of conversation can feel perfectly natural. Getting good ones, when we're describing something that matters to us, typically feels normal, comfortable—even wonderfully supportive. That's why professional caregivers, from therapists to attorneys to journalists, use them as tools of the trade.

There are profound moments, rare situations, times of extreme personal attachment in daily life when most people have *given* reflections automatically, immediately, intuitively. Those times when we confront another's intense self-disclosure can leave us speechless except for somehow acknowledging that we have, indeed, registered the message. Our visceral reaction is to show we are on their side. We reflexively say something to confirm that their discomfort or happiness has been taken in and taken seriously.

SHE: This letter says I didn't get the job. Damn, they didn't even interview
  me. It's not right! They never gave me a real chance.

243

HE: I can't believe it. That's really not right. It's so unfair. Without even giving you an *interview*!

I've witnessed such "natural" reflections in everyday settings where expressions of disappointment, anger, shock, or excitement were reflected or paraphrased by friends. They aren't used often in daily life but take on terrific importance when they demonstrate empathic understanding of big feelings. I've been curious about natural reflections for years—hunting them in others' conversations like a bird-watcher hunting for species that don't show up often. Since they occur mostly during private moments between close acquaintances, my capture rate is low. For some undetermined reason, I've spotted more of them in adolescents than in adults. Adolescents seem to use reflections through sheer enthusiasm.

SHE: He said yes for Saturday on the party. He's going out with me— *really*! I mean, *really*!
FRIEND: So he's *really* going out with you—Gawd!

I wish there were some serious research on this natural stuff, but it's extremely difficult to study. Even so, I strongly suspect that the best natural reflectors are parents whose children are learning to talk. Here's a favorite example.

TODDLER: *(Scurrying toward mother across the beach, waving a just-discovered seashell above his head)* Mommy, Mommy! Shell! Mine shell. Mine!
MOTHER: *(Empathic, reflecting)* A shell, a real shell—and it's *yours*. All yours!

This spontaneous, intuitive communication between mother and child creates an emotional bond for an important moment. More reflections will sustain the bond, strengthen the child's security and sense of being understood, and support the child's development and willingness to explore. Mother finds a double gratification as she both vicariously enters her child's excitement and then communicates that private knowledge to the child's satisfaction. It's heavy-duty connecting—great stuff for a kid's mental health. But what about the kid's mental health ten years later when understanding is needed for some adolescent "discovery" that doesn't thrill mother? The child still needs that sense of being inwardly understood, but Mom doesn't intuitively enter the excitement for the latest teenage fashion, haircut, media idol, or weekend tragedy of not getting the car or party invitation. Reflections don't come as naturally when we're not immediately touched by the other's experience. That's why they're sadly underused in family life, friendships, and work settings.

I'm not the only professional who bemoans the weakness in our national talk style. Just about every mental-health scholar and practitioner specializing in human relations or intimacy would like to see greater use of reflections in our close communications.

So I'm going to make a pitch for the increased use of reflections in daily life. *And quiet or shy people, take note:* For your less-active conversational styles, using reflections will let you contribute meaningfully, at your pace, without trying to be a quick, clever, frequent talker. Just think, if you're more comfortable letting others carry the conversational ball, you can use reflections to fill long or awkward silences when others finish talking, you can provide encouragement through reflections for others to expand on their topics, and you can use reflections to complement the strengths you probably already have—allowing plenty of room and paying attention. These reflections that follow instead of lead are a great fit for your passive talk styles—but passive here doesn't imply weakness at all. As you've seen, these unassuming reflections—done consistently—shape conversation profoundly. They're the most useful addition to the talk style of people who are reserved, slow-talking, shy, or just sparing of words.

Whether you're a quiet person or not, I hope you're persuaded by now to spend some time learning how to use reflections. If you can't find an interested partner, consider showing your mate, child, lover, or colleague some short sections of chapter 2: The "Nosh" story near the beginning of the chapter might sway a parent regarding the importance of reflections in child rearing; a disinterested male with insecurity about his capacity to empathize might get an eye-opener from the research in the section "Who Has Empathy, and Who Doesn't?" There are also brief sections on the role of reflections in lovemaking, at the workplace, in psychotherapy, in group settings (and on television), for unlodging secrets, and for unclogging repetitious, boring conversations.

I mostly dislike being in the role of salesman for reflections, like those professionals who hawk the benefits of exercise, good diet, patient sex, and those other aspects of life that require counterintuitive behavior. But after all, strictly following impulses—"doing what comes naturally"—would lead some of us to avoid exercise, eat fatty, salty, sugary foods, and seek quick unilateral gratification in lovemaking. Applying reflections to the "uninteresting" concerns and discoveries of people close to us doesn't mean faking interest or being polite; it means simply taking time to *emotionally* understand why something is psychologically salient for that significant person in your life—and then to *communicate* that understanding. It doesn't require hours of intense concentration. Say your good friend buys a dumb car in an awful color and wants you to understand his pleasure. Put aside your judgment, tune into the fun, and give feedback with a reflection, and *then* complain. Empathizing and reflecting doesn't preclude registering your disapproval. All it does is show you also can take a minute to appreciate a friend's pleasure.

It usually doesn't take long to reflect spontaneous disclosures if they're not blockbusters. For more serious disclosures, bigger ones about significant problems or passions, it may take longer, but the principle is the same: Learn to focus *first* on the quality of another's experience rather than your disapproval or disinterest; that can strengthen any relationship.

Using reflections deliberately for minor acts of understanding before registering opinion, interpretation, or disclosure can cut down on conflict. Using reflections for *major* acts of understanding—for large, serious issues—requires reshaping the conversational tone with a series of reflections that can create a sustained episode of understanding. The only negative aspect of this talk tool is that it can't be learned in a few minutes. It's not that reflections are difficult to grasp as an idea but that the learner must go beyond that counterinitiative, against-the-grain feeling to a place where they become more natural. A bright, motivated person can produce usable reflections within an hour of practice. Better-quality reflections will take several hours of practice after reading the next section. Subtle, penetrating reflections that skilled pros use on the touchy topics of their patients, parishioners, clients, or customers require months—even years—of experience.

A THREE-STEP WAY TO MASTER REFLECTIONS

Good reflections allow you to enter the most private and vulnerable inner lives of others with safety and understanding. In the dialogue sample that follows, a nonprofessional group leader named Dorothy has taken the method I teach to heart: She employs three-step reflections to assist another member of her self-help mutual support group, Alice, relate vital feelings about the decline of her husband, Sidney, from Alzheimer's disease.

Members of the Philadelphia group, all of them mates of Alzheimer's victims, were coping with the enormity of losing the mind and emotional company of someone very close—in some cases, an intimate partner of 20 to 30 years. Their discussions made some painfully isolated people feel a lot less alone—less strange about suffering from insomnia, less agonized by making all the decisions for someone who was bright and capable just a few years back, less frustrated at answering their confused mates' repeated questions, less hurt at being isolated from relatives, less stupid about not institutionalizing their bewildered, wandering mates, less embarrassed when coping with the victims' bizarre acts in public. Those issues had caused many surviving partners to question their mental health—until they entered the special conversations of the support group.

Members of the group received some communication training, including the three-step reflection technique from my audiotape program.

The three steps that Dorothy will apply in this reflection sample are:

- Active waiting.
- Empathizing.
- Finding the words.

Step One: Active Waiting

This is like clearing your mind to sit down and listen, to be a respectful, attentive audience. You wait with aggressive attention. Sounds odd, but it only means saying nothing, or helping the message sink in. As the message sinks in and triggers your memory or current feeling, remember your reaction. Keep track of your reaction. So, doing reflections requires *not* thinking about what you want to say next, *not* making evaluative judgments of good or bad about what you're hearing. Deliberate concentration has to be placed on the other's message. That message must be apprehended without distortion. If the message is a problem the other has, the challenge is to seize the problem and think little about possible solutions. It's taking on an attitude that feels unnatural to an ordinary talker. The typical way of responding to a problem is to judge what's heard, turn attention to formulate a response, and give in to the urge to advise or interpret. Only a few inexperienced communicators can do a decent active wait on the first try.

Step Two: Empathizing

Empathizing, feeling as if you were the other person, doesn't come easily for some people. (See the section "Who Has Empathy, and Who Doesn't?" in chapter 2.) But there's a trick that helps: After actively waiting and gathering some information, turn your attention away from the disclosure *momentarily* and move into your own memories, to a time when you experienced something similar. If you want to empathize with someone's mixed feelings about, say, taking on the responsibilities of a corporate management job, you take a moment to search your mind for an experience in which you had mixed feelings about taking on new responsibilities in *any* job or situation. It's not the same *situation* you're looking for but the same *experience* (in this case, the same mixed feelings about new responsibilities). It could even be mixed feelings about taking over a Boy Scout troop, as compared to taking on a management job, as long as a similar feeling is there.

If your discloser is experiencing shame, terror, or anger, search for a similar level of shame, terror, or anger in your memory, regardless of where or when it occurred. If the other person is talking about his terror at parachuting out of an airplane and you've never jumped from a plane, perhaps you've felt something similar jumping from a high diving board into a pool. Let your attention in this phase bounce between the discloser's experience and your search for a similar feeling. Parts of the other's message will be missed at first, but that's to be expected when learning. (Feeling into others' feelings is a talent that varies widely among adults. Some can empathize almost without trying, while others have to regulate their empathic reflexes downward to avoid being overwhelmed. Children have difficulty experiencing the kind of empathy described here; so do immature or troubled adults. Serious mental illness is often associated with a dysfunction of empathy.)

Step Three: Finding the Words

Try a reflection (even a clumsy one, if you're a beginner). Nothing fancy or profound. Just try feeding back the heart, the essence of the other's message. Try to simplify it somewhat; shave off some of the clutter, take the other person's point of view with an emphasis on feelings. For beginners, only a bit of progress should be expected. In fact, all that's needed much of the time is a *little* paraphrase of the message to demonstrate understanding and direct the discloser to deeper layers of experience.

The following excerpts between Dorothy and Alice begin after Alice has told how she dealt with Sidney's inexorable loss of mental abilities from Alzheimer's disease. She had to live through his intellectual decline and emotional deterioration before living through his physical death.

ALICE: You wanna hear something crazy? My mind just leaped back 32 years to my high school art class. The assignment was to make a poster from a proverb of our choice. We were learning to do fancy Roman lettering. A long proverb meant long hours of fussy work. *(She laughs)* So I chose a short one, but it had a long word. I can still see it: "Procrastination is the thief of time." Those thick black India ink letters are hanging in my head 'cause right now I'm thinking that procrastination is stealing away my days.

DOROTHY: Sounds like you were saying that word to yourself over and over again until it hooked up with a 32-year memory. "Procrastination. Procrastination. Procrastination. Procrastination is the thief of time." And right now it's robbing your time.

[Dorothy's competent, somewhat overdone reflection gives me the feeling that she wants to throw all her attention at Alice. There's no attempt at brilliance, but her description of Alice repeating the word "until it hooked up with a 32-year memory" is apt and vivid. It would certainly make *me* feel understood. Notice Dorothy's phrase "Sounds like you were saying. . . ." It represents an effort to paraphrase the message. Many people who learn reflections and use them deliberately in bunches wind up prefixing reflections with "It seems that you're thinking . . ." or "Sounds like you mean . . ." That's a way of saying, "I'm being guided by your message. *You're* the authority. It's your feeling, not

mine." I see no problem in habitually starting reflections with prefixes
like, "If I hear you right, you're feeling. . . ." They might start sounding repetitious, even unimaginative, but they are reminders of who owns
the message; that's easy to forget when lots of reflections are in the air.
Try alternating them when you gain a little skill. At any rate, Alice was
hearing her private, *internal* feelings condensed and displayed *exter-
nally*—as if a computer screen printed out: "And right now procrastination is robbing your time." That display verifies a registered message
and moves Alice closer to confronting her procrastination and the fear
tucked behind it.]

ALICE: It *is* robbing me. Robbing me of the time I need for putting
        my life back together. Well, uh . . . It'll never get back to-
        gether like it was. But I'm not even getting a *little* more to-
        gether by delaying . . . holding back. There's something I'm
        not dealing with—not dealing with openly with others. It's
        'cause I procrast—*(Long pause)* Hell! It's because I'm *scared*
        to let it surface. Scared of the disruption, the discomfort, the
        embarrassment, and disgust. Like vomiting. I fought against
        vomiting all my life. Stubbornly. Scares me. I only did it five
        or six times.

DOROTHY: So it's not pure procrastination—it's fear of letting it out of
         you, like your fear of vomiting. That fear is keeping you from
         putting your life back together again. *(Pause)* Ah, at least, as
         you say, putting *some* of it together.

[Here's a summary of Alice's message topics in the preceding dialogue,
including confirmation of Dorothy's message on procrastination as a
thief: "It *is* robbing me." Then Alice moves through never getting her
life together as it was; not even starting because of avoiding that "something"; renaming her procrastination as a resistance to disclosing or
purging fear, which she likens to the physical act of vomiting; and using
the vomiting metaphor to show how she also stubbornly doesn't get rid
of that fear.

[It took me about five minutes to prepare the preceding summary of
Alice's message topics. I had the benefit of seeing her words transcribed
in print and 25 years of experience analyzing reflections. Yet it only took
Dorothy 3 seconds to start reflecting, and 14 seconds to complete her
comments. There's no way she could have done it without clearing her
mind and actively waiting to catch the meaning. The simile of someone
actively waiting to catch a ball parallels the situation of preparing to
receive a message for empathy. It's a remarkable event that any reasonably bright mind can do with some practice. I'm not saying Dorothy's
reflection was state-of-the-art or a superb re-presentation of every nuance of Alice's message—but it was an effective and uncluttered delivery
of empathic understanding. Sure, there are some very skilled therapists
and other language virtuosi who could have collected all of Alice's meaning, packaged it into a brilliantly clear reflection and delivered it with
the art of a poet. But there's also a beauty in what Dorothy has done. I

like the way she zeroed in on the discovery that procrastination is a cover word for fear instead of trying to paraphrase the sequence of topics in order of presentation. And I thought it useful for her not to get side-tracked by that vivid vomiting metaphor. She moved right to the issue of how fear was holding up progress.]

ALICE: Yeah, being scared is holding me back. Not only in the group, but with my friends. I need them for me to get better, but I turned away from everyone soon after it happened. It was so sudden and horrible that it didn't add up. So much was going on inside me that I had to lock it up. Even sensitive people became dangerous . . . 'cause anyone could burst that tight shell around me . . . and expose my hurt and confusion. Even a kind look could penetrate the shell and drag me back, force me to remember. Because their eyes were saying, "Poor thing. She must be suffering so. What a tragedy." *(Pause)* I guess the compassion in their faces made me relive some of the horror of his illness.

DOROTHY: You've needed people, but even kind people made you relive the horror of Sidney's dying mind. Even a kind look could penetrate the shell and shake your emotions. So you turned away from everyone, but now you need them.

[This reflection retold the story in a third of the time Alice took. If I carefully try to do that summary from a written transcript of Alice's disclosure, it takes many minutes. But finding the words in the flowing give-and-take of conversation takes seconds, if you key on significant words or themes like: "Relive the horror . . ." or "Penetrate the shell. . . ." Finding the words becomes easier when you look for them with an active wait.]

ALICE: It's been months. I'm feeling guilty about losing my temper so much when they nagged at me to talk. I've had bad dreams about screaming at innocent people. *(Pause)* And it's lonely. God, it's confusing. I'm afraid of seeing them again. See, I'm still angry . . . and the temper . . . but I don't know why. They all think I've turned against them, but I didn't! It's weird— I know they love me and want me out of my shell and I'm not against them. I'm really not. I'm *not*.

DOROTHY: You're really not against them, even though they think so. But you're still angry and afraid of losing your temper. And . . . uh . . . you're, let's see, lonely and guilty and you've had bad dreams about screaming at people—all kinds of confusing emotions except that you're really not against them.

[When you look at Dorothy's repetition, "You're really not against them" in print, it might look a little dumb. Saying the same words after Alice has pounded away at the point might sound mechanical. It might sound mechanical even if you heard a tape recording of their exchange. But it probably didn't sound that way to Alice. Repetitive or echoic para-phrases of critical or confusing messages can be gratifying to receive if you're sorting out an emotional puzzle. In this case, Alice repeated a disclosure she made ten minutes earlier ("I haven't turned against my friends") that somehow never got reflected by Dorothy. That is, Alice didn't get the satisfaction of hearing her protest understood and accepted—a frustration that stuck around under the surface of the conversation for ten minutes until Alice repeated the message. She was trying to repair a missed connection and seemed satisfied when Dorothy registered receipt of the feeling with a reflection. Repeating unregistered messages is a common process in *any* conversation—and an *urgent* process in important conversations. Typically, the repeat occurs within seconds of a missed connection, but it can take minutes in a case such as Alice's. Sometimes repeats are done after long stretches; the cause is usually a missed connection, no matter who is at fault. So Dorothy's repeat may look dumb, but it's competent. It was undramatic, not especially clever, but it gave Alice a small dose of the experience of being known. Dozens of doses add up to important psychological medicine for exploring rough emotional territory. Being clever and dramatic isn't the task of reflections. They should simply show that a feeling or thought exists in two minds. Now the air is cleared for Alice to go deeper.]

ALICE: How could I be against them when it's so obvious that they care and are worried about me? You know, I was pretty much inside myself with grief. The shell was closed tight. I was practically mute except for yelling when they prodded to know how I was feeling—what was happening inside. I *couldn't* tell them. How *could* I?

DOROTHY: They were worried about you being so much inside yourself with grief. But you *couldn't* tell them because it hurt so much to talk about—

ALICE: *(Interrupting)* No, it wasn't the hurt. I couldn't tell them because I didn't *know*. Everything was jumbled, numb. There was a strange person inside of me—she was like a strange dream, but she was *me*. How could I tell them about the strange me I didn't know? So I closed up.

[Alice's disclosure about not being able to communicate painful feelings to friends is easy to misunderstand as not wanting to relive the agony. It's common to keep quiet about touchy topics as a way of avoiding emotional pain. But Alice wasn't keeping quiet for that common reason. And Dorothy made the wrong assumption. So Dorothy's bad guess created an inaccurate reflection and Alice felt misunderstood and rushed in with an interruption to set things straight. People are usually eager to correct inaccurate reflections. It happens frequently and reveals how serious disclosers are about receiving understanding. When a reflection sticks extremely close to the meaning of a message, such errors don't happen. Adding extra meaning, exaggerating, or watering down are distortions that reduce accuracy. An accurate reflection works better than a pretty one.]

DOROTHY: Oh, so hurting wasn't the thing. You couldn't say because you

just didn't *know* for sure what was going on inside. You were
a stranger to yourself, some peculiar person was inside that
you didn't recognize.

ALICE: Exactly! I didn't recognize her. She was strange because something was cut out of her life. She didn't have his crazy, clever
joking, his competence, his worrying about me. She was the
one who knew Sidney's mind was dead and gone better than I
did. But, in a crazy way, I couldn't recognize myself in her. I
just couldn't swallow losing him. Couldn't stand the horror.
I guess the stranger . . . I guess I made her a secret hiding
place for my terror. Dumping my terror on her allowed me to
walk around feeling nothing for a while. She helped me forget—as if a part of me wasn't really missing.

[Dorothy picks up the figurative image—the metaphor of a stranger inside, and the reflection helps Alice think more clearly about her terror
and emotional numbness and how this stranger inside was a hiding place
for the terrible truth that her husband's mind was disappearing. The
image of not knowing how it felt inside transformed to having a strange
person inside and then to some peculiar person that wasn't recognized.
The image bounces between them and is allowed to become even more
real in the next response, as Dorothy's reflection shows Alice that now
she also knows what that stranger inside was doing.]

DOROTHY: She was the one who felt the horror of his illness for you. You
secretly put your terror in her so you could get relief in being
numb. Nobody knew. And that numb part of you couldn't even
recognize her. She swallowed much of your pain. Allowed you
to walk around at times like nothing was missing.

ALICE: As if nothing was cut out of my life. I could forget for moments
that a part of my mind and body were just sliced away—cut
away with a scalpel.

DOROTHY: This imaginary stranger helped you forget that parts of you
had been amputated.

ALICE: Oh, God, *yes*—that's it. *Amputated* from me. It felt as if my
wound was bleeding badly and hurting badly. I guess my little
stranger made it more bearable. I'd have gone crazy without
her. . . . I was grateful that I could imagine her and use her.
I wanted to protect her because that meant protecting the hiding place for my terror. . . . I wanted to share her with my
friends, but I didn't know how.

DOROTHY: You were grateful because she made your wounds more bearable and kept you from going crazy. . . . *(Long pause)* She
protected your terror and you protected her. You wanted your
friends to know her but couldn't figure out how to tell them.

[Dorothy's repeated reflections have allowed Alice to dig into unex-
plored territory. Alice's imaginary inner woman has not been questioned
or judged in the least by Dorothy. Both women stick to the basic theme

with little distraction. Dorothy's simple re-presentation about Alice wanting her friends to know about her stranger but being unable to figure out how to tell them about her, produces a surprisingly strong reaction.]

ALICE: Yeah, how could . . . if I didn't . . . know her well enough . . . oh, God. *(Breaks down, starts sobbing softly; long pause)* It's a lie. I didn't want them to know and I *did* know how to tell them. I was scared to give her up. I was feeling like a little girl playing with a doll that became a pretend refuge for my overwhelming feelings. I've been lying to myself . . . and to them. And I started lying to you. It's just that I've been so ashamed of worrying everyone around me, ashamed of using an imaginary character like a kook, ashamed of screaming at people 'cause I was afraid they'd want me to stop imagining things. *(Long pause, then almost whispering)* And I've been ashamed of *lying*.

DOROTHY: So you kept your secret and let them worry and now you're ashamed. You were afraid they'd think you were a kook and make you stop imagining her.

ALICE: Yes . . . yes. And it's time to tell them before they're alienated forever. I'm gonna tell them.

DOROTHY: You want to tell them why you couldn't tell them, oops, why you *refused* to tell them.

ALICE: *(Pauses a long moment, then smiles at Dorothy)* Almost missed that one, Dorothy. *(They both laugh)*

Even though this dialogue displays an "amateur" reflector, I wouldn't rank the talent as at all average. Dorothy is outstanding. She was the best communicator in the self-help support group.

I'd guess that 1 out of 50 people who learn reflections gets as good as Dorothy after using them several months. She's gifted. But I've seen unusually motivated people do some good ones after only weeks of practice. I advise playing around with the first two steps instead of trying to run off a string of usable reflections right away. Finding opportunities to do active waits and empathy isn't hard. In my experience, people who do that eventually become frustrated and *need* to find the words. Practicing on someone who's willing to put up with your early, awkward reflections can sharpen your skill more rapidly and, if you become good, the session could surprise you with a partner who's opened up more than expected. These reflections have a way of sneaking up on people in a nice way, even when you're just practicing.

PRACTICING

Investing time to acquire reflection skills typically yields interpersonal profit within weeks. Especially for people in "high-talk" work, and parents (particularly parents of adolescents), and intimate couples who aren't afraid of intense communication. Learning reflections is easy for any bright, normal adult who's not a stranger to empathy. If you love an adult or child (even a *pet*), you've already felt plenty of empathy. Without empathy, there's no intimacy; without intimacy, there's no love. Warning: Learning to do good reflections can be a lot tougher if you're currently going through a personal crisis or troubled emotional time. Honing this skill seems to require some serenity, a conflict-free mind able to play around with empathy. In addition, if your personality or current interpersonal style tends toward being detached or preoccupied with self, with busily seeking personal identity, the task will be tougher. Over the years, I've learned that practicing empathy isn't easy, familiar or even pleasurable for people who are currently coping with severe, self-absorbed narcissism or are experiencing a loss of appetite for intimacy or are in a state of emotional "flatness" or feeling turned off to acting nurturantly. So if you're into a period of coolness toward the human race or suffering a spell of aloof "nonattachment," learning reflections will take extra work.

(Anyone who tries the exercises in this section might profit from taking another look at the sections "Step One: Active Waiting," "Step Two: Empathizing," and "Step Three: Finding the Words" near the beginning of this chapter and the section "Who Has Empathy, and Who Doesn't?" in chapter 2.)

"Mirror, Mirror"

For groups or pairs. This exercise can take from 15 minutes to an hour for groups and about 10 minutes for a pair. Sometimes it's cumbersome for groups, but it works so well that it's worth the trouble. It's easier for a pair. In some ways, Mirror, Mirror sounds more complicated in print than it is in reality. And done repeatedly, the exercise can probably do more than any other to develop reflecting skills. Participants will need note-taking materials.

Purposes

1. Creates an excellent, *safe* practice arena for trying out the wait/empathize/find-the-words sequence for performing reflections.
2. Demonstrates how even "artificial" reflections given in a manufactured setting have the power to effectively penetrate knotty personal problems and touchy topics.
3. Combines recreation with a communication skill workout. It can be used as a family game or a party game with minor revisions. (The games require making only *light* disclosures.)

Method

1. For a *pair*: Create a seating arrangement in which the two of you can be close enough to talk quietly. Do *not* face each other. Back-to-back chairs is one possibility.

   For a *group*: Create an arrangement in which the group is equally divided into an inner circle closely surrounded by an outer circle containing the same number of people. Everyone faces the center. Inner circle people take on the role of disclosers; outer circle roles are as reflectors. This works for from 4 to 16 people. Consider arranging pillows on the floor or placing chairs in two concentric circles.

2. For a *pair*: Decide who will be the first discloser. That person makes a self-disclosure that can ramble for about 90 seconds after spending a thoughtful silent minute preparing the message. The disclosure can range from mild, unresolved problems to candid, here-'n'-now disclosures (what you're thinking or feeling—right *now*) to deeply private, risky disclosures (depending upon the pair's level of intimacy, current mood, and current capacity for handling serious revelations). Be sure the discloser also tells how he or she feels about making that revelation right now. Don't use risky disclosures in the early going of this exercise—it can be psychologically dangerous.

   For a *group*: Decide on the appropriate level of disclosure for the setting. For a game atmosphere, it's best to start with very mild but real problems or here-'n'-nows. Very real, risky disclosures can be okay for a close family or well-established self-help group. Start with a volunteer and limit disclosures to about a minute—not much less and no longer. A group facilitator or coordinator should remind each discloser to also reveal here-'n'-now feelings about the disclosure.

3. For a *pair*: The reflector, using the wait/empathize/find-the-words method, takes notes on the disclosure. Note-taking is the key to making this exercise effective and comfortable. Taking plenty of time, the reflector creates a carefully worded, briefer mirroring of the disclosure—a re-presentation in shorter form that mirrors back what's been heard. The challenge is to create a reflection that's neither exaggerated nor attenuated and will leave the discloser feeling accurately mirrored. You can ask the discloser to rate (from 1 to 10) or comment on the accuracy of the re-presentation.

For a *group*: Same as above, except that the reflector only has 30 seconds to create a *written* re-presentation, and the discloser rates accuracy (i.e., how well the reflector captured the essence, heart, crux, essential meaning of the message). After that, remaining group members also rate the reflector's accuracy. When extremely low scores occur, I like to stop for a few minutes and ask the entire group to *kindly* describe why the reflection was inaccurate. Some groups cheat and use a minute to do their written re-presentations. That's okay at first, but the shorter time comes closer to what's really needed when doing reflections in the flow of conversation.

4. For a *pair*: After rating the reflection, switch roles and repeat the sequence. Consider alternating roles two or three times, but decide first exactly how many rounds you will do. Ending the exercise in a raggedy way can spoil the enjoyment.

For a *group*: After rating a reflection or describing an inaccuracy, move on to the next volunteer. Avoid arbitrary round-robins. One complete round is usually enough, especially for groups larger than six. After that it's good to take a break and return as a group later for a free-for-all discussion. I've found the free-for-alls to be valuable and often amusing. Avoid open discussions that exclude participants who had to leave or prefer to stop. Specifying a brief time limit of 15 minutes or an hour (or whatever feels comfortable) encourages everyone to take part and brings a "clean" psychological closure to the event. Be sure to see the following section before starting.

HINTS AND A VARIATION

It helps to start these exercises by notifying the first few disclosers about how much time they used so participants get the feel of disclosing for 30 or 90 seconds. Kitchen or wristwatch timers are helpful. Assigning one person as group leader smooths the process. Arranging for people to read this chapter or parts of it can elevate this exercise into a basic, repeatable routine for running self-help sessions on occasion or organizing communication around a chronic family problem. (For a group, consider copying all or parts of this chapter for distribution.) Seasoned couples can also do a dozen or more rounds on the point of mutual distress or any relationship issue. The exercise cuts down dramatically on misunderstanding, distortion, and unnecessary pain in conflict resolution.

The most effective variation of the exercise has the outer and inner group exchanging places and rerunning the entire procedure. That usually takes too much time for a single session with a group that's larger than four or six. Of course, one solution is to switch circles on another occasion. It's best to maintain, if possible, the same pairing during the second session. A common, minor irritating problem occurs when the discloser becomes frustrated or otherwise stimulated in the middle of the reflector's mirroring. It happens surprisingly often. I've found that if participants agree to a simple signal (like showing the palm of the hand to the interrupting discloser), the reflecting person can do the task with much less distraction. You can create other variations for this exercise, but, as usual, try my field-tested version first. It's been used thousands of times and remains the safest way to begin.

"The Deferred Reflection System"

I call this a system instead of a method because it's an ongoing, organized operation. With its several parts, it sort of runs itself, once established. The system can reshape human relations in a family, work setting, or couple—significantly and for the better. But it does require that participants be able to do reflections and fuss with note-taking, tape recorders, or answering machines. The trouble is worth it—I've seen deferred reflections save marriages and dramatically reduce conflict in small work staffs (less than a dozen people).

PURPOSES

1. To maximize understanding and sharply reduce distortion when vital communication is tense or filled with conflict or in need of repair. Deferred reflections can break into the cycle of accelerating damage within a distressed relationship.
2. To elevate close relationships into superb arenas for empathic understanding.
3. To demonstrate (to human service students or self-help groups, for example) that meticulously prepared reflections can repair conflict, lower the rate of broken-record messages, and eventually create greater openness.
4. To introduce a brand-new channel of communication that upgrades intimacy and keeps important issues active and "working" within relationships.

METHOD

1. Each participant first learns to do at least rudimentary reflections (at minimum by reading this chapter and practicing a little).
2. Figure out a way to capture and preserve *important* disclosures (by writing them down or recording them on a tape machine or answering machine). Do what's necessary to allow the disclosure to come out complete and unrushed. This meticulous reception of the disclosure is an extreme exaggeration of the initial active waiting phase when doing three-step reflections during the actual flow of conversation.
3. Now the captured disclosure is dwelled upon, stewed over, absorbed, studied, and leisurely felt into, so that it becomes an easy target for a penetrating empathy or an imaginary "co-experience" (mentally re-creating the disclosure in familiar terms to render it real). That is, if the disclosure is too foreign, too painful, too revolting for a natural empathic connection, try imagining yourself going through the motions—even forcing your imagination into strange, unpleasant territory. Push the disclosure into your mind somehow and try to let some of it soak through to your feelings.
4. After the disclosure is mentally reproduced, find the words that demonstrate deep understanding. Create a careful reflection. It's best to write them out and even edit your sentences; create clear expressions of how the disclosure

registered in your mind, or lived for a moment in your heart.

JUSTIFYING THE DELAY

The deferred reflection system changes the fast-moving wait/empathize/find-the-words sequence into a slow, extended sequence: record the disclosure meticulously; let it stew in your mind; write out the reflection with care. Three-step reflections that typically take less than a minute to perform can take hours or days this way. The extra time and fussing could be a small price to pay for reducing distress.

This system can be reduced to a technique that comes to the rescue of stressed interaction or painful failures to communicate simply. All that's needed is an agreement between a pair for a single sequence of disclosures to reflect. I know dozens of couples who occasionally defer reflections during episodes colored by intense emotions or extended conflict. It's precisely such occasions that require the use of subtle meaning and careful messages to repair the customary miscommunication. The deferred reflection approach became so important to the quality of talk in one family (previously in therapy with me) that family members continue to report its impact by preparing a list of "stewed" reflections which I receive in the mail every Christmas.

If you look hard at the nature of conflict in close relations, it becomes evident that talk (or "shout" in emotional circumstances) is colored by self-absorption, bias, refusal to listen, fights for attention, and other elements that adversely affect clarity. Defective communication usually makes a bad situation worse. Problems are compounded when the battle is active for days or weeks. Deferred reflections help reduce distortion and allow emotions to defuse. They work as safety valves and allow people to remain in meaningful contact in the midst of conflict. They can save a relationship.

Take a look at the "Disclosure Bank" method in chapter 7 for hints on setting up the system. Also, don't use deferred reflections for ordinary disclosures (unless you're just practicing) because the procedure can become boring without important issues at stake.

"Empathy Overkill"

PURPOSES

1. A marvelous three-person exercise that serves as an arbitrator for arguments between kids (especially feuding siblings), parents and their children, or any pair debating a personal matter of moderate or minor consequence.

2. It can cause antagonists to examine their own exaggerations during a debate while demonstrating the value of reflections for simplifying arguments.

3. Empathy overkill is a formidable weapon against an intimate enemy's "erroneous," unmoving, "rigid" attitude on an interpersonal issue.

METHOD

The whole idea is to have a mediator who represents both sides by reflecting each message *to* the opponent before the opponent replies. The mediator hears his message to her and then reflects it to her. When she responds, the mediator reflects that response to him . . . and so on. The "overkill" part is the exaggeration that flavors each of the mediator's reflections. It's the exaggeration of feelings, the amplification of emotions behind the message that brings insight and humor to the debate. Don't be preposterous with this. All that's needed is a mild increase in amplitude, like turning the volume up.

Say that someone complains during an observed argument: "You borrow my books, you use my pens and paper and hardly ever ask permission—and you don't have a right to! I just don't like it! It's not *fair*." The mediator might amplify the annoyance into anger, or the anger into mild rage with an exaggerated first-person reflection: "You constantly rip off my property behind my back. You've disregarded me and violated my rights and I *hate* it! You've been reckless with my life—*cruel*."

Well, my example is overdone a bit for effect. Overkill works best when the exaggeration starts slowly. Let it creep up so the debaters might feel satisfaction from the first few mild distortions. I won't specify a format because you can use dozens of procedures—even spontaneous entry into an argument. (But absolutely stay away from spontaneous entry into serious conflict; the overkill might be believed and do psychological damage.) If you think this technique might help people (especially children) in painful contention, move in slowly with a few *accurate* reflections before turning to overkill. I recommend it as a safe procedure with one critical warning: Always make absolutely sure that *everyone* knows exactly what you're doing and why you're doing it. Withholding your intention or hiding your technique when entering a serious conflict could feel worse to the combatants than being "manipulated." It could be experienced as treachery. I've heard of awful consequences where empathy overkill was used recklessly. As an interpersonal game, though applied to less serious issues, it can be silly and even cause the dueling pair to break up with laughter. (My wife and son have lost track of what they were arguing about on several overkill occasions.) The embellished reflections can easily loosen an opponent's entrenched positions, quell hostile passion, and stop namecalling. I love to do it myself because everyone usually ends up winning.

"Rogerian Talk"

The late Carl Rogers was a major influence on the way professional caregivers—especially therapists—talk to their clients. His simple, powerful ideas about how people get close and help each other are used around the world. (See "People Who Write about Talk," on page 353.) He was my academic mentor. He was also the source of my inspiration for studying language in close relationships. So I know if he were alive, reading this casual recipe for using his ideas would tickle him a little because he was ambivalent about teaching techniques separate from the attitudes behind them. I can hear him saying something about how the attitudes, the essential caring, the empathy, and the commitment to honest talk are more important than technique. Then I'd answer with a minor lecture on how using new technique can pave the way for caring, honest attitudes. He'd have strong answers. Strong enough to slow me down, but he'd end with, "I suppose your stuff just might work. Anyway, when you try it, I'd like to learn what *you've* learned. Maybe I'll change my mind." And he would mean it.

PURPOSES
1. To get a little taste of what client-centered (or Rogerian) psychotherapy is like.
2. To learn a context in which *strings* of reflections serve a discloser's personal exploration.

3. To demonstrate how the practice of technique (in this case, using talk tools) can eventually reveal or establish a new "stance," a new attitude or set of values on how to help someone through serious difficulties.
4. To provide profound help for distress.

METHOD

1. Start practicing Rogerian Talk in a two-person, half-hour setting. When you have a good feel for it, go to an hour, or try the method in more complex groups like your family, work team, or self-help group. However, everyone should know what you're doing—and why.
2. Put yourself in a frame of mind where you want to give help and provide support and care little or not at all about getting psychological benefit for yourself, like showing off, satisfying your curiosity, offering solutions, indulging your impatience, covering your blunders, or letting your mind drift—especially into thinking of how effective your reflections might be. The idea is to focus so completely on the person you're helping (the discloser) that your sense of self recedes into the background. You become a follower, a psychological servant, an empathic understander, giving back the meaning of what is received. Hard to do. Sounds almost spiritual, like a religious act, but the task here needs even more than belief or commitment to a helping attitude for an hour. It requires putting yourself in a psychological frame of mind that can feel strange and awkward at first—especially if you're a man who resists giving up to others.
3. Make reflections your dominant or sole talk tool for the full session. An occasional self-disclosure is okay after you've tried it a few times, but be wary of distracting the discloser. (See chapters 1 and 7 if you get serious.) Give plenty of silence responses, allowing behavior, while avoiding crowding behavior like interruptions and overtalk. (Glance through chapter 6 and take to heart chapter 12.)
4. During the helping session, remove from your conversational diet the following talk tools: advisement, all five varieties; interpretations (even soft ones); and questions. Even just one of these taboo tools uttered at the wrong moment could destroy the psychological safety of your helping. Beginners frequently slip off this diet restriction.

APPROACHING STATE-OF-THE-ART

I've never seen anyone develop their method to near its maximum in less than six months. Fortunately, though, even minimum skill with Rogerian Talk goes a long way. Here are some practice tips toward excellence; I hope you refer to them frequently.

- Use a tape recorder and listen to your mistakes and to exactly how your reflections took the discloser deeper into himself or herself. Relistening can also help disclosers examine their struggle toward clarity.
- Ask the discloser for feedback on the accuracy of your reflections. Don't be discouraged if you're told that the reflections felt unnatural at first. Even professionals hear that from their clients, and they know that the feeling fades shortly.
- Use three-step reflections and keep them very accurate, or even on the mild or watered-down side. Exaggerated or amplified reflections are disruptive in the hands of a beginner. Later on, you might try reflecting just a little ahead of the discloser by concentrating on the leading edge of his or her feeling. It's like reflecting the unspoken emotions they're moving toward. It's a tricky technique because if you get too far ahead, the mood is broken as you become an interpreter (see chapter 9).
- Use plenty of time before each reflection even if it feels awkward or causes you to lose your talking turn. It's better to miss a turn than to crowd.
- Aim toward using nothing but reflections the first time or two.
- After a few sessions, play around with using metaphors, similes, or physical images as they occur to you, e.g., "When he asked you to live with him, you had a feeling of being captured—almost as if he held a cage in front of you with an open door." Using such rich language to represent complex feelings can be terrific, but it's too much to try during the first few sessions. Wait until you're comfortable with the basic mechanics.
- During the second or third session, start making your reflections shorter than the messages they represent. The goal is to show empathic understanding and then get out of the way so exploration can continue with little disruption.
- After several sessions of practice, you may wish to reflect messages given outside the main theme. Reflect the discloser

saying things like, "This might sound silly, but . . ." or "I'm not sure I want to continue with this . . ." or "I just don't know what to say." That is, reflect those here-'n'-now messages *about* messages—they usually are important.

• Don't force reflections if your discloser doesn't give you much opportunity at first; continue reflecting silently—under your breath. Most disclosers want all of the attention during the first part of the first session or two. After that, people start expecting reflections—*wanting* them, in fact. If you can't clearly empathize with a discloser, simply give a silence response—even if it means waiting for *minutes*. I mean it. Don't let your fear of silence push you to make a "dutiful" reflection. A pretending helper is poison in high trust conversations designed to encourage risky disclosures.

Avoiding "Begging" Reflections

At heart, reflections are nothing more than disclosed empathy. They tell. They are *not* questions. But beginners frequently end reflections with an upward inflection. Maybe it's insecurity with a new powerhouse talk tool that makes learners put a question mark in their voice. These questions-in-the-service-of-reflections actually ask the discloser for confirmation: "So you're saying that right now you're confused and *tired*?" Translation: "I'm not quite sure you're confused and tired and don't want to be presumptuous, so would you please give me feedback and confirm that I'm right?"

The problem is that begging reflections request reassurance from the discloser, who may be hard at work exploring some difficult issue. That's why they can be obtrusive and demanding. The begging for confirmation forces the discloser to switch attention from an inner personal journey to an outside evaluation of the reflector's performance.

Perhaps I'm making it sound like an obnoxious act unfairly. After all, part of the questioning reflector's motive can be to show respect for the discloser as an authority on his or her feelings. Beginners can't avoid using begging reflections at least occasionally; that's no disaster. But using them *repeatedly*, even frequently, will badly distract the discloser and ruin the flow of experiencing. Imagine an hour session (which typically holds around 25 reflections) that interrupts the discloser 15 times. Too much. It wrecks the mood. So please be on guard for begging reflections—especially after you've had an hour or two of practice under your belt. What I don't want is for beginners to worry about excluding them so much it slows learning the basic technique. But as skill comes, these insecure devices should disappear.

CHAPTER 9

MASTERING INTERPRETATIONS

THE DOUBLE-EDGED nature of interpretations allows them to serve both hostility and nurturance. That's why my presentation of the damn things has always been nagged by warnings. In the best of hands, interpretations can quickly turn from well-intended instruments for letting loved ones know exactly what's wrong with them into cruel weapons for hurting with a negative personality diagnosis. So please keep in mind that the help-intended methods described in this chapter can inadvertently be used carelessly to injure as well as to cut to the core of problems.

Used with the intention to help (not hurt), interpretations can give the gift of new possibilities. They can help uncover mysteries and stimulate fresh solutions to old problems. Even when a well-intentioned, empathic personal interpretation is somewhat wrong—"Maybe he left early because he saw your shyness as coldness toward him"—it can stimulate thought toward a useful insight: "No, we already talked about my shyness at length and he knew I liked him—but now I remember explaining how I get overloaded spending too much time with new people. I bet he was just being considerate in leaving early. That puts a new slant on things. I'll call to see what really happened."

My example is too perfectly pat, but it does illustrate the unpredictable and important function of creating new meaning with kind intentions. All interpretations attempt to create new meaning for the listener. Even if they are dead wrong or angry, the goal is to give news—unknown facts. That's why the attitude of the interpreter and the context in which the interpretations are exchanged become critical to their utility. Given in a context of mutual trust (like serious friendship, loving concern, or professional caretaking), these talk tools are interpersonal gifts. At times, they can be like gifts of hard-to-swallow medicine. They can melt meaninglessness and change lives in minutes. That's also exactly why they can so easily become cruel or nasty when given out of anger or cold, mean indifference. Here's lesson one, then, in applying interpretations to beneficial purposes: Use them only when feeling generous and in a calm context. Giving a *personal* interpretation aimed at changing someone's view of their own behavior or mental process can be difficult if suspicions arise that the change serves the interpreter's needs first. Biased, self-serving personal interpretations abound within close relations. That's why some seek the supposedly "objective" view of an impartial therapist or mutual friend.

The personal interpretation is where person A faces person B and offers a new explanation of B's personality, motives, feeling, thinking, behavior, or character. Basically, A implies knowing something about B that B doesn't know. Quite a presumptuous act, even where unbiased generosity and calm prevail. The presumptuous act easily becomes an outrageous insult in the midst of passionate, crowded debate. Adrenaline and good personal interpretations don't mix. (Personal interpretations are emphasized in this chapter because they are more salient for solving relationship problems than the group, third-party, or general interpretations described in chapter 3.)

The most common practical application for interpretations is where you observe someone not recognizing an important truth about themselves or about something that touches them. It could be a husband who comes home and yells at his wife once a week. The wife figures out that their conflicts occur somewhat systematically on Monday nights. It happens that Mondays are hell-day at the office for the husband. He seems unaware of the truth about Monday nights being so clouded with family fights. How does she present her interpretation so it "takes" (is taken as a possible truth—a new way to view himself)?

I've had difficulty getting my adolescent son to accept my interpretation that his grumpy noontime moods result from a no-breakfast, low-blood-sugar morning. The difficulty has been my own doing, my own impatience when presenting my findings with certainty—a pronouncement of truth about his body and mind. I gave him a *hard* interpretation.

ME: Sasha! That's the third time I've asked what happened to the remote control [for the TV], and I'm getting frustrated.

SASHA: I didn't hear you, 'cause I'm reading. *(Sarcastically)* Do you mind?

ME: Ah, c'mon. I practically shouted in your ear. You're just grumpy and wanting to start trouble 'cause you ate that dumb stuff for breakfast. And now low blood sugar has vacuumed all the energy from your brain.

SASHA: That's all you know, low blood sugar all the time—you've got sugar on the brain.

ME: And you're a vacuum brain.

You'd think that I'd know better than to initiate a nasty name-calling exchange with my son, but the combination of hard interpretations and impatience caused my fall from grace. Sometimes I do better, remembering to use a *soft* interpretation. Honest. Here's a Frisbee-tossing occasion when I held back on the temptation for hard interpretations.

ME: Maybe I'm imagining it, but it seems like you've been moody for the last hour. Usually, you don't get so annoyed when my shots go wild. I really threw some ugly ones, but I've done it before and all I got was pity—not being called "stupid" or "ox paws." Maybe your body needs some more fuel? Did you remember to do a good breakfast?

SASHA: Mom made me French toast, but it was just too yucky inside, so I had orange juice and stuff.

ME: Stuff?

SASHA: A couple of chocolate cookies.

ME: *(Resisting fatherly outrage)* Well, you know, that's not gonna nourish you all the way to lunch—maybe I'd better make you a cheese sandwich now. It could be something else, but a bad breakfast might be giving you a bad mood. I can't be sure that's it, 'cause—

SASHA: *(Interrupting)* Ah, c'mon, you *can* be sure. I'm sure. You're just trying to say it nice so I'll understand. *(Smart kid)*

The "soft" interpretation I used was characterized by a tentative, respectfully submitted, fact-supported explanation about his behavior and feelings. This deferent, watered-down talk tool is the only way to go when telling others our view of how they are as humans.

CREATING SOFT INTERPRETATIONS

Here are basic recommendations for reducing the explosive impact and dangerous aftereffects of interpretations.

1. Offer *every* observation as a *hunch*. Don't just *think* of it as a hunch, but say so. Call your effort a guess, speculation or a tentative thought, *before* telling someone what they are, what they did, or how they think, feel, or behave. Softening your interpretation makes messing with someone's self-image immensely less tricky and much more respectful. Presenting yourself as an authority with the correct conclusion creates mischief. So if someone rejects your brilliant idea, try something daring—let them. Getting frustrated when your firm belief in an unquestionable truth is lightly regarded or politely dismissed usually ruins the help-giving. All you have to do is remember the word "hunch" and act on it.
2. The next word to remember is *evidence*. It's a reminder to explain how you arrived at the hunch. If the evidence is partial and you admit to your incomplete knowledge, it'll enhance trust. Describing even minor evidence for your hunch shows that it's more than pure imagination or fantasy.
3. Then there's *doubt*. You give your hunch, describe evidence for it, then express doubt. Actually, the exact order is unimportant as long as you use all three elements of the soft interpretation. Even if you're positive that you've cornered the truth with some interpretation, I advise you to force disclosure of some minor doubt. (Think of times you've been sure of your facts and turned out to be dead wrong.)

If you can remember *hunch/evidence/doubt* and express them all, there's little danger in using this potentially hurtful talk tool. The three elements create the awkward acronym HED (think of head). Bad spelling, but a good reminder to soften personal interpretations and respect your listener's sensitivity and intelligence.

HED APPLIED

The following dialogue was sent to me by two couples from Queens, New York, who were trying to save their marriages. One of the big issues for them was exaggerated emotions pumped up by hormones distributed by premenstrual syndrome (PMS). They found each other at a local PMS workshop that helped them form a self-help, mutual support group. The couples used an audiotape training program I helped develop at UCLA (Common Concern Program) which taught, among other things, the proper use of soft interpretations. On their own, they also brought psychodrama techniques into their self-help group, in which one couple would re-create an argument in front of the group. Then the others offered soft interpretations based on the reenactment. Their invention has worked effectively for several other groups. I'm told that its title, "Two HEDs Are Better," was inspired by the HED method and New York state dry sherry. To reduce confusion, I've assigned fictional names that connect each couple: Rina and Robert, Vickie and Victor. We enter midway through their 14th session. Rina and Robert are already arguing over a past argument—and the reenactments haven't even started.

RINA: Our fight started when you said that I was always ready to jump on you every time you—

ROBERT: *(Interrupting)* No, no, no! It was when we had to do an early decision about Kevin's summer—

RINA: *(Interrupting)* Robert, Kevin's summer school was decided way before the fight. I distinctly remember getting mad the first time you started that crap about me *always* jumping on you.

ROBERT: Well, my dear, once again your *distinct* memory has failed to . . . *(etc.)*

Couples approaching reenactments bring real emotion that can spill out even before they start their replay. After five minutes of such premature debate between Robert and Rina, the couple began the actual psychodrama. (Throughout this transcript, the self-help group refers to their dramatic reenactments as psychodrama. They've also nicknamed soft interpretation as "interps.")

Rina and Robert's psychodrama depicts a brief, harsh argument that occurred in their home two weeks earlier. It's evening. He's on the phone as she enters the room. Rina assumes he's talking to Braddie, who helps him run a small chain of yogurt parlors. He and Braddie are on the phone several times a day, discussing business, usually enthusiastically. They enjoy each other, and Rina has felt jealousy over their animated conversations.

RINA: Don't you think you ought to be getting off the phone and resting? It's been a hard day. Is talking to Braddie so important right now?

ROBERT: *(Cupping his hand over an imaginary phone mouthpiece and putting on a contemptuous face)* Whataya talkin' about, Rina?

RINA: About you getting some rest. About giving up already before surgery is required to detach that phone from your ear.

ROBERT: And what's this about Braddie?

RINA: Couldn't it wait till tomorrow? Haven't you had enough time with her today?

ROBERT: Why the hell do you assume I'm talking to Braddie, and why are you so damned worried about my health all of the sudden? *(Quickly shifts focus, addresses imaginary phone)* Please hold a minute. *(Returns angry attention to Rina)* What the hell are you doing to me? I'm trying to solve a rotten payroll problem with *Ed*. Is that okay with you? Do I have your *permission*?''

RINA: Well, I don't know who you were—it might as well have been Braddie because—listen, you're gonna be sick if you don't rest because—

ROBERT: *(Interrupting)* No, just listen. Dammit, I'm so tired of you *always* jumping to conclusions before getting the facts. You *never* worry about getting good facts before doing one of your insane jealous numbers.

RINA: Why don't you talk about *your* insensitivity and preoccupation with Braddie? It might as well have been her. What's the difference? Why should I worry about you when all you do is treat me like a taken-for-granted piece of furniture? Spend *all night* on the phone, you stupid schmuck. And then flush yourself down the wire. *(She stomps away from Robert with a touch of feigned overacting for humor, even though it's obvious to all observers that they both relived some real anger from two weeks ago)*

Rina and Robert need a few minutes to cool down and talk to the other group members about how the couple play-acted more rationally and less provocatively than in the real event. Then Victor rewinds the tape recorder so the group can listen from the beginning. At my request, a second tape recorder remains operating to capture the entire process. This wonderful little self-help group has invented a procedure that could help other couples cope with PMS or any relationship-threatening problem. The rules are to stop the playback anytime anyone has a reaction or a soft interpretation about what the argument means. After hearing the first few exchanges on tape, Vickie says she's ready to interpret Robert. The rules call for no interruption of an interpretation in midstream.

VICKIE: Uh, hi Robert. *(Laughs)* Okay, here's one for what you did to me last month with the kitty. *(Group laughs)*

["Kitty" refers to an interpretation Robert had offered Vickie about her substituting a cat for the baby she wants. His interpretation helped clear up a conflict between Vickie and Victor over the new pet.]

VICKIE: Let's see, uh—I've got a *hunch*—only a hunch—you were ready to jump all over Rina that night. That you had a chip on your shoulder and that's why you screamed at her instead of simply informing her that she was mistaken. Okay, now the evidence. The evidence, uh, comes from kinda the way she seemed generally concerned about your stress-out. I mean, it's unlike you to be so inconsiderate that you absolutely pay *no* attention to the loving part of her message. *(Pause)* And also you've been irritable more often lately with all the payroll screwups, and Rina said you had a rotten day or something. So that's my evidence for you being cranky with a chip on your shoulder. So, uh, that's the evidence and then comes the doubt. So, uh, that's the evidence and then comes the doubt. My doubt, well, maybe you were cranky about something else, like your phone conversation. Maybe you and Rina had a fight earlier. *(Long pause)* Maybe something about not wanting Rina to worry—not being able to accept her kindness right then. Ah-h, let's see, that's all.

ROBERT: Thanks, Vickie dear. Your lovely interp is—*(Dramatic pause)* wrong. *(Group laughs)* But, but—seriously, one part, about not being able to accept her kindness at that moment, was right on. Ya see, Rina's kindness was sorta like a cover for her, her—what shall I call it—her jealous dig. She's had Braddie-on-the-brain lately and it's wearing thin. Like every time I talk to Braddie it seems I'm hurting Rina, and when she—when Rina comes on strong trying to get me off the phone with Braddie when I'm having a serious talk with Ed, I blow up. It's infuriating. So that's the chip on my shoulder from Rina's jealousy. I suppose I shoulda thanked her for her concern about my bad day and I shoulda been more understanding about her green-eyed monster, but sometimes it drives me up the wall. Maybe I lost patience because of the bad day, too, like you say, Vickie, but the nagging was mostly what did it. But, maybe it's fair to say I had a chip on my shoulder from her jealousy. Or a touchy sore spot that provoked me to blow up instead of answering Rina more reasonably.

Even though Vickie's full explanation was rejected, some parts of it started Robert thinking about his knee-jerk reaction to jealousy. Also, note how easy it is to reject soft interpretations. Much of the ease is from the familiarity between Vickie and Robert, but imagine the same game with Vickie coming on strong as a true believer, positive about her truth while offering no evidence. Hard interpretations are hard to reject. They create awkward or hostile situations.

Hard interpretations are taboo when playing Two HEDs Are Better. The rules are that *two* soft interpretations be given per couple. Robert received his, so now someone in the group must give a formulation about Rina's motives or behavior that would explore *her* thinking. Victor had an eye-opener for Rina. He joked about it requiring a man to see behind the behavior of women because women share the same blind spots and miss each other's defense mechanisms. I don't endorse his view, but I've noticed a very high proportion of men choosing to interpret women and vice versa while playing Two HEDs Are Better. (It seems about 80 to 90 percent of the interps are directed at the opposite sex.)

VICTOR: *(Speaking rapidly with excitement about his new idea)* Rina! I think you overblended—what's the word? Fused—uh, mixed two messages as I see it, from the replay you guys did. Like the caring was there all right, but you were also complaining at the same second, the same moment. Ya know? Like it sounded like all you were doing was worrying about Robert's exhaustion, but you were also worrying, you also cared about not wanting him talking to that Braddie. You were trying to—

VICKIE: *(Interrupting)* Hold it! This thing is supposed to be a *hunch*. Remember? You're coming off sounding like some damned arrogant analyst telling a woman some secret about her soul. This game's supposed to be HED, Mr. Know-It-All-about-Women. So how 'bout getting off your high horse. Better not lose *your* head. *(Group laughs)*

VICTOR: *(Clutches a hand to his chest and rolls his eyes upward in mock anguish)* Okay. Okay. She's right. Let me do that as a hunch. *(Long pause)* It struck me that you possibly, uh, might have emphasized your caring in order to slip in a complaint about Braddie. Wait. What I mean is that it was hard, it might have been hard for you to say, "I don't like you talking to Braddie and I wish you'd stop. I'm jealous." Like maybe that was just too damned difficult, uh, embarrassing. So, uh, maybe you unconsciously hid it and worried about Robert's working too late. So that's it. That's my hunch.

Now what's "E" stand for again? Oh, *evidence*. Well, Rina, you were saying stuff about "it might as well have been Braddie" and him spending all night with her on the phone and that he treats you like furniture. And then, then you even started, like early in the psychodrama about it, about does he have to talk to

Braddie now? But maybe the replay was different from what happened. I guess it's right that you assumed it was her without even checking. What I'm saying is that maybe the jealous feelings sort of dominated your mind and being kind to Robert was a second thought. Maybe a distant second? *(Pause)* That's it. And now it's time for my humble doubt. I know I can be all wet, Rina. Just like last month when everyone got so mixed up at *our* replay. Remember? We screwed up. So maybe something's wrong with my conclusions. Or maybe you weren't even trying to cover up your annoyance and just had two feelings at the same time.

Rina bought it. Almost all of it. She admitted to sort of using her worry as an excuse but insisted her worry was also genuine. She began talking to Robert right there and told him she could see why he flew off the handle. They resolved to work out a more direct way of handling the problem. And they actually began facing their dilemma later that session. The soft interpretation did its work.

When it comes to repairing tattered feelings after an argument, the situation can sometimes be eased by reporting *real* facts instead of using interpretations that are *disguised* as facts. Say a husband complains that his wife is not paying attention to what he's saying, and she looks up from a book and says, "Huh?" There's little room for doubt that he is conveying validated, verifiable, nonspeculative information. I call that a "report."

Making distinctions between the knowable assertion of a report and the frequently vague, untestable assertion of an interpretation can save grief as angry couples try to get past their trouble spots, as in: "I watched you eat the whole bag of cookies tonight." [Report] "So you must be feeling nervous again." [Interpretation]

PRACTICING

The best practical advice on using interpretations is to keep them away from immediate, emotionally charged conflicts because they add fuel to the fire. If you must tell someone what you think of him or her, use HED to water down the arrogance. Done tentatively, in a calm setting, a brilliant, eye-opening idea has, at best, a 50–50 chance of being well accepted.

Finding the right time to unveil that hard-to-swallow, ego-bruising interpretation isn't easy. So, if you want more than resistance, denial, and dirty looks, take ten minutes to do it right. Otherwise your hasty explanation or classification will reveal more about *your* motivation than your listener's personal life. Because the interpretation is a cousin to advisement and frequently carries implied guidance, the two talk tools behave somewhat similarly as psychological stimuli. (If this stuff is important for your personal or career life, see the first two small sections in chapter 10 for some advisement characteristics that are relevant for interpretations.)

"Two HEDs Are Better"

This technique and its innovators are described in the previous section. I'll just summarize and offer variations briefly here. Allow about 45 minutes per couple. For groups of two to four couples.

PURPOSES

1. Provides an unusually safe setting for exchanging potentially threatening personal interpretations.
2. Allows couples in conflict or couples coping with chronic talk breakdowns to use peers as helpers in repairing relationship damage.
3. Can also be a practice arena for honing soft interpretation skills.

METHOD

1. One couple volunteers to "replay" a real argument or conversation that doesn't yet make clear sense or remains unresolved. Reenact only relevant parts and maintain the psychodrama from five to no longer than ten minutes. All of it must be recorded via audiotape or videotape.
2. Members of the "audience" listen with full antennae, looking for missed motives, unnoticed behavior, denied feelings—anything useful that the replay couple may have overlooked. When the recorded conversation is played, anyone with an idea should stop at a spot that can be interpreted. Usually the interpretation is directed at one member of the pair, unless a strong idea occurs that cannot be addressed to a single person. Both members of the replay should be interpreted only once during each round. They should never interpret each other.
3. Use only *soft* interpretations using the HED method de-

scribed in the previous section. Everyone involved must be assertive in reminding interpreters not to stray into hard interpreting (expressed as truth rather than a *hunch* supported by *evidence* and offered with *doubt*). Hard interpretations are frequently rejected under any circumstances.

4. Allow each couple about 15 minutes to discuss interpretations between themselves. Invite group members to occasionally chime in. Make sure *both* people are discussed. You may be tempted to exceed 15 minutes and siphon time and energy from interpreting other couples. If so, it may be best to reduce the number of rounds for the session. This procedure can be emotionally draining. The post-interpretative discussions are meant to stimulate future constructive exchange for the couple, so keep strict limits unless it seems extended discussion during the session is very important and demands striking while the iron is hot.

VARIATIONS

These involve (1) doing replays at home and bringing the recording to the sessions (a timesaver); (2) exchanging recorded replays to take home so that each couple has leisure to prepare interpretations for the next meeting. The Queens self-help group played around with several convenient formats with reported success. Apparently, Two HEDs Are Better can be shaped to many circumstances as long as the interpretations are *soft* and the group maintains a fair distribution of attention among couples. Don't let one couple consistently take the limelight—or do hard interpretations of each other.

"The Low-Provoke Mode"

PURPOSES

1. To reduce emotional abuse and curb conflict during ordinary arguments and family fights.
2. To maintain control of angry passion during debate without stifling full expression of negative interpretations (like telling others what's wrong with them).

METHOD

1. It's simple: Try to use soft interpretations as discord begins. Don't attempt to suffocate fault-finding or expressions of pain or anger. This technique is for putting a lid on irrational squabbles and thoughtless insults, not forceful contention.
2. Ideally, both parties should know how to give soft interpretations (hunch/evidence/doubt). If a contestant sees his or her partner lapse into childish name-calling or outlandish claims in midbattle, it should be challenged with stuff like: "Where's the evidence?" "Is that a fact or your hunch?" "Can you stay with that without any doubt?"

AN OBSERVATION

I've got a *hunch* that couples who have had a *single* experience of soft-interpreting each other (in a practice session on noninflammatory topics) have greater success using the Low-Provoke Mode. My evidence comes from about a dozen families at Berkeley's Institute of Human Development. Of course, there is doubt, because two or three couples described the technique falling apart in midargument—even after earlier HED practice during a calm period.

"Soap Opera Analyst"

PURPOSES

1. To provide a convenient, no-pain workout session for semi-serious soap fans (daytime or nighttime) who wish to enhance their interpretative abilities. (Passionate soap fans are advised to skip this exercise or risk turning into name-calling J.R.'s.)
2. Offers an opportunity to observe the ease by which we can apply a variety of divergent (and apparently appropriate) interpretations to the same situation. This exercise can vividly demonstrate the blind-men-and-elephant phenomenon that plagues the act of interpretation. A good classroom assignment.

METHOD

1. Zero in on a single soap character by taking casual notes on his or her motives, blind spots, inconsistencies, deceptions, indifferences, or inadequacies of character.
2. Do it by yourself or with someone beside you, or make ar-

rangements to compare notes with a friend watching somewhere else.

3. At the end of the episode, review your notes and write out as many explanations or diagnoses as you can. Imagine that the character wanted insight from you or help in self-understanding. Don't try to be consistent. Let your mind work without constriction and make your interpretations short. It will probably take more than one episode to generate some good interpretations. You'll need a familiar character.

4. Compare interpretations with a partner or simply compare your own interpretations over several episodes. Just performing this exercise was a fine learning experience for me.

5. If you want an easy opportunity to practice soft interpretations, add hunch/evidence/doubt to a few. It can really help, even when the characters are cartoonlike. Soap writers specialize in teasing viewers (or hitting them over the head) with hints about the characters' blind spots or interpersonal stupidities.

VARIATION

If you have a VCR, consider recording episodes until you find some behavior that can be easily interpreted in many ways. Then play it for others (maybe at a party) and ask them to privately write interpretations. The challenge here is to search for hidden motivations, blind spots, subtle traits that mark a character, etc. As soon as they're done, collect the interps and read them out loud. It can be fun. If people are feeling strong, turn the tables and ask the group to interpret the interpretations. That process can be very revealing—sometimes embarrassing. This specialized high-impact talk tool (the *personal* interpretation) is only useful within a narrow band of human activity—offering people insight into themselves or stimulating the opening of new mental routes for others.

Third-party interpretations are frequently used for back-biting, and I haven't developed any exercises for that skill—yet. Group interpretations are terrific professional tools for running seminars, work meetings, and TV talk shows. (Oprah Winfrey nicely interprets her audiences on the spot, Phil Donahue also does it frequently, Johnny Carson makes humor out of group interpretations ["We've got a mean, hungry group out there tonight"], and David Letterman uses them like a slightly embarrassed farm boy worrying about his performance.) Athletic coaches and teachers can also use them to settle things down or as motivation. (If you want to understand group interpretations, read the section "Group Interpretations—for Contemplation, Inspiration . . . and Perspiration" in chapter 3.)

General interpretations are another matter. They're usually generalizations about human nature or society or the physical universe. The art of using them as instructional devices is as broad as the art of teaching. (See the sections "General Interpretations and the Proliferation of Half-Truths" and "Old Proverbs Never Die; They Don't Even Fade Away" in chapter 3.) But the art of understanding another person by his or her use of general interpretations in social discourse is specific and easy to learn. Observing someone's feeling of personal attraction, willingness to be compliant, masked annoyance, assessment of you, or degree of eagerness to get close can be facilitated by knowing how general interpretations work in conversations. The dialogue between Angie and Larry (in the section "Early Signals of Personal Attraction" in chapter 3) contains practical illustrations for converting these interpretations into self-disclosures. I'm a bit ambivalent about recommending such "manipulative" ways to observe others, but it seems we all do some of it anyway, without trying. Angie and Larry can help you do a lot of it—if it's worth the work to you.

CHAPTER 10

MASTERING ADVISEMENTS

A SOPHISTICATED array of advising talk tools exists for persuading, influencing, reducing conflict, maintaining love, managing staffs, dismissing complaints, suggesting solutions—any form of guiding imaginable. But we chronically just plain screw things up with these advisement tools, using them in the wrong way, for the wrong reason, at the wrong time.

The screwups can cause good advice to be rejected. When it's everyday, garden-variety, automatic advice, certain complications are created, including the wounding of pride or the frustration of having a decent piece of advice blindly dismissed. Those complications are usually without longterm effects; the wounded pride and frustrated deed are eventually forgotten. No big deal. But the complications coming from rejected advisements in serious, life-altering situations can be costly to the point of ruining relationships or careers. So demonstrating a method for reducing the rejection of advice is one of the goals of this chapter. The idea is to make *serious* advice palatable. (I'll stay away from easy stuff like guiding friends to favorite restaurants and movies.)

Teaching communications has taught me that most people want to spend time sharpening skills for *giving* important advisements, but few are interested in learning to accept and effectively *use* guidance. We seem less effective in carefully considering unpleasant advice than in getting rid of it.

One of the pleasures of adulthood is to reject advice with a vengeance whenever possible. After a childhood of family pressure to heed the advice of parents and social pressure to obey the commands of teachers, we can just turn our backs on advice-givers. Sweet revenge for those years of compliance. Of course, the price paid can be the loss of valid, well-meant, and even important life-enhancing guidance due to blind rejection.

On the other hand, there's also a price to pay for the blind *acceptance* of advice sought when desperation or some rushed expedience ruins our reasoning. We can become promiscuous consumers of shoddy counsel when feeling at the end of our rope. Our urgent psychological hungers cause us to swallow without tasting. Unmet needs for relief and love lead to a helpless gullibility. The gullibility is a by-product of desperation, which leads us to succumb to the unknown and abandon discrimination. So, from stubborn (and sometimes costly) blind rejection to gullible (and often costly) blind acceptance, the way we consume advisement seems to suffer from extremes. That's why a second goal of this chapter is to demonstrate a method for discriminating usable from useless (or even dangerous) advice.

A WISE GUIDE ON THE GIVING AND TAKING OF ADVISEMENT

Effectiveness in giving and receiving advice can be a matter of luck, but being effective consistently over the years depends on managing the advising situation. Spending a couple of careful minutes deciding if you should swallow or discard important advice is *wise*. The same is true for giving it. Whether it's a crisis, a decision point, or a profound confusion makes no difference. A high-quality, wholesome exchange of guiding information requires the presence of four interpersonal conditions. By a stunning stroke of fate, the four conditions happen to create the acronym WISE:

W. *Willingness* to receive advice. Is the mood receptive? Is there energy to hear about a new way of doing it?

I. *Information* about the person and the problem. Has the adviser learned what the advisee has already tried?

S. *Success* in dealing with a similar situation. Is the advice about to be given backed up by evidence of success? Is it a sure thing or a longshot?

E. *Empathy* for the feelings and thoughts involved. Can the adviser tune into the other person's experience? Is there deep understanding of the advisee's discomfort at hearing how to do it right, or his feelings of embarrassment?

Using all or even part of the WISE guide as a checklist increases the odds of getting vital personal advice accepted. It also can guide you when deciding whether to use or discard help-intended advice for serious problems. I've even used the guide for telling friends and my student therapists why their advice was difficult to accept or missed the mark.

This four-part conceptual gadget may look like it asks for a lot: perfect conversational conditions for giving and getting advice. But please don't discard it as cumbersome. I don't mean for it to be used rigidly in an all-or-none manner. In some situations, the *S* (evidence of success) may be impossible to give or expect. Maybe the *E* (empathy) can be overlooked when the advisement is more cut-and-dried or businesslike. WISE must be adapted to situations and personal possibilities. The big payoff in taking the trouble to memorize this guide lies in knowing exactly what's available and missing before *any* important advising transaction. If you learn the four conditions and remember them, WISE can also be used as a diagnostic tool for what went wrong when help was rejected (or what went right when it was accepted). The primary *S* I can offer as inducement for trying the formula comes from observation of UCLA students in my communication classes. Every year, a dozen or so confront critical situations when advisement has to be given or received, and they remember to use WISE. They report (in student journals) varying degrees of success, from moderate to strong. I hear of few outright failures. Now and then, I get letters from some long-gone students describing a dramatic use of the formula for breaking through barriers. Overall, they've had good luck with WISE, and so have I during some critical personal and professional incidents. It's helped me to appropriately reject some passionate but myopic career advisements from a few well-meaning colleagues at UCLA. I've used it to melt some of my resistance to hearing uncomfortable guidance about my chronic workaholic problem. Most dramatically, WISE has helped me give guidance as a father. I'll swear an oath on it as a great device for getting kids to hear caring, careful advisement from fathers and mothers. (The *W* and *E*, in particular, do the trick.) I've also had bad luck when my unthinking urge to advise pushed

patience aside as I asserted some dumb guidance with a missing
I or a weak *S*.

I'll end my pitch for memorizing WISE with a final *S*, coming
from participants in a dozen self-help groups for women in their
forties and fifties coping with rough adjustments to divorce. The
groups were trained by a program (Common Concern audiotapes) that teaches WISE. Tape recordings of their self-help
conversations reveal abundant examples of effective advice exchange *after* they practiced the four key conditions. I heard one
woman half-jokingly mutter, "WISE" before giving a difficult
advisement.

The Catastrophe of Quick-Cure Advising

The dialogue that follows is from two young women who had
never heard of WISE. The situation, I admit, is quite unusual,
but it vividly displays the dynamics of advising. Their conversation was part of a video experiment dreamed up by a friend,
a TV producer. He wanted to capture conversations where one
person helps another. It was to be naturalistic, with nonactors
talking about somewhat serious, real-life problems. The women
were strangers who volunteered out of curiosity and camaraderie. The videotaping took place in a comfortable living room
in the producer's home. The situation was casual and low-key,
with a dozen people who volunteered. One, Ruth, took the role
of "helper" and the other, Markie, became a problem-discloser.
Even in front of the camera, Markie was able to give some fairly
risky disclosures. Here's how it went.

MARKIE: *(Nervously, with a delicately high-pitched, soft voice)* See, I see
myself as a more mature person than others do, a lot of others.
It's this . . . uh, childlike quality I have sometimes.

RUTH: Uh huh. I've noticed it.

MARKIE: *(Scrunching up her face in disappointment)* You *have*?

RUTH: Yeah, I mean, I'm not, uh, I'm not judging you or anything. But
you do have kind of a little girl quality.

[Ruth *is* judging her with a personal interpretation, and a critical one at
that. Ruth has delivered a personality diagnosis at the 23-second mark
in their conversation: "Yes, Markie, you do act immature." Pretty fast,
but not remarkable for someone inexperienced in playing the role of
helper. After all, the exercise asks her to help Markie explore a personal
concern, so Ruth has grasped the obligation. Her posture and tone of
voice have become more authoritarian than during the earlier warm-up

talk. Within minutes, her natural manner is transformed into the stereotype of a benevolent, expert helper as if she were acting in a movie. I've seen such transformations hundreds of times as "civilians" assumed the role of therapeutic helpers during communication exercises. The way in which a great variety of people have taken on the role of an almost parentlike, kindly, firm, self-assured—even lofty—provider of help is thoroughly predictable. It's provided a sharp picture of what must be the popular conception of a psychologically helpful person: a considerate but stern expert on human relations who's able to give uncomfortable insight in the form of interpretations and unpleasant advisements with cool commands, self-confident suggestions, and advising questions that carry a biblical tone. Somehow, as a society, we've erroneously validated the idea that a psychologically helping person must be an authoritative adviser.]

MARKIE: *(Sagging)* Yeah . . . that little girl quality.

RUTH: Well, you're admitting the problem. That's a big step.

[Ruth bestows approval with another personal interpretation.]

MARKIE: Do ya think so? I hope it's a big step. Ya know, it's especially bad in my work. People, especially men, the fathers at work, don't take me seriously sometimes. They treat me like . . . I don't know . . . I, uh, just want to be stronger so that—

[I can't tell if it's the demand of the exercise or if Markie actually wants to hear more. Either way, she gives Ruth a green light to proceed. A clear *W* is established. That frees Ruth to present her first advisement, a hard command.]

RUTH: *(Interrupting)* You can be. You have to keep asking yourself, "Am I doing it now? Do I wanna be doing it? *No!*—so I'll stop doing it."

MARKIE: Well, I've been trying to do that, but it doesn't seem to help.

[Oops. Ruth neglects to create one of the WISE conditions, the *I*—getting informed about what's already been tried. Her irresistible urge to advise has nothing to do with any exercise by now—she's *determined* to prescribe a quick cure.]

RUTH: Oh, you know what I think would help? Assertiveness training. It would help you get out of this, this stereotype of the Golden Girl, ya know, the blonde Beach Bunny. It can take a jolt to break out of that rut. Really. Sometimes it takes outside help to give you that jolt and push you in the right direction. Then once you're making progress, you can keep telling yourself not to give in to it. Right?

[I get exasperated hearing someone repeatedly advise without becoming informed. It's an easy step to miss in the helping process. I admit to skipping the *I* on occasion, but rarely when the issue is serious. When doing therapy, capturing the *I is my first goal*.]

MARKIE: Uh . . . yeah, but I *did* do that. A therapist gave me behavior therapy, and I did this thing . . . uh, like telling myself what to—like, did you ever hear of self-talk?

RUTH: Sure, it's—

[*The ill-informed advisements have stirred Markie's assertion as she cuts in for a long disclosure, as if to force the facts into her shoot-from-the-hip adviser.*]

MARKIE: *(Interrupting)* Well, I did that a lot for six weeks. Do it now and it helps me take care of me. I tried all sorts of things: assertion books, practicing with friends, but ya see, I, I just don't feel as strong as a coach. *(She runs an "age-group" swim team with 90 kids from ages 6 to 16)* Maybe I listen to them too much. They use up gobs of time talking about ways to do a little less work, and I'm such a halfhearted policeman . . . uh, police-woman that when—

RUTH: *(Interrupting)* So the assertion training didn't help with—

[*Markie breaks in again; maybe she's hoping to stave off another Ruth advisement.*]

MARKIE: Oh, I can clamp down on 'em, even threaten 'em, but it's joyless coaching. Ya see, I so wanted to help 'em love to learn strokes—that's the thing. That's where I'm weak. It's in motivating, so I don't, uh, I don't want ever to *force* kids to work out more. Some of the parents get angry. I lost one last week 'cause I, uh, 'cause they complained about light workouts. Damn, you can't do a lot of yards when you do stroke-work and for stroke-work, there's, well, I *play* with 'em, get in the water with 'em, so they see me as even more childlike—

RUTH: *(Interrupting)* Wait, I don't understand. What does playing in the water have to do with stroke-work, or who is it who sees you as more childlike?

[*Finally. After giving two pieces of badly informed bad advice, Ruth asks an innocent question. Markie responds with a 12-minute dissertation on coaching junior Olympic adolescent swimmers, explaining that stroke-work means teaching technique, while also detailing how swim parents are impossible to please and capable of getting coaches fired. Now she's about to end that flooded disclosing by returning to the original problem. She rambles some about her "falsetto, high-pitched, teen-ager voice" being the culprit for her youthful image. (Her voice is unusually high pitched, and her articulation is exquisite. The assertion in her speech is almost canceled out at times by her special voice qualities.) After mumbling something about maybe having erred in bringing up the topic, she continues attacking her students' parents.*]

MARKIE: Like I say, there's no trick in pushing these kids 3,500 yards—good for endurance, longer races, ya know. But these kids need technique now before they develop lifelong bad habits. And with stroke-work added, they only have a 1,600-yard workout. But some parents want everything. They're worse than Little League fathers. Honest. They abuse their kids emotionally. Push, push, push. They make them hate swimming and burn out young. They really do. Top Olympic swimmers never worked out so much so young. Push 'em at 12 and 13 and they burn out at 14 and 15. It's really child abuse. Parents say they do it so maybe the kid can get a college scholarship. Big bucks, yeah. But really, these deadhead overweight parents live vicariously through the kids *too* much. The old folks really are emotionally retarded and walk around behind my back wondering "if our young lady coach needs a bit of maturing"—just 'cause I'm warm with the kids. Can you believe? Racehorses—like they own a racehorse. It can be awful, heartbreaking. Driven parents pushing workouts almost every day, sometimes seven days a week! Sometimes twice a day! Would you believe it? And they want *my* cooperation. And when I play with the kids out of caring, they call me "girlish." And then they want me to do 3,500 instead of playing even a little so they learn to appreciate good stroke technique. Swimming should be fun, too. And they think *I'm* immature. God. Too much. Let 'em get Rambo.

RUTH: That's quite a scene. Poor kids. Why don'tcha try telling 'em that they're gonna burn out their kids if they don't ease up? Wouldn't it be helpful to explain it to 'em carefully?

[Here Ruth tries a couple of less insistent advising questions, instead of her earlier commands. But once again she's neglected her *I* (information). Markie didn't say whether she'd already tried talking to the parents. Worse, Ruth shows no *E* (empathy) for Markie's frustration and is miles away from offering anything like an *S* (successful precedent). This exercise in helping has even lost Markie's *W* (willingness). Gentle Markie now starts raising her voice to her adviser.]

MARKIE: Are you *kidding*? Explain it to 'em? They're experts! They know it all and they don't care. They rationalize—talk themselves into it like addicts. Ya think they're gonna listen to *me*? You don't know hard-core swim parents. They're deranged! Listen, I've got four or five of 'em and they've got all the rest too scared to speak. Why do ya think there's so much turnover of swim coaches? Hard-core parents that think coaches who don't do twice-a-day 3,500s and want kids to have fun are immature. Immature! *(Long pause as her anger recedes into hurt, her eyes flood and she wipes them)* Oh, honest, I'm so tired of this. It happens everywhere I work.

The conversation was mercifully terminated after Ruth asked a couple of concerned and courteous questions, as if to demonstrate—finally—some empathic understanding for Markie's discomfort. At least she learned enough not to try more advice.

These newly met women walked away from their experimental conversation knowing they didn't hit it off. No advice was taken. I don't think they liked each other much, but no animosity was evident in their moment of polite small talk afterward. They separated quickly and started conversations with others in the group. Their talk had revealed the impact of ill-informed, poorly offered advice. It suggested a cause—bad advising—for an effect—failure to connect: Markie's risky self-disclosure was made as a call for some help in a situation that turned out to be low in WISE conditions. We saw precisely why the advisement was pushed away. We saw Markie experience "discloser's remorse." Ruth's insistence on advising time after time based on weak information *(I)* and practically no empathy *(E)* illustrated how bad advice disconnects people. And viewing their conversation against the Intimacy Index produces a low score on symmetry—no shared experience or common attitude about the topic or the conversation's process (see chapter 7).

Also no empathy—Ruth wasn't tuned into Markie's internal frame of reference. She didn't move into her point of view. Markie unveiled a rather risky disclosure, but it wasn't reciprocated by Ruth. She could have revealed some of her feelings about having her advice rejected or being obliquely criticized by Markie's adamant lecture. But none of that happened because Ruth's advising was without method. So these new acquaintances experimented with un-WISE advising and ended up disconnected.

Other pairs continued the experiment throughout the afternoon without much more success. One pair elected to disregard instructions requesting "a sincere attempt to give and take help" with a real-life, serious-as-possible personal problem. Their topic was pros and cons of buying a station wagon over a standard sedan. I thought in that case the help was useful, even without much WISE present. (The adviser remembered an article in *Car & Driver* magazine.) The remaining pairs tried more substantial stuff and *all* translated the phrase "give and take help" into the act of advising. No surprise—few people think of helping with such responses as me-too advisements and reflections. So, the TV experiment produced a bunch of conversations containing fairly risky disclosures followed by ill-informed, invalidated, and often unempathic advice-giving. Somewhat vulnerable disclosers facing earnest but unskilled advisers giving top-of-the-head guidance. A combination doomed to failure.

A State- of- the-Art Example of Advice-Giving

The producer was having the volunteers do "seconds," in which disclosers made another try at solving their problem with a new helper. As I watched the pairs continue their struggles (like neophyte dancers stepping on each other's toes while smiling politely), the image of poor Markie with her exquisitely hurt voice returned to me. It seemed that her special feminine vocal cords (her "girlishness") and her concern about how overly competitive swimming can dehumanize children made her the easy victim of the vicarious ambitions of parents, along with some old-fashioned sexism. My impulse was to volunteer as her second helper, but I couldn't. (It wouldn't have been appropriate, as a professional, to mix in directly with the experiment, and it wouldn't have been ethical, as a professional, to risk "recruiting" her as someone who might want further consultation when I couldn't offer that.) Then it struck me that my friend Barbara, who had tagged along that day out of curiosity, would be an excellent choice. She was a former student of mine, visiting from New England where she was dean of students at a university. Barbara is a skilled communicator open to trying something new. She agreed readily. Markie was confused at first—probably because of her debacle with Ruth. But the group urged Markie to give it another try, and she reluctantly agreed.

Markie and Barbara walked to their seats in front of the camera, both unusually tall, solid-looking women. They sat facing each other squarely. Markie made an exaggerated frown, as if to say, Is this going to be awkward again? Barbara, maintaining direct eye contact, smiled kindly and used a reflection to capture the meaning in Markie's scowl.

BARBARA: I see you're expecting trouble. Or maybe just saying with your expression, "Why am I doing this again?"

MARKIE: *(Losing her frown)* Well, uh . . . Yeah. That's what I was sort of saying. I mean, my face was . . . *That's* what I was feeling. *(Smiles)* Yeah, it was awkward, not because of Ruth, because of . . . well, she came . . . she came, well, uh, on strong without . . . but it was my . . . *(Long pause)* This thing is hard to talk about. And it's hard for *anyone* to help. What more can I do? All the things she [Ruth] said were things I'd already tried and, uh, *look* at me. So that's right, what you said. Why am I doing this? It's like, maybe if you help, if you keep talking about it, it can do some—maybe it's at least, healthy. . . . So I, so, here I am.

[Markie's disfluencies and stumbling come from being almost shocked by Barbara's reflection of her frown. Coming off Ruth's advice barrage, it's momentarily disorienting to get this shot of empathic understanding. It's like Markie is thinking to herself, My God, this woman's right *there*, with me.]

BARBARA: Like taking medicine or doing a workout when you're tired. You've tried everything, but what the hell—it's better to keep talking. So here you are.

[Another reflection clarifying Markie's message, at first with a metaphor (taking medicine) and then more literally. As a dean for eight years, Barbara has learned how to help students in trouble. She's had to break bad news often and learned the "real" causes of her students' failures. I'll take some credit for her habit of reflecting the message in gestures and using WISE, but she was outstanding even as a beginner. She was in the minority of clinical psychology students who believe that "natural" talk from an empathic heart wasn't enough for helping someone in need. My position is that a warm, accepting, open, understanding attitude is great for starters, and that a theory of helping adds perspective—but without a solid set of talk tools the great attitude and nifty theory are worth little. That made sense to Barbara, so she retooled her talk repertoire. In her conversation here, she blends talk technique with sincere caring and respect. I know the idea of bringing high-tech talk to the complexities of vulnerable emotions is a troubling act to some. The concern is that some technique or science might dominate an intimate process—that the head might crowd out the heart. That *can* happen, but Barbara demonstrates that it doesn't have to.]

MARKIE: Exactly. Here I am, getting medicine, with little hope it'll help. Actually, Ruth was right about the assertiveness. But the training was just a bunch of tricks. Like for manipulating people. I, uh . . . Fooling people isn't gonna—really becoming assertive isn't that simple! Ya see, it's not just my childlike voice, it's the childlike part of me—inside. Understand? Sometimes I *am* what I sound like. And I *like* it. I want to be childlike, too, but sometimes she, uh, *it* causes problems. . . . Sometimes big problems.

BARBARA: So, you have two childlike parts—your voice and something inside . . . like a little "she" inside. And sometimes that's okay and sometimes it's big problems.

[Barbara is sticking quite close to Markie's meaning, which is yielding some *I* (information). And providing close company that creates safety. The reflection starts out as superb paraphrase, even catching the "she" slip by Markie, but then fails to make an important distinction. People on the verge of opening up want precise understanding, so Markie sets the record straight.]

MARKIE: No, it's not okay. I mean, my voice isn't okay—yet. I can get a vocal coach for that next summer. It's the "little" one inside that's sometimes okay and sometimes a problem. The damn voice is *always* a problem. Well, almost always. Some guys love it.

BARBARA: I see, the childlike voice is almost never okay—it's the little one inside that sounds okay at times, other times, uh, not okay at all. Is that it? No, I forgot the part about sometimes guys love your voice.

[Nice literal reflection. Barbara isn't advising yet, but the information *(I)* is pouring in, thanks to her accurate reflecting. Listening to these impressive-looking women talking about voice fascinated those of us observing because Markie's super-soprano was dramatically contrasted by Barbara's soothing baritone.]

MARKIE: Yeah, they do . . . At least they say they do. "What a sexy voice." Or sometimes they say things like, "Cute." Sometimes I hate it, what they say. But it depends on the guy. Ya know, it's hard just to not say anything 'cause the voice is so unusual. You must have that, too, like with your voice. Just like the other—

BARBARA: *(Interrupting)* Yeah, but the opposite. Once, someone said, "Sexy." Once, someone said, "You sound like Bea Arthur." *(Both laugh)* Nobody ever said "Cute." *(Both laugh again)* On the phone a stranger may call me "Mister." *(Both laugh at length, acknowledging the almost comedic contrast between their voices)* So I usually throw in my name early. . . . *(Long pause)* So, but you were saying it's hard to avoid talking about your voice sometimes.

MARKIE: Oh, yeah, but my point was that I'm getting too old to be "cute." *(Laughing)* Sexy is okay, but cute—like with me, it suggests, uh, terminally cute. Look, I really want to be *both* a woman and a girl. I wanna be a strong woman in full bloom and sometimes it's also great fun to be a girl. *(She sings)* "Girls just wanna have fun." *(Regular voice)* The girl in me is more spontaneous, helpless, irresponsible, she lets "Daddy" decide—lets the guy take over and do the work and decide what she'll do. Let's him do things to her. The girl doesn't know how to get long-lasting joy, and she, she, uh doesn't know about pride—like having self-pride, I mean, I mean self-respect or how to protect herself. So, her quick fun doesn't last, 'cause she's sorta linked into what others want and when they change she's out. Know what I mean? So I only wanna be a girl with my *real* daddy, my *real* mom, or someone that really loves me. The rest of the time I'd like to be a decisive grown-up woman who sorta controls her own destiny and her own physical needs and gets long-term satisfactions instead of quick excitements that drop you fast. It's like, uh, what I mean is that I want both.

BARBARA: Whew! That sounds grown-up to me. Here's what I heard—uh, let's see . . . You want to be both . . . because the little girl gets you more fun, quick fun . . . but the woman gets you more, uh, long-term joy and steering your own life. I got that. But then you say the girl likes, um, giving in; she lays back and goes on the guy's ride—*(Laughs)* wait—not literally. *(Both laugh)* I mean the guy's *trip*. But that can be self-destructive. I guess . . . I guess you mean if done too much? Oh, if it's done where's there's no love. Right. So, you want to control more of your own destiny, your own life and body more. But you want to be girlish too; you want both.

[Sometimes in having the advantage of reading dialogue, readers feel reflections are just restating the obvious. In fact, Barbara, in the rush of what Markie's telling her, has done an excellent job of reflecting the big picture. Conversation is a messy business, especially when trying to get at sensitive, ongoing personal troubles. Barbara's reflections are driving at what might not have quite crystallized in Markie's own mind, much less Barbara's or anyone else's who heard it. Ultimately, the result will be more tidiness of thought and feeling. The reflections will help contain the chaos.]

MARKIE: Exactly. Both. But right now, the damn girlish part gets, uh, she takes over too much. Ya know? It's almost sometimes like I give in to my voice, the way others hear it and I become what they think. It's easier that way, to let *her* take over. Even with the team at times. They like it. The girlish part gets people to like me—not the slave-driving parents but lots of others. *(Pause)* I want them to like me, but it's not worth it. Not worth it.

BARBARA: It's just not worth being liked to give up so much to be liked. The girlish part takes too much of you. "She" even gives in to your own voice, to the way others hear it and uh . . . it's not worth it. *(Long pause)* It costs too much.

MARKIE: Oh, yes, much too much. God, I never let myself think that before—it's, it's costing me my *womanhood*. I guess I never thought before how much it costs.

BARBARA: It's a new way of thinking about the big price for being sweet and agreeable. The price could be your womanhood.

[It's as if Markie has been taking small steps on potentially dangerous ice, but senses that each step is supported. The impact can be seen in her next response—after a 45-second pause in which Barbara didn't so much as twitch a lip.]

MARKIE: Ah-h-h-h . . . It's almost numbing. It's costing me my own womanhood. It's like seeing part of myself in a different way. . . .

[Barbara's relentless reflections are giving Markie the experience of being known. Not only is the conversation much safer than Markie's talk with Ruth, it's more profound and the repeated reflections bring out all sorts of background information on the assertiveness problem. So the safety creates greater willingness *(W)* and abundant information—she's dotting her *I.*

[The pair continues for about ten minutes on the "costing my womanhood" issue, and eventually moves to a new episode with Barbara asking an innocent question about what Markie has tried with her tyrannical swimming-crazed parents. After describing the failed attempts, Markie returns to her anger at the parents. She seems to be moving farther from finding what she originally yearned for: a "plan for action." Barbara offers a me-too disclosure that carries a dose of vitamin *E* (empathy). The *E* quenches Markie's repetition of complaints.]

BARBARA: Ever since we started this thing, a little memory trace has tingled to this High School Scholar's Program I regretfully . . . *(Laughs)* started seven years ago. Your trouble with the parents reminded me. It was for high-achieving 12th graders, to get a taste of some college courses. Well, it was also for recruiting. *(Hushed voice in mock secrecy)* Don't tell anyone. *(Regular voice)* The 12th graders were carpooled to us and audited freshman classes. They were a pleasure to see—so playful, like they were starving to learn and to talk with classmates who wouldn't be bored or disdainful of their curiosity, their hunger to learn. You know, gifted kids are denied what they need in most high schools; it's really sad. I really don't regret starting it, except for the parents. Honestly, some of them are awful. Dealing with them was more work than all the kids and professors *combined*. *(Distorts face, nasal whine)* "Why can't my kid take advanced English II?" "Why didn't Sally get in? She's just as smart as Mary Jo." "My kid feels alienated from all those stuck-up college kids." *(Regular voice)* It was gruesome, Markie. Not all the parents, just 20 or so out of 90 that couldn't handle their kids' talents. They were going to sue me and the university and write to the chancellor and write letters to the newspapers and withdraw their kids—and the gentler I was, the rougher they got. It went on and on, but I really know how it feels to be attacked by mad-dog parents who sabotage the good things you're doing for kids.

[A me-too disclosure to the rescue. It's lucky that they both had to face parents in their work, but any similar experience of frustration when trying to do conscientious work or receiving unjust complaints from clientele could have been used. The me-too disclosure goal is to demonstrate that you have personal knowledge of a salient part of the other's experience. If that can be done honestly, an empathic link can be forged. Empathy alone is not a credential for delivering life-altering advice, but it's usually a necessary ingredient. Markie thinks so.]

MARKIE: So, *you've* had it, too! You know what it's like to be sabotaged by mad-dog parents. *(Laughs)* Boy, that's pretty rough lang—that's more than I've ever called mine, but it's good. It's nice to hear someone else say it. Mad dog! They *do* sabotage, don't they?

BARBARA: Yeah. Not on purpose, but from passion and wearing blinders and sort of feeling they've got to fight for their kids with a frenzy even when there's no need. Some live through their kids. I, uh, I know that's a natural way, part of parenting—but some live *too* much inside their kids. They fill up some of their own emptiness by using their kids' success as belonging to them. They sort of feed too much on—

MARKIE: *(Excitedly interrupting)* I know *exactly* what you mean. These overweight parents screaming their lungs out at meets as their skinny little athletes paddle furiously—it's perfect. And the frustrated dads and moms who wanted to be stars when they were young and didn't for one reason or another—God, their poor kids being controlled in so many little ways by passionate . . . and, uh, you're right—mad-dog parents. . . . Then *(Wistfully)* So you've had to deal, I mean, you really know how parents can get overinvolved living vicariously off their kids' achievements. But what did you *do*? Did you get better? Did you figure out something?

[She's asking for the successful coping *(S)* evidence. She's asking for advice because the *W* and *I* and *E* are firmly in place. This conversation is an unusually good example of how WISE conditions establish a climate for important advising, even with the *S* missing. If Barbara failed to come up with a success story now, her efforts to establish the other conditions would still have significant by-products for Markie: discovery of the loss of womanhood issue; exploration of how she enjoys the "girlishness" though it sometimes entraps her; perhaps a better readiness for attacking the "mad-dog" parents. I hope you see that WISE does more than ensure an effective exchange of vital advice. Even when a letter is missing, the by-products often advance the advisee's position for problem-solving.]

[Barbara is about to answer Markie's question burst about *S*. Note that its tone is more like a self-disclosure response to empathy than an attempt to advise, to guide.]

BARBARA: *(Laughing)* Hey, wait—too many questions. Ah-h-h, let's see, yes, it, uh, did get better. Yeah. I did figure out a way. Not to get rid of them, or even change them; actually, it was several things, like really, really trying to understand what's in their hearts, where they're coming from. Then really, really understanding my own exasperation. Then I started sort of a monthly open letter. Kind of like a newsletter with quotes from authorities on the danger of pushing kids too hard and tips for fitting in with older classmates and my own stuff. The letter communicated ideas that were hard to get across one to one, and then I—

MARKIE: *(Interrupting)* I could Xerox this great article from *Swimmer's World* about burnout in age-group swimmers and how parents shouldn't push.

BARBARA: Yeah—stuff like that. But first it's best to spend some quality time thinking hard about where they're coming from and what's burning you. Do that first and all your, what, your action proposal?

MARKIE: Plan for action.

BARBARA: Yeah, your plans for action will be better after you dig into them, and *you* first really do it and save grief.

This was Barbara's first direct advisement: a soft command. What a contrast between this WISE-based act of guidance after 25 minutes and Ruth's earlier attempt at a life-altering command after 23 seconds. Barbara believed some contemplation was needed before the "plan for action." And Markie listened carefully; she started outlining ways for "getting beyond the mad-dog snarl." No mock acceptance of advice here.

Barbara went on to suggest building a stronger parent support organization, methods for pulling strength from the "good" parents, and arranging parent discussions for establishing balanced goals for the kids. Markie listened to her older, more experienced adviser with little or no resistance and much gratitude. It was clear to all observers that she would probably implement the new ideas—these weren't frivolous New Year's resolutions. It wasn't just girlish enthusiasm; more like a woman about to try some serious changes. I was impressed and left with a lump in my throat.

PRACTICING

Frieda Fromm-Reichmann was a wonderful psychotherapist who believed that people in trouble need advice last—first they need a moving experience. She held hands for hours with hospitalized mental patients in back wards before trying to guide them. Her belief in providing the experience of attachment before advising (and her success) came to mind while writing about Markie and Barbara. Markie was provided the experience of empathic understanding, patience, and openness that established an atmosphere of psychological safety. The experience made her ready—even eager—for Barbara's advice.

Fromm-Reichmann's psychology of advising could be thought of as a dictum for interpersonal skill: Don't give important advice before providing an important experience. Translating from my point of view yields: Don't expect an eager W before giving the I, S, and E.

When it comes to getting practical about advisement, curbing the urge is the best first step for most people. It's a habit hard to extinguish. There are many rewards and automatic triggers attached to advising. So simply deciding to cut down won't work if you're an advising addict. Here's an exercise designed to provide an experience à la the Fromm-Reichmann dictum.

"Advice Abstinence"

This simple exercise works in any conversation where you hear a complaint or an unresolved predicament, or feel the urge to advise without WISE. It's especially useful if you're an advising-prone parent of an adult or semi-adult. It can take from a couple of minutes up to hours.

PURPOSES

1. Starts the process of cutting down on unsolicited advising.
2. Provides impressive evidence that people may simply wish to self-disclose and can comfortably leave you without expectations that their discomfort must be solved by advice.
3. Allows practice in being more friend and less parent to a child willing to learn from his or her own mistakes.
4. Provides a nonthreatening first step toward better communication for self-acknowledged advice addicts.

METHOD

All I can do is offer hints, because this holding-it-in task is tough for advising addicts and overly nurturant parents. Start by thinking of people who frequently reject your suggestions and commands or fail to follow up on your ideas. Figure out a way to initiate a conversation where you'd typically want to advise, or try to remember this exercise the next time the situation occurs naturally. Another good strategy is to target a person and begin thinking of him or her as off-limits to your advice for a week or a month. Censoring your "perfectly good" or "vital" advisement is easier said than done. This exercise has a moderate failure rate. Short of biting your tongue, please:

1. Put a time limit on suppressing your urge to advise during any conversation at first. Even an accurately timed five minutes can work for starters. If you target an off-limits person, make sure your campaign has a clear point to end. For some-

one you see daily, a two- or three-day campaign should be enough.

2. Concentrate on establishing a solid *I* (information on the background of the problem); and a big *E* (empathy for the other's discomfort *and* empathy for the other's satisfaction gained from simply disclosing discomfort).

3. Be direct when possible, and tell how you will purposely stay away from advising in favor of trying to take in a better understanding of the problem.

4. Even ask someone to help you practice abstinence by disclosing for a fixed time. Sounds peculiar, but my students report success—especially if the exercise lasts longer than 15 minutes.

5. Read the section "Behind the Urge to Advise" in chapter 4 before trying this exercise. If you plan on abstaining with your adult child, try locating the WISE-effective book *Once My Child . . . Now My Friend* by Elinor Lenz.

SUCCESS STORY

One of my patients was having a rough time with her 20-year-old daughter. After a lovely child rearing and peaceful adolescence, the daughter became fiercely independent and sometimes rebellious. "She seems to resent me before a word is said," the mother said. "Even when I show how much I care, there's a tension in our talks. I'm an experienced professional, and I have so much to give [the daughter followed her mother's career as a graphic illustrator], so many ways to help her avoid mistakes."

My patient was coping with the common, painful problem of giving up her "little girl" and making friends with her young, professional daughter. The transition was terrible because the daughter was struggling and needed a sounding board; the mother was failing because the old advisement urge swamped every conversation. Unsolicited advice was ruining their relationship (see the section "Ask the Talk Doctor" at the beginning of chapter 4).

One night after a therapy session with the despairing mother, I met with a close friend. The friend was caught in a research dilemma and faced a deadline. As a more experienced researcher (and compulsive caretaker), I began to advise her without checking her *W*. She tried hearing my fast-paced list of solutions but had no energy for taking in any more data. She wanted some mild compassion, not research consultation. Being in touch with what was happening, she gently disclosed that all she needed was my sustained attention to her complaint: That kind of reserved caring was easier done with my patients than with a friend. Over the next few days of her thrashing, I invented some of these methods of advice abstinence, and they worked pretty well. The next week I offered the techniques to my patient. She had good luck and added her own twists. Since then others have tried and revived the methods with varying degrees of success.

Note: If your tendency is to overadvise, remember that chapter 4's "Ask the Talk Doctor," "Behind the Urge to Advise," and "Shaping Others Out of Love and Necessity" sections have ideas that can assist in cutting down. Consider showing any of these sections to someone close who specializes in advising.

If advising others for your own goals gets you in trouble, take another look at the section "Machiavellian Manipulation" in chapter 4.

If you're a chronic caretaker—someone with an overdeveloped nurturance gland (like me), who goes around telling people to button up when it's cold, to think twice before ordering bacon, to tune in to that terrific thing on the tube, and so on until friends laugh at you—remember chapter 4's "The Secret Wish of the Pure Complainer" and "Maintaining Love." (I did. Really. Rereading them didn't cure me, but it helped cut my promiscuous parenting advice notably.)

Here's another experiment designed to provide better experiences when you deal with *getting* advice, particularly from "authorities"—physicians, mechanics, teachers, government officials, etc.

"Advice-Consumer's Guide"

PURPOSES

1. Develops a personal technique for approaching professionals and obtaining the best possible advice.
2. To learn if the technique helps overcome timid feelings, intimidation, passivity in gathering information.
3. To provide a technique for use by various self-help, mutual support groups that are self-governing and desire technical advice from authorities on their common concern.

METHOD

1. During a peaceful moment, make a list of *everything* you want to know from a specific professional source.
2. Translate the list into the briefest set of cogent questions. Do a second draft of the questions so that they're open, closed, or multiple-choice—depending on how much time will be available to spend on the issues (see the sections ''Open Questions for Longer Answers,'' ''Closed Questions for Short Answers,'' and ''Multiple-Choice Questions for Multiple-Choice Feelings'' in chapter 5).
3. On a separate sheet, write what can be done to expedite the WISE conditions. Spell out what you've already tried or specify the background in a sentence or two. Prepare a question for learning what's worked and what's failed in the past. Give your feelings *if* they're essential to getting good advice.
4. If you plan to use the phone, do ''conversational contracting.'' Get a commitment for the time you need: ''When can you give me five minutes to talk about the strange noise in my engine?''
5. If it's going to be in person, boil down your questions and WISE expediters and use them openly, explaining your goal of getting good advice—''If you don't mind, doctor, I'd like to cover these three things that have been on my mind about the diet.'' Preferably, you'd have ''contracted'' for a certain amount of time in advance.
6. After the conversation, figure if you'd have been better off improvising without written questions or WISE expediters. After all, it is an experiment. (You might be one of the 20 percent who think on your feet well enough so that the written preparation gets in the way more than helping. My casual finding is that over 80 percent claim that writing in advance is a significant help.)

JUSTIFICATION

Recent research has made it painfully obvious that communication breakdowns between professional service providers and their clients hurts everyone. Inadequate gathering of advice is a key element in poor patient compliance with medical guidance, misunderstanding, and mistrust in care maintenance and repair, lost opportunities between teachers and parents. I'd bet the majority of problems between physicians and their patients comes from communication maladies. My former student, Professor

William Stiles of the University of Miami, Ohio, found serious gaps in the ways typical patients gather factual information from physicians. Often, patients fail to cooperate because certain courtesies or modesty or minor intimidation keeps them from driving a hard bargain for the specific detailed guidance wanted. Scientists are recognizing this "noncompliance" as a major health problem. My UCLA colleague, Professor Bertram Raven (in collaboration with Professor Joel Brown, University of California, Berkeley) found that patients who felt empathy from their physicians ("I took the same thing when I had your illness") were able to cooperate better. They were less cooperative when doctors used their usual hard commands: "Take this twice a day and don't use any dairy products." Apparently patients of women physicians were able to pull out more empathy because they cooperated significantly more than those treated by male doctors. So getting some E from a professional helper encourages clients to cooperate.

It's the same with S and making sure the pro advisers have lots of I from you. Unfortunately, too many people think it's silly, even stupid, to spend five or ten minutes preparing and editing a careful documentation of their car problems or medical condition. That frustrates me—I'm convinced that for a large majority, communicating important needs off the top of their heads produces all sorts of wasted time, poor outcomes and, in some cases, serious consequences. So, if you can't be bothered to take ten minutes to jot down ideas for expediting WISE or making your presenting problem crisp, consider the hours, days—sometimes months or years—thrown away because of a single significant piece of bad advice.

This next experiment ties in with Advice-Consumer's Guide. It shows how anyone can "force-fit" casual or even careless advice from an authoritative person.

"Advisement Oracle"

Approaching professionals such as physicians, therapists, lawyers, and the clergy when we are frightened, distressed, or desperate leaves us vulnerable to their advisements. A busy, expedient, or fatigued professional is subject to making errors—sometimes blatant ones. Accepting bad advice against our better judgment occurs more when we're in a predicament.

This odd experiment needs at least three people. It can also be done with a large group. Advisement Oracle is good for a healthy family and great for an adult party. It can be done in 10 to 15 minutes.

PURPOSES

1. Demonstrates how anyone can "force-fit" inappropriate advice.
2. Can bring insight to someone who tends to easily accept guidance, suggestions from "experts" and persuasive strangers.
3. If it works well, demonstrates the danger of accepting vital advice from a professional without using WISE as a consumer's guide.

METHOD

1. Start with someone willing to ask seven questions about a mild personal problem. It's important to discourage serious, sensitive problems before selecting someone. Avoid volunteers who are feeling touchy or are in a bad mood, because this experiment involves talk subterfuge. The question-asker should be a robust person in a good mood. Select someone who can tolerate getting fooled.
2. Tell the "asker" that you and others will provide a yes/no answer for each question by a secret method that cleverly involves a famous (or knowledgeable) person. Explain that you will reveal the method later and ask any skeptics to suspend their disbelief to help the experiment work. Two or more of you will have to leave the room for a couple of minutes after each question.
3. After leaving the asker, flip a penny (Lincoln is the famous person you're involving) to obtain a yes/no answer. Return and announce the answer with no further comment.
4. Request the asker to give his or her reaction to the answer out loud. That will allow everyone to observe how we "fit" advice into our thinking—especially the kind that goes against the grain. Even if the asker is amused or suspects artifice or reacts playfully, he or she will likely demonstrate some of the thought processes involved in absorbing advisement without evidence that the adviser is informed, successful, or empathic. If you note serious discomfort or signs of distress, stop immediately and explain everything, and use your most caring talk skills to help the asker become comfortable.

5. After hearing reactions, request another question, leave the room, flip the penny, return and announce the answer without comment. Request disclosure of the asker's reactions. Repeat process for seven questions.

6. Disclose the entire procedure to the asker in a way that doesn't distance him or her. Reveal the purpose. The game is now over and won't work for the others. Consider the experiment as a takeoff point for discussing the ways each of you accepts difficult-to-fit advice from people who appear authoritative. Mention advice from salespeople, columnists, media therapists. Talk about being desperate for advice and gullible.

FAILURE STORY

The Advisement Oracle exercise copies a superb sociology experiment designed by UCLA Professor Harold Garfinkle. He asked students to partake in research to ". . . explore alternative means to psychotherapy."[1] Each student was seen by an experimenter who falsely represented himself as a "counselor." After discussing the background of a person's problem, the student was allowed to ask a series of closed questions—yes or no—on an intercom system connecting two rooms. The "counselor" heard the question, gave a standard pause, and then announced his yes or no answer. After hearing the answer, the student was able to disconnect the "counselor" and talk his reactions into a tape recorder. After that, the counselor was connected again to hear a new question. The process was repeated several times. The sequence of answers was predetermined from a table of random numbers and evenly divided into yes and no. Garfinkle was interested in how the students would interpret the answers. He wanted to catch their method of "fact production in flight." For me, Garfinkle's experiment demonstrates our tendency to resort to wild interpretations to squeeze improbable counsel from an "authority" into our thinking; it illustrates how we accommodate difficult-to-fit "expert" advisement into our beliefs— even when the advice is dumb or dangerous.

SUBJECT: *(Student)* Okay, this is the situation that I am presented with. I happen to be of the Jewish faith and I have been dating a Gentile girl now for about two months. My dad is not directly opposed to this situation, but I feel at the same time that he is not exactly pleased with it. Mother feels that as long as Dad is not directly opposed to this situation that I should go ahead and continue dating until he makes some direct statement to the contrary. My reason for feeling why he is not too pleased with this is that he has never said don't date her, but at the same time he will come up with digs and sayings that make me feel very ill at ease about dating the girl. My question is, do you feel under the present circumstances that I should continue or stop dating this girl? Let me put that in a positive way. Do you feel that I should continue dating this girl?

EXPERIMENTER: *("Counselor")* My answer is no.

[A lucky break for Garfinkle's experiment that the random numbers produced a "no," because the counselor appears to be taking sides with a popular sentiment prohibiting fraternization between young men and women with differing religious backgrounds.]

SUBJECT: *No?* Well, that is kind of interesting. I kinda feel that there is really no great animosity between Dad and I, but, well, perhaps he feels that greater dislike will grow out of this. . . . Or maybe it is easier for an outsider to see certain things that I am blind to at this moment.

[Note his puzzlement, a reaction to what he interprets as the counselor's concern that interfaith dating will generate father/son animosity—even though none exists now. The counselor's expert objectivity, he begins to believe, can capture a truth beyond his own grasp. They move on to the student's second question.]

SUBJECT: Do you feel that I should have a further discussion with Dad about this situation or not?

EXPERIMENTER: My answer is yes.

[Could you imagine the intellectual struggle that would have occurred in our student's mind if the random answer had been "no"? My guess is that the struggle would end with the student accepting the advice as sound. Anyway, he accepts the command for further discussion with his father, and asks another question.]

SUBJECT: If after having my conversation with Dad and he says to continue dating her, but at the same time he gives me an impression . . . he really does not want me to date her, but he is only doing it because he wants to be a good dad . . . should I still date the girl?

EXPERIMENTER: My answer is yes.

[Oops. The student was almost begging for a "no" here.]

SUBJECT: Well, I am actually surprised at the answer. I expected a "no" answer on that . . .

The student then attempts to bridge the dissonance in his thinking between his anticipated "no" and getting the "yes." By noting the counselor is missing some salient information on his father, he points out a missing *I* (information) and then provides the details to fill in.

The interchange continues for five minutes as the student strains to accept the inconsistent, ill-fitting advice. Sometimes we attribute an automatic *S* (success potential) to the advice of authorities who take our money for their guidance—as if paying makes it valid. And we may not even expect *E* (empathy) from someone who *knows* our problem so well he doesn't have to feel into it. I suspect many of us tend to accept, to swallow, expert guidance a bit too easily.

A bit later, the student hears some more unexpected, almost bewildering yes/no guidance and responds: "Well, once again I am surprised." He grapples with the incongruence, asks another question and once again has difficulty swallowing the ill-fitting advice: "Well, no? Well, this has me stymied."

Near the end of the experiment, the student becomes more emboldened after coping with the growing weight of what could have seemed incompetent advice from a certified UCLA counselor: "Well, I really don't know if I agree with that or not." He offers a tentative argument, then finally backs off with, "I suppose that only time will tell. . . ."

After the interchange ended, the student was asked for final reactions. He revealed his profound ambivalence, including an urge to reject that was overcome by a deference for professional authority: "Perhaps I did not hear what I really wanted to hear, but perhaps from an objective standpoint they were the best answers because someone involved in a situation is blinded to a certain degree and cannot take this objective viewpoint."

He went on to express respect for the counselor's competence: "I honestly believe that the answers he gave me, uh, I believe that he was completely aware of the situation at hand . . ."; for the concern and empathy: "I mean, it was perhaps what I would have expected from someone who fully understood the situation. And I feel that it made a lot of sense . . ."; and for effectiveness: "His answers as a whole were helpful . . . had a lot of meaning for me . . . did help in understanding the situation. . . ."

The respectful doubts were expressed cautiously: "One or two of them did come as a surprise to me, and I felt the reason perhaps he answered these questions the way he did is for the reason that he is not aware of the personalities involved and how they are reacting or would react to a certain situation." Even at that, this student's expressed ambivalence toward incongruous, unexpected advice from an authority figure showed some mildly assertive aspect of his nature. Other students accepted bad advice with much less hesitation—even when it threatened to dramatically alter their lives. When I first read how students reacted in Professor Garfinkle's experiment, I was incredulous at the magnitude of their gullibility and their deference to wrenching advisements. At first, I suspected their reaction was a form of "passive/aggressive" resistance that produced a mock acceptance that could be discarded later. But later on, my own experience with students participating in exercises persuaded me that such advice is often taken very seriously.

The following example of another participant in Garfinkle's experiment boggles my mind. The random yes/no answers advised him that it would be imposible to develop good study habits, that he would never get a degree in physics, that he should, in fact, quit college. To the question "Will I ever get a degree in anything?" the answer turned up "no." So this poor guy, trying to be brave, appeared to be seriously considering changing his life on the basis of 13 random answers from a "counselor." It makes me think of the vulnerable client in actual therapy with an advice-happy therapist—dangerous business.

The student's comments: "Well, as far as what I got from the conversation, it is rather foolish for me to pursue my work any further as far as getting a degree in anything. Actually, I have felt all along that the type of work I am interested in, which is inventing, is not something that requires a degree necessarily. . . . I also get the impression that my study habits will never improve as much as I'd like them to anyway. I will not get a degree. I will get a [military] commission, and it is fruitless for me to study either at home or at school."

Could you imagine the consequences if Professor Garfinkle had allowed these students to leave without explaining the tricks? It would resemble the awful consequences of accepting incongruent, uninvestigated, erroneous advice from a confused family physician, a careless therapist, or any ill-advising "expert."

Now, back on the other side: I want to get practical about situations in which you *must* give advice—at work, as a parent, or as a friend. You want to sharpen techniques. This next experiment is partly make-it-up yourself.

"Talking Pairs Technique"

This exercise requires a like-minded friend, colleague, employee, or anyone willing to donate time for your self-improvement. The procedure is simple, effective, and can be revised as you wish. I've watched it work successfully for 15 years. Keeping chapter 4 at your elbow, do time-limited conversations in the roles of adviser and help-seeker. No longer than 30 minutes at first, even if the limit frustrates you. Keep the problems mild so they don't dominate the learning. Limit yourself to one or maybe two kinds of advisement at first. Figure out some way to keep the WISE conditions in mind. Let yourself make mistakes. A tape recorder can reveal things you'd never notice otherwise. Especially if you listen two, three, or even five times. Terrific learning occurs when two or more people listen to tapes and stop often to discuss. And don't think you can get away with two-hour practice conversations at first. I'm very serious. The burnout can be worse than nothing. Start with half an hour using a wristwatch alarm or kitchen timer so you don't have to keep glancing at a clock. Clock-watching can ruin concentration and seems to encourage talking overtime. When the time-limited conversation between adviser and help-seeker ends, spend some time discussing what happened. Was the advice usable? How acurately did you perceive each other's feelings during this conversation? Did either uncover any fresh views on how advice works in human relations? My rule of thumb is to spend at least half as much time *discussing* Talking Pairs as it took for the exercise. You can almost guarantee some serious learning by recording and listening to parts of the exchange. Variations can come from your imagination, such as limiting yourself to only one advisement per 15 minutes or withholding advice until you're almost sure it meets all WISE conditions or forcing yourself to give shoot-from-the-hip quick advice (to a strong understanding partner) or holding back until the last five minutes to give a single well-crafted me-too or even a self-confident hard command. If you are part of a couple where the flow of advisement is mostly one way, you might be motivated to create your own version of Talking Pairs.

A management consultant invented his own version for use by pressured corporate heads who tend to be overconfident in the validity of their initial decisions. It requires the executive adviser to produce a piece of advice or two, even top-of-the-head advice during the first 5 minutes of conversation. After that, the task is to patiently establish WISE over 20 to 40 minutes and then revive the early advisement to check out its appropriateness. This variation has given executives an eye-opening experience about the ineffectiveness of rushed advising—a common hazard at the workplace. I'm told that this experiment has taught managers that they can save time by slowing down. I'm not making any scientific claims here—just reporting one enthusiastic *S*.

Another variant of the Talking Pairs Technique involves deciding to forgo *any* advising if all of WISE cannot be strongly established in 30 minutes. This version has been quite successful when participants are asked to read the section "A State-of-the-Art Example of Advice-Giving" earlier in this chapter. For those who need it, this type of exercise can develop an impressive advisement technique in three or four sessions. State-of-the-art skill might require more work, depending on your interpersonal intelligence (yes, there is such a thing, according to several human intelligence authorities) and the intensity of your exercises. As for giving dumb advice with great technique—no problem: A commitment to WISE eliminates such ugly disasters.

CHAPTER 11

MASTERING
QUESTIONS

I ANALYZED the conversational styles of some television talk show hosts several years ago for *TV Guide*. The magazine wanted a story that compared communication skills of national media conversationalists. As in this book, I emphasized flexibility in using talk tools. For TV interviews, that meant doing something more than asking a dutiful, predictable question every time the conversation slowed for a moment. After all, if you asked most viewers what talk show hosts do, they'd probably say, "Ask questions." The best ones, though, do a lot more—they're adaptable in using reflections, interpretations, self-disclosures, silence responses, even advisements. Less skilled hosts tend to mechanically ask one routine question after another, leaving little room for the rich range of talk tools that color any good, natural living room conversation, which is what we want on TV: living room conversations with unusual people. Our dependence on questions simply crowds out the variety of language needed for full-bodied, spontaneous talk. (That's probably why the three hosts who displayed the greatest flexibility and no overriding question habits were still on national TV forums as this book went to press.)

The three who stood out were Johnny Carson (who used questions only 38 percent of the time), Phil Donahue (32 percent), and Dick Cavett (40 percent). The question-abusers were Mike Douglas, Merv Griffin, Dinah Shore, and Tom Snyder. While these four obviously possessed exceptional public appeal and some unusual talk skills, my limited sampling indicated they were heavy-handed question users. Tom Snyder, for example, was capable of using questions 90 percent of the time with a guest when he enthusiastically pursued a point:

"When you were a little kid . . . what was your homelife like? I mean, were you locked in a closet or anything like that?"

"No."

"Tied to the bed?"

"No."

"Hit on the head?"

"No."

"Spanked excessively?"

"No."

His interrogation of a young man suing his parents for malpractice sounds like that of a courtroom prosecutor. Interesting for small stretches, but tiresome throughout an entire conversation on TV—or, for that matter, in a living room.

Excessive question use also limited the TV talk styles of such warm, veteran media personalities as Douglas, Griffin, and Shore. Merv was clocked at 77 questions during a 25-minute segment! And even though his queries carried a tone of innocence that sometimes helped to penetrate his guest's armor, his style suffered from question monotone. (I called him TV's "innocuous-question king," which, I heard, prompted him to call me something you couldn't put in *TV Guide*.)

Carson, Donahue, and Cavett, on the other hand, mixed their talk tools like salads, with questions as basic lettuce: the reflections, advisements, disclosures, and interpretations were the tomatoes, carrots, and dressings that complement the basic ingredient. All three hosts used a surprisingly large portion of reflections—19, 16, and 14 percent, respectively—compared to the rare occurrence of reflections in everyday talk. Those high percentages could match the number of reflections used by psychotherapists. Self-disclosures were also in generous supply: 13 percent for Carson and Donahue, 26 percent by an exposed Cavett. None of them was shy about giving advice (28, 19, and 14 percent) or cordially interpreting their guests' inner lives (5, 12, and 5 percent). I also observed more allowing behavior (see the section "The Power of Positive Waiting" in chapter 6) as they waited fractions of seconds longer between talking turns, and interrupted less. In the *TV Guide* story, I illustrated Carson's allowing behavior by describing his three minutes of patient listening to a dedicated actor (Peter Strauss) who was reliving the creation of a prison movie. Three minutes of pure listening is an eternity—and a luxury—in talk show time. Just like in too many living rooms.

THE SAGA OF THE SHY QUESTION-ABUSER

The *TV Guide* story allowed me the pleasure of slipping in some favorite advice on talk problems to a huge national readership. Reacting to it, some journalists did follow-ups, and one, Sara, turned the tables, giving me *her* story on the consequences of question abuse. During the interview, she disclosed her puzzlement about some talk show hosts' techniques; she also interpreted some of their personalities, reflected my observations, and gave me long wait-times. Her questions were reserved for small details.

I ended up telling her more than any of the other hyper, questioning journalists, and I didn't realize what she was doing until we were nearly finished. She had gone so far as to *practice* my techniques for three weeks and use them on me. She went to the library and located a technical article I did on the talk tools, studied it, used the method in interviews with other story subjects, and quickly developed superior skills. Remarkable. The first part of her crash course was to simply resist questions. That was half the battle in broadening her interview style. Using fewer questions is often the first important step in improving professional interviewing style.

About a year after her interview with me, Sara called again, needing psychological consultation on a story she was writing. Afterward, we talked about her trick on me. She claimed to have reduced her professional question usage to 10 percent— very hard to believe for a fact-hungry journalist. But as she continued describing her self-help effort, I was convinced she really made a substantial, permanent reduction. Her question diet also emphasized ''open'' questions and allowed room for plenty of reflections, disclosures, and general interpretations, with a smattering of advice. The change brought dramatic improvement to her information-gathering capacity. She was asking less and learning more from the interviews. Her stories improved. Sara said it was ironic—asking fewer questions brought more data. That reminded me of my bumper sticker aphorism: "Questions can be the world's worst way to gather information."

As the conversation broadened, Sara explained that she was rather shy in social contexts, especially with new acquaintances. I've known other successful writers and editors who use a reserved talking style. Low-profile interviewers can exude a permissiveness for the uncrowded free expression and risky self-disclosing of their informants. Thus, Sara's shyness turned into an advantage in her work, but it was causing stress in her personal life. This professionally admired journalist who interviews public figures with aplomb had a history of painful shyness in social settings, especially with new men. Sometimes she acted more like a girl than a woman; for years she held the misguided belief that her spontaneous social talk had to be full of cute submission.

Later Sara wrote me that she discovered her "mousy, conventional, self-conscious conversations with new guys were filled with squeaky questions aimed to serve the authority of the mighty man." She treated her dates like her magazine story subjects by deferring with succumbing questions. (Shy people often employ routine questions to fill the void, turn the attention spotlight away from their immediate sense of vulnerability, and elicit more action by the other person. Very useful as anti-anxiety medicine. Also very addictive.) Sara greatly reduced her "helpless, humiliating, seductive, little girl" questions and strengthened her talk style with such tools as general interpretations, self-disclosures, reflections, and some soft personal interpretations. Getting away from anti-anxiety question addiction, she said, allowed her to move a lot closer to "being a full person free of female coyness."

QUESTION-BARRAGE BACKLASH

Anti-anxiety questions frequently turn against their owners. Sara's repeated use of insincere, manipulative questions to play little girl made her life worse until she broke her habit. Those talk show hosts who were fearful of dull moments and forced filler questions on their guests turned out some dull shows. Done deliberately or reflexively, anti-anxiety questions will eventually bring a sad backlash. They can leave shy people even more vulnerable and cause eager interviewers to miss more pertinent facts. They produce paradoxical effects by inhibiting a free exchange in conversation, thereby increasing anxiety. Like other abused tools, these semi-innocent questions seem to produce short-term situational relief but risk long-term personal damage.

Question barrages do their damage more quickly. Unlike ordinary question abuse that pretends honest interest while crowding color out of conversation, question barrages virtually force people to retreat from conversation. They repel victims by pounding on them. They pressure listeners with a rapid succession of small, relentless demands.

Question barrages are conversational episodes that persistently ask and ask and ask. Motivated by excitement, eagerness to connect, or just plain habit, a parade of questions marches out. Not infrequently, the barrages attack the serenity or privacy of the other with their rat-a-tat-tat intrusiveness. We use them with surprising regularity in states of high anxiety and when we sense serious interpersonal disconnection.

Sometimes we're driven to it by a concealed partner who guards information, frustrating our need for attachment. Whether you're a perpetrator or the victim of a question barrage, chances are there's a disconnection of intimacy. Barraging can be a symptom, a signal that someone is eager to close a breach. Sometimes the symptom appears too late for curing underlying damage that dooms the relationship.

The following story dramatizes how that breach is widened by barraging. It also suggests a method for reconnecting with reluctant partners. The grandmother in this story drove almost 60 miles twice a month to visit her only grandchild, Stevie, 12. Their relationship had been unusually close, but now it was a case of one-way adoration; Steven was learning to be a cool kid. Like many preadolescents, he hadn't yet sorted out his early acts of personal independence from acts of disregard or downright rejection. So sometimes he was aloof and careless with Grandma's feelings.

On the other hand, two minutes ago he gave her a favorite ceramic bowl he made. And he genuinely missed her during the previous year's fishing trip. Even so, Grandma, a widow, was suffering from his recent coolness. He was developing autonomy and seemed detached. She typically couldn't get him to talk for more than a few minutes before the boy found an excuse to slip away. Sometimes he withdrew into uncharacteristic silence. The awkwardness of this typically talkative pair had been going on for months. Stevie's mother (Grandma's daughter), Karen, was troubled by it, blaming his indifference on "early onset of adolescent cruelty," and Grandma sadly agreed. Both overlooked the insidious impact of Grandma's bimonthly question barrages.

Karen was my graduate student, a budding talk scientist, and thus capable of shameless eavesdropping. She did a good job of capturing a conversation between her mother and son with the aid of shorthand. (Afterward, the pair was told the theft was for science; they'd seen Karen snooping into talk before when fulfilling assignments for me. Mom got permission to show me the transcribed version.) Here is some of it.

GRANDMA: Did you guys try for bluegill at Pine Lake?
STEVIE: Yeah—uh huh.
GRANDMA: Any luck?
STEVIE: Yeah, a few.
GRANDMA: Big ones?
STEVIE: Naw, just regular.
GRANDMA: Did you get some?
STEVIE: Only one.
GRANDMA: And your mother?
STEVIE: She got two I think. Yeah, two.
GRANDMA: I see, That's nice, because when your mother was a girl, she adored breaded bluegill. I hope you had enough for a supper. *(Pause)* Did you?
STEVIE: Yeah. We each had two or three. Uncle Paul had maybe three or four. I think four, maybe.

[Here Stevie tries to engage her with more language, but her inquiry doesn't allow much substance to an uninspired boy. Also, he seems lulled into short answers by her barrage of mostly closed questions, which demand brief answers. (See the section "Closed Questions for Short Answers" in chapter 5.)]

GRANDMA: That's where your mother learned to love bluegill—from Uncle Paul's fishing expeditions. He loves 'em more than steak. Did ya know, he even likes 'em for breakfast?
STEVIE: Yechhh. That's sick. *(Pause)* Gross!
GRANDMA: Why should that disgust you? It's just eating the same food at a different time.
STEVIE: I dunno. Sounds *gross*.

Grandma continues her question barraging for another eight minutes, trying to draw Stevie into engaged conversation, but it's only succeeding in separating the pair. Grandma's maneuvers for enriching exchange are countered by Stevie's maneuvers for getting free. Her cascade of questions is hardly satisfying.

Stevie finally flees by excusing himself to go to the bathroom. When Grandma says, "Take your time. I'll wait here," his face drops.

When he returns, Stevie brings a toy rocket he's built and proceeds to explain how it functions, how he built it from a kit, and how well it flies. At first, she asks questions about the danger and difficulties in building it, and he responds at length. But Grandma's tactical question barrage is less stimulating as she moves to the rocket's color scheme, danger in shooting it off near the school playground, and budgeting his allowance to afford rocket fuel cartridges. The thrill is gone. He wants to relive watching his toy in action, in flight. But instead of the rocket's red glare, he gets questions on budget management. Grandma moves out of his frame of reference. There's no way she can move readily into his meaningful experience with her contrived questions. She doesn't realize that he needs good company in order to maintain conversation across generations. So talk stalls.

Grandma is frustrated. Her longing for closeness produces dysfunctional behavior; she starts another barrage that drives a deeper wedge between them. All she wants is to enact her love for the boy, but she ends up boring him to distraction. The aversive quality of her question barrage in full flight isn't apparent to Grandma. It's hard for any of us to notice the discomfort we inflict while pounding someone with earnest interrogation.

GRANDMA: Summers used to go fast for me, too. Only three weeks left?
STEVIE: A little more.
GRANDMA: Four weeks?
STEVIE: I dunno exactly, Grandma—like three and a half weeks.
[He could be thinking: Who cares if it's three or three and a half weeks. Jeez! What does she want from me? The ordinary emotional radar that 12-year-olds come equipped with can easily pick up questions contrived to draw them out. Grandma's manipulation motives are showing.]
GRANDMA: Well, you could do a lot of rocket flying in three and a half weeks.
STEVIE: I'll do some, but I wanna save fuel for when school starts to show my friends.
GRANDMA: Will you be ready for math when school starts? Did your mother help you get over the confusion?
STEVIE: Uh huh.
GRANDMA: Really?
STEVIE: Uh huh.
[This may be painful to read—even hard to believe that someone wanting more contact could punish so unwittingly. However, most of us are

capable of doing the same without noticing the futility. Grandma here regroups her forces for the next overdose.]

GRANDMA: You still get good grades in English?

STEVIE: Yeah—pretty good.

GRANDMA: I hope you're still writing that lovely poetry. Are you?

STEVIE: A little. Not much this summer.

GRANDMA: Oh, Stevie, you should. The one about seeing the moon in the early morning was so sweet. Don't you see you've got a natural talent with words? You shouldn't quit. Will you promise me you won't quit?

STEVIE: I promise.

And I promise to spare you any more of this. Karen, who was eavesdropping across the room behind a newspaper, told me the conversation was turning into a grueling event for both participants when Stevie crudely claimed he needed to return a friend's call and rushed out of the room. His lie hung in the air. Grandma poignantly pretended everything was okay, but Karen knew better. Nothing was said.

A rare redeeming feature of the question barrage is its ability to warn all within earshot that there may be some disturbance in the balancing act between ostensibly close pairs. Grandma and Stevie were out of balance in their demonstration of empathy. She didn't do a good job of expressing empathy for his skyrocket enthusiasm, among other things. And Stevie's empathic abilities are still undeveloped—like most 12-year-olds, he has a distinctly limited ability for feeling into many of an older person's experiences. Their self-disclosure imbalance was also painfully obvious, but Stevie wasn't the only reluctant, self-protective participant—Grandma never came close to revealing her honorable, natural here-'n'-now impulses for sharing experience with her grandson. If she were administered a truth serum, she'd have to confess, "I'm just wanting us to talk with each other in a pleasant way. I'd really like to know what's important to you, but I don't know how to make that happen. So I'm being tactical. I'm pretending an exaggerated interest in what you say with my question barrage, and I'm distressed it's not working. My questions are less from curiosity than from wanting to get closer."

Grandma eventually disclosed her distress to daughter Karen, diagnosing Stevie as "withdrawn." When Karen translated her shorthand notes of the complete conversation, Grandma was mortified because "I sound like Grand Inquisitor instead of Grand Mother." She wondered what made her do it and reluctantly asked Karen for help. A month later, they visited me with the typed conversation in hand, and I gently gave Grandma my "truth serum" interpretation of her unspoken thoughts during that distressing conversation. (Please note that it was a soft interpretation, expressed as a hunch with evidence and a note of doubt. The technique is outlined in chapter 9.) It was accepted with embarrassed humor, which turned into more self-criticism, and then a concern about what she had been doing the past year: "Poor Stevie is the innocent victim of grandson-bashing." She was genuinely undefensive.

I admired her flexibility in wanting to change. We discussed the impact of question barrages on kids *and* adults. Kids tend to associate the relentless onslaught of questions with being grilled about being naughty: "Why are you watching TV instead of finishing your homework? Don't you know your grades are slipping? If I didn't find out, were you gonna tell me about the TV? Don't you know I've been worrying about your being behind in math? Are you really listening to me?"

Question barrages can leave anyone pinned to the wall. The interrogation can cause victims to say things like, "Aw c'mon, you just want me to say what you already know!" Barrages frequently contain veiled admonitions and can produce all sorts of aversive reactions stemming from guilt, shame, self-protection, and other reasons we might have for hiding like little boys and girls.

Dealing with the Barrage Instinct

Grandma understood. She wanted some concrete suggestions for improving the situation. I responded with my habitual cautions about how the communication gap couldn't be closed overnight, then offered her a list of procedures for transforming some of the disengagement into intimacy. The long-term problems that produce guarded relations (where reluctance is the rule and question-barraging the futile response) can't be solved by the following list. But the recognition of barraging as a symptom and the resulting modification of talk patterns can reduce tension and open possibilities. Grandma got the concealment door open using these ideas.

- Both sides have to at least recognize the pattern of barraging and concealment *without* getting into a futile debate about who's to blame or who started it. Grandma mentioned the matter to Stevie, almost casually. He took it with a cool shrug and said something like, "You sure can ask a lot of questions sometimes, Grandma."

- Even though it's painful or infuriating, the question-barrager should try to ask less over a designated period of weeks *or months*. That resolution should be known by both people. Grandma posted yellow stick-'em notes proclaiming "Ask Less" and "Don't Barrage" around her house. (She said it curbed her habit but still left her with the sense of being closed out.)

- Expect discomfort from backing off and from the persistence of the other's refusal to open up. Sometimes the lack of pressure over weeks or months eventually allows the closed person enough release to volunteer more disclosure. I've only seen this happen when both people are clearly aware that the needy barrager *is* working to give up the habit. If the reluctance to reveal does start to melt, it should be greeted with much allowing behavior, reflections, disclosures—but hardly more questions. Lay off the little demands.

- If the concealment continues—even with less pressure—the resentment from being left out may generate an urge to barrage again. Relapse is a real danger for question-barragers. That didn't happen with Grandma because she brought the problem to light. It was a prominent issue in their interchange. They frequently joked about the matter as Stevie pretended strong reactions to even mild questions. Grandma's new and *expressed* caution about overasking gave Stevie a sense of autonomy—as if his will were being respected.

  Eventually, Grandma altered the entire relationship by entering Stevie's world of interest, watching *his* favorite TV programs, taking him shopping at the hobby store.

- Question barraging in adult couples can be a sign of a serious information gap. The reluctant partner may be caught in a reveal/conceal ordeal (see chapter 1)—wanting to disclose out of love, yet fearing vulnerability. Some revelations can threaten the survival of a relationship and are not made even after the barraging partner suspects the secret. So I have no neat answers for those agonizing adult tug-of-wars that go on under the surface for years. But I do know that the primary *symptom* is the recurring question barrage. Couples coping with an unspoken or unmentionable taboo topic that fosters barraging may find some of the following ideas useful.

- Assuming both people either vaguely sense or clearly recognize the cycle of concealment and barraging, consider making the cycle itself a frequent topic of *no-blame conversation*. Talking about the clashing set of needs or habits, without dwelling on the touchy topic itself, has had some good results, in my experience. Such conversation takes vigilant monitoring but can ease tension by acknowledging the fact that a communication gap exists without creating pressure to bridge it immediately. There is much to gain in discussing the range of causes for holding back information. Concealment might be motivated by lifelong training in the hiding of feelings by a family, a culture, an occupation, or special circumstances. Holding back might be from the repeated experience of being made to feel like a child by confessing deep privacy or from the notion that removing mysteries will dull a partner's interest (a dangerous myth) or from not wanting to relive a buried memory that might bring shame or lowered self-respect.

Of course, some secrets are kept to hide a betrayal of trust or a relationship-busting treachery. The tragedy of maintaining the illusion of being worthy of trust by deceptive concealment is that it drives an invisible alienating wedge into intimacy. For many, it may be better to live an illusion of intimacy than to end a relationship. The discomfort of not being fully known or living with a mate's suspicion or coping with a few question barrages is the price that must be paid.

Sometimes *self*-concealment, denial, is the psychological dynamic that makes a partner seem reluctant. Tampering with denial takes much patience, empathy, and mutual disclosure. It requires a big act of love. The potential rewards for such open, patient empathy could be significant relief from the urge to know *now*; a reduction in the frustrated feeling of being left out and its concomitant anger; and sometimes, the beginnings of more disclosure from a reluctant partner.

- The reluctant partner's understanding of the motives behind question barrages also requires an act of patient, empathic love. And that can be hard to do after feeling badgered by a barrager making a last-ditch attempt at intimacy. Attending to the barrager's need to share privacy—to feel deeply connected by "knowing everything about you"—can reveal an impressive amount of caring. For some, the need to conceal or the fear of being found out or the powerful drive toward secrecy may be a clue to some deeper reluctance about being *too* close, *too* intimate at that point in the relationship. Feeling open is a major part of feeling close.

Finding out there's caring behind those "gimme, gimme" interrogations can be a sobering experience. Maybe that "badgering" is coming from a wholesome need to reconnect some severed intimacy. And if that's true, why is there reluctance? Is it really a reluctance to get closer? To keep away from the waiting intimacy? (Passive behavior is under increasing scrutiny by communication scholars—those cases where conversational passivity [silence or giving very brief answers] turns into *aggression* as a means of discomforting the more outgoing—and resented—person. In other words, where passivity is used frequently as a weapon.)

- If you're either the barrager or the reluctant self-discloser, try showing the other person this section as a catalyst for discussion. Also consider the sections "The Reveal/Conceal Ordeal in Romance" and "Disclosure-Matching" in chapter 1. There's a game in the "Practicing" section of this chapter that has proved helpful for couples coping with the concealment of matters that are not threatening to the relationship's survival. It's called 20-Question Tag and is discussed in the section "Question Tag."

Back to Grandma. She read some literature that I gave her on self-disclosure and tried out some here-'n'-now disclosures on friends. That was when she told Stevie everything she discovered about her barraging habit. She was talking about talk—metacommunicating—good stuff that frequently starts cleaning up an interpersonal mess. Stevie got the drift and seemed relieved.

At last report, Grandma was a "recovering questionaholic." She started reading some of Stevie's science fiction books and discussed the plots and characters with him. Repairing the relationship became a project for her that involved sacrifice (some of the science fiction bored her) and an investment of time that many adults in relationships couldn't afford or wouldn't give to each other. I suppose the grandparent/grandchild relationship presents a particularly good prospect for repairing talk breakdowns that would severely challenge the more enmeshed and complicated connections between spouses and lovers. Stevie eventually told her plenty about his private thoughts on friends and school—and his mother's "unfair attitude" when assigning him household chores.

Several months after our initial talk, Grandma wrote me a letter I had requested describing their progress. She admitted some "early skepticism for those 'artificial' talk exercises. They struck me as very mechanical. Nevertheless, I resumed my practicing until my habit got much better. I am not saying it's a complete elimination, but rather a substantial improvement." The letter ended with "I just have to tell you this, Dr. Goodman: Last night Stevie called *me*. That was the first time he ever called just to talk. He was ever so eager to tell me about this adventure game he wanted to buy and play with me. . . . Well, I was floored when he asked when I was coming to visit again. It was only three days since we had seen each other. I told him I planned to be there in about two weeks. My darling grandson then said 'Aw, Grandma, why can't you come *this* Saturday?' "

Grandmother went. After all, she and Stevie had a lot to talk about.

GETTING GOOD ANSWERS
BY DUMPING DUMB QUESTIONS

Beyond the boomerang effects of barrages, mistakes in using questions typically involve poorly formed inquiries, just plain unnecessary ones, and questions that inappropriately barge into another's sensitivities. In my view, though, the costliest kind of "dumb" questions in the long run are those that ask a willing partner for too little information when a lot is wanted or for too much information when just a little is wanted. These misasked questions produce minor frustrations all over the place.

At the most fundamental level, "closed" questions—which can be answered with a simple "yes" or "no" or something almost as brief—are often used when we want more: "Are you feeling okay about what I just said?" That closed question isn't the thing to do if a detailed answer is wanted. An "open" question—"How do you feel about what I just said?"—would work better. The misuse of closed for open questions often happens in bunches, turning what looks like small problems into major ones.

On the other hand, probably even more of an ongoing communication problem is created by asking open questions when short, direct answers are in order. Frequently, the cause is the desire to avoid being blunt, pushy, insensitive, or presumptuous with queries that make a pointed demand. Sometimes the open-for-closed substitution serves interpersonal politics, as when my son avoids a direct "Can we go to the movies tonight?" by asking, "When's the last time you saw a good comedy?" Since I don't share his enthusiasm for weekly film outings, he finds it easier to broach the subject with a more roundabout open query. Such maneuvering (done half in jest in his case) can become a permanent part of adult talk styles, a mannerism born of caution. Thus, an odd etiquette is served when our need for simple answers seems abrasive or self-centered. An academic journal editor asks: "How's the writing coming along on the article?" I give him five minutes of detail on my efforts in simplifying a messy academic idea before he interrupts to ask the closed question originally on his mind: "Will you be finished with it by the February deadline?" Trouble is, the intention to be "considerate" can easily become an unthinking bad habit—substituting open questions for straightforward closed ones muddies the smooth exchange of sincere conversation.

My guess is that people rarely recognize question misuse as the reason for their discomfort if they repeatedly get too much (or too little) information. Good examples of major frustrations in those areas are in chapter 5 in the sections "Closed Questions for Short Answers" and "Open Questions for Longer Answers." Professionals interested in creating more effective interviews can get some help by reading the first six sections of chapter 5 or trying this chapter's "Question-Matching," "Innocent Questions Game," and "Question Tag" exercises. Professionals who *must* ask questions in emotionally laden situations or emergency contexts might also benefit from reading chapter 5's "Multiple-Choice Questions for Multiple-Choice Feelings."

Please understand that sharpening your ability to ask questions doesn't require constant vigilance. Just reading this chapter and doing a practice routine once usually starts a change process.

PRACTICING

"Question-Matching"

This can be used as a one-shot "drill" for getting a good feel of open and closed questions in action. You'll need a willing collaborator for at least 15 minutes. As an alternative, Question-Matching can be done as a spontaneous routine in ordinary conversation, limited to 5-minute shots. (The time limits are vital for keeping away from the aversive aspect of extended question barrages.)

PURPOSES
1. To match your question use to your immediate state of mind; to match your momentary need for brief, pointed answers with the use of closed questions or your need for expanded answers with open questions.
2. To demonstrate the satisfying experience of managing your questions and gathering just the right amount of information to fit your need.
3. To demonstrate how a *series* of discriminating questions can provide a better, and more comfortable, way of "finding out."

METHOD
1. Find a collaborator willing to answer your questions for a *fixed* period of time. Fifteen minutes is usually easy to donate and is long enough for a first (or only) practice. Agree on a topic that is both comfortable and easygoing enough to last 15 minutes. Avoid disclosing your specific interest in open/closed questions, but do tell about practicing language skills—people can become justifiably angry at being fooled in this way for more than a few minutes.
2. If you prefer practicing in a more "natural" context, consider limiting your question matching to five minutes without disclosing the practice. But be careful not to try it during any talk that might be important for your partner. For a first practice, using a willing collaborator has proven more effective than this "natural" method.
3. Don't worry about matching precisely what you want to know with question type at the start. Begin with a few open questions to get your partner going.
4. When you feel the exchange starting to flow, slow down a

bit. Silently ask yourself what you want to know next—
something either brief and pointed or longer and even rambling—and *match* your wants to an open or closed question.
5. If your open or closed question doesn't get what you want,
don't switch. For example, if you use an open question like,
"Would you tell me about it?" and it doesn't work well, try
another open question like, "What were you thinking when
you read the letter?"

VARIATION

This is a more sophisticated version for the professionals or
those who have learned to use open and closed questions with
facility. Add the multiple-choice question to your repertoire (see
the section "Multiple-Choice Questions for Multiple-Choice
Feelings" in chapter 5) and use it when you want answers longer
than those pulled by closed questions and shorter than the ram-
blings received from your open inquiries. Multiple-choice questions control less than closed questions and more than open
questions; they can be very efficient when you want someone to
answer from a *list* of possibilities. They also can be an unusually
considerate way to question touchy topics (as illustrated in chapter 5). Learning to match them with your thoughts makes questioning more sensitive and efficient. They are much more difficult
to use than open/closed questions and can mess up a beginner's
practice with Question-Matching.

"Innocent Questions Game"

For a pair or a group. Time varies from 20 minutes to an hour
or more for a large group. It also works well in a classroom, but
absolutely requires reading of chapter 5. It's a helpful device for
quarreling couples and can also work in ordinary work conversations or leisure talk where your communication practice
doesn't jeopardize important matters.

This method of limiting inquiry to innocent questions has
been used by thousands of people using my SASHAtape program. A cross-section study of 300 adults indicated these exercises were typically regarded as "very useful." Research with
self-help groups suggests open-question exercises stimulate improvement in the way people help each other with life-disrupting
problems like divorce and widowhood. Those playing this game

over the years recommend emphasizing open questions at first because that reduces the frequency of loaded questions.

PURPOSES

1. It can bring insight into the ubiquitous need for *telling* our thoughts and feelings with questions.
2. It provides an experience in maintaining an exceptionally sincere questioning style that enhances possibilities for earning trust. Innocent questions reduce anger in talks between conflicting people—especially couples.
3. Assuming that participants will occasionally fail to use innocent questions in this game, it can illustrate the peculiar uses and impacts of some loaded and semi-innocent questions.

METHOD:

1. All participants should read chapter 5, or at least glance through it. In classes, teachers might get away with handing out brief summaries a few minutes before starting; that's had mixed results. Very good results have been reported when one member of a couple takes the time to teach the question types to his or her partner before playing.
2. Regardless of context (whether organized pairs, groups, or ordinary conversation), the same basic rule applies: Ask only questions that are direct, sincere, "unloaded" attempts to gather wanted information. Eliminate loaded questions that *tell*, that maneuver with extra baggage for advising, interpreting, or disclosing. (The section "Loaded Questions" in chapter 5 points them out.) Eliminate semi-innocent questions that beautifully imitate innocents but subtly perform important jobs like complaining, requesting approval, resisting demands, softening surprise, starting flirtation, bragging, reducing anxiety, and softening persuasion. (All of these are illustrated in chapter 5.) The only job your question should do here is *find out*.

VARIATIONS

1. Use any of the group games, exercises, or experiments described in the "Practicing" sections of chapters 7 through 10 that can emphasize questions, or set up an open group discussion with the goal of finding out new things about each other. College and high school teachers have suggested non-

threatening topics like digging into each other's tastes in movies, TV, food, cars, etc. Select topics or issues that are engaging below the point of passion.

2. Couples can also borrow procedures from earlier chapters or play a cross-examination game. The problem of stirring emotions that distract from practicing innocent questions is greater for couples than groups. Consider doing time-limited (20-minute), in-depth interviews on personal preferences for specific leisure time activities.

Interrogations on hot topics such as past romances or current dissatisfactions are guaranteed to diminish the percentage of innocent questions. I've heard of good results from limiting conversation to innocents during an evening out or during just part of a trip.

"Question Tag"

This important exercise was developed by my former graduate student, Dr. Ruth Taylor, for helping small groups reduce question misuse. It rarely fails. The basic idea is so simple, effective, and flexible that it can be tailored to specific problems that plague a group or a pair. I'll detail some of the dozens of possibilities in this section. It's hard to give you the precise time required, but figure roughly 15 minutes to an hour or more per small group. Question Tag is terrific for classrooms—from sixth grade to graduate school. It's okay for pairs that can handle the intense demand, but limit your exchange to 10 minutes at first.

PURPOSES

1. To devise an engaging, light-hearted format for quickly learning about individual talk habits and gathering information.
2. It's capable of focusing on several types of question misuse in a single session.
3. It can provide a vehicle for classroom instructors to do experimental teaching on most aspects of the question as a major communication tool. It can introduce participants to every type of question.
4. One variation demonstrates advantages and disadvantages of substituting other talk tools for questions. Question Tag can

provide experience where questions are the least effective way for eliciting critical information.

METHOD

1. The basic procedure for groups and pairs starts with a set of rules for topics of inquiry *appropriate to the setting*. Groups of strangers can be limited to particular topic areas that are mildly personal, or they can simply be cautioned to stay away from potentially embarrassing issues. Close friends, colleagues, and self-help groups may wish to concentrate on common concerns or even touchy topics.

2. In the group, start with a volunteer directing a question or other talk tool inquiry at another member of his or her choosing. Make sure the volunteer prefaces the inquiring by first announcing the name of the talk tool to be used. For example: "This will be an innocent question" or ". . . a self-disclosure *replacing* a question." The person selected to answer the question (the question "receiver" or "tagged" person) responds freely, and then tags another, by asking a new question. In brief, anyone tagged with a question must answer and then tag someone else. If any question hits a vulnerable spot or causes discomfort, it can be "vetoed" and replaced with another. That's it.

The game takes on a dramatic range of complexions, depending on which variation of rules you select for asking and responding. Here are some of my field-tested favorites.

Basic Question Tag. Prepare a short list of question types with one-sentence definitions taken from chapter 5 and make copies for everyone. Allow participants to use any question that strikes their fancy after announcing its name. If you insist on playing the game with participants who haven't read chapter 5 or don't have a list, try explaining the difference between innocent and loaded or open and closed questions. It might work, but a good game requires that participants have *some* understanding of how questions work.

Semi-Innocent Question Tag. This starts with innocent questions, then someone may try to slip in a semi-innocent without getting caught. But semi-innocent questions cannot be tried until the group first does a string of a least three sincere, information-gathering innocents. After a "semi" is asked, the group must do three innocents, before anyone else tries a sneaky, manipulative semi. You'll need a judge to stop arguments on outlandish semis. Use my list of semi-innocent question motives (to brag, complain, flirt, etc.) near the end of chapter 5. We designate the winner to be anyone capable of slipping two undetected semis past the group. That can take 45 minutes or more in a group of six.

Controlled Question Tag. With this version, tag participants are allowed to dictate the class of question used by the person he or she tags. The results are usually funny, especially when the assignment is a loaded or semi-innocent question. When players cannot respond or they ask an innocent question, they're "out." The winner is the last survivor. This is a good game for students learning about communication. It produces some bizarre questions and is *not* recommended for any family or self-help group addressing serious problems.

Spotlight Question Tag. For elementary school and junior high students. The idea here is to ask anything, but the tagee answers only if he or she pleases. Younger kids have played it with flashlights in the dark (at camp) or quasi-dark (in a classroom with lights off and blinds closed). People are tagged as the light beam strikes them. (Those older, more "sophisticated" junior high kids prefer to point.) When a player prefers not to answer, he or she merely disregards the tag and asks a question of another.

Here-'n'-Now Question Tag. Exciting isn't too strong a word for this version when played by an intimate couple, a close group of friends, or advanced students. All questions and answers must be about *immediate* experiences—here-'n'-now thoughts about each other. The game can be about stimulated memories or anything that enters the player's head and heart. It can be extremely revealing, so remember the veto rule. This version has been terrific for families wanting to find out more about each other without getting involved with deadly confrontations. It has also proven itself as a good relief exercise for intense sessions in self-help groups.

Other versions. Alternate between two question types; for example, the player tagged with an open question must ask a closed. Not great fun, but a good way to start with people that you don't want to challenge much.

A support group for cancer survivors invented "question-quelling tag" (their name). The group alternates between innocent questions and self-disclosures. That is, every other inquiry is made by a disclosure, such as, "I haven't asked how your new medication is working because you've seemed sad lately," or "I've always wanted to know what kind of kid you were in high school." The group claims that the game has permanently changed their atmosphere by "quelling" question use so that members do less interrogating and advising behind the facade of a question.

Another variation requires participants to alternate asking a question with using another talk tool. After being tagged and asking a question, the participant's next turn must give up questions in favor of disclosure, advisements, reflections, or interpretations that *elicit information*: "I suggest you explain the unflattering side of your breakup with Allen [advisement]." "About five minutes ago you were saying how much you wanted a vacation this spring—like you were even dreaming about getting out of town [reflection]." "Your answer to that last question was more clever than informative—you used cleverness to disguise the fact that your answer was weak [interpretation, on the nasty side]."

A professor at Vanderbilt University splits her classes into opposing sides for a question contest. Opponents ask any kind of question they like on a nonthreatening topic. They announce the kind of question before asking. Respondents must not cheat by resisting the demands that the questions make on them. The side gathering more information wins. I'm told that the game turns into a farce, but students enjoy it and solidify their booklearning about question use.

One final variation, 20-Question Tag, is a good game for couples needing to inquire about touchy topics without finding out too much, too soon. It's really not very effective for gaining communication skills, but the limited number of questions can be comfortable when disclosing about difficult issues. I recommend it for couples coping with mild or moderate concealment problems. When the unknown information is potentially explosive, limit the game to five or ten questions. Disregarding the limit can make things worse for a strained relationship. Please be careful. This *must* be played as a two-way tag where questions can be asked *about* questions. The veto rule is of critical importance here. So is a resolute agreement to stick within the limits. To my surprise, several couples have reported that announcing the question type before each inquiry can have a comforting effect on the sometimes tense interaction. I don't know why. The key to success here is restraint and the selection of *innocent* questions. (Open questions usually are less controlling than closed questions.) If possible, do something distracting or part company for a while after finishing.

If you can't arrange to do the practice exercises in this chapter because of an unwilling partner, consider showing him or her one of the first six chapters. Some partners, reluctant to try talk games, might join you in analyzing the way talk is used or abused by talk show hosts or movie characters. A good experience in making sense of some safe figure on the screen might stir interest in trying some person-to-person talk exploration.

CHAPTER 12

MASTERING SILENCES

ONCE UPON a time, I believed that individual talk styles were rather permanent personality traits. The way a person talked seemed an almost unalterable aspect of his or her temperament. So the shy person's reticent, quiet, uncrowding manner, or the extrovert's fast, sometimes loud, sometimes pushy pattern struck me as rather fixed feature in their lives. Without thinking it through, I just sort of assumed that our talk styles were deeply established by our families, our regional subcultures, and our genes. Talk *was* temperament. And, oddly, I somehow kept believing in the unchangeable nature of talk styles, even when my career early on as a therapist rested on a belief in profound personality change.

But all that has changed. I've seen many people move away from unwanted, "entrenched" talk habits. Now I know that gentle souls who allow too much—people who compulsively submit, follow, and get pushed around—can change their passive patterns. And I've also been persuaded by watching habitual crowders—who impatiently rush talk—achieve a significant shift in attitude. I wouldn't assert that lifetime talk styles can be reshaped rapidly, but they are less resistant to change than is commonly believed. Crowding behavior and overallowing habits can be altered without heroic struggle.

First, those who overdo allowing. It might come as a surprise after my argument for conversational allowing in chapter 6 that I'd regard a lot of silent waiting as a problem. And it isn't a problem if it means the generous, competent, deliberate act of allowing someone the time needed to think it through and say it well. Waiting—on purpose, at the right time, with a sense of engagement—is a conversational skill that opens up tentative talkers, gives permission to guarded voices, and even brings reluctant people back for more. But good waiting doesn't mean detached, self-protecting passivity. Or inept, angry freezeouts. Or fearful muteness. Or helpless, dependent submission that eventually makes a talk partner resentful. Addicted allowers typically store up grievances from being disregarded and pushed around. How could they be so mistreated when they're seemingly generous about *giving* attention? It's tough for verbally passive people to see the psychological dysfunction in their one-sided interactions. They are often rewarded for following. Their tendency toward seducing others into taking over the conversational floor doesn't fit their desire to be nonmanipulative, quietly sincere people.

Chronic crowders, on the other hand, specialize in interruptions and urgent talk episodes. Some are driven to dominate conversation. They need to give up some control to get better balance in their relationships. They need to stop *taking* so much attention and elbowing noncombatants out of the conversation.

Wait. Just wait. Wait another second before rushing in each time he pauses. Wait just a couple of seconds so she can say it all. Wait a minute and I'll give you a good answer. Wait a few minutes for him to gather his composure. These little gifts of waiting are hard to give if you've got an unmanageable urge to crowd.

There's plenty of hope, though, for getting rid of bad habits, whatever side of the silence scale they fall on. The "Practice" section in this chapter offers some methods for anyone willing to admit they might go too far, one way or the other. People who allow too much can examine their attitudes and try on new skills. They can learn how talk tools used against them might be necessary in their own repertoire for taking their turns as full participants in conversation. Crowders, by using silence responses and longer wait-times before taking a talking turn, can discover the benefits *and* pleasures of waiting. One immediate benefit is the crowder's knowledge that he or she is no longer alienating people by monopolizing attention.

SKILLFUL SILENCE

Over the years, I've found it more difficult to teach people to stop crowding than to stop chronic allowing. Some of my UCLA students get uncomfortable when they have to sit silently through audiotapes I play that illustrate the value of conversational allowing. One tape involves a turning point in the life of a young woman. This was a session of experimental psychotherapy I did while at the Institute of Human Development on the Berkeley campus of the University of California. For me, it was also a personal turning point in reaffirming that people in chronic psychological trouble need lots of conversational allowing: long wait-times, unrushed responses, and freedom from interruptions. The very same allowing ingredients, in fact, that people with big emotional problems need in everyday conversation between friends and family members.

Sometimes, before starting that tape, I read my student therapists excerpts from the noted session by the late Carl Rogers (see the section "The Power of Positive Waiting" in chapter 6), in which he waited at one point over 17 minutes for a schizophrenic patient. Their reaction is usually along the lines of, "It's strange to think of him waiting in silence for so long as a way of helping, but maybe it worked because severe disturbances respond to severe communication." Then they hear me on tape with a patient who is *not* severely disturbed, and again there are long wait-times, and their minds race far ahead with speculation about what the patient's "real" problem is, what she's thinking as I wait for her, and when I'm finally going to ask a question that they all want to ask of her.

Linda (pseudonym) was an intellectually gifted, shy, physically beautiful, quietly desperate 19-year-old woman from a Chinese-American family. When she came to me for therapy, she was secretly terrified of her father, "trapped" by her passivity, preoccupied with her "intimacy phobia," and just plain scared of people in general. She was rarely able to go out after sundown. She had daily tension headaches. Linda was also feeling "disgusted and drained to the point of emptiness" because of her sexual promiscuity, yet felt ambivalently proud that "my one-night stands said I was the kind of girl who drove guys wild."

Linda was my patient for 27 sessions spanning six months. The critical session was the sixth. Years later she wrote me a letter about that "silent" session: "It was knowing you would wait for me for as long as I needed—for the whole damn hour if I wanted—that gave me the security to let bad memories come back. Without the waiting, I would still be living with all the terrible things that went with '*it*' [her awful secret]."

Linda saw the transcript I've excerpted from that sixth session and asked me to disguise a couple of things; otherwise, it's intact.

In addition to the impact of waiting, this session further illustrates the use of reflections, which offer the kind of support that says, "I'm giving you deep attention. I'm following you. I'm not wandering. I'm trying to feel what you feel. Right now whatever you say is more important than what I think." Reflections are kindred to the silence of waiting because they also require us to succumb to our partner's conversational will. Reflections submit to the talk of others. Combined with allowing behavior, they form a powerfully seductive environment for helping people dig deep into the most fearful recesses of their minds (see chapter 2). The combination of long, attention-filled wait-times with empathic reflections from a trusted partner can feel like an enactment of love.

Linda was hunched in a chair, still wearing her heavy winter coat.

LINDA: I don't even know what to talk about today. *(Silence, 5 seconds)*

[That's about 4 seconds longer than typical wait-times in typical conversations. Pay attention to the changes in the lengths of these silences.]

GOODMAN: You sorta feel like you usually feel when you come here. *(2 seconds)*

LINDA: Um-m-m, the things I've already talked about are the things I wanna talk about. . . . The other things, I don't wanna talk about them . . . they, uh, hurt. *(6 seconds)*

GOODMAN: You stayed away from some of the more painful issues in your life, or only touched on them? *(1 second)*

LINDA: I've stayed away from them, mostly. *(3 seconds)*

GOODMAN: Uh, huh. They're just very hard to talk about. *(15 seconds)*

[She was breathing rapidly and occasionally sighed. This was longer than any of our previous wait-times, but neither of us felt awkward. It was *her* time. She was becoming accustomed to controlling our conversations. She used the silence to think about the futility of talk as an aid for her chronic problems. I knew she was wrong, but my talk wasn't to challenge her assumptions—it was to wait, empathize, and tell her what I heard.]

LINDA: I've never talked about things I can't change. . . . Doesn't make me hurt any less. Doesn't change anything. Doesn't erase them. *(5 seconds)*

GOODMAN: Talking doesn't wipe out things or make them different for you. *(6 seconds)*

LINDA: Don't know why I should feel bad about things . . . *(Mumbling)* that aren't my fault anyway. *(0.5 second)*

GOODMAN: That what? *(0.5 second)*

LINDA: Aren't my fault anyway. *(0.3 second)*

GOODMAN: Uh, huh. *(2 seconds)*

LINDA: If something's not my fault, I shouldn't feel bad about it anyway. But I *do* feel bad when I talk about it. *(8 seconds)*

GOODMAN: If it's beyond your control—

LINDA: *(Interrupting)* It *was* beyond my control. It's *not my fault!* *(2 seconds)*

[Linda was adamant about declaring that this thing happened—this "it"—could not have been prevented by her. I wanted her to know I understood.]

GOODMAN: You did *nothing* to make it happen. *(40 seconds)*

[My reflection underlining her point put Linda into silent mental activity. It was our first extended wait-time of the session. The scattering of 3- to 15-second silences earlier would be unusually long for social conversations, but not for therapy conversations. Her 40 seconds of cogitating suggested the issue of who was responsible for "it" was significant. She needed more time, but I interrupted her thoughts with an expanded reflection of her feelings; I should have waited till she was finished.]

GOODMAN: I guess you're saying you can talk about it and analyze it . . . get down to the root of the thing and it won't do much good. *(0.8 second)*

LINDA: *No-o-o.* I don't think it's gonna change much . . . about my phobias. My pathetic sex life . . . my headaches . . . I can't change what happened. *(4.5 seconds)*

GOODMAN: You don't feel you can change what has happened—or what happens *now?* *(0.3 seconds)*

LINDA: What *has* happened. *(5 seconds)*

GOODMAN: It's like a historical fact. *(4 seconds)*

LINDA: It's so . . . you can change something if you do something; if you have a habit, maybe you can talk about it and maybe it'll stop. But for something that happened, something that's not happening now, I don't know what you can do. . . . It makes me not like myself. *(28 seconds)*

[Here, I definitely break into her long silence because I need to sink down deeper into her experience of self-dislike.]

GOODMAN: It's done. It's with you. It *is* you and you don't like yourself and you're feeling helpless to change. *(3 seconds)*

LINDA: The way I feel about it is sad. Because it's not my fault . . .

not right to feel guilty and disgusted about things that aren't your fault. It's dumb. *(Pause, 30 seconds)* I'm dumb. *(21 seconds)*

[Note that the silences often last longer than the talk. The pattern establishes my allowing attitude and brings a sense of uncrowded openness to our session. This uncrowded atmosphere might not work during an initial therapy session or an important conversation among friends who are accustomed to crowding. Long wait-times in social or family settings are best introduced gradually. If not understood, the allowing can cause pressure and awkwardness.]

GOODMAN: Sometimes you feel rather foolish, blaming yourself, feeling guilty about things that you really have no right to feel guilty about.

[That did it. My repeated reflections about who's responsible for "it" finally connected well with this one. She went into her feelings again—exploring difficult territory.

[After almost *4 minutes* of silence, Linda looked up at me with a painful expression. She tried to talk but failed. She slouched back and looked down. I reflected her nonverbal communication.]

GOODMAN: It's just *extremely* hard to talk about—painful—thinking about them . . . as if . . . *(Stumbling for words)* Sounds like you're almost . . . as if it's tough enough to just sit there and think about them. *(30 seconds)*

[While waiting, my mind tried to scan her here-'n-now experience about some terrible "it" that infiltrated her mind and changed her self-concept for the worse. I watched and tried to feel the importance of "it" not being her fault, the sense of being trapped, miserable, helpless. It was hard for me to sustain the painful empathy; I had to escape and let my attention wander. Then I remembered that it was only an hour for me, but it was an ongoing feeling for her. That thought helped me return to her feelings and made me want to give her emotional company. I didn't want to wait passively or escape my uncomfortable attachment to her pain. There was little room in my mind for sustained curiosity about what "it" was. My students can't understand why the curiosity didn't overwhelm me; it dominates them whenever I play the session. Some students experience frustration at not knowing and start guessing. I don't tell them. They also fidget and want me to crowd her during the long wait-times. A few first-year grad students begin to obliquely question their professor's skill during the previous 3-minute, 42-second silence. Students typically prefer that I would have asked her outright about the horrendous "it." Their curiosity pushes aside thought about what's best for the client. That impatient priority is a problem for therapy students who bring crowding habits from a lifetime of "civilian" conversations.]

LINDA: I get a headache thinking about it. *(7 seconds)*

GOODMAN: You've got a headache now? *(0.3 second)*

LINDA: Yes. *(4 seconds)*

GOODMAN: Just thinking about it turns the stuck feeling into a headache. *(3 seconds)*

LINDA: It's one thing . . . that's gone wrong I can't get rid of. I can get rid of my family and I maybe can get rid of feeling afraid of people, get rid of feeling I'm not as good as people—I am as good as people. I can get rid of all those things 'cause I can see myself getting better, but this thing's immovable. *(3 seconds)*

GOODMAN: You experience it as a never changing thing. You're helpless against it. *(0.2 second)*

LINDA: *(Sniffles a bit as a few tears slowly roll down her face)* There's nothing I can do! It's *there* and there's nothing I can do to change it! And it's not even my *fault*. It's my *parents'* fault. They think that taking care of your children or protecting them is taking them to school and making sure they don't say bad words and making sure they go to church on Sunday, but they don't really . . . *(Pause, 3 seconds)* They don't really protect against one of the things that really hurts people. They wanna make sure you're polite and show manners and play the violin for guests. But they just didn't protect me from something that ruined my *whole life*. *(2 seconds)*

GOODMAN: They just weren't careful about the really destructive things. *(2 minutes, 37 seconds)*

[Some students in my seminar are unable to empathize with her anguished resentment during this silence. They need to know *what* ruined her whole life and try to solve that puzzle instead of experiencing some of her distress. The waiting is too much for their active minds. They know I'm watching them wiggle and they expect my interpretation of their impatient, and sometimes unfeeling, behavior, but some still can't help making their own interpretations about "it." Their imaginations run wild. It dawns on a few that the meaning of "it" during these minutes is of little consequence compared to the reflections and the waiting. They start learning that topics ("it") are sometimes less important than processes (like long silences and reflections) when giving serious help.]

LINDA: I can't even talk with my father anymore and say, "Look what you've done . . . and haven't you made a mess of my life?" I can't talk with him anymore. *(10 seconds)*

GOODMAN: Are you saying that he wouldn't understand? *(0.7 second)*

LINDA: He'd be *horrified*. I can't talk about . . . there's nothing to talk about with him, really . . . uh . . . *(0.7 second)*

GOODMAN: Wouldn't change a thing. *(1 second)*

LINDA: Would make things *worse* . . . just something he wouldn't . . . no one took care of me. *(4 seconds)*

GOODMAN: Nobody protected you when it mattered. . . . *(Pause, 5 seconds)* They took care of the small, unimportant things—pretty clothes, violins, modeling lessons, things for appearance. *(0.2 second)*

LINDA: Not the crucial things that . . . *haunt* me now. Kids get beat up every day. I forgot who I fought with on the playground. But I'll never forget what my parents caused. That's why I can't stand them; they think they're good parents, but they've messed me up. *(3 seconds)*

GOODMAN: They caused something awful to happen to your life and they walk around now feeling good—not knowing it ever happened. *(1 minute, 41 seconds)*

LINDA: I just can't talk about it. *(5 seconds)*

[Linda looked up at me from her hunched position. She opened her mouth, then turned back to stare at her knees. I reflected her gesture.]

GOODMAN: You want to, but it just hurts too much. It's not that—

LINDA: *(Interrupting)* But I can't *do* anything about it.

GOODMAN: What's the use of saying what hurts—it won't change a thing. *(6 minutes, 48 seconds)*

[Imagine waiting in an empathic silence for someone bottled up with an agonizing memory. It made my palms moist. Both of us were frozen in the moment. But it was just what she needed to free her. The long silence turned out to be significant because the meaning of "it" was about to be disclosed. Knowing that, before my students hear her disclosure, I try getting them to wait with concentrated empathy. I urge them to try reexperiencing her feelings for the duration of the long silence. They try, but some confess to wandering thoughts. Engaged waiting is an acquired skill. They aren't sure that these extreme waits are necessary. My students usually trust me when I put them into odd communication situations, but the trust is strained for many at this point.]

LINDA: Hm-m-mph . . . Say something.

GOODMAN: I was thinking about what you're going through, but you need me to say something to take your mind off it.

LINDA: I don't wanna think about it 'cause it makes my head hurt. I get angry and I wanna *ha* . . . I wanna ha . . . hit people and wanna hit my father and . . . *(2 seconds)*

GOODMAN: I think you were going to say "hate." It makes you hate and you don't wanna hate.

LINDA: No, I don't wanna hate. I shouldn't hate people too much. . . . I could almost *kill*—for, for what . . . I . . . *(Sighs)* *(5 seconds)*

GOODMAN: *(Almost whispering)* It's unforgivable. *(10 seconds)*

LINDA: *(Haltingly, tearfully, breathlessly)* Nothing . . . too awful . . . angry with people, but . . . I've never wanted to . . . kill anybody—there's *one* person I want to kill. *(4 seconds)*

GOODMAN: Want to wipe off the face of the earth.

LINDA: I want to shoot him dead a hundred times, drag him to the ocean so the gulls can *eat every part of him*! Till there's *nothing* left. *(0.9 second)*

GOODMAN: Destroy him so there's nothing left. *(1.1 seconds)*

LINDA: This drooling man. My rotten, smiling, vicious *uncle*. Drooling all over a 10-year-old. *Acting* like he loved me—saying it was good—giving me root beer, having his way with me, making me scared to tell. And my parents kept *thanking* him. For taking care of me. *(Long sigh)* Oh-h-h, God, a great babysitter, all right. Went on for months . . . *(7 seconds)*

GOODMAN: They were blind, couldn't see what he really was? *(1 second)*

LINDA: No! No! They couldn't have been. . . . All those signs . . . they must have . . . *suspected*. . . . How could they? I don't think they wanted to face it. . . . They just made their suspicions disappear. . . . *(Pause, 12 seconds)* How can one sleazy, sick, selfish man make someone unhappy all their life? . . . *(Pause, 6 seconds)* They run around putting people in the gas chamber for this and for that—why don't they go around and collect all the molesters and gas *them*? *(0.4 second)*

GOODMAN: You want him dead—need revenge to get rid of some of this awful pain and hate. *(1.5 seconds)*

LINDA: I can't forgive him. Can't. I still see him at Christmas. God, I shouldn't be so afraid of him, but I am. *(0.8 second)*

GOODMAN: He still terrifies you. *(6 seconds)*

LINDA: I'm afraid he'll kill me. 'Cause I just hate him with every ounce of me—he's *filth*! *(3 seconds)*

GOODMAN: Disgusting . . . maybe even more than disgusting. *(7 seconds)*

LINDA: I get sick when I think of it. He's made me vomit. I want him dead. *(8 seconds)*

GOODMAN: Just hard to accept the fact he's living at this moment. *(0.1 second)*

LINDA: He should never have been born. *(0.8 second)*

GOODMAN: Should never have existed. *(3 seconds)*

LINDA: He's damaged my whole *life*. That's why I'm afraid of people now. Why I'm afraid of feeling my body . . . afraid of feeling my sex. . . . That's why I keep trying with anybody that comes along, even when it's scary. I try everything . . . with almost every guy but I can't really *feel* it. *(3 seconds)*

GOODMAN: He's made your sex into something numb. And made you afraid of people. *(0.5 second)*

LINDA: He made me feel dirty. . . . *(Pause, 6 seconds)* Oh, I *hate* him. If you ever feel dirty, you can never feel clean again. . . . And my stepmother never knew what was wrong with me. *(Mockingly)* "What's the *matter* with you, why can't you be like *other* people?" *(10 seconds)*

GOODMAN: Your stepmother never knew what disgusting thing had happened, the bad thing that contributed . . .

[Linda started sobbing and continued for more than 6 minutes. When the crying stopped, she looked me straight in the eye, made a wan little smile, pointed both hands at me, palms up as if asking, Can you really know how I feel?]

GOODMAN: You're asking, I think, how could I know what you've experienced? How could I know how bad you feel now?

LINDA: Yes . . . *(Pause, 12 seconds)* but maybe you do know some of it. . . . That's important, but I still can't forget it. Wish part of my brain was gone so I could forget what happened. Help me forget so that I don't have to feel it for one more minute. *(She laughs a bit out of her crying and reaches for my hand)*

GOODMAN: Could we have it operated on?

LINDA: *(Laughing more)* Yeah. There's the solution. *(Pause, 42 seconds)* I'm sure these things happen to other people and they go on living. Maybe I can learn to live through this. . . . At least I've told *you*. I guess that's a start. . . .

At this point my students understand that impatient probing questions about the nature of "it" had no place in the conversation. They begin to believe that vigilant, consistent waiting can loosen tightly compressed secrets. And they usually see how the empathic process, via reflections, can keep a listener too busy to get curious *at first* about the events that caused feelings. It gives me pleasure to hear students discuss how the quick satisfaction of curiosity about Linda's "it" might have closed her up for the duration of the therapy, if not for the rest of her life. After the impact of this session hits them, some are eager to try out the process of waiting for someone in emotional trouble. I hope reading it triggers the same reaction.

The session continued as I waited for her, following her experiences and reflecting her feelings. She spoke of how her uncle's abuses caused her to develop a habit of lying, and a pattern of profound mistrust toward any man offering care. She sobbed, out of relief, at the end of the session, saying, "I've been saying things out loud today that I haven't been able to say to myself."

Linda's story took several happy turns after some difficult coping with her problems. She had some painful family confrontations, managed to turn away from her compulsive sexual activity, survived the awkwardness of her first lengthy romantic relationship, and eventually got rid of her daily headaches. After we ended therapy, she joined a support group of women who'd had similar childhood experiences. Within a year, she was organizing groups for other women.

My session with Linda is an extreme example of how silences

can be used as a skill in combination with other talk tools. (Reflections work very well, and so can self-disclosures and soft interpretations.) But the psychological dynamics that were operating in our therapy conversation can be seen in conversations at home where intimate pairs need unrushed talk.

IN APPRECIATION OF CREATIVE CROWDING

With all of the emphasis I put on appreciating noncrowding behavior, it hasn't come as a surprise that I've been accused at times of lacking regard for the way some crowded conversations produce warmth, camaraderie, and sheer fun. A woman from Miami wrote me a few years ago—in response to a magazine piece called "Slow Talking in the Big City"—to say I apparently didn't understand from first-hand experience about the spontaneous combustion of ideas and humor that can happen in the midst of steady interruptions and overtalk. Ouch. I wrote back and tried to explain that I've been having enjoyable fast conversations like that all my life.

What really stung was when a New York linguist went so far as to call me a decontextualized strategist. Where I come from (Detroit), those are fighting words. But I kept my mouth shut, and even read a book by the linguist Deborah Tannen called *That's Not What I Meant*. She writes provocatively about how talk habits are shaped by social contexts. Two Boston people, for instance—because of habits shaped over the years by social context—might enthusiastically interrupt each other for hours as a way of rubbing shoulders, latching onto each other's emotions, becoming unguarded and emoting feelings. (The Charlie/Phil conversation in chapter 6 illustrates some affectionate crowding.) That style can be fun and healthy exercise. As Professor Tannen observes in her innovative research, regional and ethnic differences play a significant role in what you can get by with, and where.

So Tannen is right—my problems with crowding behavior don't fit contexts where two or more crowders are good-naturedly having at each other with what she calls machine-gun questions, along with rushed responses, simultaneous talk, and other lively forms of verbal jostling. But I don't believe that crowding someone who isn't inclined, or able, to crowd back is bilateral fun. Those one-way verbal assaults are like duets with a trombone and harmonica—the trombone player has a responsibility to adjust the volume down a little. Few things are as irritating as a decontextualized trombonist.

THE CASE FOR CONSCIOUS CROWDING

People who get pushed around a lot in conversation—mostly slow-talking, quiet souls—might never get their fair share of attention by waiting for the kindness of crowders. Sometimes the only recourse is to crowd in return. As a practical matter, crowding—on purpose, at critical moments—is just as much a skill as the act of conscious allowing. Bereft of tools for occasionally crowding back, some people are left at the mercy of others' wills. Indiscriminate passivity in talk is definitely not a skill. The silent minority who consistently shun attention and the conversational spotlight may not antagonize others as quickly as chronic crowders, but they—and the people around them—can wind up robbed of robust *two*-way conversations.

There's a big difference between the kind of active, engaged allowing that goes on when close attention is required and the kind that simply disengages—for whatever reason. The reason could be just shy withdrawal, the wish to speak deliberately or not at all, self-protecting quietness, or an ambivalence about overcoming lifelong habits of giving up the floor. Passive allowing as a habit can ultimately wind up causing as much resentment in our partners as habitual crowding. Here's a typical scenario.

Pete dates Terri and appreciates the way she seems to supply generous attention for whatever he has to say. They spend more time together and he continues to appreciate all of the room she gives him. They move in together and things seem pretty much the same . . . except, somehow, he doesn't feel as eagerly heard. It starts dawning on him that she might not be as generous with her attention as she is withdrawn. All of the special attention that he's received doesn't sound so special when it turns out to be the result of indiscriminate or chronic passivity. The warmth of being allowed begins turning, in his mind, into the lonely coolness of one-way talk. Terri's quiet, catering talk demeanor still works well with casual acquaintances and strangers, but to Pete, she's holding back the sort of active involvement he expects from an intimate. If it's supposed to be a special quality she shares with him, how come she also seems to do it with strangers? And when he tries to discuss all of this, she's genuinely perplexed—why would her gentle giving be viewed negatively now? Chronic allowers can be stubborn in accepting complaints about the disengagement and loneliness that result from their habits. Most of them aren't even aware there's a problem. They've felt so much resentment in their lives at being crowded out that they have a hard time considering how they cause resentment.

It's tough. I've seen some slow-talking, long-term quiets thoroughly confused by the idea that they could be victimizing not only themselves but also people they're close to. Sometimes their passivity comes from fears—of being awkward, losing serenity, showing soft spots, or looking pushy. Sometimes, though, when silence is used as a *weapon*, the behavior becomes hostile—a manipulative, relentless, passively aggressive reluctance that strikes the victim's consciousness as disengagement. That sort of indirect nastiness is often hard to spot at first. (A passive-aggressive acquaintance once told me that his chronic quietness was his way "of playing it safe so that other people can make asses of themselves first.")

Let's face it, some quieter folks need to take more chances, to recognize that they might be consistently managing attention *away* from themselves. That passive habit isn't benign or victimless. Conscious crowding, used judiciously, is a skill that can save relationships by balancing them better.

PRACTICING

This practice section has tips and exercises for dealing with both habitual allowing and crowding.

Hints for Reluctant Talkers Who Want to Get More Aggressive

Trying more conscious crowding at first typically results in very small increases in assertive conversation behavior. That's to be expected. It's not going to happen overnight. Overcoming a livelong habit of allowing too much can't be forced too rapidly. I've seen shy people, inspired by a magazine article on assertion or a New Year's Eve resolution, turn into talk terrors during a couple of weeks of crazed crowding as they attempt to over-zealously establish their rights. Warning: Overcorrection can cause conflict that sends the passive talker into deeper patterns of overallowing.

For starters, take time to simply observe the exchange of attention in several of your conversations. That'll be distracting at first. The self-consciousness usually turns into a comfortable self-awareness after a few tries. Don't attempt to become a roaring extrovert over a weekend. Just observe how often you are interrupted and how often you *do* interruptions. Watch for two small but critical incidents in the talk: filled pauses and unfilled pauses.

Filled pauses are brief moments of self-interruption where the talker says things like "Uhmmm" or "ahhh" or "let's see" or "ya know." Linguists study how we use these fillers to hesitate, feel doubt, collect thoughts—and to let our partners interrupt. They're the second favorite spot for interrupting, an invitation to interact.

Unfilled pauses are the favorite place for interrupting. They're just the silent lulls of a second or two in the midst of a verbal sentence or paragraph. They're choice moments to jump in.

A great way to enter the arena without feeling pushy or on the spot is to offer reflections. Verbally demonstrating empathic understanding rarely is an either/or situation—it's more like a win for both sides. At the very least, reflections are more neutral than interpretations or advisements. And they have a proclivity for slowing down the pace of your partner, which provides additional chances to chime in comfortably without rushing.

Hints for Stopping Crowders

This is aimed at fending off casual acquaintances and strangers in a nonviolent manner. I don't recommend the methods for close relationships (unless you inform your friend, the crowder, beforehand). These are best used for protecting yourself from a busy or paternalizing authority figure (physician, lawyer, psychologist, smooth-talking salesperson) or fast-talking colleagues or meetings full of overtalk, and in similar settings where your train of thought is important and gets sidetracked. The following devices are thought of as last-resort efforts rather than durable skills.

My favorite way to shut down habitual crowding is to do a metamessage—*talk about the talk*—that says something like, "Oops, I didn't get to finish my sentence." The idea is to respectfully refocus the crowder's attention onto his or her process without name-calling, accusation, or direct advice.

There's something about being "forced" to focus on the process of crowding that leaves an unalterable impression. A heartfelt disclosure about your need to finish an idea often does the job without embarrassment or debate. For the really self-absorbed crowder, you may need a follow-up metamessage or two: "I wasn't able to explain . . ." "I need a little more room to tell you . . ." "I've got some leftover reactions to what you were saying a few minutes ago. . . ."

If you stick with self-disclosures that show the way you two are talking, there may be no need for tricks, like fighting interruptions with interruptions, a defense that usually makes conversations deteriorate into contests. Even if you win by cleverly cutting in at filled or unfilled pauses, the attention gained is usually second-rate.

A more severe form of metamessage than self-disclosing about the talk itself is interpreting the conversation. It can be a showstopper. Interpretive metamessages can generate small shocks: "We're talking all over each other so much there's no chance to think," or "You've been so eager to tell me about it that you've been cutting me off in midsentence." Interpretations carry more potential to be insulting than disclosures.

One more option is to go for a straightforward piece of insistent advice: "Wait a minute—give me a chance to finish," or "If you stop interrupting me for a while, I'll let you know what I think." Commanding another to talk differently may feel too assertive to some people, but there are plenty of times when it beats walking away or attempts to manipulate.

For me, metamessages work much of the time. Putting a spotlight on the process of crowding sometimes contributes to the clutter right at the moment; long-range, though, I like it better than condescending a crowder with a feigned interest and switched-off mind—or demeaning myself while someone blathers all over me.

Hints about Communicating with Busy Professionals

Most of us grew up learning that we should quietly wait for some people—parents, elders, teachers, for example—to have their say before jumping in. As adults, many of us act that way around "experts"—anybody who's supposed to know a lot more than we do about the ways certain things work, even if it's our own body.

Based on a study by researchers Sheldon Greenfield and Sherrie Kaplan (UCLA School of Public Health), the typical doctor interrupts patients six times per visit. It's not only frustrating to have our worrisome complaints cut off in midstream by the physician, it can be a serious interference in providing adequate health care. Missing a critical bit of information, a small symptom, can distort a diagnosis. In addition, the rushed, confused patient is less likely to follow medical directions.

It doesn't mean doctors—and other professionals we rely on—aren't conscientious. Virtually all of the physicians-in-training or practicing doctors I've dealt with in communication classes (even a few of the lawyers and realtors) have believed they needed to get better information from their clients or patients to do their jobs effectively. But the psychological history of doctor/patient relations over the years is mixed, at best. Consider the psychology of it.

You go into the office with various feelings from worried to terrified, from confused to distressed. You're paying for help from a professional who's supposed to get a fix on the most private physical aspects of your life, not to mention your personal feelings about those private functions. It's one-way intimacy, in which you're asked to succumb to the physician's control for your own good. There may be things you don't understand but must do on faith; physicians need compliance. So the nature of the transaction puts the patient in a vulnerable position; you give up some control; you submit in some ways like a child submits to parents; the necessities of the situation demand trust and deference. But that doesn't mean the doctor can't be challenged to listen to your complete story. In the Greenfield/Kaplan study, 200 patients—utilizing 20 minutes' worth of training—cut their physicians' interruptions from six to three per visit. The patients also increased their own average of interruptions from one to four per visit.

A story in the *Los Angeles Times* quoted Greenfield's appraisal of how managing attention benefited the patients: "A group with hypertension showed decreases in their blood pressure levels. Patients with ulcers also improved. It was very dramatic. We think it happened because the patients were getting a much better sense of control over their own care and a sense of collegiality with the doctor."

Some medical schools, to their credit, are starting to teach communication skills to residents. Dr. Richard Frankel, a sociologist at Wayne State University's Medical School, has been teaching such fundamentals as "to shut up" during the first part of the interview and then "to solicit additional concerns from the patient." Research indicates that both the trained residents and their patients wind up more satisfied and that the health care is "better and more comprehensive."

Forcing Physicians—and Other Pros—to Listen

These techniques are specifically aimed at dealing with doctors, but they can be adapted to apply to other people you go to for expert help—attorneys, nurses, mechanics, accountants, realtors, etc.

PURPOSES

1. To serve as a preparatory procedure and conversational guide for enhancing the physician's capacity to diagnose.
2. To enable patients to get a clear set of instructions for using medications and executing self-care regiments.
3. To reduce apprehension and anxiety about medical visits.
4. To provide a bit of support, a little pep talk, for anyone approaching hospitalization, anticipating serious health problems, or caring for a fearful child who's facing medical treatment.

METHODS

The Patient's Problem List. Consider preparing a brief list of symptoms, questions, special requirements or anything important that needs careful understanding. Obviously, the advantage is to put things in writing during a calm mood, with plenty of time to think, remember, observe, and phrase communication carefully. The list also allows you to add items over a period of hours or days. I've found it best to scribble out my list, let it rest in case forgotten symptoms or new questions come to mind, and then rewrite or type it with an eye toward clarity. Condense it to half a page if possible.

These patient problem lists are wonderful aids when anxiety is present, but they can also help when you simply want your physician to know all the facts during a rushed office visit. In my own little informal poll of 16 doctors, almost half of them actually preferred that the list be handed directly to them; the rest preferred that their patients read the list out loud, embellishing upon request. This simple aid has improved medical interviews significantly, according to both patients and physicians I've talked to. I'd like to see patient problem lists become routine in medical practice.

Slipping into pauses. The simplest way to combat crowding and get a word in edgewise is to aim a quick sentence into an unfilled, silent pause. If none are available, try a filled pause (see descriptions earlier in this chapter). This procedure is done unwittingly by many in the ordinary flow of conversation, but it may need to be used deliberately in the unnatural rush of medical interviews.

If your "expert" never pauses. In this case, think about using that expert remedy—the self-disclosing metamessage. Tell your doctor, for example: "I'm feeling too rushed to remember everything I needed to say." That's a respectful, effective disclosure about the way you two are talking that works most of the time.

If disclosure metamessages don't get his or her attention. It might be necessary to use bold interpretive metamessages such as, "We've been talking so fast that I haven't had a chance to describe all the details," or "You seem so rushed that it's tough to answer carefully." Or a last-ditch effort might require an advisement metamessage: "Give me just a couple of minutes to explain it better."

Some physicians might not react well to getting such guidance or interpretation about conducting a medical interview. But if you avoid a nasty tone, I'd like to think most would accept the honesty and respond by slowing down their pace, even if they've forgotten that *you* are paying *them*.

"Dominance/Submission Game"

The capacity for enjoying a range of dominance/submissive behaviors is a requisite for mental health. Within a relationship, being able to responsibly take over, control, influence, and assert—*or* to appropriately yield, defer, let go, and be dependent—is a condition of mature love. That's not a philosophical position but a psychological assertion held by most people who study human relations for a living. It's an obvious and extremely practical fact that becomes clouded by denial and embarrassment in our struggle to connect closely with each other. This game can stimulate a couple or a small group into thoughts about their capacity for aggression and passivity within an intimate relationship. Its initial purpose is to heighten awareness about the experience of submitting attention and dominating attention in conversation. In my view, our individual styles for giving and getting attention say much about our styles of loving.

PURPOSES

1. To provide several immediately contrasting experiences of completely controlling attention and then selflessly succumbing to another's control during a single conversation. The game has an especially good track record for stimulating important insights for both crowders and chronic quiets. But the possibilities for insights and some amusement are there for any pair (or small group) feeling good about each other.
2. To serve as a rough self-assessment device for how "ambidextrous" or psychologically comfortable you are in dominating and submitting during conversations. It's also a training routine for getting more comfortable with either controlling or being controlled.
3. To introduce the ideas of attention-management and turn-taking as interpersonal processes to students or intellectually curious pairs or groups.
4. To help adjust attention balance. It often encourages more fairness among familiar talkers. It can apply to work teams, self-help groups, therapy groups, and especially families and couples that have drifted into an imbalance of conversational control.

METHOD

1. The person talking controls *all* the attention and is not interrupted until he or she wants to relinquish the floor and clearly points to the next conversation "controller."
2. The duration of control for an individual ranges from about one to seven minutes in the self-help groups I've timed. With couples, it usually goes on a little longer. Occasionally someone feeling playful or needy tests the limits in a group by going on for 10 to 15 minutes. (I've heard one instance where a habitually shy, passive woman controlled her dominant partner into mute attention for 90 minutes in a mutually satisfying reversal of roles.) If overcontrol by an eager domi-

nator is a concern, establish limits before starting: 5 or 10 minutes in a group, 10 to 15 minutes for couples seems about right. Otherwise, simply limit the game itself to an hour.

3. Before starting, give permission for controllers to maintain very long silent pauses (even for minutes if they wish). Controllers must not be hampered by guilt. They should give themselves permission to dominate attention as they please without regard to other's impatience or eagerness to grab the floor. Listeners must pay strict attention and not show signs of disrespect or employ nonverbal communication— especially funny gestures that disrupt concentration. (That last rule creates temptation because this game is a natural vehicle for playfulness. A little troublemaking is okay, but frequent mischief might distress quiet types who are feeling earnest about their controlling roles.)

A VARIATION FOR KIDS

Since children know a lot about submitting their attention to parents, teachers, and older kids, they take to the dominance/ submission game with gusto. Once, at a summer camp, a group of 10- to 13-year-old children played this game for *three hours* before being sent to bed by their counselors. Shy children took increasingly longer times in the controller role. The effects even generalized to the remainder of their camp stay, according to counselors. Controlling and submitting attention with peers and without chaos seems to provide pleasure (and learning) for pre-adolescents and early teenagers. I haven't tried it, but the game might also be useful for developmentally disadvantaged and hyperactive children in special classrooms or at home with family.

"Painful Silence/Golden Silence"

This has been field-tested over many years as an eye-opener on how crowding stifles personal exploration in groups. The exercise has been used in a variety of settings, from college courses to self-help groups and large families. It's been done thousands of time as a requirement of my SASHAtape program. I estimate that it fails to gel about 25 percent of the time—usually because group members can't get comfortable. Despite that hefty failure rate, when it does succeed, the results are impressive. This isn't for couples or groups of less than four. It takes 35 to 45 minutes and requires the services of a nonparticipating timer.

PURPOSES

1. To illustrate the effect of extreme crowding and allowing on small group behavior—especially help-intended and help-seeking behaviors.
2. To provide a quick method for starting sessions and stimulating interaction in established groups. For them, it can be used repeatedly.

METHOD

1. It requires two adjacent ten-minute periods, except when used as a routine group starter where two periods of five minutes are adequate. The topics of conversation should be engaging, because the flow of spontaneous talk must occur during the "painful silence" episode.
2. Start with the painful silence episode by selecting one or two topics that touch the lives or stir the emotions of most participants.
3. Consider reading the following instructions on painful silence to the group:

   This exercise asks you to stretch imagination and put yourself in a world where giving and getting information—quickly—is a strong urge. Please pretend you have an irrational passion for gathering facts about each other, as if your lives depended on it. If the leader hasn't suggested a stimulating topic, try introducing things of personal interest that can keep the conversation lively. Take a little risk if you're in the mood. Assume an attitude of hunger for information that only has ten minutes to find satisfaction. Talk as often as you can without worrying about monopolizing attention. Silences are awful. Pretend they give you pain. They are wasted moments. Imagine the group as a team joining forces to achieve more information exchange than other groups. Please give up any natural inclinations toward quiet courtesy, reserve, or the avoidance of pushiness. Putting yourself in this strange world for ten minutes can provide some good learning.
4. Consider getting permission from all group members to use an audio tape recorder for the exercise. The tape can be utilized later for either group discussion or tending to individual members, or both. Replaying it is often an educational experience in itself.
5. Arrange the group in a tight circle, if possible, and let members talk at will for exactly ten minutes, then stop them

(abruptly, if necessary). Be sure to explain they will continue discussing the same topic in a minute. Insist they remain mute for half a minute (it might be difficult to quiet them), then ask the group to start another ten-minute episode in the "golden silence" condition. Tell the group to start immediately after you instruct them. You may want to read the following paragraph out loud:

The group's task for the next ten minutes is to take on an attitude exactly opposite from that of the previous ten minutes. It's an abrupt change and should challenge your capacity for switching attitude. No need to change the topic of conversation; just your attitude about rushing to capture many facts in little time. Please become part of a new world now where silence is golden and what you say is less important than what you hear. So listen deeply and turn away from urges for quick replies. Allow several seconds to pass before responding to each other. Give very long wait-times. At first, maybe count silently up to ten before talking after someone has stopped. Never interrupt. Listen deeply and peacefully without feeling that you must remain completely silent. Simply playing mechanical games with who can shut up the longest will ruin the benefits. If long silences feel awkward, try turning the mild tension into a pleasurable pause by giving yourselves permission to be peacefully still at times. The rule here is: Don't compete for the floor. Be the *giver* of attention; only take attention when others don't seem to want it. There's no room for even a hint of pushiness during the next ten minutes. Any volunteer can now start talking, *slowly*, about where you left off when I interrupted you. Good luck.

6. Gently stop the group after ten minutes of the golden silence exercise. An abrupt ending is not necessary this time. Ask the group to take a brief break, then open a discussion about the contrasting personal experiences between the painful and golden silence episodes. See if members can describe differences in group behavior over the two episodes besides the obvious crowding and allowing activity.

CRYSTALLIZING THE EXPERIENCE

A common observation of participants is that there is a deeper exploration, less defensiveness, and more frequent exchange of personal thoughts during the golden silence episode. When that happens, groups are usually interested in discussing the general issue of conversational crowding and allowing in their lives. Some people may be interested in reading this chapter for how-to material and chapter 6 *after* completing the exercise. Reading the section before starting will ruin the learning experience.

It has proven extremely valuable to play a random minute or two of recorded audiotape from the painful silence episode—*immediately* followed by a few minutes from golden silence. Whether you taped or not, here are some questions for stimulating discussion.

- How did you feel *being* interrupted and *doing* interruptions? Describe the differences. Was some of it enjoyable? Frustrating? Friendly?
- Are you able to see why raising touchy topics during crowded arguments can amplify hurt feelings? How much does the process of crowding add to the damage done in arguments?
- Even though this exercise was self-conscious and manufactured, did anyone notice how people tended to match each other's pace? Can anyone recall conversations where crowding begot crowding or allowing begot allowing? Are these conversational qualities contagious in typical talk?
- Which episode went more against the natural grain of your temperament? Describe the feelings.
- For any admitted crowders: Have you the real *freedom* to be comfortable when allowing others to monopolize attention?
- For anyone admittedly shy or distinctly reserved: Are you capable of deliberately crowding to get your message heard? Can you do it with a dominating person?
- Do you tend toward being more of a crowder or an allower when with familiar friends? Children? Strangers? Your boss? Subordinates? Your dentist? Your physician? Do you have a habit of crowding a little more or allowing a little more than the people you love?

APPENDIX

People Who Write about Talk

IF YOU'RE curious about someone mentioned in this book, or you want to dig deeper into a special area of talk, glance through this section. It's a broad, opinionated sampling of writing by scholars, journalists, and impassioned amateurs.

Some of the writing is technical, loaded with jargon, but reading *this* book should make the big ideas understandable. Popular books based on sound information are included. The goal here is to provide a resource for tracking down anything you want to know about talk. The alphabetical listing does not include every important writer, but you will find one or two representatives for each area of writing on talk. Some writers are included just because I like them, or because their work uses my thinking.

D. A. were the initials of an anonymous seventeenth-century writer on talk—an early conversation analyst. It seems D. A. wrote the world's first talk book. Fascinating stuff. He took a radical stance by actually inviting women readers. You won't find it in your local bookstore, but rumor has it that a mutilated copy exists somewhere in the Yale library. Intact first editions can be read at a few major research libraries such as UCLA's Clark Library. It's title: *The Whole Act of Converse: Containing Necessary Instructions for All Persons, of What Quality, and Condition Soever, with the Characters of the Four Humours, of the English and French, as to Their Way of Conversing* (Joseph Hindmarsh, 1683, London).

The secretive Mr. A. observed how bad conversational habits, in the 1690s, destroyed friendships. He urged readers to improve their talk by cutting down on boasting, monopolizing attention, criticizing neighbors, being endlessly witty, talking too much, and speaking before thinking. (Things haven't changed much in 300 years.) Readers are warned not to talk of trifles nor debate with inferiors. He classified ordinary women as inferiors: "[Distracting, uncivil talk], is yet more ordinary amongst women, than among men, because they are generally an unthinking sort of creature, and scarce reflective on what they say, being easily over-rul'd by their passions, and commonly not capable to revenge themselves otherwise than with their tongues" (page 14). The book frequently uses women to document examples of terrible talk. Its sometimes violent sexism is in sharp contrast to Jonathan Swift's brilliantly written complaint about the frequent exclusion of women from male conversation, written a few years later. (Swift's work is covered later in this section.)

Anyone interested in a disturbing picture of talk between the sexes back then, or the author's analysis of how personality affects talk style (personality equals "sanguine, cholerick, melencholy, or phlegmatick"), or the differences among early English, French, Italian, and Scottish conversational style, can order a photocopy edition from University Microfilms International, P.O. Box 1307, Ann Arbor, MI 48106. They also take credit card phone orders; phone 1-800-521-0600. Request Reel 45, Item 2, Wing 3A.

Mortimer Adler, America's favorite popular philosopher, has come to the conclusion that learning how to talk better is more important to happiness than learning how to read or write better. That's a dramatic disclosure, since Adler is a master educator in adult reading and writing methods. He backed up his belief about the importance of talking by writing *How to Speak/How to Listen* (Macmillan, 1983). It does a good job of placing talk in the context of social history and offering a rudimentary classification of conversations into playful versus serious, personal versus impersonal, theoretical versus practical. It may be a good starting point for people thinking about conversation and culture, but Adler offers little insight into the inner workings of talk and fails to honor the promise of his title. His brilliance rarely slips beneath the surface of talk, but he does demonstrate the powerful role of conversation in the functioning of civilization.

Maybe it takes more than being a fine philosopher to become a fine talk scholar.

Charles Berger studies interpersonal communication, in contrast to **Steven Chaffe's** speciality, mass communication. Nevertheless, they are joint editors of *The Handbook of Communication Science* (Sage, 1987). Talking to millions on TV and talking to a friend are events that share some common features in the management of messages, the "production, processing, and effects of symbol and signal systems." The book is aimed at specialists and would be a struggle for laypeople. But any "civilian" deeply interested in the last word on communication research or theory, or topics like conflict, persuasion, family process, consumer behavior, children's talk, public opinion, or professional mass communicators (like journalists) might be able to absorb some of the material. The jargon is thick and the writing is often unskilled.

Karen Blaker does a call-in radio program on the East Coast. Her experience with call-in secrets led to a long personal investigation of self-disclosure and concealment described in *Intimate Secrets* (Little, Brown, 1986). A clearly written section on the development of secrecy patterns from infancy to late adolescence could be a practical guide for parents, teachers, and therapists. The material on teen secrets seems interesting enough to be read by teenagers themselves. A section on adult secrecy explores the extremely difficult necessity and danger of high-risk disclosing in intimacy. Some of her opinions about not giving or expecting total honesty in primary intimate relationships are controversial and opposed to the thinking of major interpersonal thinkers. Her conceptions of privacy and secrecy become blurred at times. Overall, her book can serve as a self-help manual for what I call "promiscuous disclosers" (see chapters 1 and 7 of this book) and chronic concealers. She shows how the secretive soul is linked to a lifetime of denial.

Sissela Bok explores talk that conceals and discloses. Her books *Lying* (Pantheon, 1978) and *Secrets* (Pantheon, 1982) are rather scholarly but not technical examinations of betrayal and openness in family life, friendship, work, religious confession, politics, science, journalism, corporations, police work, and military talk. She addresses the frequently overlooked connection between deceptive talk and self-deception.

Roger Brown is the author of the venerable *Words and Things* (Free Press, 1968), a classical introduction to the psychology of language. It's old-fashioned, but still good for getting acquainted with the history and big ideas of the science—if you're a student of language. Sometimes the reading gets bogged down with jargon, but Brown's command of the field and his warm wisdom compensate.

Bonnie Burstein spends most of her time teaching people to help others help themselves. She creates programs at the California Self-Help Center at UCLA. Her doctoral dissertation studied talk that is intended to help. She believes most people don't realize how much of their daily talking is aimed at making things better for others—even if it's not altogether altruistic. Burstein explains how the "help-intended" communicator tends to ask many questions, overdo explanations, and ruin exploration with interruptions. Helpers just talk too much to help most of the time. She taught people to expand their options in using all of the six "talk tools" used in this book. Two methods were used: (1) published manuals combined with audiotapes (the SASHAtape program); and (2) specifically trained "live" group leaders teaching the same six talk tools. Both methods enriched actual performance skills as the participants demonstrated new helping habits that included reflections, self-disclosures (yes, disclosures are effective as helping tools), and better use of silence—less interrupting and less overall talking. Her big surprise was that the "do-it-yourself" learners did just as well, and sometimes better, compared to those learning from in-person leaders. Burstein's dissertation, *The Structure of Helping Language as an Outcome of Two Communications Skills Training Programs: Live versus Automated* (UCLA, 1982), is available from University Microfilms International, P.O. Box 1307, Ann Arbor, MI 48106. For phone orders, call 1-800-521-0600.

Leo Buscaglia has been called everything from "a frothy, prancing spellbinder for desperately dull souls" to "a significant social force for opening up millions of Americans to the practical joys of loving . . . a secular antidote for our violent culture." His best-sellers and widely distributed lectures focus on the enactment of love—the communication of love. Disdain and even ridicule by professionals have hardly dampened his appeal. Some say that Buscaglia has had more psychological impact on the public than all of the psychotherapists in this country. *Bus 9 to Paradise* (Ballantine, 1986) is loaded with evocative and sometimes simplistic tales supporting the ethic that the maintenance of intimacy requires work in the form of sitting down to really talk. This impassioned man is on a mission to motivate people to take risks in disclosing love (see the discussion of risky disclosures in chapter 1 of this book.) He is unarguably effective and influential, but neglects *specifying* methods and pitfalls involved in the open expression of affection. "Sitting down to really talk" needs more than an inspired resolution. Saying what we mean is a skill that needs knowledge about face-to-face talk. Despite that weakness in his work, Buscaglia's earnest psychology couched in junior-high language continues to inspire people in trouble. It can be a useful stimulant that may penetrate the cynicism of some isolated teenagers and adults.

Paula Butler writes about silent talk. She wants to give people permission to listen in on their own internal conversations. Her book *Talking to Yourself* (Stein & Day, 1981) takes a cognitive-behavioral approach to personal problem solving. It's a self-support manual describing internal troublemakers called "The Self-2 Judge," "Drivers," "Stoppers," and "Confusers." Butler's examples of self-talk can take an added meaning when classified as talk tools: "I'm an idiot" (interpretation); "Am I making the right decision?" (closed question); "I shouldn't feel guilty taking the evening off" (advisement); "I don't want to feel scared" (self-disclosure). Knowing exactly *how* to talk to yourself might make her method even more interesting.

Gordon Chelune wants researchers to do a better job of measuring self-disclosure (see chapters 1 and 7 of this book.) He believes knowledge of the phenomenon is limited by the lack of consistency in definition among scientists. His technical book *Self-Disclosure: Origins, Patterns, and Implications of Openness in Interpersonal Relationships* (Jossey Bass, 1979) has chapters by 11 scholars who regard disclosure as a key in understanding romance, family talk, personality disorder, and therapy technique.

Andrew Christensen studies the ways couples shout at each other. He has spent years analyzing how unhappy couples get caught in a marital rut. An important pattern: One person (usually the woman) demands more engagement, more talk, and the other withdraws, resists disclosing. It's reminiscent of the reveal/conceal ordeal described in chapters 1 and 7 of this book. Christensen sees talk avoidance as a damaging feature of chronic marital conflict. The damage is fed by the mythical belief that "it will get worse if we talk about it." Christensen's solid, scientific book, scheduled for publication late in 1989, is tentatively titled *Vicious Cycles and Imcompatible Differences*. It offers guidance for resolving communication breakdowns without further professional assistance. (Dr. Christensen is in the UCLA Department of Psychology.)

Robert Craig is interested in the practical aspects of communication research. He edited *Conversational Coherence* (Sage, 1983) with colleague **Karen Tracy**. She's interested in the skills for talking well. Their book, with chapters by 15 conversation researchers, introduces the latest methods for studying talk: how conversationalists influence each other; the extent to which talk messages are consciously produced; the prejudices that talk scientists bring to their observations; and the influence of gesture, crowding, and allowing behaviors on verbal behavior. The book displays how a growing group of young, bright scholars are moving the field of talk analysis out of its adolescence into a grown-up scientific discipline.

Valerian Derlega and **John Berg** are social psychologists who collected the latest thinking in *Self-Disclosure: Theory, Research, and Therapy* (Plenum Press, 1987). Their chapters are written by academics *for* academics, but a few contain important information (put in plain language) on special topics that can be immediately useful to the lay reader. Mary Fitzpatrick's chapter on verbal intimacy in marriage is low on jargon and offers useful ideas for traditional and more independent couples. William Stiles does a brilliant essay on the paradox of disclosure as a symptom of psychological dysfunction and as a healing act. (More illumination of that useful fact is found in chapter 1 of this book.) An aggressive reader personally concerned with special aspects of openness or concealment can find chapters grappling with disclosure and loneliness, distress, psychopathology, relationship disengagement, gender, self-consciousness, brain function, and psychotherapy. Some of it is ponderous and exceedingly academic, but if that's your cup of tea, there's nothing better in print.

Robert Elliott used to be infatuated with metaphors, but then he studied response modes (the academic name for talk tools) at UCLA and became a professional observer of therapy talk. Along with five kindred colleagues, he studied a variety of response-mode systems in search of the best set of language tools for making sense of conversation in any kind of therapy. Their study adds scientific support to the framework of six talk tools used in *The Talk Book*. The other researchers are William Stiles, Miami University; Alvin Maher, University of Ottawa; Clara Hill, University of Maryland; Myrna Friedlander, State University of New York, Albany; and Frank Maigison, Central Manchester Health Authority, England. (Their findings were reported in "Primary Therapist and Response Modes: Comparison of 6 Rating Systems," *Journal of Consulting and Clinical Psychology*, vol. 44, no. 2, 1987.) Each of the researchers had developed an independent set of talk tools, a system for analyzing therapy talk. The simplest system divided talk into 8 parts; the most elaborate looked at 35 parts of language. All systems contained the six talk tools used in this book, and a couple of systems were derived from a framework purposed by Goodman and Dooley ("A Framework for Help-Intended Communication," *Psychotherapy: Therapy, Research, and Practice*, vol. 13, 1987). The research focused all of the systems on the same group of seven recorded therapy sessions, ranging from Jungian dream analysis to behavior therapy. When the investigators were finished with their months of computations, they concluded, "The present results suggest that a set of fundamental response-mode categories or dimensions underlies a variety of systems with different [various] origins and purposes." That is, validity was found for a set of *primary* talk tools for making sense of conversations about personal problems. Those primary tools are the same ones used over the years in my communication framework—and in this book— with the addition of a category called "Information" (termed "Reporting" and discussed in chapter 3). Such research underlines the essential nature of questions, advisements, self-disclosures, interpretations, and reflections for understanding and enhancing face-to-face talk. (The study did not use the difficult-to-measure events of interruption, allowing behavior, and overtalk contained in chapters 3 and 9.)

Peter Farb plays with language across cultures, like an anthropological linguist ought to. He brings theories of play to the analysis of language and intellectually wanders across phenomena and societies. The guy loves talk curiosities, and his book *Word Play* (Knopf, 1974) is filled with them. English-speaking people who are bilingual can get extra fun, and insight, from Farb's observations by simply consulting their own experience.

Eugene Gendlin *was* one of our country's eminent award-winning psychotherapy researchers. He quit after "studying some questions psychotherapists don't like to ask out loud." In *Focusing* (Bantam, 1981), Gendlin asked, "Why doesn't therapy succeed more often? Why does it so often fail to make a real difference in people's lives? In the rare cases when it does succeed, what is it that those patients and therapists do? What is it that the majority fail to do?" After studying thousands of recorded sessions from many forms of therapy, he found a crucial difference between successful and unsuccessful patients: "The difference is in *how* they talk." Not *what* they talk about, but their ability to talk about what they do inside themselves—to systematically come into touch with their feelings in a new way and then self-disclose (see chapter 7 in *The Talk Book*). That powerful discovery turned Gendlin's life around. He wanted to teach people the inner act of *focusing* on experiences with a technique that creates change. He wanted to empower people to help themselves and each other without using therapists. As expected, many professionals aren't thrilled by Gendlin's research and self-help promotion—even though subsequent research supports much of his claim. His book has gone through several printings, and studies of the procedure are now appearing in research journals. If you pick up his book, see chapter 11, "The Listening Manual," which describes four kinds of face-to-face helping. His helping methods can be understood more completely and even expanded by applying techniques from *The Talk Book*—especially those in chapters 7, 8, 9, and 11.

Erving Goffman was a dominant talk theorist—one of the great analysts of language. The late sociolinguist heavily influenced linguists, sociologists, psychologists, and anthropologists of his generation. Much of his thinking (and most of his dense writing style) is inaccessible to the lay reader. In some ways, his profound, semiobscure, brilliant, tireless examinations of discrete talk events is reminiscent of Georg Simmel (described later in this section). Goffman loved to show how talk takes its meaning from the situation, the context. If you can tolerate an extremely specialized academic style, "Replies and Responses" in *Forms of Talk* (University of Pennsylvania Press, 1981) can take you into the twilight world of question usage. But don't try it before reading the two chapters on questions, 5 and 11, in this book.

Thomas F. Gordon is editor of *Communication Abstracts*

(Sage, March, June, September, and December), which offers ample summaries of the world's literature on almost every kind of communication—interpersonal, small group, organizational, media. Very comprehensive and available in college, university, and large public libraries, it's a good resource for tracking down special interests.

Charles Hanson is a down-to-earth psychologist specializing in talk that helps. He is interested in empathy, and he studied its impact in the research project described earlier, in the section on Bonnie Burstein. Hanson found that even those people who appear sympathetic and sensitive do not convey much empathy when they interrupt a lot, ask many questions, explain frequently, and talk as much as a typical person trying to help. His impressive doctoral dissertation, *Measuring Empathy as an Outcome of Training in Help-Intended Communication* (UCLA, 1979), should make sense to laypeople, and it offers an elegant way to look at the psychological process of empathy. The method explained in his dissertation can teach those with weak or moderate capacity for expressing empathy how to do a better job. His dissertation is available from University Microfilms International, P.O. Box 1307, Ann Arbor, MI 48106. For phone orders, call 1-800-521-0600.

Marion Jacobs doesn't only write about better ways to talk in a self-help group, she *talks* about the matter at length on six audio cassettes. They are part of a program that can guide a group of strangers into becoming a fully functioning mutual support system (the Common Concern Program, Harbinger Press, San Francisco; it is also available to Californians on a free-loan basis from the California Self-Help Center, UCLA, Los Angeles, CA 90024; phone 213-825-1799). Common Concern was developed and narrated by Jacobs, Goodman and associates. It uses the same set of talk tools that shape this book and has proven successful in a recently completed field study. Almost any small group of people with a shared predicament can learn to manage their sessions and communicate with skill by interacting with the program over 12 sessions. Specialized tape inserts customize the program to specific needs—for bereaved parents, incest survivors, families and friends of people with Alzheimer's disease, hospice and oncology workers, parents who were physically abused as children, people coping with fertility problems, recent widows, recently divorced women in their forties and fifties, and women coping with breast cancer—

but the talk skills are for any problem. There are guides for helping an individual recruit and select members. Every detail is covered.

Stanley E. Jones specializes in the kind of talk that goes on in small groups. He joined **Dean Barnlund** and **Franklyn Haiman** in writing *The Dynamics of Discussion* (Harper, 1980), which traces the influence of talk style and talk competence on group cohesiveness, apathy, conflict, decision making, and leadership, along with the abuses of discussion.

Sidney Jourard wrote the first book about the role of self-disclosure in healthy human relations. *The Transparent Self: Self-Disclosure and Well-Being* (Van Nostrand, 1964) is dated, but reads easily. Almost single-handedly, Jourard opened a field of scientific inquiry into the revealed talk of intimacy. He died tragically at an early age and left disclosure researchers without the support of his powerfully playful mind. Students should see his early research efforts in *Self-Disclosure* (Wiley, 1971).

Harold H. Kelly works to establish a new science of interpersonal relationships. He is an eminent social psychologist who studies the cooperation, competition, and conflict that shape talk. Kelly leads a group of scholars that is establishing "close relationships" as a field of specialization within psychology (*Close Relationships*, with Berscheid, Christensen, Harvey, Huston, Levenger, McClintock, Peplau, and Peterson; W. H. Freeman, 1983). The book is a bit too technical for the lay reader, but the summaries are clear enough to show how scientists probe intimacy. They want to identify psychological laws that cut across relationships formed by lovers, mates, families, close friends—even close co-workers. A key is the interdependence of gratification—sort of a complementarity that comes from exchanging gifts, information, services, and companionship frequently and strongly over long time spans. In a way, Kelly and his colleagues look at the exchange of intimate commodities (as this book looks at the interdependent exchange of risky disclosures, advice, "allowing" behaviors, interpretations, empathy acts, and information gathering). It doesn't take a scientist to know such things are vital to maintaining closeness and mental health, but it does take a scientist to spot vital, overlooked details or to connect events into larger pictures disregarded by the public.

Kelly makes that point nicely in his introduction to *The Emerging Field of Personal Relationships*, edited by Robin Gilmour and Steve Duck (Lawrence Erlbaum, 1986). Kelly's introduction is free of jargon and can provide some practical thinking tools for anyone strongly motivated to zero in on close relationships. The book is an excellent source for learning about communication in social groups, loneliness, the first year of marriage, juvenile friendship, deteriorating relationships, the impact of losing a partner, jealousy, and distress in marriage. Don't expect glib advice, simplistic solutions, black-and-white pictures, or easy reading. This stuff is science; an academic like me would call it the real thing.

Mark L. Knapp is a major catalyst for the field of interpersonal communication. He is editor of a book series, past editor of the journal *Human Communication Research*, wrote a couple of books on talk, and co-edited with **Gerald Miller** the important *Handbook of Interpersonal Communication* (Sage, 1985). Miller (another prolific writer) and Knapp crafted a lucid, low-jargon introduction to their handbook that is the best quick overview of the entire field. It's an excellent starting place for beginning students. The ideas of two dozen specialists are gathered into four sections that represent four very logical ways that scholars, or anybody, can think about communication: (1) basic positions, perspectives, values, and motives for approaching talk; (2) fundamental units, categories, and classification schemes for dividing talk into manageable pieces; (3) basic processes, sequences, flows, and dynamics of talking; (4) contexts, situations, and settings that shape face-to-face talk. It provides a nice way to organize vantage points. The handbook also contains a nice set of references covering just about every piece of pertinent literature in that area. It's practically a substitute for going to the library. Overall, it's an outstanding resource with some surprisingly good writing. In addition, Knapp's colorful little textbook, *Interpersonal Communication and Human Relationships* (Allyn & Bacon, 1984), is engaging and intellectually accessible to high school graduates.

Robin Lakoff wrote an influential book, *Language and Women's Place* (Octagon, 1975). Her dedication expressed hope that the next generation would transcend the inequities between men and women, as evidenced by linguistic discrimination. It looks like her wish won't be realized. Sexism in language may have melted a little—thanks to the observations and goading of people like Lakoff—but most of the demeaning talk habits she described are still frozen solid in conversation between the sexes and in our references to women. She writes about some awful ways women talk to women, "women's language," the stifling effects of "polite" interchange, the talk customs that frame women as objects—sexual and otherwise—and the peculiar overuse of questions that hedge assertion (I call them "self-subordinating" questions and sometimes "semi-innocent" questions, as in chapter 2 of this book). Lakoff is easy to read, except for a few outbursts of technical linguistic jargon, but her thinking is strong. Sometimes anger enters, but the reasoning remains intact. A wonderful book for couples.

Dale Larson is obsessed with giving psychology away—especially the kind that helps people talk better. He's one of our best general experts on the variety of small group communication training programs for coping and for helping others. His book *Teaching Psychological Skills* (Brooks/Cole, 1984), illustrates 14 programs covering the range of methods for delivering practical psychological knowledge—including my SASHAtape program. Each program is systematically described by its developer. It's the premier consumer's guide for selecting mental health enhancement programs. It's easy to use, and the writing is often colorful.

Linda Costigan Lederman has written a book that is easily the most beautifully illustrated introductory text on human communication—*New Dimensions* (William C. Brown, 1977). It's filled with photos, cartoons, charts, and poems that illuminate the text in prize-winning fashion. It emphasizes concepts a lot more than skills. The ideas are soundly organized around themes of "The Listener," "The Sender," and "The Message." Her writing is sophisticated and the material is sometimes advanced. It's a strange book—serious, strong, even difficult ideas on splashy, magazine-like pages.

Matthew McKay argues that talking skills ought to be taught in elementary schools because "parents are often dismal role models." His textbook, *Messages* (New Harbinger, 1985), written with Martha Davis and Patrick Fanning, is almost simple enough to be read by a bright junior high student. It focuses on discrete skills for getting close, resolving conflict, connecting with family, and talking in public. It's a bright, uncrowded book with examples that should appeal to teenagers.

Margaret McLaughlin, a scrupulous scholar and conversational analyst, has studied awkward silences, conversation between strangers, and sex differences in storytelling. She wrote a formidable book on conversational skills, turn-taking, and other linguistic machinery that allows us to exchange messages coherently: *How Talk Is Organized* (Sage, 1984). It's an important contribution for scientists and graduate students. A very ambitious amateur talk scholar, willing to struggle, could learn a lot from her. McLaughlin's goal, shared by many of us, is to "dredge up" talk rules that lie beneath the surface of awareness. Sometimes her strain toward precision produces strange language, as in "Argument: A discourse unit built around the expansion of an initiating speech act or proffer, and its dispreferred reply." It's hard to write both precisely and plainly about the way we talk.

Robert Norton, in *Communicator Style* (Sage, 1983), examines the real possibility that the *manner* in which we communicate reveals our essential uniqueness—our personality. He is the first scholar to devote an entire book to talk style. It's easier to read than most "hard-nosed" talk books and offers intriguing ideas on how our personal talk styles are created from patterns of listening, self-disclosure, attraction, metacommunication (talk about talk), and nonverbal communication. His chapter on "Social Magnetism" is lively and important.

William O'Barr has done research that doesn't support some scientific thought about the separateness of women's language. He's an anthropologist at Duke University who studied courtroom trial talk and found that a witness's occupation and experience told more about talk styles than whether the witness was male or female. The research is described in his book *Linguistic Evidence* (Academic Press, 1982).

Carl Rogers, ingenious thinker and great talker, has had more influence on the way we think about communication in close relationships than anyone in this half of the century. His profound, simple, scientific thought stimulated and shaped psychologists, educators, philosophers, and other professionals around the world; they, in turn, have influenced their students and the public. Rogers's ideas (even specific language), published in the 1950s and 1960s, have turned up consistently in popular psychology books ever since. *This* book was influenced in vital ways by him; he was my professor and friend. He died in 1987. *A Way of Being* (Houghton Mifflin, 1980) is an extremely readable story of his experience as an obsessive talk watcher, his founding of a humanistic psychology and major therapy system, his philosophically clear thinking about psychological "reality," his starkly personal disclosures about growing old, his searing analysis of American education, and his futuristic exploration of the twenty-first-century person. And his classic, *On Becoming a Person* (Houghton Mifflin, 1961), is essential, down-to-basics reading for understanding the evolution of psychological ideas.

William Safire, whose enduring column "On Language" in the *New York Times Magazine* (and in syndication) is usually about language in print, sometimes writes penetratingly about person-to-person talk.

Nathalie Sarraute, France's leading avant-garde novelist at 87, writes about phrases and words with the kaleidoscopic vividness of Gertrude Stein—but in some ways, she's more evocative. (*The Use of Speech*, translated by Barbara Williams and published by George Braziller in 1983, has a misleading title.) Common phrases, like "See you very soon," "And why not," "Don't talk to me about that," and "I don't understand" are poetically examined in a hall of mirrors that can send a cooperative reader into reveries about the connection between talk and humans. Sarraute's fiction is almost obscurantist as it reveals familiar emotional facts of mundane language. It's musty stuff. The fairy tales on "The word love" and "My dear" journey through a dozen scenes where meanings change with contexts. The book won't work for passive or impatient readers. There is a clear message about the strange array of multiple meanings that spread from a fixed phrase. (See chapter 5 in *The Talk Book* for a demonstration of the chameleonlike behavior of "loaded" and "semi-innocent" questions.)

Emmanuel Schegloff is searching for bedrock "rules" that govern conversation everywhere (see chapter 6 in this book). He's a talk scientist establishing a new discipline called "conversational analysis." Schegloff is a heavyweight thinker who prefers to write for other scholars. Anyone earnestly interested in learning how a group of scientists are struggling to untangle the second-to-second complexities of conversation could read the "Conversational Analysis" chapter in *Pragmatics*, edited by Stephen Levinson (Cambridge University Press, 1983). It's tough going for beginners.

Saul Schiffman has researched the ways therapists learn to talk with patients, including differences between those who've had special emphasis on the six talk tools and those who haven't. Just as with "civilians," budding therapists, it turns out, can benefit from paying attention to basic units of communication. Schiffman says that, overall, student therapists (in UCLA's Clinical Psychology Department) "with up to three years of clinical training were no more empathic or accepting, no more able to promote client exploration, and no different in interview style than those who were just entering training. . . . Thus the data suggest that clinical training [in itself] has no effect whatever on the variables measured" ("Clinical Psychology Training and Psychotherapy Interview Performance," *Psychotherapy*, vol. 24, 1987). In contrast, 13 of the 46 budding therapists studied "showed dramatic differences in interview style. . . . The expert judges rated them as significantly more empathic and accepting . . . giving less advice, asking fewer closed questions, and making more use of reflections. More than their clinical peers, they focused on the clients' feelings." Those 13 had participated in a program (the Psychotherapy Process Lab, or PPL) designed to teach them how to use the six basic talk tools (via the SASHAtape audio series that was a precursor to this book). "The pattern of results," writes Schiffman, "is what impresses: on nearly every measure, the PPL trainees were more like senior psychotherapists. . . . It is surprising that a single training experience should seem effective when a much more extensive training regimen was not." Schiffman speculates that the training in talk tool use works "because it gives trainees a means of monitoring their own behavior. One cannot regulate a [communication] behavior that one cannot reliably observe. Much therapist training deals in difficult-to-observe abstractions—'rapport,' 'countertransference,' 'confrontation.' By breaking the complexities of therapist behavior into observable, changeable units, training [in talk tool use] may provide a powerful tool for behavior change."

Wallace Shawn, playwright, wrote a screenplay that was put together out of real conversations. He wanted it to be "just talk, as people really do." His conversations with Andre Gregory created *My Dinner with Andre* (Grove Press, 1981). Their wonderful script and movie came to life, as Gregory puts it, because it "struck me that the most necessary and appropriate piece that one *could* possibly do at this particular moment in history would be a piece about two friends sitting and talking to each other." I prefer the script to the film. In the reading is where pieces of language show themselves in full color—especially the various hues of questions. And the range of interpretations helps to show

how these inventive minds create meaning and classify experience. Their minor arguments are fueled by advising, while reflections reveal their caring and drawn-out vulnerable disclosures.

John Shlien has skill as a talker that has dazzled students who have listened to my audiotape of him in a therapy conversation. Sometimes his writing dazzles with subtle ideas about intuition, an examination of erotic feelings in therapy relationships, thoughts on the nature of psychotherapy—especially client-centered psychotherapy—and speculations about talk that makes excuses, masks images, and defends our vulnerability. His evocative chapter "Secrets and the Psychology of Secrecy" is about disguises, adventures, and the intricacies of talk that toys with truth telling. (It's found in *Client-Centered Therapy and the Person-Centered Approach*, edited by Shlien and Ronald Levant; Praeger, 1984.) The therapist's attitude toward his or her client's secret life is described as a key to the way therapy works. It's a strong conceptual tool for knowing the nature of any form of psychological help.

Shlien likes the idea that "It is not the total falsehood but the half-truth that corrupts completely." That notion touches on my discussion about the tyranny of half-truths told, "sneaky" manipulations, and disclosures-in-the-service-of-a-secret (decoy disclosures) in chapters 1 and 7 of this book. The issue is also important for the "semi-innocent" question in chapters 5 and 11. The ways we veil and unveil with talk during our intimacies in order to flirt, seduce, bond, disengage, and enhance self-worth are processes worthy of research. Shlien is inviting psychologists to study secrecy, to ". . . describe the phenomenon and to explain (1) the *motives* that keep secrecy alive, and (2) the *purposes* it serves, both well and poorly."

Georg Simmel (pronounced *Gay'-org Zim'-el*) did his impressive observations on human relations as an unpaid lecturer and then ordinary professor at the University of Berlin around the turn of the century. He was admired in small circles. Now, scholars around the world regard him as a flat-out genius. Simmel is a scholar's scholar. His penetrating analyses of "social games," conversation, coquetry, lies, coercion, adornment, secrecy, silence, and the "stranger" stirred his students. The capacity to see beneath the surface brought fame to his unfinished writing after his death in 1918. He has inspired many major sociological thinkers. A good source for getting a glimpse of his unique mind is *The Sociology of Georg Simmel*, translated by Kurt Wolff (Free Press, 1950). Simmel's two paragraphs on the essence of female flirtation ("Coquetry") have never been surpassed. It's well worth the price of rereading the dense translation several times. And an honored essay on the poignancy of human wandering and connecting to someone both close and distant, someone "outside," oddly attached, uncommitted, expected to move on, is entitled "The Stranger." Simmel shows how the "stranger" combines qualities of nearness and remoteness to become abstract. It's eye-opening stuff for understanding intimacy. Much of the writing can bring insight into our motives for talking. Warning: Between the heavy food for thought and the tortuous German sentences, one paragraph can take a month to digest.

Dennis Smith and **Keith Williamson** believe that it's best to learn talking skills by both feeling and doing them. They wrote a textbook emphasizing both experience and behavior: *Interpersonal Communication* (William C. Brown, 1977). The writing seems geared to early college, but it could be suitable for bright high school students. There are good sections on interpersonal crowding, healthy and unhealthy talk traits, and pseudointimacy.

William Stiles, my former student, describes the workings of talk tools (termed "response modes" in the scientific literature) in medical interviews and psychotherapies; in conversations between parent and child, professor and student, and married couples; and in debates by politicians in presidential primaries. Stiles is especially interested in "the frame of reference" or viewpoint, and the focus of experience, in talking. He also sees psychological importance in acts of edification (called "reporting" in this book) that represent facts and in confirmations that express agreement, disagreement, and shared experience. Such thinking led to an expanded version of the original response modes. (See his chapter, "Development of a Taxonomy of Verbal Response Modes," in *The Psychotherapeutic Process*, by Greenberg and Pinsof; Guilford, 1983.) Stiles is also an innovative self-disclosure theorist who uses a human "fever" metaphor to explain the dynamics of disclosing as a symptom *and* cure for emotional distress (see chapter 1 of this book).

Jonathan Swift satirized human conduct with an ingenuity unmatched in the English language. He mocked politics and human relations in seventeenth- and eighteenth-century Ireland with an artful distance that seemed to come from passionate caring. It's obvious that he cared about the waste of human spirit caused by the ineffective ways people talked to each other. There is little satire in his impassioned "Hints toward an Essay on Conversation" (in *A Book of English Essays*, by S V. Makower and B. Blackwell; Norwood Editions, 1979). It is a historical gem describing the timeless abuses of face-to-face talk and the ugly conversational sexism in polite Irish society. Many of his observations could also apply to current talk. Swift was indignant over the disregard his society had for improving their talk skills. He complained that ". . . so useful and innocent a pleasure [as talking with each other], so fitted for every period and condition of life, and so much in all people's power, should be so much neglected and abused." He continued, describing passionately how ". . . human nature is most debased [by neglecting to improve] that faculty which has held the great distinction between men and brutes." Swift backed up his point with quaint but penetrating descriptions of conversational crowding (". . . an impatience to interrupt each other; and the uneasiness of being interrupted ourselves"), flooding listeners with self-indulgent talk, overemphasizing the importance of being witty, using jargon to show off, and the custom of pushing women aside during serious discourse (". . . degeneracy of conversation [is caused by the same attitude that] excludes women from any share in our society, farther than in parties, at play, or dancing, or in the pursuit of amour"). Swift's observations on the damage done to human relations by bad talk habits and conversational sexism remain relevant. They point to issues I explore in this book.

Deborah Tannen is an unusual linguist who translates for the public academic knowledge on miscommunication that's caused by cultural or regional differences. She writes about many aspects of linguistics for popular magazines and the *Washington Post*. Some of her writing seems appealing enough to recruit young people into the study of language. Tannen believes the useful insights of linguistics are too often hidden in scholarly journals. She does a great job of disseminating information on the anatomy of talk between men and women. Her lively little book, *That's Not What I Meant* (Morrow, 1986), can help those who must talk across a cultural gap.

Candace West studies talk between women and men. She's especially interested in the way men do most of the interrupting (chapter 6 of this book examines talk between the sexes). Her book *Routine Complications* (Indiana University Press, 1984) reveals some persistent problems in physician/patient talk—especially when the physician is male and the patient is female. A conversation analysis of interruptions, questions, and laughter leaves her without a villain or hero. Readers may feel differently.

William Wilmot focuses on talk in one-to-one relationships (called "dyads" in our business). He has studied the dissolution of romantic relationships and talk about talk (metacommunication), and written a popular, clear textbook, *Dyadic Communication* (Random House, 1987). It's meant for the college classroom but could introduce most people to the major academic ideas on relationships. It contains references for over 500 articles and books pertinent for one-to-one communication sessions.

Bernie Zilbergeld made an assault on those 45-minute conversations called psychotherapy. The dust jacket of his book *The Shrinking of America* (Little, Brown, 1983) quotes some eminent therapist/researchers who figure his study ". . . will be unenthusiastically received by devotees of psychotherapy . . . [and] would strongly advise therapists and their clients to reconsider their myths and prejudices.—Albert Ellis, Ph.D." "By taking the wind out of extravagant expectations, he points to a more humane and realistic way of thinking about ourselves.—Arnold Lazarus, Ph.D." "Rescues the American public from its helpers by introducing a much-needed bit of reality into the highly romanticized and quasi-religious world of psychotherapy. The book itself is psychotherapy of a high order . . . —Bernard Apfelbaum, Ph.D."

This is strange praise by people who do therapy. Maybe their kind comments arise from the cognizance that Zilbergeld's assault comes from a position of concern for therapy consumers. Too many believe that a rented conversation characterized by one-way intimacy is the best or only way to solve personal problems. Zilbergeld wants us to do a better job of working through difficulties by talking to friends or mates, joining self-help groups, reading judiciously selected self-help books, and perhaps organizing personal-change groups guided by audiotape programs.

Surprisingly, *The Shrinking of America* is a constructive guide to selecting a 'brand" of therapy (out of 131 varieties) and testing for incompetencies in therapists. It may be the best thing to read *before* entering a series of therapy conversations. Zilber-geld debunks the major myths: There is one best therapy; it's equally effective for all problems; behavior change is therapy's most common outcome; great changes are the rule; the longer the therapy, the better the results; therapy changes are permanent, or at least long-lasting; at worst, therapy is harmless; one course of therapy is the rule for most clients; only specially trained professionals can help people change. This is a good list of common beliefs that have been contradicted by research. Unfortunately, Zilbergeld himself perpetuates the popular myth that suggests that "doing what comes naturally" is all it takes to make private talk into mutually helpful talk. I hope he will get rid of that fixed, false belief after reading *this* book.

NOTES

Chapter 1

1. Mark Knapp and Gerald Miller, eds., *Handbook of Interpersonal Communication* (Beverly Hills, Calif.: Sage Publications, 1985), 72.
2. William Stiles, "I Have to Talk to Somebody: A Fever Model of Disclosure," in *Self-Disclosure—Theory, Research, and Therapy*, V. J. Derlega and J. Berg, eds. (New York: Plenum Publishing, 1986).
3. Mark Knapp and Gerald Miller, eds., *Handbook of Interpersonal Communication*, 225.

Chapter 2

1. Ezra Stotland et al., *Empathy, Fantasy and Helping*, Sage Library of Social Research, vol. 65 (London: 1978), 179.
2. Nancy Eisenberg and Randy Lennon, "Sex Differences in Empathy and Related Capacities," *Psychological Bulletin*, vol. 94, no. 1 (1983), 101 31.
3. Martin Buber, *I and Thou* (Edinburgh, England: Rand R. Clark, 1923).
4. Dr. Lewis is a former classmate and longtime friend of mine. The verbatim transcript was published in a professional book, *Case Studies in Counseling and Psychotherapy*, by Arthur Burton (New York: Prentice-Hall, 1959), 212 16.

Chapter 3

1. These things aren't really identical. Proverbs and mottos are usually one-liners of unknown origin with smooth language polished across generations. Aphorisms and their pompous predecessors, maxims, are longer, popular sayings from known

373

authors. Stefan Kanfer described the maxim as "a personal observation inflated into a universal truth . . ." ("Essay," *Time*, 11 July 1983, 74). Slogans are created slick and short and exist across months instead of generations. The differences between these bits of language are real but become trivial when considering psychological impact because all of them are joined by a common denominator—they're all general interpretations.

Chapter 4

1. Richard Christie and Florence Geis, *Studies in Machiavellianism* (New York: Academic Press, 1970).

   These social psychologists brought together most of the scholarship on people who habitually influence and maneuver others in conversation. The authors scrutinized 50 studies on power and opportunism in human relations and made a lasting contribution to the intimate science of interpersonal communication.

Chapter 5

1. Mathilda Holvman, "Interrogative Patterns in Children's Speech," *Journal of Psycholinguistic Research*,, vol. 1, no. 4 (1972), 37 49.

Chapter 6

1. Daniel Stern, *First Relationship: Mother and Infant* (Cambridge, Mass.: Harvard University Press, 1977).
2. Starkey Duncan, "Some Signals and Rules for Taking Speaking Turns in Conversations," *Journal of Personality and Social Psychology*, vol. 23 (1972).
3. Emmanual Schegloff, "Conversational Analysis," in *Pragmatics*, Stephen Levinson, ed. (New York: Cambridge University Press, 1983).
4. Mary Budd Rowe, "Waiting in the Classroom," *Science and Children*, Spring 1978.

Chapter 7

1. Sidney Jourard, *Self-Disclosure* (New York: John Wiley & Sons, 1971), 173 80.
2. Sidney Jourard, *Self-Disclosure*, 173 80.
3. Irving Janis, "The Role of Social Support in Adherence to

Stressful Decisions,'' *American Psychologist*, February 1983, 893 917.

Chapter 10

1. Harold Garfinkle, *Studies in Ethnomethodology*, (New York: Prentice-Hall, 1967).

INDEX

Note: Page numbers referring to entire chapters appear in **bold-face** type.

377

About the Author

GERALD GOODMAN, Ph.D., associate professor of psychology at UCLA, is co-director of the nonprofit California Self-Help Center, which uses his Common Concern audio tape to improve the communication abilities of self-help group members throughout the state.

GLENN ESTERLY is a frequent contributor to *TV Guide* and has also written for *Rolling Stone, California Magazine*, and *Los Angeles Magazine*.